Popular Tales of the West Highlands

PRINTED BY R. & R. CLARK,

FOR

EDMONSTON AND DOUGLAS, EDINBURGH.

LONDON . . HAMILTON, ADAMS, & CO.
CAMBRIDGE . MACMILLAN & CO.
DUBLIN . . W. ROBERTSON.
GLASGOW . . JAMES MACLEHOSE.

POPULAR TALES

OF

THE WEST HIGHLANDS

ORALLY COLLECTED

𝕎𝔦𝔱𝔥 𝔞 𝔗𝔯𝔞𝔫𝔰𝔩𝔞𝔱𝔦𝔬𝔫

BY J. F. CAMPBELL

VOL. I

MYTHOLOGICAL TALES, FABLES, AND OSSIANIC BALLADS.

EDINBURGH:
EDMONSTON AND DOUGLAS.
1862.

CONTENTS.

LIST OF ILLUSTRATIONS.

———◆———

ERRATA.

Page	24	line	22	for	dhuibhsee	read	dhuibhse
„	25	„	19	„	dhoar	„	dhaor
„	26	„	1	„	mò	„	mo
„	37	„	5	„	'n	„	'm
„	—	„	9	„	'm	„	'n
„	46	„	2	„	seire	„	seirc
„	—	„	16	„	darusd	„	dorusd
„	47	„	8	„	,	„	'
„	48	„	26	„	turc	„	torc
„	51	„	15	„	n'	„	'n
„	69	„	9	„	d' en	„	de 'n
„	102	„	20	„	chiud	„	chuid
„	—	„	—	„	ionnsaidh	„	ionnsuidhh
„	103	„	16	„	ruim	„	rium
„	104	„	14	„	mae	„	mac
„	106	„	39	„	b	„	bi
„	118	„	14	" What is (the reason of) thy coming from the land?" read, " What is thy land's produce?"		
„	121	„	4	„	doirn'eig	„	doirneig
„	—	„	7	„	mhorbhadhsa	„	mharbhadhsa
„	—	„	11	„	gad	„	gad
„	125	„	9	„	Craohh	„	Craobh
„	—	„	19	„	marbh	„	mharbh
„	131	„	6	„	an	„	a'
„	139	„	17	„	chrainnaibh	„	chrannaibh
„	142	„	14	„	Brembhaig	„	Breubhaig
„	155	„	10	„	chu	„	cha
„	163	„	6	„	Gruagach	„	Ghruagach
„	165	„	15	„	ghleantna	„	ghleannta
„	169	„	12	„	Gruagaich	„	Ghruagaich
„	—	„	18	„	un	„	an
„	175	„	15	„	os riun	„	as ruin
„	178	„	31	„	mniun	„	muin
„	227	„	22	„	Deogh	„	Deagh

Page	231	Note	5	for	ghaoidheadh	read	ghlaoidheadh
„	240	line	27	„	the	„	thee
„	243	„	6	„	Treanghaisgeach	„	Treunghaisgeach
„	245	„	36	·,	bharragh	„	barragh
„	—	„	88	„	dheag	„	dheug
·,	246	„	5	„	sbluisd	„	soluisd
„	—	„	16	„	haislean	„	uaislean
„	—	„	37	„	ainmeanan	„	ainmeannan
„	251	„	24	„	ceanu	„	ceann
„	265	„	84	„	anam	„	annam
„	294	„	22	„	Leomham	,	Leomhan
„	295	„	4	„	min	„	mìn
„	805	„	14	„	Fhian-ta	„	Fhìannta
„	809	„	80	„	Leagalh	„	Leagadh
„	313	„	9	„	sind	„	siud
„	817	„	6	„	lasgara	„	lasgarra
„	—	„	12	„	ficheud Ghaidheal		fichead Gaidheal
„	—	„	20	„	Eiroinn	„	Eirionn
„	819	„	4	„	airnn	„	oirnn
„	—	„	19	„	gaisge'	„	gaisg'
„	326	„	21	„	about around	„	around
„	841	„	20	„	phiathar	„	phiuthar
„	—	„	27	„	phiathar	„	phiuthar

„ 364, at the top. The Lay of Magnus was written from the dictation of Alexander MacDonald, and subsequently compared with the recitation of the other authority.

„	364	„	14	„	Beìth	„	Beithe
„	367	„	16	„	om'	„	am'
„	—	„	18	„	non	„	nan
„	876	„	14	„	gruagch	„	gruagach
„	377	„	14	„	carr-shiuflach	„	carr-shiubhlach
„	884	„	6	„	"like blade's daughter the smith's shop," read, "like blade the smith's shop's daughter"		
„	387	„	15	„	mis	„	nis
„	391	„	19	„	chuinir	„	chuimir
„	392	„	9	„	fheail dhaoise	„	fheoil dhaoine
„	894	„	80	„	they had before;	„	; they had before
„	397	„	28	„	jun	„	gun
„	—	„	38	„	played	„	placed
„	898	„	8	„	iomagain	„	iomagain
„	—	„	15	„	comihairle	„	comhairle

It may be some excuse for this long list of errors, and for the

Gaelic orthography, that the printers do not understand Gaelic, the scribes dwell far from them, the penmanship is sometimes indistinct, and the usual spelling of words is often wilfully modified, to express the pronunciation of various districts, while adhering to the rules of Gaelic orthography.

The variations are often of philological value, as for example—FAIL is the Islay value of FAR—*where*, and it seems to be a very ancient form of Gaelic, which is not in any modern book, even mine, for the scribe did not venture to take such a liberty. But in an Irish MS., written prior to 1150, quoted p. 49 of the Transactions of the Ossianic Society, is this line—

> " Baile i tegtis fecht fir."
> " In the place where men were wont to pass."

Or perhaps,

> " *The town where*, come past men."

Thus FAILE, *where*, is equivalent to *ans a'* BHAILE, in the town where; and so, Balla, a wall; Baile, a town, or a farm, or any collection of houses; is made to have the same meaning as Faile, a definite place, distinguished from an indefinite place, such as the site of a wanderer's camp would be. The change then from FAIL to FAR, and the preservation of FAIL in one locality, and the relation of *Far* to *baile*, are worth the departure from a system not yet fixed.

LVIII.

THE RIDER OF GRIANAIG,[1] AND IAIN THE SOLDIER'S SON.

From Donald MacNiven, a lame carrier. Bowmore, Islay, 5th July 1859. Written down by Hector MacLean.

THE knight of Grianaig had three daughters, such that their like were not to be found or to be seen in any place. There came a beast from the ocean and she took them with her, and there was no knowledge what way they had taken, nor where they might be sought.

There was a soldier in the town, and he had three sons, and at the time of Christmas [2] they were playing at shinny, and the youngest said that they should go and that they should drive a hale on the lawn of the knight of Grianaig. The rest said that they should not go; that the knight would not be pleased; that that would be bringing the loss of his children to his mind, and laying sorrow upon him. "Let that be as it pleases," said Iain the youngest son, "but we will go there, and we will drive a hale; I am careless of the knight of Grianaig, let him be well pleased or angry."

They went to play shinny, and Iain won three hales from his brethren. The knight put his head out of a window, and he saw them playing at shinny, and he took great wrath that any one had the heart to play shinny on his lawn—a thing that was bringing the loss

of his children to his mind, and putting contempt
upon him. Said he to his wife, "Who is so impudent
as to be playing shinny on my ground, and bringing
the loss of my children to my mind? Let them be
brought here in an instant that punishment may be
done upon them. The three lads were brought to the
presence of the knight, and they were fine lads.

"What made you," said the knight, "go and play
shinny upon my ground and bring the loss of my
children to my mind? you must suffer pain for it."

"It is not thus it shall be," said Iain ; "but since
it befell us to come wrong upon thee, thou hadst best
make us a dwelling of a ship, and we will go to seek
thy daughters ; and if they are under the leeward, or
the windward, or under the four brown boundaries of
the deep,² we will find them out before there comes
the end of a day and year, and we will bring them
back to Grianaig."

"Though thou be the youngest, it is in thy head
that the best counsel is, let that be made for you."

Wrights were got and a ship was made in seven
days. They put in meat and drink as they might
need for the journey. They gave her front to sea and
her stern to land, and they went away, and in seven
days they reached a white sandy strand, and when
they went on shore there were six men and ten at
work in the face of a rock *blasting*, with a foreman
over them.

"What place is here?" said the skipper.

"Here is the place where are the children of the
knight of Grianaig ; they are to be married to three
giants."

"What means are there to get where they are?"

"There are no means but to go up in this creel
against the face of the rock."

The eldest son went into the creel, and when he was up at the half of the rock, there came a stumpy black raven, and he began upon him with his claws, and his wings till he almost left him blind and deaf.[4] He had but to turn back.

The second one went into the creel, and when he was up half the way, there came the stumpy black raven and he began upon him, and he had for it but to return back as did the other one.

At last Iain went into the creel. When he was up half the way there came the stumpy black raven, and he began upon him, and he belaboured him about the face.

"Up with me quickly!" said he, "before I be blinded here."

He was set up to the top of the rock. When he was up the raven came where he was, and he said to him.

"Wilt thou give me a quid of tobacco?"[5]

"Thou high-priced rogue! little claim hast thou on me for giving that to thee."

"Never thou mind that, I will be a good friend to thee. Now thou shalt go to the house of the big giant, and thou wilt see the knight's daughter sewing, and her thimble wet with tears."

He went on before him till he reached the house of the giant. He went in. The knight's daughter was sewing.

"What brought thee here?" said she.

"What brought thyself into it that I might not come into it."

"I was brought here in spite of me."

"I know that. Where is the giant?"

"He is in the hunting hill."

"What means to get him home?"

"To shake yonder battle-chain without, and there is no one in the leeward, or in the windward, or in the four brown boundaries of the deep, who will hold battle against him, but young Iain the soldier's son, from Albainn, and he is but sixteen years of age, and he is too young to go to battle against the giant."

"There is many a one in Albainn as strong as Iain the soldier's son, though the soldier were with him."

Out he went. He gave a haul at the chain, and he did not take a turn out of it, and he went on his knee. He rose up, he gave the next shake at the chain, and he broke a link in it. The giant heard it in the hunting hill.

"Aha !" said he, "who could move my battle chain but young Iain the soldier's son from Albainn, and he is but sixteen years of age; he is too young yet ?"

The giant put the game on a withy, and home he came.

"Art thou young Iain the soldier's son, from Albainn ?"

"Not I."

"Who art thou in the leeward, or in the windward, or in the four brown boundaries of the deep, that could move my battle chain, but young Iain the soldier's son, from Albainn ?"

"There is many a one in Albainn as strong as young Iain the soldier's son, though the soldier should be with him."

"I have got that in the prophesyings."

"Never thou mind what thou hast got in the prophesyings."

"In what way wouldst thou rather try thyself ?"

"When I and my mother used to be falling out with each other, and I might wish to get my own will, it was in tight wrestling ties we used to try; and one time she used to get the better, and two times she used not."

They seized each other, and they had hard hugs, and the giant put Iain on his knee.

" I see," said Iain, " that thou art the stronger."

" It is known that I am," said the giant.

They went before each other again. They were twisting and hauling each other. Iain struck a foot on the giant in the ankle, and he put him on the thews of his back under him on the ground. He wished that the raven were at him.

The stumpy black raven came, and he fell upon the giant about the face and about the ears with his claws and with his wings until he blinded him, and he deafened him.

" Hast thou got a nail of arms that will take the head off the monster ?"

" I have not."

" Put thy hand under my right wing, and thou wilt find a small sharp knife which I have for gathering briar-buds, and take the head off him."

He put his hand under the raven's right wing and he found the knife, and he took the head off the giant.

"Now Iain thou shalt go in where is the big daughter of the knight of Grianaig, and she will be asking thee to return and not to go farther ; but do not thou give heed, but go on, and thou wilt reach the middle daughter ; and thou shalt give me a quid of tobacco."

" I will give that to thee indeed ; well hast thou earned it. Thou shalt have half of all I have."

" I will not. There's many a long day to Bealtain."

" The fortune will not let me be here till Bealtain."

" Thou hast knowledge of what has passed, but thou hast no knowledge of what is before thee ; get warm

water, clean thyself in it; thou wilt find a vessel óf
balsam above the door, rub it in thy skin, and go to
bed by thyself and thou wilt be whole and wholesome
to-morrow, and to-morrow thou shalt go on to the house
of the next one."

He went in and he did as the raven asked him.   He
went to bed that night and he was whole and wholesome in the morning when he arose.

"It is better for thee," said the knight's big daughter,
"not to go further, and not to put thyself in more danger;
there is plenty of gold and silver here, and we will take
it with us and we will return."

"I will not do that," said he; "I will take (the
road) on my front."

He went forwards till he came to the house where
was the middle daughter of the knight of Grianaig.
He went in and she was seated sewing, and she (was)
weeping, and her thimble wet with her tears.

"What brought thee here?"

"What brought thyself into it that I might not
come into it?"

"I was brought in spite of me."

"I have knowledge of that. What set thee
weeping?"

"I have but one night till I must be married to
the giant."

"Where is the giant?"

"He is in the hunting hill."

"What means to get him home?"

"To shake that battle chain without at the side of
the house, and he is not in the leeward nor in the
windward, nor in the four brown boundaries of the
deep, who is as much as can shake it, but young Iain
the soldier's son, from Albainn, and he is too young yet,
he is but sixteen years of age."

"There are men in Albainn as strong as young Iain the soldier's son, though the soldier should be with him."

He went out, and he gave a haul at the chain, and he came upon his two knees. He rose up and gave the next haul at it, and he broke three links in it.

The giant heard that in the hunting hill.

"Aha!" said he, and he put the game on a withy on his shoulder, and home he came.

"Who could move my battle chain but young Iain the soldier's son from Albainn, and he is too young yet; he is but sixteen years of age?"

"There are men in Albainn as strong as young Iain the soldier's son, though the soldier should be with him."

"We have got that in the prophesyings."

"I care not what is in your prophesyings."

"In what way wouldst thou rather try thyself?"

"In hard hugs of wrestling."

They seized each other and the giant put him on his two knees.

"Thine is my life," said Iain, "thou art stronger than I. Let's try another turn."

They tried each other again, and Iain struck his heel on the giant in the ankle, and he set him on the thews of his back on the ground.

"Raven!" said he, "a flapping of thine were good now."

The raven came, and he blinded and deafened the giant, giving it to him with his beak, and with his claws, and with his wings.

"Hast thou a nail of a weapon?"

"I have not."

"Put thy hand under my right wing, and thou wilt find there a small sharp knife that I have for gathering briar-buds, and take the head off him."

He put his hand under the root of the raven's right wing, and he found the knife, and he took the head off the giant.

"Now thou shalt go in and clean thyself with warm water, thou wilt find the vessel of balsam, thou shalt rub it upon thyself, thou shalt go to bed, and thou wilt be whole and wholesome to-morrow. This one will be certainly more cunning and more mouthing than was the one before, asking thee to return and not to go further; but give thou no heed to her. And thou shalt give me a quid of tobacco."

"I will give it indeed; thou art worthy of it."

He went in and he did as the raven asked him. When he got up on the morrow's morning he was whole and wholesome.

"Thou hadst better," said the knight's middle daughter, "return, and not put thyself in more danger; there is plenty of gold and of silver here."

"I will not do that; I will go forward."

He went forward till he came to the house in which was the little daughter of the knight; he went in and he saw her sewing, and her thimble wet with tears.

"What brought thee here?"

"What brought thyself into it that I might not come into it?"

"I was brought into it in spite of me."

"I know that."

"Art thou young Iain the soldier's son, from Albainn?"

"I am; what is the reason that thou art weeping?"

"I have but this night of delay without marrying the giant."

"Where is he?"

"He is in the hunting hill."

"What means to bring him home?"

"To shake that battle chain without."

He went out, and he gave a shake at the chain and down he came on his hurdies.

He rose again, and he gave it the next shake, and he broke four links in it, and he made a great rattling noise. The giant heard that in the hunting hill; he put the withy of game on his shoulder.

"Who in the leeward, or in the windward, or in the four brown boundaries of the deep, could shake my battle chain but young Iain the soldier's son, from Albainn; and if it be he, my two brothers are dead before this?"

He came home in his might, making the earth tremble before him and behind him.

"Art thou young Iain the soldier's son?"

"Not I."

"Who art thou in the leeward, or in the windward, or in the four brown boundaries of the deep, that could shake my battle chain but young Iain the soldier's son, from Albainn? and he is too young yet, he is but sixteen years of age."

"Is there not many a one in Albainn as strong as young Iain the soldier's son, though the soldier were with him?

"It is not in our prophesyings."

"I care not what is in your prophesyings."

"In what way wouldst thou like thy trial?"

"Tight wrestling ties."

They seized each other and the giant set him on his haunches.

"Let me go; thine is my life."

They caught each other again; he struck his heel on the giant in the ankle, and he laid him on the shower top of his shoulder, and on the thews of his back on the ground.

"Stumpy black raven, if thou wert here now!"

No sooner said he the word than the raven came. He belaboured the giant about the face, and the eyes, and the ears, with his beak, and with his claws and with his wings.'

"Hast thou a nail of a weapon?"

"I have not."

"Put thy hand under the root of my right wing and thou wilt find a small sharp knife that I have for gathering whortle berries, and take his head off."

He did that.

"Now," said the raven, "take rest as thou didst last night, and when thou returnest with the three daughters of the knight, to the cut (edge) of the rock, thou shalt go down first thyself, and they shall go down after thee; and thou shalt give me a quid of tobacco."

"I will give it; thou hast well deserved it; here it is for thee altogether."

"I will but take a quid; there is many a long day to Bealtain."

"The fortune will not let me be here till Bealtain."

"Thou hast knowledge of what is behind thee, but thou hast no knowledge what is before thee."

On the morrow they set in order asses, and on their backs they put the gold and the silver that the giants had, and he himself and the three daughters of the knight reached the edge of the rock: when they reached the edge of the rock, for fear giddiness should come over any of the girls, he sent them down one after one in the creel. There were three caps of gold on them, made up finely with "daoimean" (diamonds); caps that were made in the Roimh (Rome), and such that their like were not to be found in the universe. He kept up the cap that was on the youngest. He was waiting and waiting, and though he should be waiting still, the creel would not come up to fetch him. The rest went on board, and away they went till they reached Grianaig.

He was left there, and without a way in his power to get out of the place. The raven came where he was.

"Thou didst not take my counsel ?"

"I did not take it; if I had taken it I should not be as I am."

There is no help for it, Iain. The one that will not take counsel will take combat. Thou shalt give me a quid of tobacco."

"I will give it."

"Thou shalt reach the giant's house, and thou shalt stay there this night."

"Wilt thou not stay with me thyself to keep off my dulness ?"

"I will not stay; it is not suitable for me."

On the morrow came the raven where he was.

"Thou shalt now go to the giant's stable, and if thou art quick and active, there is a steed there, and sea or shore is all one to her, and that may take thee out of these straits."

They went together and they came to the stable, a stable of stone, dug in into a rock, and a door of stone to it. The door was slamming without ceasing, backwards and forwards, from early day to night, and from night to day.

"Thou must now watch," said the raven, "and take a chance, and try if thou canst make out to go in when it is open, without its getting a hold of thee."

"Thou hadst best try first, since thou art best acquainted."

"It will be as well.'

The raven gave a bob and a hop and in he went, but the door took a feather out of the root of his wing, and he screeched.

"Poor Iain, if thou couldst get in with as little pain as I, I would not complain."

Iain took a run back and a run forward, he took a spring to go in, the door caught him, and it took half his hurdies off. Iain cried out, and he fell cold dead on the floor of the stable. The raven lifted him, and he carried him on the points of his wings, out of the stable to the giant's house. He laid him on a board on his mouth and nose, he went out and he gathered plants, and he made ointments that he set upon him, and in ten days he was as well as ever he was.

He went out to take a walk and the raven went with him.

"Now, Iain, thou shalt take my counsel. Thou shalt not take wonder of any one thing that thou mayest see about the island, and thou shalt give me a quid of tobacco."

He was walking about the island, and going through a glen; he saw three full heroes stretched on their backs, a spear upon the breast of every man of them, and he in lasting sound sleep, and a bath of sweat.

"It seems to me that this is pitiable. What harm to lift the spears from off them?"

He went and he loosed the spears from off them. The heroes awoke, and they rose up.

"Witness fortune and men, that thou art young Iain the soldier's son, from Albainn, and it is as spells upon thee to go with us through the southern end of this island past the cave of the black fisherman."

He went away himself and the three full heroes. They saw a slender smoke (coming) out of a cave. They went to the cave. One of the heroes went in and when he went in there was a hag there seated, and the tooth that was the least in her mouth would make a knitting pin in her lap, a staff in her hand, and a stirring stick for the embers. There was a turn of her nails about her elbows, and a twist of her hoary hair about her toes, and she was not joyous to look upon.

She seized upon a magic club, she struck him, and she made him a bare crag of stone. The others that were without were wondering why he was not returning.

"Go in," said Iain to another one, "and look what is keeping thy comrade."

He went in, and the carlin did to him as she did to the other. The third went in, and she did to him as she did to the rest. Iain went in last. There was a great red-skulled cat there, and she put a barrow full of red ashes about her fur so as to blind and deafen him. He struck the point of his foot on her and drove the brain out of her. He turned to the carlin.

"Don't, Iain! these men are under spells, and in order to put the spells off them thou must go to the island of big women and take a bottle of the living water out of it, and when thou rubbest it upon them the spells will go and they will come alive."

Iain turned back under black melancholy.

"Thou did'st not take my counsel," said the raven, "and thou hast brought more trouble upon thyself. Thou shalt go to lie down this night, and when thou risest to-morrow thou shalt take with thee the steed, and shalt give her meat and drink. Sea or land is all one to her, and when thou reachest the island of big women sixteen stable lads will meet thee, and they will all be for giving food to the steed, and for putting her in for thee, but do not thou let them. Say that

thou wilt thyself give her meat and drink. When thou
leavest her in the stable, every one of the sixteen will
put a turn in the key, but thou shalt put a turn against
every turn that they put in it. Thou shalt give me a
quid of tobacco."

" I will indeed."

He went to rest that night, and in the morning he
set the steed in order, and he went away. He gave
her front to sea and her back to shore, and she went in
her might till they reached the island of big women.
When he went on shore sixteen stable lads met him
and every one of them asking to set her in and feed her.

"I myself will put her in, and I will take care of
her; I will not give her to any one."

He put her in, and when he came out every man
put a turn in the key, and he put a turn against every
turn that they put into it. The steed said to him that
they would be offering him every sort of drink, but
that he should not take any drink from them but whey
and water. He went in and every sort of drink was
being put round about there, and they were offering
each kind to him, but he would not take a drop of any
drink but whey and water. They were drinking, and
drinking till they fell stretched about the board.

The steed asked him before she parted from him
that he should take care and not sleep, and to take his
chance for coming away. When they slept he came
out from the chamber; and he heard the very sweetest
music that ever was heard. He went on, and he heard
in another place music much sweeter. He came to the
side of a stair and he heard music sweeter and sweeter,
and he fell asleep.

The steed broke out of the stable, and she came
where he was, and she struck him a kick, and she awoke
him.

"'Thou didst not take my counsel," said she, "and there is no knowing now if thou canst get thy matter with thee, or if thou canst not get it."

He arose with sorrow; he seized upon a sword of light that was in a corner of the chamber, and he took out the sixteen heads. He reached the well, he filled a bottle and he returned. The steed met him, and he set her front to sea and her back to shore, and he returned to the other island. The raven met him.

"Thou shalt go and stable the steed, and thou shalt go to lie down this night; and to-morrow thou shalt go and bring the heroes alive, and thou shalt slay the carlin, and be not so foolish to-morrow as thou wert before now."

"Wilt thou not come with me to-night to drive off my dulness from me?"

"I will not come; it will not answer for me."

On the morning he reached the cave, "FAILTE DHUIT, all hail to thee, Iain," said the carlin; "FAILTE DHUIT's, all hail to thee, but CHA SHLAINTE DHUIT not health to thee."

He shook the water on the men and they rose up alive, and he struck his palm on the carlin and scattered the brains out of her. They betook themselves out, and they went to the southern end of the island. They saw the black fisherman there working at his tricks.* He drew his palm, and he struck him, and he scattered the brains out of him, and he took the heroes home to the southern end of the island. The raven came where he was.

"Now thou shalt go home, and thou shalt take

* Here the narrator has evidently forgotten some of the adventures. A similar character to the black fisherman appears in other tales, and his adventures should be added here, if the story were mended.

with thee the steed to which sea and shore are alike. The three daughters of the knight are to have a wedding, two to be married to thy two brothers, and the other to the chief that was over the men at the rock. Thou shalt leave the cap with me, and thou wilt have but to think of me when thou hast need of it, and I will be at thee."

"If any one asks thee from whence thou camest, say that thou camest out from behind thee; and if he say to thee, where art thou going? say that thou art going before thee."

He mounted upon the steed, and he give her front to sea, and her back to shore, and away he was, and no stop nor stay was made with him till he reached the old church in Grianaig, and there there was a grass meadow, and a well of water, and a bush of rushes,⁸ and he got off the steed.

"Now," said the steed, "thou shalt take a sword and thou shalt take the head off me."

"I will not take it indeed; it would be sad for me to do it, and it would not be my thanks."

"Thou must do it. In me there is a young girl under spells, and the spells will not be off me till the head is taken off me. I myself and the raven were courting; he in his young lad, and I in my young girl, and the giants laid DRAOIDHEACHD magic upon us, and they made a raven of him and a steed of me."⁹

He drew his sword, he turned his back, and he took the head off her with a scutching blow, and he left the head and the carcass there. He went on forwards and a carlin met him.

"From whence didst thou come?" said she.

"I am from behind me."

"Whither art thou going?"

"I am going before me."

"That is the answer of a castle man."

"An answer that is pretty answerable for an impudent carlin such as thou art."

He went in with her and he asked a drink, and he got that.

"Where is thy man?"

"He is at the house of the knight seeking gold and silver that will make a cap for the knight's young daughter, such as her sisters have; and the like of the caps are not to be found in Albainn."

The smith came home.

"What's trade to thee, lad?"

"I am a smith."

"That is good, and that thou shouldst help me to make a cap for the knight's young daughter, and she going to marry."

"Dost thou not know that thou canst not make that."

"It must be tried; unless I make it I shall be hanged to-morrow; here thou hadst best make it."

"Lock me into the smithy, keep the gold and silver, and I will have the cap for thee in the morning."

The smith locked him in. He wished the raven to be with him. The raven came, he broke in through the window, and the cap was with him.

"Thou shalt take the head off me now."

"It were sorrow for me to do that, and it would not be my thanks."

"Thou must do it. A young lad under spells am I, and they will not be off me till the head comes off me."

He drew his sword, and he scutched his head off, and that was not hard to do. In the morning the smith came in, and he gave him the cap, and he fell asleep. There came in a noble-looking youth, with brown hair, and he awoke him.

"I," said he, "am the raven, and the spells are off me now."

He walked down with him where he had left the dead steed, and a young woman met them there as lovely as eye ever saw.

"I," said she, "am the steed, and the spells are off me now."

The smith went with the cap to the house of the knight. The servant maid betook herself to the knight's young daughter, and she said that there was the cap which the smith had made. She looked at the cap.

"He never made that cap. Say to the lying rogue to bring hither the man that made him the cap, or else that he shall be hanged without delay."

The smith went and he got the man that gave him the cap, and when she saw him she took great joy. The matter was cleared up. Iain and the knight's young daughter married, and backs were turned on the rest, and they could not get the other sisters. They were driven away through the town with stick swords and straw shoulder-belts.

[1. Maclean writes as follows :—

Got this tale from Donald M'Niven, Bowmore, who learnt it from an old man of the name of Neil Mac-Arthur, who died some twenty years ago or more.

Donald MacNiven is over forty years of age, is a cripple, but is sometimes in the habit of acting as a carrier, and driving a cart from Bowmore to Port Ellon and Port Askaig. He is of a fair complexion, a demure expression, and evidently loves the wonderful. I do not think he can either read or write. I was informed that he could recite a considerable number of tales, but he tells me he has quite forgot them, from having given up reciting them.

RIDIRE GHRIANAIG. The word Ridire, as explained elsewhere, now means a knight, but it probably meant a minor king in the olden time.

GHRIANAIG is the genitive of Grianag, which has been corrupted into Greenock.

That town is called by its Gaelic name throughout the Highlands. It is derived from *Grian* the sun, pronounced GreeAn, which is probably the root of many names which are now sounded " *green*," such as *Grisnez* in France, *Crinan* in Argyllshire, and other places which are green and sunny in other countries. I might translate the words freely, the kinght of Greenock, the knight of the sun, or the Ritter of Sunnynook, but acting on the principle with which I set out, I give the knight his Gaelic name, and so avoid drawing doubtful conclusions.—J. F. C.

2. NOLLAIG is Christmas, and is also used for New Year's day. The derivation is probably NODH, new; LA, day; French, *noël;* Welsh, *nadolig;* Irish, *nodhlag;* Manks, *nollick;* Breton, *nadolig.* The Highland customs which prevail at this season smack rather of pagan times. Processions of boys go about on New Year's eve shouting curious rhymes, some of which are full of the names which pervade the Ossianic poems; curious ceremonies are performed, and the singers are rewarded with food. I hope some day to be in a position to say more about these old Christmas customs; they are mentioned in Chambers's nursery rhymes.

The game of shinny is usually played at this season, and the great game used to come off on the day of the great "nollaig," New Year's day, old style. The game is played in all parts of the United Kingdom as "hocky," "hurling," etc., and something like it is still played in the far east on horseback. To drive the ball

from one goal to the other is called LETH BHAIR, a
"half hale ;" to drive it back again is BAIR, a "hale ;"
and to win a goal at the man's game is nearly as great
a feat as to gain a battle.   In some parts of the Highlands hundreds used to be engaged, all excited to a
degree that those who have been at a public school, or
who have read Tom Brown's account of football, may
perhaps understand.

3. FHIORRACHD FHUARRACHD, etc.   This phrase is
(according to Maclean) frequently used, though few
know what the words literally mean.   The common
meaning attached to them is, "Not to be found anywhere." May they not be corrupt forms of IOCHDRACHD
and UACHDRACHD, it is not in the higher or lower
regions.

I have given a different rendering ; I have heard
very similar words used by boatmen for beating to windward and running to leeward, and veering is an English sailor's word still.

RANNAN is used for rainnean, divisions, in this tale.
This form of the word in this sense is obsolete in Islay,
and I suspect elsewhere.   It now signifies verse, which
is no doubt so called from being divided into lines and
stanzas.   We still use it in the genitive, thus, An
Rainn, the Rhynns ; Ceann shios na ranna, the farthest
down part of the Rhynns ; An rugha Rannach. —
H. M'L.

4. The raven attacking the man in the basket might
be a picture drawn from nature. Boys are often lowered
over rocks in the Western Highlands to take birds'
nests, and the old birds occasionally resent the injury.
I have myself seen sparrow-hawks, terns, and other
birds stooping viciously at men who had gone near

their nests. I have heard of a man having his head laid open by enraged sea-swallows ; and there are all manner of stories current of adventures with birds in rock climbing.—J. F. C.

5. The quid of baccy needs no explanation, when it is remembered that the common fee for the story-teller is a quid. An old man long ago was teaching a boy to play the fiddle, and the following dialogue is recorded :—" Which finger shall I raise ?" " Hast thou tobacco ?" " No ; which finger shall I lift ?" " Hast thou got tobacco ?" " No." " Then lift and lay them down as it may please thyself." There is a hunger-ing after tobacco amongst those who are given to it, and cannot get it, which must be felt to be understood.

6. CEAP may have been substituted for CURRACHD, a cap, which was the old Gaelic name for all head-dresses, male or female.—H. M'L.

I have no doubt that the man who told the story meant a cap, and I have so translated the word, but the Gaelic word means a trap or gin, and many things besides. An old man who told me a story exceedingly like "the Fisherman" in the Arabian Nights, introduced the character who resembled the young king of the Black Isles, not as a man half marble, but as a man with his head in a *ceap*, and on being interrogated, ex-plained that this was a kind of head-dress used for punishment or torture, in which the head of the victim was fastened. Such head-dresses, made of rusty iron, may be seen in museums, and ceap may have meant something like a helmet, whose machinery bears some resemblance to a rat-trap.

7. GODARLEUM (page 31).—This is a new word to

me. The reciter could give no explanation of it farther than that it was darting off very abruptly, which the context leads a person to think. Godadh is a quick, somewhat violent shake of the head. I find the reciters at Bowmore speak a more corrupt dialect than others whom I have met. They use English words very frequently for Gaelic words still in common use. This gives an idea of the manner in which English words and forms of speech may have gradually replaced Gaelic ones in these tales, MacNiven alternately used FORES-MAN and UACHDARAN in speaking of the overseer of the sixteen men that wrought at the rock.—H. M'L.

The flapping stone door occurs in a book called the "Romance of History," and I think the magic cave was placed somewhere in Spain. I have an impression that I have heard of it elsewhere.—J. F. C.

8. TOM LUACHARACH, a bush of rushes, perhaps a rushy knoll.

9. FO GHEASAN. Irish writers who take the historical view of these traditions, translate geasa by vow or promise. This seems to fix the meaning at MAGIC.

I have translated this passage as literally as my knowledge of the two languages enables me to do it, because the language, which is simple every day Gaelic, seems, when considered with its meaning in this passage, to throw a light on past beliefs. The enchanted steed, and men at the present day when they speak Gaelic, talk of themselves as if they were something different from their bodies. In English it is said, "*I am* an old man;" in Gaelic, "I am *in my* old man."

The form of words is the same when the speaker says "I am in my old clothes," and this form of speech is here used together with DRAOIDH-eachd (?), *druid*-ism, magic, and a *transformation* is effected by *steel* at a *well*, in a *grass meadow*, near a *rushy knoll*, beside *an old church* at *Gria*naig.

Something to do with GRIAN the sun, is mixed up with magic and worship, at an old church, and with druidism, and wells, and magic metal, and green meadows and rushes, things which usually have to do with magic, and with metempsychosis, which is supposed to have been a druidical doctrine; and all comes direct from a man who cannot possibly know anything about such things except as traditions, which are supported by similar traditions found elsewhere. I believe this tale to be founded on Celtic mythology.—J. F. C.

The following Gaelic words used in this tale are very near to the English, LENA, lawn ; GRUND, ground ; SGIOBAIR, skipper ; PEANAS, penalty ; BLASTADH, corruption for blasting ; SAIL, heel. SPAISDEAIR-ACHD is not in English, but it has relations in Italian, andar *a spasso*, and in Norse and German, spazieren.

The incidents may be compared with those in the Big Bird Dan, Norse Tales, page 442 ; the King of Lochlin's Three Daughters, vol. i., page 236 ; but though these have much in common, I know nothing quite like this story anywhere. To me it suggests a succession of vivid pictures, perhaps because I understand the intention of the narrator from my knowledge of the landscapes which he clearly had before his mind.]

RIDIRE GHRIANAIG.

BHA aig Ridire Ghrianaig (1) tri nigheanan, nach robh 'n leithid ra fhaotainn, na ra fhaicinn an aite sam bith. Thainig beisd o'n chuan, 's thug i leath' eud, 's cha robh fios de 'n rathad a ghabh eud, na cait an racht' a 'n iarraidh.

Bha saighdear anns a bhaile, 's bha tri mic aige, 's an am na nollaig (2) bha eud aig iomain, 's thuirt am fear a b-oige gun rachadh eud agus gun cuireadh eud bair, air leuna ridire Ghrianaig.

Thuirt cach nach rachadh, nach biodh an ridire toilichte, gun biodh siod a toirt na chuimhne call a chloinne, 's a cuir duilichinn air. "Biodh sinn 's a roghainn da," urs' Iain am mac a b-oige, "ach theid sinn ann, 's bheir sinn bair, tha mise com' airson ridire Ghrianaig biodh e buidheach na diombach."

Chaidh eud a dh' iomain 's bhuidhinn Iain tri bairean air a bhraithrean. Chuir an ridire cheann a mach air uinneig, 's chunnaic e eud aig iomain, 's ghabh e corruich mhor, gun robh chridh' aig h-aon sam bith dol a dh' iomain air a leuna, ni bha toirt call a chloinne na chuimhne, 's a cuir miothlachd air. Thuirt e ra bhean. "Co tha cho miobbail 's a bhi' g iomain air mo ghrunndsa toirt call mo chloinne 'm chuimhne! biodh eud air an toirt an so, a thiotamh, 's gun rachadh peanas a dheanadh orra." Chaidh na triuir ghillean a thoirt an lathair an ridire, 's bha eud nau gillean gasda.

"De thug dhiubsee," urs' an ridire, "bhi cho miobhail 's dol a dh' iomain air a ghrunnd agams', toirt call mo chloinne 'm chuimhne! Feumaidh sibh peanas fhuileann air a shon."

Cha n ann mur sin a bhitheas," urs' Iain, "ach o'n thuit duinne tigh 'n cearr ort, 's fhearra dhuit fardrach de long a dheanadh dhuinn, agus folbhaidh sinn a dh' iarraidh do nigheanan; 's ma tha eud fo 'n fhiorrachd na fo 'n fhuarrachd, na fo cheithir rannan ruagh' an domhain, (3) gheobh sinn' a mach eud, ma 'n d' thig ceann lath' a 's bliadhna, 's bheir sinn air an ais eud do Ghrianaig."

"Gad is tu 's oige, 's ann a 'd cheann a tha chomhairl' a 's fhearr Bidh sinn air a dheanadh dhuibh."

Fhuaireadh saoir, 's bha long air a deanadh ann an seachd lathan. Chuir eud a stigh biadh is deoch mar dh' fheumadh eud airson an turais. Thug eud a h-aghaidh ri muir, 's a cul ri tir, 's dh' fholbh eud 's ann an seachd laithean rainig eud traigh gheal ghainbheich, agus nur a chaidh eud air tir bha se fir dheug ag obair ann an aodann creige blastadh, 's uachdaran orra.

"De 'n t-aite tha 'n so?" ursa 'n sgiobair.

" So 'n t-aite bheil clann ridire Ghrianaig. Tha eud ri bhi posd' air tri famhairean."

" De 'n doigh air faotainn far a bheil eud ?"

" Cha 'n 'eil doigh sam bith ach dol suas anns a chliabh so ri aodann na creige."

Chaidh am mac a bu shine anns a chliabh, 's nur a bha e shuas aig leith na creige thainig fitheach gearr dugh, 's thoisich e air le a inean, 's le a sgiathan, gus nach mor nach d' fhag e dall bodhar e. (4) Cha robh aig ach tilleadh air ais.

Chaidh an darna fear sa chliabh, 's nur a bha e shuas leith an rathaid, thainig am fitheach gearr dugh 's thoisich e air, 's cha robh aig ach tilleadh air ais mur a rinn am fear eile.

Chaidh Iain ma dheireadh sa cliabh. Nur a bha e shuas leith an rathaid, thainig am fitheach gearr dugh, 's thoisich e air, 's ghread e ma 'n aodann. "Suas mi gu clis," urs' esan, "ma 'm bi mi dall an so." Chuireadh a suas e gu braigh na creige. Nur a bha e shuas thainig am fitheach far an robh e, 's thuirt e ris.

" An d' thoir thu dhomh greim thomhaca ?"

" A dhoar shlaightire ! 's beag comain agad orm airson sin a thoirt duit."

" Na biodh amhail agad da sin bidh mise 'm charaid math dhuit. Nis theid thu do thigh an fhamhair mhoir, 's chi thu nighean an ridire fuaghal, 's a meuran fliuch le deoir."

Ghabh e air aghaidh gus an d' rainig e tigh an fhamhair. Chaidh e stigh. Bha nighean an ridire fuaghal.

" De thug an so thu ?" urs' ise.

" De thug thu fein ann nach fhaodainnsa tigh 'n ann ?"

" Thugadh mis' ann gun taing."

" Tha fios agam air an sin. Ca bheil am famhair ?"

" Tha e sa bheinn sheilg."

" De 'n doigh air fhaotainn dachaidh ?"

" An t-slabhraidh chomhrag ud a mach a chrathadh 's cha n 'eil san fhiorrachd, na 's an fhuarrachd, na 'n ceithir rannan ruagh' an domhain, h-aon a chumas comhrag ris, ach Iain og Mac an t-Saighdeir, a Albainn, 's cha n 'eil e ach se bliadhn' deug a dh' aois 's tha e tuillidh a 's og a dhol a chomhrag ris an fhamhair."

" Tha iomadh h-aon an Albainn cho laidir ri Iain Mac an t- Saighdeir, gad a bhiodh an saighdear leis."

Chaidh e mach. Thug e tarruinn air an t-slabhraidh, 's cha d' thug e car aisde, 's chaidh e air a ghlun. Dh' eiridh e suas, thug e 'n ath chrathadh air an t-slabhraidh, 's bhrisd e tein' innte. Chual am famhair sa bheinn sheilg e.

"Aha!" urs' esan, "co b-urrainn mò shlabhraidh chomhraigs' a charachadh, ach Iain og Mac an t-saighdeir e Albainn, 's cha n 'eil e ach se bliadhn' deug a dh' aois, tha e ra og fhathasd."

Chuir am famhair an t-sitheann air gad, 's thainig e dhachaidh.

" An tusa Iain og Mac an t-saighdeir a Albainn ?"

" Cha mhi."

"Co thu ? san fhiorrachd, na san fhuarrachd, na 'n ceithir ranna ruagh' an domhain, a b' urrainn mo shlabhraidhs' charachadh ach Iain og Mac an t-saighdeir a Albainn ?"

Tha iomadh h-aon an Albainn, cho laidir ri Iain og Mac an t-saighdear, ged a bhiodh an saighdear leis."

" Tha siod san fhaidheadairachd agamsa."

" Coma leam de tha san fhaidheadaireachd agadsa."

" De 'n doigh air am math leat thu fhé' fheuchainn ?"

" Nur a bhithinn fhé 's mo mhathair thar a cheile, 's a bhiodh toil agam mo thoil fhé fhaotainn ; 's ann an snaomannan cruaidhe carachd a bhitheamaid a feuchainn, 's aon uair a gheobhadh i chuid a b' fhearr, 's da uair nach fhaigheadh."

Rug eud air a cheile, 's bha greimeannan cruaidh' aca, 's chuir am famhair Iain air a ghlun.

" Tha mi faicinn," urs' Iain, " gur tu 's laidireacha."

" Tha fiòs gur mi," urs' am famhair.

Chaidh eud an dàll a chèile rithisd, bha eud a caradh, 's a tarruinn a cheile. Bhuail Iain a chas air an fhamhair sa mhuthairle, 's chuir e air slaitidh a dhroma, foidhe air a ghrunnd e. Ghuidh e gum biodh am fitheach aige. Thainig am fitheach gearr dugh, 's ghabh do 'n fhamhair s an aodann, 's ma na cluasan, le a inean, 's le a sgiathan, gus an do dhall, 's an do bhodhair e e. " Am bheil tarrunn airm agad a bheir an ceann de 'n bheisd ?"

" Cha n 'eil."

" Cuir do lamh fo m' sgeith dheis-sa, 's gheobh thu corc bheag bhiorach ann, a bhios agam a buain nam braonanan, 's thoir an ceann deth."

Chuir e lamh fo bhun sgeith' dheis an fhithich 's fhuair e chorc 's thug e 'n ceann de 'n fhamhair.

" Nis Iain theid thu stigh far a bheil nighean mhor ridire Ghrianaig 's bidh i 'g iarraidh ort tilleadh, 's gun dol na 's fhaide, ach na d' thoir thusa feairt, ach gabh air t-aghaidh, 's ruigidh thu 'n nighean mheadhonach, 's bheir thu dhomhsa greim thombaca."

" Bheir mi sin duit gu dearbh 's math a choisinn thu e, gheobh thu leith 's na th' agam."

" Cha 'n fhaigh gu dearbh ; 's iomadh la fada gu bealtainn."

Cha lig am fortan gam bi mìs' an so gu bealtainn."

Tha fiòs agad air na tha seachad, ach cha 'n 'eil fiòs agad air na tha romhad. Faigh uisge blath, glan thu fein ann, Gheobh thu ballan iocshlaint as cionn an doruisd, rub rì 'd chraiceann e, theirig a laidhe leat fhé', 's bidh thu gu slan fallain am maireach, 's am maireach gabhaidh tu air t-aghaidh gu tigh na h-ath te.

Chaidh e stigh 's rinn e mar a dh' iarr am fitheach air. Chaidh e laidhe 'n oidhche sin, 's bha e gu slan fallain, sa mhaidinn, nur a dh' eiridh e.

" 'S fhearra dhuit," ursa nighean mhor an ridire, "gun dol na 's fhaide, 's gun thu fhé chur an tuillidh cunnairt, tha na leoir de dh' or 's de' dh' airgiod an so, 's bheir sinne leinn 's tillidh sinn."

" Cha dean mi' " sin urs' esan, " gabhaidh mi air m' aghaidh."

Ghabh e air aghaidh gus an d' thainige gus an tigh an robh nighean mheadhonach ridire Ghrianaig. Chaidh e stigh, 's bha ise na suidhe fuaghal, 's i caoineadh, 's a meuran fliuch le a deoir.

" De thug thusa 'n so ? "

" De thug thu fhè ann nach fhaodainnsa tigh 'n ann ? "

" Thugadh mise gun taing ann."

" Tha fhiosam air an sin, de chuir a caoineadh thu ? "

" Cha 'n 'eil ach aon oidhch' agam gus am feum mi bhi posd air an fhamhair."

Ca bheil am famhair ?

" Tha 's a bheinn sheilg."

" De n doigh air fhaotainn dhachaidh ? "

" An t-slabhraidh chomhraig sinn a mach taobh an tigh chrathadh, 's cha n 'eil e 's an fhiorrachd, na san fhuarrachd, na 'n ceithir rannan ruagh' an domhain, na chrathas i, ach Iain og Mac an t-saghdeir a Albainn, 's tha e ra og fhathasd; cha 'n 'eil e ach se bliadhna deug a dh' aois."

" Tha daoin' ann an Albainn, cho laidir ri Iain og Mac an t-saighdeir, gad a bhiodh an saighdear leis."

Chaidh e mach 's thug e tarruinn air an t-slabhraidh, 's thainig e air a dha ghlun. Dh' eiridh e 's thug e n' ath tarruinn urra, 's bhrisd e tri teineachanan. Chual am famhair siod 'sa beinn sheilg.

" Aha ! " urs esan, " 's chuir e 'n t-sitheann air gad air a ghuall-ainn, 's thainig e dhachaidh."

" Co b' urrainn mo shlabhraidh chomhragsa charachadh ach Iain og Mac an t-saighdeir a Albainn, 's tha e ra og fhathasd ; cha n 'eil e ach se bliadhn' deug a dh' aois."

" Tha daoin' ann an Albainn cho laidir ri Iain og Mac an t-saighdeir, gad a bhiodh an saigdear leis."

" Tha siod anns an fhaidheadaireachd againne."

" Tha mise coma de th' anns an fhaidheadaîreachd agaibhse."

" De 'n doigh air am math leat thu fein fheuchainn ?"

" Ann an cruaidh ghreimeannan carachd."

Rug eud air a cheile 's chuir am famhair air a dha ghlun e.

" 'S leat mo bheath," urs' Iain, " 's tu 's treise na mise. Feucha-
maid car eile."

Dh' fheuch eud a cheile rithisd 's bhual Iain a shàil air am
fhamhair sa mhuthairle 's chuir e air slaitidh a dhrom' air
ghrunnd e.

" Fhithich," urs' esan, " bu math dallanach dhiot anis."

Thainig am fitheach, agus dhall agus bhodhair e 'm famhair, a
gabhail da le a ghob, 's le a inean, 's le a sgiathan.

" A bheil tarrunn airm agad?"

" Cha 'n eil."

" Cuir do lamh aig bun mo sgeithe dheissa, 's gheobh thu ann
corc bheag bhiorach a bhiòs agam a buain nam braonanan, 's thoir
an ceann deth."

Chuir e lamh fo bhun sgeithe dheis an fhithich, fhuair e chorc, 's
thug e 'n ceann de 'n fhamhair.

" Nis theid thu stigh, glanaidh thu thu fein le uisge blath, gheobh
thu 'm ballan iocshlaint, rubaidh tu ruit fhe' e, theid thu laidhe, 's
bidh thu gu slan fallan am maireach. Bidh i so gun taing, na 's
seoltacha, 's na 's beulaiche, na bha 'n te roimhid, aig iarraidh ort
tilleadh, 's gun dol na 's fhaide, ach na d' thobhair thusa feairt urra,
's bheir thu dhomhsa greim thombaca."

" Bheithir mi, dearbh 's airidh air thu."

Chaidh e stigh 's rinn mar a dh' iarr am fitheach air. Nur a dh'
eiridh e 'n la'r na mhaireach bha e gu slan fallan.

" 'S fhearra dhuit ursa nighean mheadonach an ridire, tilleadh
's gun thu fhe' chur ann an tuillidh cunnairt, tha na leoir de dh, or, s
do dh' airgiod an so."

" Cha dean mi sin gabhaidh mi air m' aghaidh."

Ghabh e air aghaidh gus an d' thainig e gus an tigh anns an
robh nighean bheag an ridire, chaidh e stigh, 's chunnaic e ise
fuaghal 's a meuran fliuch le deoir.

" De thug thusa 'n so ?"

" De thug thu fhe' ann ! nach fhaotainnsa tigh'n ann."

" Thugadh mis' ann gun taing."

" Tha fhios'am air an sin."

" An tu Iain og Mac an t-saighdeir a Albainn ?"

" 'S mi, de 's ciall duit a bhi caoineadh ?"

"Cha n 'eil agam dàil gun laidhe leis an fhamhair, ach an oidhche so."

"Ca bheil e ?"

"Tha e 'sa bheinn sheilg."

" De 'n doigh an' air a thoirt dachaidh?"

" An t-slabhraidh chomhraig ud a mach a chrathadh."

Chaidh e mach 's thug e crathadh urra, 's thainig e nuas air a mhasan. Dh' eìridh e rithisd 's thug e 'n ath chrathadh urra 's bhrisd e ceithir teineachan innte, 's rinn e toirm mhor. Chual am famhair siud sa bheinn sheilg. Chuir e 'n gad sithinn air a ghuallainn.

"Co 's an fhiarrachd, na san fhuarrachd, na 'n ceithir rannan ruagh an domhain a b' urrainn mo shlabhraidh chomhragsa chrath-adh, ach Iain og, Mac an t-saighdeir a Albainn, 's ma 's e th' ann tha mo dha bhrathairsa marbh roimhe so."

Thainig e dhachaidh na dheann, a cuir an talamh air chrith roimhe 's na dheigh.

" An tu Iain og Mac an t-saighdeir?"

" Cha mhi."

" Co tha san fhiorrachd, na san fhuarrachd na 'n ceithir rannan ruagh' an domhain, a b' urrainn mo shlabhraidh chomhragsa chrath-adh ach Iain og Mac an t-saighdeir a Albainn 's tha e ra og fhathasd; cha n 'eil e ach se bliadhn' deng a dh' aois."

" Nach iomadh h-aon an Albainn cho laidir ri Iain og Mac an t-saighdeir, gad a bhiodh an saighdeir leis."

" Cha n 'eil e san fhaidheadaireachd againne."

" Coma leam de tha san fhaidheadaireachd agaibhse."

" De n doigh air am math leat t-fheuchainn ?"

" Snaomannan cruaidhe carachd."

Ghlac eud a cheile 's chuir am famhair air a thoin e.

" Lig as mi 's leat mo bheatha "

Rug eud air a cheile rithisd, bhuail e shàil air an fhamhair sa mhuthairle, 's leag e air e fras mhullach a ghuaille 's air slaitith a dhrom' air an lar e.

" Fhithich ghearr dhuigh, na'm biodh thu 'n so anis."

Cha bu luaithe 'thuirt e 'm facal, na thainig am fitheach. Leadair e 'm famhair ma 'n aodann, 's ma na suilean, 's ma na cluasan, le a ghob, 's le a inean, 's le a sgiathan.

" A bheil tarrunn airm agad."

" Cha n 'eil."

" Cuir do lamh fo bhun mo sgeith dheis 's gheobh thu corc bheag bhiorach ann a bhios agam a buain nam braoilleanan 's thoir an ceann deth."

Rinn e siod,

"Nis urs' am fitheach gabh fois mar a rinn thu, 'n rair, 's nur a thilleas thu le tri nigheanan an ridire gu bearradh na creige, theid thu fhè sios an toiseach, 's theid eudsan sìos a 'd dheigh, 's bheir thu dhomhsa greim thombaca."

"Bheir gu dearbh 's math a 's airidh air thu; so dhuit air fad e."

"Cha gabh mi ach greim, 's iomadh la fada gu bealtainn."

"Tha fiòs agad de th' as do dheigh, ach cha n 'eil fios agad de tha romhad."

An la r na mhaireach chuir eud an ordugh asaicheann, 's chuir eud air am muinn an t-or 's an t-airgiod a bh' aig na famhairean, 's rainig e fein agus tri nigheanan an ridire bearradh na creige. Nur a rainig eud bearradh na creige, 'n earalas gun tachradh tapadh-cion do ghin de na nigheanan, chuir e sios eud te an deigh te, anns a chliabh. Bha tri ceapannan (6) oir orra air an deanadh suas gu gasda, le daoimean ceapannan a rinneadh ann 's an Roimh, 's nach robh 'n leithidean ra fhaotainn anns an domhan. Ghleidh e bhos àn ceap a bh' air an te b' oige. Bha e feitheamh, 's a feitheamh, 's gad a bhiodh e feitheamh fhathasd, cha d' thigeadh an cliabh a nios a iarr-aidh. Chaidh cach air bord, 's air folbh a ghabh eud, gus an d' rainig eud Grianaig.

Bha esan air fhagail an siod, 's gun doigh aig air faotainn as an aite. Thainig am fitheach far an robh e.

"Cha do ghabh thu mo chomhairle."

"Cha do ghabh; na 'n gabhadh cha bhithinn mar a tha mi."

"Cha n 'eil arach air Iain, an t-aon nach gabh comhairle gabh-aidh e comhrag, Bheir thu dhomhsa greim thombaca."

"Bheir."

"Ruigidh thu tigh an fhamhair agus fanaidh thu ann an nochd."

"Nach fhan thu fhe' leam a chur dhiom mo chianalais."

"Cha 'n fhan cha fhreagair e dhomh."

"An la r na mhaireach thainig am fitheach far an robh e."

"Theid thu nis gu stabull an fhamhair, agus ma bhiòs thu tap-aidh tha steud an sin a 's coingeis leatha muir na tir, a dh' fhaodas do thoirt as na càsan so."

Dh' fholbh eud comhla 's thainig eud gus an stabull. Stabull cloich' air a chlaghach a stigh ann an creig, agus dorusd cloiche ris. Bha 'n dorusd a clapail gun stad, air ais 's air aghaidh, o mhoch latha gu h-oidhche, 's o oidhche gu latha.

"Feumaidh tu nis faire," urs' am fitheach, "agus cothrom a ghabh-ail feuch an dean thu dheth dol a stigh nur a bhios e fosgailt gun e dheanadh greim ort."

" 'S fhearra dhuits' fheuchainn an toiseach o 'n a 's tu 's eolaiche."
" Bidh e cho math."

Thug am fitheach beic, agus godarleum (7) as 's chaidh e stigh, ach thug an dorusd it' e bun a sgeith, 's sgreuch e.

" Iain bhochd na 'm faigheadh thusa 'stigh cho beag doruinn riumsa, cha bhithinn a gearan."

Ghabh Iain roid air ais, 's roid air aghaidh, thug e leam as a dhol a stigh, rug an dornsd air 's thug e leith a mhais deth.

Ghlaoidh Iain, 's thuit e fuar marbh air urlar an stabuill (8). Thog am fitheach e, 's ghiulain e e air barraibh a sgeith, mach as an stabull, do thigh an fhamhair. Leag e air bord air a bheul 's air a shroin, chaidh e mach, chruinnich e luigheannan, 's rinn e ceirean a chuir e ris, 's ann an deich laithean bha e cho math sa bha e riabh.

Chaidh e mach a dhol a ghabhail sraid, 's chaidh am fitheach a mach leis.

" Nis Iain gabhaidh thu mo chomhairle, 's cha ghabh thu ionghantas de ni sam bith a chi thu feadh an eilean, 's bheir thu dhomhsa greim thombaca."

Bha e spaisdireachd feadh an eilein, 's a dol romh ghleann; chunnaic e tri lan laoich na 'n sineadh air an driom, sleagh air uchd a h-uile fir dhiu, 's e na shioram suain chadail, 's na lòn falais.

" Their leam fhé gur deisneach so; de choire a bhiodh ann's na sleaghannan a thogail diu ?"

Chaidh e agus dh' fhuasgail e dhiu na sleaghannan. Dhuisg na laoich, 's dh' eiridh eud a suas.

" Fhianuis air an fhortan, 's air daoine, gur tu Iain og Mac an t-saighdeir a Albainn, 's gu bheil e mar gheasaibh art dol leinne romh cheann ma dheas an eilein so, seachad air uamh 'n iasgair dhuigh."

Dh' fhalbh e fhe 's na tri lan laoich, Chunnaic eud smuid chaol a mach a uamh. Chaidh eud gus an uamh. Chaidh h-aon de na laoich a stigh, 's nur a chaidh e stigh bha cailleach an sin na suidhe, 's an fhiacaill a bu lugha na beul dheanadh i dealg na h-uchd, lorg na laimh, agus maide brosnachaidh do'n ghriosaich. Bha car da h-inean ma h-uilt, 's car da falt liath ma laghwaran, 's cha robh i aobhach ri amhrac urra.

Rug i air slachdan draoidheachd, bhuail i e 's rinn i carragh maol cloiche dheth. Bha ionghantas air an fheadhain a bha mach de chuir nach robh e tilleadh.

" Theirig a stigh," urs Iain ri fear eile, " 's aimhric de tha cumail do chompanaich."

Chaidh e stigh 's rinn a chailleach air mar a rinn i air an fhear eile. Chaidh an treas fear a stigh 's rinn i airsan mar a rinn i air cach. Chaidh Iain a stigh ma dheireadh. Bha cat mor claghann ruagh an sin, 's chuir i bara de 'n luaith dhearg ma cloimhe an los a bhodhradh sa dhalladh. Bhuail e barr a chois urra, 's chuir en t-ionachainn aisde. Thug e lamh air a chaillich.

"Iain na dean. Tha na daoine sin fo gheasaibh agus airson na geasan a chur dhiu feumaidh tu dol do dh' eilean nam ban mora, 's botall de 'n uisge bheo, thoirt as, 's nur a rubas thu riu e, folbhaidh na geasan 's thig eud beo."

Thill Iain air ais fo dhuibthiamhas.

" Cha do ghabh thu mo chomhairle," urs' am fitheach, " 's thug thu tuillidh dragh ort fein, Theid thu laidhe nochd, 's nur a dh' eireas thu maireach, bheir thu leat an steud, 's bheir thu biadh is deoch dhi. 'S coingeis leatha muir na tir; 's nur a ruigeas thu eilean nam ban mora, coinneachaidh se deug de ghille stabuill thu, 's bidh eud air fad air son biadh a thoirt do 'n steud, sa cuir a stigh air do shon, ach na lig thusa dhaibh. Abair gun d' thoir thu fhe' biadh a 's deoch dhi. Nur a dh' fhagas thu san stabull i, cuiridh a h-uile h-aon de 'n t-se deug car 'san uichair, ach cuiridh thusa car an aghaidh h-uile car a chuireas eud ann. Bheir thu dhomhsa greim thomhaca."

" Bheir gu dearbh."

Chaidh e laidhe 'n oidhche sin, 's anns a mhaidinn chuir e 'n steud an ordugh, 's ghabh e air falbh. Thug e h-aghaidh ri muir, 's a cul ri tir, 's dh' fholbh i na deann, gus an d' rainig eud eilean nam ban mora. Nur a chaidh e air tir, choinnich se gille deug stabuill e, 's bha h-uile fear aig iarraidh a cuir a stigh s a biadhadh.

"Cuiridh mi fhè stigh i, 's bheir mi 'n aire dhi, cha d' thoir mi do h-aon sam bith i."

Chuir e stigh i, 's nur a thainig e mach chuir a h-uile fear car san iuchair, 's chuir esan car an aghaidh h-uile car a chuir eud innte. Thuirt an steud ris gum biodh eud a tairgse h-uile seorsa deoch dha, ach gun' esan a ghabhail deoch sam bith uatha ach meug a 's uisge. Chaidh e stigh 's bha h-uile seorsa deoch ga chuir man cuairt an sin, 's bha eud a tairgse gach seorsa dhasan, ach cha ghabhadh esan deur de dheoch sam bith ach meug a 's uisge. Bha eudsan ag ol, 's ag ol, gus an do thuit eud na 'n sineadh, man bhord.

Dh' iarr an steud airsan ma n do dhealaich i ris, e thoirt an aire 's gun cadal, 's a chothrom a ghabhail airson tigh 'n air folbh. Nur a chaidil eud s an thanaig e mach as an t-seomhar, 's chual e 'n aon cheol a bu bhinne chualas riabh. Ghabh e air aghaidh agus chual e ann an ait' eile ceol moran na bu bhinne. Thainig e gu taobh staighreach 's chual e ceol na bu bhinne 's na bu bhinne, agus thuit e na chadal.

Bhrisd an steud a mach as an stabull, thainig i far an robh e, bhuail i cic air 's dhuisg i e, "Cha do ghabh thu mo chomhairl," urs ise, "'s cha n' eil fhios a nis am faigh thu do ghnothach leat na nach fhaigh." Dh' eiridh e le duilichinn. Rug e air claidheamh soluisd a bha 'n oisein an t-seombair, s thug e na se cinn deug a mach. Rainig e 'n tobar, lion e botall 's thill e. Choinnich an steud e, 's thug e h-aghaidh ri muir 's a cul ri tir, 's thill e gus an eilean eile. Choinnich am fitheach e.

"Folbhaidh thu agus stablachaidh thu 'n steud, 's theid thu laidhe nochd, 's am maireach theid thu agus bheir thu beo na laoich, 's mar bhaidh thu chailleach, 's na bi cho amaideach am maireach 's a bha thu roimhe so."

"Nach d' thig thu leam a nochd a chur dhiom mo chianalais."

"Cha d' thig cha fhreagair e domh."

An la'r na mhaireach rainig e'n uamh.

"Failte dhuit Iain," urs' a chailleach.

"Failte dhuits' ach cha shlainte dhuit."

Chrath e'n t-uisg' air na daoine, 's dh' eiridh eud beo; Bhuail e bhas air a chaillich, a 's spread e 'n t-ionachainn aisde. Ghabh eud a mach, 's chaidh eud gu ceann deas an eilean. Chunnaic eud an t-iasgair dugh an sin ag obair ra chuilbheartan. Tharruinn e bhas 's bhuail e e, 's spread e n t-ionachainn as, 's thug e na laoich dhachaidh do cheann deas an eilean. Thainig am fitheach far an robh e.

"Nis theid thu dhachaidh 's bheir thu leat an steud; 's coingeis leatha muir na tir. Tha tri nigheanan an ridire ri banais a bhi ac-a, dithisd ri bhi posd air do dha bhrathair, agus an te eile air a cheann-abhart a bh' air na daoin' aig a chreig. Fagaidh tu 'n ceap agamsa, 's cha bhi agad ach smaointeachadh orm, nur a bhios e dhith ort, 's bidh mi agad. Ma dh' fheorachas h-aon diot co as a thainaig thu abair gun d' thanaig thu as do dheigh; 's ma their e riut ca' bheil thu dol, abair gu bheil thu dol romhad."

Chaidh e air muinn na steud, thug e h-aghaidh ri muir, 's a cul ri tir, 's air folbh a bha e 's cha d' rinneadh stad na fois leis gus an d' rainig e 'n t-sean eaglais ann an Grianaig, 's bha lòn feoir, an sin, agus tobar uisge, agus tom luachrach. Thainig e bhar na steud.

"A nis," urs' an steud, "gabhaidh tu claidheamh, agus bheir thu 'n ceann diomsa."

"Cha d' thobhair gu dearbh, bu duilich leam a dheanadh, 's cha b' e mo chomain e."

"Feumaidh tu dheanadh, 's ann a th' annamsa nighean og fo gheasaibh, 's cha bhi na geasan dhiom gus an d' thoirear an ceann diom. Bha mi fhe' sam fitheach a suiridh, esan na ghill' og, 's mis' am' nighinn oig, 's chuir na famhairean draoidheachd oirnn, 's rinn eud fitheach dhethsan agus steud dhiomsa."

"Tharruinn e chlaidheamh, thionndaidh e chul, 's thug e 'n ceann dith le sgath bhuille, 's dh' fhag e 'n ceann sa chlosach an siod. Ghabh e air aghaidh. Choinnich cailleach e.

"Co as a thanaig thu?" urs ise.

"Thanaig mi as mo dheigh."

"Ca bheil thu dol?" Tha mi dol romham.

"Sin freagairt fir caisteil."

"Freagairt gu math freagrach air cailleach mhiobhail mur a tha thusa."

Chaidh e stigh leatha 's dh'iarr e deoch. Fhuair e siod.

"Ca bheil t-fhear?"

Tha aig tigh an ridire aig iarraidh or is airgiod a ni ceap do nighean og an ridire, mar a th' aig a peathrairchean, 's gun leithid nan ceapannan ra fhaotainn an Albainn."

Thanaig an gobha dhachaidh.

"De 's ceaird duit oganaich?"

"Tha mi 'm ghobha."

"'S math sin, 's gun cuideachadh thu leamsa ceap a dheanadh do nighean og an ridire, 's i dol a phosadh."

"Naoh 'eil fhios agad nach urrainn thu sin a dheanadh."

"'S eiginn feuchainn ris, ma 'n an dean mi e bidh mi air mo chrochadh am maireach." "So a 's fhearra dhuit a dheanadh."

"Glais mise stigh 's a cheardaich, gleidh an t-or 's an t-airgiod, 's bidh an ceap agamsa dhuit sa mhaidinn."

Ghlais an gobha stigh e. Ghuidh e 'm fitheach a bhi aige, Thainig am fitheach, Bhrisd e stigh romh 'n uinneag 's bha 'n ceap leis.

"Bheir thu 'n ceann dhiomsa nis."

"Bu duilich leam sin a dheanadh 's cha b' e mo chomain e."

"Feumaidh tu dheanadh 's gill' og fo gheasan mise, 's cha bhi eud dhiom gus an d' thig an ceann dhiom."

Tharruinn e chlaidheamh, 's sgath e 'n ceann deth, 's cha robh siod doirbh a dheanadh. Anns a mhaidinn thanaig an gobha 'stigh 's thug e dha 'n ceap. Thuit e na chadal. Thainig oganach ciatach le falt donn a stigh, 's dhuisg e.

"S mise," urs' esan, "am fitheach, 's tha na geasan a nis dhiom."

Choisich e leis sios far an d' fhag e 'n steud marbh, 's choinnich boireannach og an sin eud cho aluinn 's a chunnaic suil riabh.

"'S mis' urs ise 'n steud 's tha na geasan diom a nis."

Chaidh an gobha leis a cheap gu tigh an ridire, Thug an searbhant thun nighean og an ridire e, 's thuirt i rithe gun robh 'n siod an ceap a rinn an gobha. Dh' aimhric i air a cheap.

"Cha d' rinn e 'n ceap so riabh. Abair ris an t-slaightire bhreugach e thoirt an fhir a thug dha 'n ceap an so, air neo gum bi e air a chrochadh gun dàil."

Chaidh an gobha 's fhuair e 'm fear a thug an ceap dha, 's nur a chunnaic is' e ghabh i boch mor. Chaidh a chuis a shoilleireachadh. Phos Iain agus nighean og an ridire, 's chaidh cul a chur ri cach, 's cha 'n fhaigheadh eud na peathraichean eile. Chuireadh romh 'n bhail' eud, le claidheamhannan maide, 's le criosa guaille conlaich.

In this tale the Gaelic is written as spoken by the narrator. There are instances of bad grammar, and of corruptions, which are left as found. Teine is used for tinne, a link. Aig is a small bay or creek. Grianaig is Sun Creek. Many similar names are found in the Highlands. In Islay is Dun Naomh-aig, Holy Creek Fort ; in Barra, Breubhaig-Breitheamhaig, Judge Creek. The word is no doubt allied to eag, a notch, or a nook. —H. M'L.

FROM A STONE AT ELGIN.—*Sculptured Stones of Scotland*, Pl. xvi.

[Under the following numbers I have grouped together a few traditions, etc., relating to the Campbell legend of Diarmaid and the boar.]

LIX.

FIONN'S QUESTIONS.

From Donald MacPhie (smith), Breubhaig, Barra, 1860.

" Fionn would not marry any lady but one who could answer all his questions, and it appears that this was rather difficult to find. Graidhne, daughter of the King of the fifth of Ullin, answered them all, and proved herself the wisest as well as the handsomest of women. Fionn married Graidhne because she answered the questions. The reciter told me that there were a great many more, but that these were all that he could remember at the time."

H. MacLean, October 20, 1860.

CEISDEAN FHINN.

[Seo na ceisdean.
Fionn. Dé 's lionaire na'm feur?
Graidhne. Tha 'n driuchd; bidh moran bhoineachan deth air aon ghas feoir.]

Fionn. What is more plenteous than the grass?
Graidhne. The dew; there will be many drops of it on one grass blade.

[Dé 's teotha na'n teine?
Ciall mnatha eadar da fhear.]
What is hotter than the fire?
A woman's reasoning betwixt two men.

[Dé 's luaithe na ghaoth ?
Aigne mnatha eadar da fhear.]
What is swifter than the wind ?
A woman's thought betwixt two men.

[Dé 's duibhe na 'n fitheach ?
Tha 'm bàs.]
What is blacker than the raven ?
There is death.

[Dé 's gile na 'm sneachd ?
Tha 'n fhirinn.]
What is whiter than the snow ?
There is the truth.

[Dé 's long ri gach luchd ?
Teanchair gobha ; cumaidh i teith a's fuar.]
What is a ship for every cargo ?
A smith's tongs ; it will hold hot and cold.

[Dé air nach gabh glas na slabhraidh cur?
Rasg duine ma charaid ; cha ghabh e dunadh na
cumail ach ag amharc air.]
What is it will not bide lock or chain ?
The eye of a man about his friend ; it will not
brook shutting or holding, but looking on him.

[Dé 's deirge na fuil ?
Gnuis duine choir nuair thigeadh coigrich an rathad
's gun bhiadh aige 'bheireadh e dhaibh.]
What is redder than blood ?
The face of a worthy man when strangers might
come the way, and no meat by him to give to them.

[Dé 's géire na claidheamh ?
Athais namhaid.]
What is sharper than a sword ?
The reproach of a foe.

[Dé 's fearr de bhiadh ?
Bleachd ; thig iomadh atharrachadh as, niotar im
a's càise dheth, 's beathachaidh e leanabh beag a's
sean-duine.]
What is the best of food ?
Milk ; many a change comes out of it ; butter and
cheese are made of it, and it will feed a little child and
an old man.

[Dé 's measa de bhiadh?
Blianach.]
What is the worst of meat ?
Lean flesh.

[De 'n seud a's fhearr ?
Sgian.]
What is the best jewel ?
A knife.

[Dé 's brisge na cluaran ?
Briathran torc muice.]
What is more brittle than the sow thistle ?
The words of a boar pig.

[Dé 's maoithe na cloimhteach ?
Dearn air an leaca.]
What is softer than down ?
The palm on the cheek.

[Dè 'n gniomh a's fhearr de ghniomhaibh ?
Gniomh ard a's uaill iseal.]
What deed is the best of deeds ?
A high deed and low conceit.

From this then it appears that Graidhne represents
quick wit and beauty, and her name seems to mean
Grádh—love.

Fionn always represents wisdom.

Mature wisdom marries young love, and in the stories which follow, love runs away with young valour.

They follow the track which has been assigned to the Celtic race. They are married in Eirinn, and in the next story, the course of their wanderings is pointed out.

———

LX.

DIARMAID AND GRAINNE.*

From Hector MacLean, July 6th 1859. Told by an old man in Bowmore, Islay, Alexander Macalister.

FIONN was going to marry Grainne, the daughter of the king of Carmag in Eirinn. The nobles and great gentles of the Feinne were gathered to the wedding. A great feast was made, and the feast lasted seven days and seven nights; and when the feast was past, their own feast was made for the hounds. Diarmaid was a truly fine man, and there was, BALL SEIRC, a love spot on his face, and he used to keep his cap always down on the beauty spot; for any woman that might chance to see the ball seirc, she would be in love with him. The dogs fell out roughly, and the heroes of the Feinn went to drive them from each other, and when Diarmaid was driving the dogs apart, he gave a lift to the cap, and Grainne saw the ball seirc and she was in heavy love for Diarmaid.

She told it to Diarmaid, and she said to him, " Thou shalt run away with me."

* The name is so spelt in this MS., and it is so spelt in Irish books.

"I will not do that," said Diarmaid.

"I am laying it on thee as a wish; and as spells that thou go with me."

"I will not go with thee; I will not take thee in softness, and I will not take thee in hardness; I will not take thee without, and I will not take thee within; I will not take thee on horseback, and I will not take thee on foot," said he; and he went away in displeasure, and he went to a place apart, and he put up a house there, and he took his dwelling in it.

On a morning that there was, who cried out in the door but Grainne, "Art thou within, Diarmaid?"

"I am."

"Come out and go with me now."

"Did I not say to thee already that I would not take thee on thy feet, and that I would not take thee on a horse, that I would not take thee without, and that I would not take thee within, and that I would not have anything to do with thee."

She was between the two sides of the door, on a buck goat. "I am not without, I am not within, I am not on foot, and I am not on a horse; and thou must go with me," said she.*

"There is no place to which we may go that Fionn will not find us out when he puts his hand under his tooth of knowledge, and he will kill me for going with thee!"

"We will go to Carraig (a crag, Carrick?) and there so many Carraigs that he will not know in which we may be."

* This incident may be compared with a German story Die-kluge Baueren-tochter. Grimm, No. 94. See vol. iii., p. 170, for numerous references to versions of the story in a great many languages. I have had two versions of the story in Gaelic—one from Mr. MacLauchlan, the other from an old man in Barra.

They went to Carraig au Daimh (the stag's crag).

Fionn took great wrath when he perceived that his wife had gone away, and he went to search for her. They went over to Ceantire, and no stop went on their foot, nor stay on their step, till they reached Carraig an Daimh in Ceantire, near to Cille Charmaig. Diarmaid was a good carpenter, and he used to be at making dishes, and at fishing, and Grainne used to be going about selling the dishes, and they had beds apart.

On a day that there was there came a great sprawling old man the way, who was called Ciofach Mac a Ghoill,* and he sat, and he was playing at DINNSIREAN (wedges.†) Grainne took a liking for the old carl, and they laid a scheme together that they would kill Diarmaid. Diarmaid was working at dishes. The old man laid hands on him, and he turned against the old man, and they went into each other's grips. The old man was pretty strong, but at last Diarmaid put him under. She caught hold of the, GEARRASGIAN, knife, and she put it into the thigh of Diarmaid. Diarmaid left them, and he was going from hole to hole, and he was but just alive, and he was gone under hair and under beard. He came the way of the Carraig and a fish with him, and he asked leave to roast it. He got a cogie of water in which he might dip his fingers, while he was roasting it. Now there would be the taste of honey or anything which Diarmaid might touch with his finger, and he was dipping his fingers into the cogie. Grainne took a morsel out of the fish‡ and she perceived the taste of honey upon it. To

* Ciofach, the son of the stranger. This personage, who plays this part in another version, is called "Cuitheach."

† Or DISNEAN, dice?

‡ There seems to be something mythical about this fish, for he appears in various shapes in the legend.

attack Diarmaid went Ciofach, and they were in each
other's grips for a turn of a while, but at last Diarmaid
killed Ciofach, and away he went, and he fled, and he
went over Loch a Chaisteil.

When Grainne saw that Ciofach was dead she
followed Diarmaid, and about the break of day, she
came to the strand, and there was a heron screaming.
Diarmaid was up in the face of the mountain, and said
Grainne—

> " It is early the heron cries,
>   On the heap above Sliabh gaoil,
>   Oh Diarmaid O Duibhne to whom love I gave,
>   What is the cause of the heron's cry ?

> " Oh Ghrainne, daughter of Carmaig of Steeds,
>   That never took a step aright,
>   It seems that before she gave the cry
>   Her foot had stuck to a frozen slab.*

" Wouldst thou eat bread and flesh, Diarmaid ?"
" Needful were I of it if I had it."
" Here I will give it to thee ; where is a knife will
cut it ?"
" Search the sheath in which thou didst put it
last," said Diarmaid.

The knife was in Diarmaid ever since she had put
it into him, and he would not take it out. Grainne
drew out the knife, and that was the greatest shame
that she ever took, drawing the knife out of Diarmaid.

Fear was on Diarmaid that the Fheinn would find
them out, and they went on forwards to Gleann Eilg.

They went up the side of a burn that was there,

* There seems to be a hidden meaning in the reply.

and took their dwelling there, and they had beds apart.*

Diarmaid was making dishes, and the shavings which he was making were going down with the burn to the strand.

The Fiantan were hunting along the foot of the strand, and they were on the track of a venomous boar that was discomfiting them. Fionn took notice of the shavings at the foot of the burn.

"These," said he, "are the shavings of Diarmaid."

"They are not; he is not alive," said they.

Indeed," said Fionn, "they are. We will shout Foghaid! a hunting cry, and in any one place in which he may be, he is sworn to it that he must answer."

Diarmaid heard the Foghaid.

"That is the Foghaid of the Fiantan; I must answer."

"Answer not the cry, oh Diarmaid;
    It is but a lying cry.†

Diarmaid answered the shout, and he went down to the strand. It was set before Diarmaid to hunt the boar. Diarmaid roused the boar from Bein Eidin to Bein Tuirc.‡

While drawing down the long mountain,
The brute was bringing Diarmaid to straits.
His tempered blades were twisted
Like withered rushy plaits.

* Glen Elg, opposite the narrows between Skye and the mainland. There are two "Pictish towers" in a glen which would answer to the description, and there are many legends of the Feinn localised about that spot.

† This is a line of the poem which follows, given as a sentence in a prose tale; and other lines occur which I have written as poetry when I thought I could recognise them.

‡ Two well known Scotch mountains.

Diarmaid gave a draw at the slasher that Lon Mac Liobhain* made, and he put it in under the armpit and he killed the boar.

This was no revenge for Fionn yet over Diarmaid. There was a mole on the sole of the foot of Diarmaid, and if one of the bristles should go into it, it would bring his death.

Said Fionn—

"Oh Diarmaid, measure the boar,
How many feet from his snout to his heel?"
Diarmaid measured the boar.
"Sixteen feet of measure true."
"Measure the boar against the hair."
He measured the boar against the hair, one of the bristles went into the mole and he fell.

Fionn took sorrow for him when he fell. "What would make thee better, Diarmaid?"

"If I could get a draught of water from the palms of Fionn I would be better."

Fionn went for the water, and when he thought on Grainne he would spill the water, and when he would think of Diarmaid, he would take sorrow, and he would take it with him; but Diarmaid was dead before Fionn returned.†

They walked up the side of the burn till they came to where Grainne was; they went in; they saw two beds, and they understood that Diarmaid was guiltless.

* This sword maker is known by this name in the Isle of Man, and is there called the dark smith of Drontheim.

† In Dr. Smith's Sean Dana, page 3 (1787), is this note on the Poem of Diarmaid. "A long dialogue concerning Cuach Fhinn, or the medicinal cup of Fingal, often repeated here, is rejected as the spurious interpolation of some later bard."

The scene is often laid on the ridge between Oban and Loch Awe, and I well remember to have heard how Fionn held his

The Fein were exceedingly sorrowful about what had
befallen.   They burned

> Grainne, daughter of Carmaig of steeds
> That never took a step aright,
> In a faggot of grey oak.

* This story then, under a very rough exterior, embodies the main incidents and some lines of the poem
which follows.

The last story, No. LIX., got in Barra, started the
heroine in Ireland.   This, got in Islay, starts her in
Ireland and brings her through Ceantire into Lorn and
to Glen Elg, opposite to Skye.

The next, the Lay of Diarmaid, got from several
people in Uist and Barra, seems to leave the place of
the catastrophe uncertain, but Bein-Gulban is the
haunt of the heroes, and Irish writers say that Bein-
Gulban is Bein-Boolban in Sligo.

In the manuscript histories of the Argyll family,
Diarmaid's sons are made to possess Carrick.

DIARMAID AGUS GRAINNE.

BHA Fionn a dol a phosadh Ghrainne nighean righ Charmaig an
Eirinn.   Chruinneachadh maithibh agus mor uaislean na Feinne
thun na bainse.   Rinneadh cuirm mhor agus mhair a chuirm seachd
lathan agus seachd oidhchean, agus nur a bha chuirm seachad chaidh
an cuirm fhe' dheanadh do na coin.   Bha Diarmaid na dhuine fior
ghasda 's bha ball seirc air aodann 's bha e cumail a churraichd

---

palms to Diarmaid filled with water from a spring which is still
shewn, and how a draught from the hollow palms would have
healed the dying warrior; but Fionn thought on Graidhne and
opened his hands and let the water drain away, as he held his
hands to Diarmaid's mouth, and Diarmaid died.

J. F. C.

daonnan a nuas air a bhall sheirc; chionn bean sam bith a chitheadh
am ball seire bhiodh i ann an gaol air. Chaidh na coin thar a cheile
gu garbh 's chaidh gaisgich na Feinn' a'n cur o cheile agus nur a
bha Diarmaid a cur nan con o cheile thug e togail air a churrachd
's chunnaic Grainn' am ball seirc agus bha i ann an trom ghaol air
Diarmaid. Dh' innis i do Dhiarmaid e 's thuirt i ris. " Ruithidh
thu air falbh leam."

" Cha dean mi sin," ursa Diarmaid.

" Tha mise cur mar ghuidhe 's mar gheasaibh ort gun d' theid
thu leam."

" Cha d' theid mi leat; cha ghabh mi 'm bog thu, 's cha ghabh
mi 'n cruaidh thu, cha ghabh mi muigh thu, 's cha ghabh mi stigh
thu, cha ghabh mi air each thu, 's cha ghabh mi 'd chois thu," ars'
esan. Agus dh' fholbh e le miochiataich, 's chaidh do dh' aite
leathoireach, 's chuir e suas tigh ann, 's ghabh e comhnudh ann.

Maidinn a bha 'n sin co ghlaoidh san darusd ach Grainne, " A
bheil thu stigh a Dhiarmaid ? "

" Tha."

" Thig a mach 's folbh leam a nis."

" Nach d' thubhairt mi riut cheana nach gabhainn a' d' chois thu, 's
nach gabhainn air each thu, nach gabhainn a muigh thu, 's nach gabhainn a stigh thu, 's nach biodh gnothach agam rint."

Bha is, eadar da bhith an doruisd air muinn boc goibhre. " Cha
n-eil mi muigh cha n-eil mi stigh ; cha n' eil mi m chois 's cha n-eil
mi air each, 's feumaidh tu dol leam," ars' ise.

" Cha n' eil ait, an d' theid sin nach fhaigh Fionn a mach sin nur
a chuireas e lamh fo dheud fhiosach 's marbhaidh e mis' airson folbh
leat."

" Theid sinn do Charraig, 's tha do Charraigean ann 's nach bi fios
aige co 'n te sam bi sinn."

Chaidh eud do Charraig an Daimh.

Ghabh Fionn fearg nur a mhothaich e gun d' fholbh a bhean, 's
chaidh e rurach air a son. Chaidh eud thairis do Chintire 's cha
deach stad air an cois, na fois air an ceum, gus an d' ranaig eud Carraig an Daimh an Cintire lamh ri Cille Charmaig.

Bha Diarmaid na shaor math, 's bhiodh e deanadh shoithichean, 's
aig iasgach, 's bhiodh Grainn' air folbh a creic nan soithichean, agus
bha leab air leith aca.

Latha bha 'n sin thanaig bodach mor cragach an rathad ris an
abradh eud Ciofach Mac a Ghoill, 's shudh e, 's bha e 'g imirt air
dinnsirean. Ghabh Grainne taitneachd de 'n bhodach. Dh' fhan e
leatha 's chuir eud an comhairle ra cheile gum marbhadh eud Diar-

maid. Bha Diarmaid ag obair air soithichean. Thug am bodach
lamh air, 's thionndaidh e ris a bhodach, 's chaidh eud an glacaibh a
cheile. Bha 'm bodach gu math laidir ; ach ma dheireadh chuir Diarmaid fodh' e. Rug ise air gearrasgian 's dhinn i ann am bunamhas
Dhiarmaid i. Dh' fhag Diarmaid eud, 's bha e folbh o tholl gu toll,
's gun air ach gun robh e beo, 's bha e air dol fo fhionna 's fo fheus-
aig. Thanaig e rathad na carraige 's iasg leis, 's dh' iarr e cead a
rosdadh. Fhuair e gogan uisg, anns an tumadh e mheuran an eas a
bhiodh e ga rosdadh. Nis bhiodh blas na meal' air ni sam bith da'm
boineadh Diarmaidh le a mheuran. Bha e tumadh a mheuran anns'
a ghogan. Thug Grainne criomag as an iasg 's mhothaich i blas na
meal 'air. An dail Dhiarmaid thug Ciofach, agus bha eud an glacaibh
a cheile car treis, ach ma dheireadh mharbh Diarmaid Ciofach, agus
air folbh a ghabh e, 's theich e, agus ghabh e thairis air Loch a
Chaisteil.

Nur a chunnaic Grainne gun robh Ciofach marbh lean i Diarmaid,
agus ma bhrisdeadh an latha thanaig i gus a chladach, agus bha
corra-chridheach a glaodhach. Bha Diarmaid suas ri aodann an t-
sleibh agus ursa Graidhne.

Gr. 'S moch a ghoireas a chorr
  Air an torr as cionn Shliabh Gaoil ;
  A Dhiarmaid O Duibhne da n d' thug mi gradh,
  De 'm fath ma n goir a chorr?

   .   .   .   .

Dr. A Ghrainne, nighean Charmaig nan steud
  Nach d' thug riabh ceum air choir,
  Se 'n t-aobhar ma 'n d' thug i 'n glaodh
  Gun do lean a cas ri lic reot.

Gr. An itheadh thu aran is feoil a Dhiarmaid.

Dr. B' fheumail air mi na 'm biodh e agam.

Gr. A laoich bheir mise dhuit e
  Cait a bheil sgian a ghearras i.

Dr. "Iarr an truaill 's an do chuir thu ma dheireadh i," ursa
Diarmaid.

Bha 'n sgian ann an Diarmaid o 'n chuir i ann i gus an so' 's cha
b' urrain e toirt as. Tharruinn Grainne as an sgian ; agus 's e 'n
naire 's motha ghabh i riabh tarruinn na sgian a Diarmaid.

Bha eagal air Diarmaid gum faigheadh an Fheinn a mach eud 's
ghabh eud air an aghaidh gu Gleann Eilg. Chaidh eud suas taobh
uillt an sin, 's ghabh eud comhnuidh ann' 's bha leab air leith aca.

Bha Diarmaid a deanadh shoithicheann, 's bha na sliseagan a bha e deanadh a dol sios leis an allt gus a chladach.

Bha na Fianntan a sealgaireachd a chois a chladaich, 's bha eud air toir tuirc nimh' a bha fairsleachadh orra. Thug Fionn an aire do shliseagan aig bun an uillt.

"Se so," urs' esan sliseagan Dhiarmaid.

" Cha 'n e cha n' eil e beo," urs' eudsan.

" Gu dearbh," ursa Fionn, " glaodhaich sinn foghaid, 's aon ait 'am bi e tha mionnaichte ris gum feum e' freagairt."

Chuala Diarmaid an fhoghaid. "Siod foghaid nam Fianntan, feumaidh mise freagairt."

" Na freagair a Dhiarmaid."

"An fhoghaid cha n' eil ann ach foghaid bhreig."

Fhreagair Diarmaid an fhoghaid 's chaidh e sios gus a chladach. Chuireadh ma choinneamh Dhiarmaid an torc a shealg. Ruaig Diarmaid an torc o Bheinn Eidinn gu Beinn Tuirc.

> A tarruinn leis an t-sliabh fhada,
> Bha bheisd a toirt Dhiarmaid a nasgaidh,
> Chasadh e lanna cruadhach,
> Mar shiefagan do shean luachair.

Thug Diarmaid tarruinn air an Leadarrach a reinn Lon Mac Liobhann, 's chuir e stigh fo a asgaill i, 's mharbh e n torc. Cha bu dioghaltas le Fionn so fhathasd air Diarmaid. Bha ball dorain air bonn cois Dhiarmaid, 's na 'n rachadh h-aon de na cuilg ann bheireadh e bhas. Ursa Fionn,

> A Dhiarmaid tomhais an turc,
> Co mhiod troigh o shoc 'ga shail.

Thomhais Diarmaid an torc.

" Se troighe' deug de dh' fhior thomhas."

" Tomhais an torc an aghaidh an fhionna."

Thomhais e n torc an aghaidh an fhionna, chaidh h-aon de na cuilg 's a bhall dorain, 's thuit e. Ghabh Fionn duilichinn nur a channaic e a tuiteam; urs' e. " De dheanadh na b' fhearr thu Dhiarmaid ?" " Na 'm faighinn deoch uisg' e basan Fhinn bhithinn na b' fhearr. Chaidh Fionn airson an uisge, 's nur a smaointeachadh e air Grainne dhoirteadh e 'n t-uisge, 's nur a smaointeachadh e air Diarmaid ghabhadh e duilchinn 's bheireadh e leis e. Ach bha Diarmaid marbh ma 'n do thill Fionn. Choisich eud suas taobh an uillt gus an d' thanaig eud far an robh Grainne. Chaidh eud a stigh, chunnaic eud da leaba, 's thuig eud gun robh Diarmaid neochiontach. Bha 'n Fheinn anabarrach duilich mar a thachair. Loisg eud

Graidhne nighean Charmaig nan steud,
Nach d' thug riabh ceum air choir.
Ann an cual de ghlasdarach.

The only points in which the tale and poem published by Dr.
Smith agree are those of the death of Diarmaid. It is so long
since I read Dr. Smith's Sean Dana that I have but a faint recol-
lection of the poem. The tale would seem to me to be partly a
parody on the poem. These old people are sometimes confused
in reciting these tales, probably much is lost, and from confusion
of memory some may be altered. At times they cannot recite at
all. Shaw, from whom I got Murchadh Mac Brian, died a few
days ago, and, so far as I can ascertain, there is none in Islay,
Jura or Colonsay, that can recite the same tale now.

H. MacLean.

Ballygrant, July 6th, 1859.

FROM A STONE IN THE CHURCHYARD OF ST. VIGEANS, NEAR ARBROATH.
Sculptured Stones of Scotland, Pl. lxix.

E

LXI.

THE LAY OF DIARMAID.

I HAVE already referred to a note by Mrs. Mac-Tavish on this subject, vol. ii. 473. She tells how she learned Dan an Dearg (the Song of the Red) more than sixty years ago, from a ploughman who used to chant it at his work ; and she adds :—

" The subject of the song is Diarmaid O Duine, or Dearg as he was sometimes called. Diarmid was, as I daresay you know, the progenitor of the clan Campbell, who are called at times Siol Diarmid, at other times Clann Duine. I never heard who his wife was, but she was esteemed a virtuous and worthy person ; yet she had enemies, who wished to persuade her husband that she did not love him, and who concerted a plot to prove her fidelity. Diarmid was a great sportsman, as all Fingalians were, and hunted wild boars, which, it would appear, were numerous in the Scottish forests at that period. The sport at times proved fatal to those engaged in it. Pretended friends persuaded Diarmid to pretend that he was killed by one of these animals. They put him on a bier, and carried him home to his wife, all bloody, as if he had really suffered as they said. She conducted herself with becoming fortitude and composure, ordered refreshments for those assembled to watch the remains of their chief, sat down along with them, and commenced singing the song which follows. It is very touching in the original. Never having been favoured by the muses, I cannot do it the justice which it deserves, or that I could wish. The translation is as literal as I can make it." *

Derg mac Derg gur i mi do bhean, Air an fhear cha dean-ain lochd, Air an fhear cha dean-ain lochd, Cha n'eil saol nach d'fhuair a dheuchain, S'truagh tha mis ad dheigh an nochd.

1

Derg, son of Derg, I am thy wife,
The husband whom I would not hurt,
The husband whom I would not hurt,
There never was a worthy who was not tried;
Wretched am I after thee this night.

* The Gaelic and music were subsequently got from the same lady.

2

Derg, son of Olla of the enlightened mind,
By whom so softly the harp was played,
By whom so softly the harp was played,
Beloved was the hero who kept no wrath,
Though Derg was laid low by a hog.

3

I see the hawk, I see the hound,
With which my loved one used to hunt,
With which my loved one used to hunt,
And she that loved the three
Let her be laid in the grave with Derg.

4

Then let us rejoice this night,
As we sit around the corpse of a king,
As we sit around the corpse of a king;
Let us be hospitable and liberal,
Thanks be to God for every thing.

1

Derg mac Derg gur i mi do bhean ;
Air an fhear cha deanain lochd.
Cha n' eil saoi nach d' fhuair a dheuchain ;
S' truagh tha mise ad dheigh an nochd.

2

Derg mac Olla chridhe 'n iuil,
Leis an seinte gu ciuin cruit ;
B ionmhuin an Laoch air nach do luidh fearg ;
Ged do thorchradh Derg le muic.

3

Chi mi n' t seabhag a's an cu
Leis an deanamh mo run sealg ;
S' an neach leis an ionmhuin an truir
Chuirer i 's an uir le Derg.

4

Bi mid gu subhach an nochd
Sin nar suidhe mu chorp Righ ;
Bi mid gu furanach fialaidh ;
Buidheachas do Dhia gach ni.

"Diarmaid, who was never conquered in battle,
was destroyed by stratagem. Some one of his enemies
took a bet with him that he could not measure the
length of a boar that he had killed by pacing its back
against the bristles with his bare soles, which gave rise
to the saying—

Tomhas n' tuirc n' aghaidh n' fhrioghain
Measuring the boar against the bristles,

when any unlikely thing is proposed. He gained his
bet, but it cost him his life ; the boar's bristles being
so strong that he bled to death. This legend is said
to be the origin of the boar's head being the crest of
the principal families of the Campbells.

MARY MACTAVISH, November 1859."

The clan MacTavish are a branch of the Campbells, and this lady, in relating a legend of her own
family, tells it as I have heard it repeatedly told, with
variations, by peasants and fishermen, who firmly believed in their own descent from Diarmaid O' Duibhn,
and in the truth of this legend.

The LAY OF DIARMAID is quoted p. 117, and men-

tioned in several places in the report of the Highland
Society on the poems of Ossian, 1805. The version
given below, though it resembles those which I have
seen in books in some respects, differs from them all so
as to make it evident that it is taken from none. I
have no doubt that it is purely traditional.

I am inclined to believe that there was a real
Diarmaid, in whose honour poems have been composed
by many bards, and sung by generations of Scotch
Highlanders, and that to him the adventures of some
mythical Celtic Diarmaid have been attributed, in the
same way that the mythical story of the apple has been
ascribed to William Tell.

Be that as it may, the Lay of Diarmaid can be
traced for a period of 300 years, and its story is known
amongst the whole Celtic population from the south
of Ireland to the north of Scotland.

THE STORY OF THE LAY OF DIARMAID.*
No. 1.

FIONN never was a king ; it was Breean, his father's
brother, who was king over the fifth which the Een
had of Eirinn, and Fionn he was Fla, the chief of
the Feene, and it was Osgar who was chief of the men.

It is Djeearmaid who was the man of the best head
that was in the Een altogether, and no arm at all
could make an impression upon him. There was
BALL DORAIN (a mole, an otter-mark) in his right heel ;
and he could not be killed unless a spike should go
into his heel in the mole.

Graine, the wife of Een, saw the BALL SEIRC
(beauty spot) that was on Djeearmaid, and she took
love for him, and he fled before her, but she followed

* In this I have tried to spell the sound of the names.

him; and they were dwelling in a cave. Djeearmaid would not approach her, and he used to put a symbol before the door, a quarter of a slaughtered animal on a stake ; and Fionn, when he saw the sign, was satisfied ; but on a day the sign was changed. A ciuthach* came into the cave, and Djeearmaid killed him with a spear, for Graine was unfaithful even to her lover.

There was an old woman there whom they used to call Mala Llee (gray eyebrow), and she had a herd of swine, and she had a venomous boar for guarding the pigs. There was no being that went to hunt this boar that came back alive. So it was that Fionn thought to send Djeearmaid to hunt him, to put an end to him.

When Djeearmaid gave out the shout of death, said Fionn to Graine—

" Is that the hardest shriek to thy mind that thou hast ever heard ?"

" It is not," said she, " but the shriek of the ciuthach, when Djeearmaid killed him."

" Ye Gods! that Djeearmaid were alive," said Fionn.

From Janet Currie, Stonybridge, September 14, 1860.—H. MacL.—Part is altered and omitted in the translation, and the Gaelic is not given, because there is nothing peculiar in the language. The legend is remarkable as containing incidents common to the story published by the Ossianic Society of Dublin in 1855.—J.F.C.

No. 2.

WHEN the Fhinn used to go to hunt, one of them used always to stay at home to watch the women. It fell upon Diarmaid on that day that it was he who

* Pr. *kewach*, described in the Long Island as naked wild men living in caves, supposed to be derived from " CIUTH, long hair behind," which word is applied in Islay to a pigtail. French, *queue*.

should stay. There was a thing which they used to call SUGH SEIRO (love juice), a kind of mark in the face of the man, and there was a helmet upon him that must not be raised, for there was no woman who might see the sugh seirc that would not fall in love with him, and Diarmaid knew that these gifts were in himself. On the day that he stayed at home he thought that no being was seeing him, and he gave a lift to the helmet; and Graidhne, the daughter of the King of Coig Ullainn, sees the face of Diarmaid. The warm soul would not be in her unless she should go with Diarmaid.

Said Diarmaid, "That will not answer for me to go with thee."

"O! we will go, or else I will tear my clothes, and I will give thee up to Fionn."

"I have no doubt of thee but that he will believe thee, because thou art his own beloved wife indeed."

They went away, and they travelled together days and three nights. They were crossing a river, and a little trout rose and struck her, and she said:—

"Thou art bolder than Diarmaid. If thou couldst go on shore!"   .   .   .   .

"Now," said he, "Fionn has come home, and they will not find us within, then they will come on our tracks, and they will get us."

"They will not get us," said she. "Whether they get us, or get us not, we will try to hide ourselves. The thing that we will do is this, we will go up to this wood up here, and the branches and leaves of the trees will hide us."

They rose up into the tree, and they went into the heart of the tree, and they drew the branches and leaves of the tree about them.

The Fhinn came to their house, and they did not find Diarmaid or Graidhne at the house.

"Here, here! lads," said Fionn, "I am without a wife, and the Fhinn without Diarmaid. We ought to go till we find them."

They went on their search, and they went over the same river. When they went over, said Fionn—

"We have now been a while walking, and since we have we will breathe a little at the root of this tree up here."

They took the advice of Fionn, and they sat at the foot of the tree."

Said Fionn—"We should turn to playing, lads."

"We are willing," said they.

Fionn and Osgar used to be the two leaders of the game. It was Diarmaid who used always to be along with Fionn. Fionn knew that Diarmaid had magic gifts at games. Now there was Osgar, and he needed a man to be with him, and it was his own father who used to be with him. They began at the games. Every game that was going, it was against Fionn that it went, and Osgar was winning. They drove three games.

Said Fionn—"I am missing Djeearmaid heavily; for it was seldom that a game went against me when Diarmaid was with me; but they are now going against me since he parted from me; but I will go against thee another time."

Diarmaid was listening. He went and he put his hand against his right side,—thus;—and he caught hold of one of the red rowan berries that were on the tree, and he let it fall down beside the tree, and the back of Fionn was against the tree. He noticed something striking him on the back, and put his hand behind him, and he caught the rowan berry, and he put it into his pouch. They began at the game, and this game went with Fionn.

" One is with me," said Fionn.

" It is," said Osgar ; " but two are wanting."

" Wilt thou go into it any more ?" said Osgar.

" I will go, I will go," said Fionn ; " try it again."

Diarmaid let down the next rowan berry, and Fionn won this one.

" Wilt thou go into it any more ?" said he.

" I will go," said Osgar.   " If thou hast two, there is one wanting."

Diarmaid let down the third one, and Fionn won the third one.

" We are now," said Osgar, " even and even ; all I won thou thyself hast taken it back again."

" Wilt thou go into it any more ?" said Fionn.

" I will go," said Osgar ; " we shall have knowledge of its good or evil at this time."

They went at it, and Diarmaid let down the fourth one, and Fionn won.

" Howsoever, it was whilst thou wert without Diarmaid on thy side I was winning.   Howsoever the matter may be, there were matters that belong to Diarmaid about thee this day before thou hast won the fourth time."

Said Oisean—" My father did not drive (the game) against us with right, my son, at all."

" I did drive it," said Fionn.

" Thou did'st not," said Oisean.

" I did ; as a proof that I did there are four rowan berries in my pouch opposite to (for) every game that I won."

He took out the four rowan berries, and when he took them out he said—

" Come down from that, Diarmaid, thyself and Graidhne, daughter of the King of Coig-Ullainn, for ye are there together."

Diarmaid and Graidhne came down; the party was made anew, and Fionn and Osgar fell out. The arms began, and the skaith began, and they were doing much harm to each other. The other part of the Fhinn were seeing that Osgar was like to win against the side of his grandfather.

Said Goll Mac Morna—"Though we had no part in the discord we should make a redding, and an umpire's parting, between the children of Treun Mhor."

Said Conan—"Let the Clann Baoisge hack each other's bodies."

Then Fionn said to Osgar to stay the arms, in case the Clanna Morna should still be after them in Alba.

Fionn took notice of Diarmaid, and he said—

> My frame, and my hand, and mine eye,
> Are longing to do honour to thee,
> Oh! Dhiarmaid O Duibhne, brave man,
> Going with my consort in secret!

There was a woman who was called Mala Lith, and she had a herd of swine, and there was a venomous boar at their head, and many a good lad went to hunt him that never came whole from the boar.

Said Fionn to Diarmaid—"Go to hunt the boar of Mala Lith on her herd of swine. Many a one went there that did not come out of the burn besides a trout." Diarmaid went to hunt the boar.

H. MacLean.

The Gaelic follows at page 78.

These two stories and the following poem give the relationships of the chiefs of that band of warriors whose exploits form the subject of all that class of old Celtic poetry which is attributed to Oisean, Osin or Ossian, and is called Fingalian in English, and Fenian in Ireland. This is the family tree as here set forth :—

TREUNMHOR (great, mighty), who gives his name to
the tribe, the children of Treunmhor, or the clan of the
BAOISGE (flashes of light, coruscations, gleams).

CUMHAL (spelt Cooal in Manx), only mentioned as
the father of Fionn. He is sometimes called Mac-
Dhughil (Macdugald), or the son of black and white
Brian the king, brother of Fionn's father, who seldom
does anything.

FIONN MacCHUMAIL (fair), flath na Finne (chief of
the Finne), married to GRAIDHNE, daughter of the king
of the fifth of Ullan.

OISEAN, the last of the Finne, son of Fionn, who
afterwards sings the departed glories of his race as a
blind old man in poverty and wretchedness.

OSGAR, his son, Flath nam Fear, chief of men.

DONN, brown, who gives his name to a tribe, clan
O Duibhne.

A SISTER of Fionn, wife of King O Dhuine, mother
of DIARMAID O DHUBHINE, the Expert Shield, the best
head in the Finne, whom all family histories and oral
traditions call the ancestor of the Campbells, but whom
I strongly suspect to be a Celtic divinity, whose attri-
butes have been ascribed to their ancestor by a Celtic
tribe.

GOLL MAC MORNA, who is only mentioned here as
an umpire in the strife, but who is a very well known
character in other poems, and is said to have been a
god in Ireland.

CONAN, who only appears to utter a bitter taunt,
and thereby supports the character always assigned to
him. MAOL, the blunt, cropped, or bald.

The FINNE, who are not here named in detail, but
are always introduced into every poem or story in which
the rest of these characters are named. Besides these
there are—

MALA LITH, an old woman, who has a magical white boar with a spike of venom in his back, invulnerable to all arms but the arms of Diarmaid.

There is a trout which Graidhne wishes to come on shore.

A savage who comes to the cave where Graidhne is, and who is killed by Diarmaid, to whom the faithless Graidhne is unfaithful.

There is the rowan tree, which is magical, and whose berries are amulets to this day ; and nearly all this is common to Irish stories, as published in 1855.

The scene is vague, and might be anywhere in Alba. It is commonly laid near Oban, in Lorne, but Bein Gulbein is the favourite haunt of these warriors, and it is generally placed in Ireland, and is said to be in Sligo, and Diarmaid turns his dying face towards Bein Gulban, wherever it may be.

This subject is referred to elsewhere ; but let. me here point out that the "Feene" are the children of beams of light, "Baoisge;" of Great Mighty, their great ancestor, and their chief is Fair, the son of Cooal, or it may be of black and white, light and darkness. That Djeearmaid might be translated "the armed god," who had yellow hair. That their standard was called the sunbeam, and that in the following short poem we have similar incidents to the loves of Venus and Adonis, the death of Achilles, etc., and that all this points rather to mythology than to a single historical incident connected with the disbanding of an Irish militia.

It is worth remark that the poem alludes to several well known adventures which are now told as stories, which may have been poems or distorted facts.

The rowan tree dwelling, verse 21, is No. xxix. in vol. ii. p. 73, or No. xxxvi. p. 168. I forget which story goes by the name. Who White Tooth may be I do not know, but Diarmaid had a son so called.

As to the date of the poem and its origin. There seems every reason to believe that it is old, and that it has been orally transmitted for centuries from generation to generation, in the islands of Scotland, wherever it was composed.

A version of it, got in Kintyre or on Lochawe-side, was printed by John Smith, D.D., minister of the gospel at Campbelton, 1787, p. 99. That version is avowedly pruned and polished.

It is printed without division into stanzas, but the rhythm here and there appears to indicate that such was the original form of the poem.

That which is now printed is so divided by me, because the rhythm generally accords, and the "assonance" and sense all point to separate verses, each complete in itself, and fit for singing to music, as these old songs are in fact sung at this day. Similar Irish poems are so divided.

Several of the lines are nearly the same in Dr. Smith's version and in this which is collected from the people eighty-four years later.

The story in the "Sean Dana" is clearly the same, though the magic is avowedly weeded from the original, and Graidhne is the faithful wife of Diarmaid, not the faithless wife of his uncle Fionn.

There is another version much older, in a MS. now in course of publication, which dates from 1539.

One specimen page has been shewn to me, and it contains one stanza and several lines almost the same as part of this "Lay of Diarmaid." It is quite certain, then, that this old song has been preserved more or less perfectly by oral tradition in Scotland amongst people who can neither read nor write, for at least 330 years, and it gives a standard by which to form an opinion of popular tradition as an aid to written history.

"The pursuit of Diarmaid and Grainne" fills the greater part of vol. iii. of the Transactions of the Dublin Ossianic Society, 170 pages; and a glance at the story as there told will shew that it is founded on the same widely spread tradition, which, as I imagine, is not a tradition of any one real event which happened at any given time anywhere; but a chapter in the mythology of the Pagan world, which may be traced far and wide in various forms.

Of the following poem, founded on this legend, the collector MacLean says:

"This Laoidh Dhiarmaid is one of the most popular of the Ossianic pieces recited in the Long Island, and is known to more individuals than any other. In South Uist I heard it recited by Angus M'Donald, Janet Currie, Allan M'Phie, and some others; in Barra by Alexander M'Donald, and Donald M'Phie (smith), Breubhaig; also by a man in Minglay. The best reciter of this and other Ossianic pieces, that I have met with, is Donald M'Phie. This M'Phie says he learnt the poem from Neill M'Innes, Cill Bharraidh, who died about twenty years ago, about sixty years of age. M'Innes could neither read nor write. M'Donald says he learnt it from his mother, Marion Galbraith; and traces it up for six generations to a maternal ancestor of his, who came from Kintyre. Janet Currie traces it to Neill Currie, her ancestor, who was Clanronald's poet. HECTOR MACLEAN."

For valid reasons, I have not given the Gaelic of all the prose stories, or the whole of them, or the whole of those of which I translate a part. J. F. C.

THE LAY OF YEEARMAID.

No. 3.

I have tried to spell the names so as to convey some idea of the
sound of the Gaelic words to English minds.—J. F. C.

1.

HEARKEN a space if you wish a lay
Of the tribe that from us are gone,
Of MacCooal and of the Feen,
And of the prince there's a woeful song.

2.

Going to Vein Goolban to hunt
The boar that the weak arms cannot wound,
That venomous boar, and he so fierce
That Gray eyebrows had with her herd of swine.

3.

GRAINE.

"Oh Yeearmaid slip not the hounds,
And trust not but this is a party of guile,
For it is hard to withstand MacCooal,
And he is in sorrow deprived of a wife."

4.

DJEEARMAID.

"O Graine wilt thou not keep still,
And for thy first love earn not shame,
I would not let slip my share of the hunt,
For all the wrath of the men of the Feene."

5.

GRAINE.

"Son of O Duine, valiant chief,
Since exploits were done through thee,
Be thou mindful of thy hand,
Here is the death to be shunned by thee."

LAOIDH DHIARMAID.

The MS. came to me without division into verses. I have so divided it, being nearly certain that I am right. The people talk of " ceathrannan," quatrains, and the metre is clear, and fits the music.—J. F. C.

1

. Eisdibh beag ma[1] 's aill leibh laoidh,
Air a' mhuinntir a dh' fhalbh uainn;
Air MacChumhail, 's air an Fhinn,
'S air mac an righ, gu 'm bheil sgial truagh.

2

Dol a Bheinn Ghulbann a shealg,
An tuirc nach dearg na h-airm chli;[2]
'S e 'n torc nimhe, 's e ro gharg,[3]
Bh' aig Mala liath[4] aig sealbh mhuc.

3

GRAIDHNE.

" A Dhiarmaid na leig na gadhair
'S na creid nach i 'n fhaghaid bhreige;[5]
'S gur deacair cur ri Mac Chumhail
A 's cumha leis 'bhith gun chéile."

4

DIARMAID.

" A Ghraidhne nach fuirich thu samhach
'S na coisinn naire dho d' cheud-ghaol;
Cha leiginn sa mo chuid de 'n t-seilg
Air son feirge fir na Finne."

5

GRAIDHNE.

" A mhic O Duibhne, a fhlaith threin,[6]
Nis o rinneadh euchdan[7] leat
Bi-sa cuimhneach air do laimh;
Seo an t-eug o 'n tearnar leat."[8]

F

6.

The monster awakened out of the sleep,
She went round about the glen,
And when she heard the din of the Feean,
East and west she turned her head.

7.

The well Skilled Shield withstood her then,
And the spear went into the belly of the boar,
It broke in the midst of the shaft again,
And the toughest head was upon the hog.

8.

The ancient blade was drawn from sheath,
With which each battlefield was won,
The son of king Guyne slew the beast,
And he withdrew himself whole again.

9.

We sent the white hog to Leodrum,
And wishful we were to go to spoil. (a)

   .   .   .   .   .
   .   .   .   .   .

10.

The fairy glen and the glen by its side,
Where used to be voice of hero and bird,
Where was the hoarse sound of the Feean
Upon the mountain after their hounds.

11.

But anger settled on Fiun of the Feean,
And he sat moodily on the mound,
About Mac O Duine of the mighty arms,
It was torture that he came whole from the boar.

6

Dhuisg an ulla-bheist[9] as an t-suain;
Chaidh i mu chuairt air a' ghleann,
'S nuair chual i farum nam Fiann
Thug i 'n ear 's an iar a ceann.

7

Chaidh an sgiath urla[10] 'na dāil
'S chaidh an t-sleagh an tar[11] an tuirc;
Bhrisd i eadar[12] an crann a rìs
'S bha 'n ceann bu righn' air a' mhuic.

8

Thairneadh an t-seann lann a truaill
Leis am buinichte buaidh gach blair;
Mharbh mac righ Dhuibhn' a' bhéist;
Thiarainn[13] e fhin 'na déigh slan.

9

"Chuir sinn a' mhuc bhàn do Leodrum
'S bu deonach sinn a dhol a 'reubadh;

.   .   .   .   .

.   .   .   .   .

10

An gleann sith, 'san gleann ri 'thaobh,
Far am biodh guth laoich a's loin;
Far am biodh torman nam Fiann
Air an t-sliabh an deigh nan con.

11

Gu 'n d' luidh sprochd air Fionn nam Fiann,
'S shuidh e gu cian air a' chnoc,[15]
Mu mhac O Duibhne nan arm aidh
Bu chràiteach leis tighinn slan o 'n torc.

12.

After he had been silent a while
He spoke, and it was ill to say,
" Oh Yeearmaid, measure the boar,
How many feet from his snout to his tail?"

13.

DJEEARMAID.

" Let us take thy counsel, Een,
Since it was grievous coming from home ;"
He measured the boar on his back,
King Guyne's son of the rounded foot.

14.

" Fifteen feet of the measure good
Are in the back of the wild swine ;" (b)

.   .   .   .   .

.   .   .   .   .

15.

FIUN.

" That is not his measure at all,
Measure him again, Oh Yeearmaid.
Against his bristles measure him,
And thou get'st each jewel (c) of a warrior proud"—

16.

" Oh, Yeearmaid, measure again,
Softly against (the hair) the boar,
And thou shalt get thy prayer from the king,
Thy choice of the tough keen spears."

17.

He rose, and that was no journey of joy,
And, as he measured the boar for them,
The venomous spike of agony pierced
The heel of the hero not mild in strife.

12

A chionn e bhith treis 'na thosd[16]
Labhair e, 's gu'm b' olc ri 'radh,
"A Dhiarmaid tomhais an torc
Co mhiad troidh o 'shoc g'a earr."

13

DIARMAID.

"Gabham-sa do chomhairl' Fhinn
O b' aithreach leinn tigh'n o'n taigh."
Thomhais e'n torc air a dhriom ;
Mac righ Dhuibhn' a bu chruinn troidh.[17]

14

"Coig troidhe deug d'en deagh thomhas
Ann an driom na muice fiadhain."[18]

. . . . .
. . . . .

15

FIONN.

"Cha'n e sin idir a thomhas
Tomhais e rithis a Dhiarmaid.
Tomhais e'n aghaidh a' chuilg,
'S gheibh thu 'laoich bhuirb gach seud."

16

"A Dhiarmaid tomhais a rìs,
'Na aghaidh, gu mìn, an torc,
'S gheibh thu t' achanaich o'n righ,—
Rogha nan sleagh ruighinn goirt.[19]

17

Dh' eirich, 's cha b'e 'n turas aidh,
'S gu 'n do thomhais e dhaibh an torc ;
Chaidh am bior nimh 'bu mhor cradh,
An sàil an laoich nach tlath 'san trod.[20]

18.

DJEEARMAID.

" Give a draught from thy palms, Oh Een,
Son of my king for my succour,
For my life and my dwelling."

FIUN.

" Ochon ! Oh king it is I that will not."

19.

" I will not give to thee a draught,
And neither shall it quench thy thirst,
And never hast thou done me good,
That thou hast not helped my ruin."

20.

DJEEARMAID.

" I have never done ill to thee,
Hither nor thither, nor east nor west ;
But travelling with Graine in a yoke,
While she planned to bring me under spells.

21.

" In the rowan tree dwelling, and thou in straits,
Bold was I for thy succour ;
At the time when death was upon thee,
It was I that went joyously to thee.

22.

" Een, 'tis to thee that my succour was good ;
Hast mind of the day of the combat of Conal ?
The Cairbre and his tribe was before thee,
And I was behind thee to help thee.

23.

" How wretched my face towards Bein Goolban !
On another day was I good for thee ;
When the white tooth was hitting thee,
I turned upon her from behind thee.

18

DIARMAID.

"Thoir deoch bhar do bhasan, Fhinn,
[21] A mhic mo righ, gus mo chobhair,
[22] Air son mo bhidh agus m' aodaich."

FIONN.

"Ochon, a righ, 's mi nach d' thobhair."

19

" Cha d' thoir mise dhuitse deoch,
'S cha mhò a chaisgeas dhe t' iota ;
'S cha d' rinn thu riamh dho m' leas
Nach do leasaich thu dho m' aimhleas."

20

DIARMAID.[22]

"Cha do rinn mis' ortsa cron
Thall, na bhos, an ear, na 'n iar ;
Ach imeachd le Graidhn' ann am braid ;
'S i tur gam thobhairt fo gheasaibh.

21

"'S a' Bhruighin chaorainn, 's tu nad' chàs,
Bu dana mise gad' chobhair ;
'S nuair a bha 'n t-eng air do mhuin
'S mis' a chaidh thugad le mcodhail.

22

" Fhinn 's ann duit bu mhath mo chobhair ;
An cuimhneach leat latha cath Chonaill ?
Bha 'n Cairbre romhad 's a mhuinntir ?
'S bha mis' as do dheigh gad' chobhair !

23

"'S gur truagh m' aghaidh ri Beinn Ghulbann !
Lath' eile bu mhath dhuit mi
Nuair a bha 'n Deud-gheal gad' bhualadh ;
Thionndaidh mi orr' as do dheaghainn,

24.

"And I succoured thee in that time!
If the women of the Feene should hear
That I was wounded on this ridge,
Dejected would be their faces.

25.

"How wretched my face towards Bein Goolban !(d)

26.

"How wretched my face towards Bein Goolban!
As I pour in a flood forth my vigour;
And though I be the son of O Duine,
Farewell be to courting for ever."

27.

There was Djeearmaid on the hillock,
Heavy the hair was and fine,
And he ever losing the (life) blood
From the wound of the spike in his sole.

28.

FIUN.

"Poor is the counsel that grew with me
To slay the son of my sister;
For Graine that ill of a woman
That never again will make my joy.

29.

"That is great the loss on the hillock,
For the price of the wild swine,
Graine king's daughter of Coig Ullain,
Djeearmaid and the two hare hounds.

24

"'S chobhair mi ort anns an uair sin!
Na 'n cluinneadh mnathan na Finne
Mis' a bhith leont' air an driom seo,
Bu tursach a bhiodh an adhart!

25

"'S gur truagh m' aghaidh ri Beinn Ghulbann!

. . . . .

. . . . .

. . . . .

26

" Gur truagh m' aghaidh ri Beinn Ghulbann
'S mi air tuil-bhruchdadh mo nearta!
'S gad a 's mise mac O Duibhne;
Soraidh leis an t-suiridh am feasda!"

27

Gu robh Diarmaid, air an tulaich,
Bu ghrinn am falt a's bu trom;
'S e ri sior chall na fala,
Le lot a bhior, air a bhonn.

28

FIONN.

"'S bochd a' chomhairl' a chinn agam,
Mac mo pheathar a mharbhadh
Airson Ghraidhn', an t-olcas mnatha,
'S nach dean i rithis mo leanmhuinn.

29

"'S mor sin a tha dh' easbhuidh na tulaich!
Air tàillibh na muice fiadhain,
Graidhne, nighean righ Choig' Ullainn,
An da ghearr chuilean, agus Diarmaid.[24]

30.

"Djeearmaid, deceiver of women,
Son of king Guyne of the brilliant hue,
No maiden will raise her eye
Since the mould has gone over thy visage fair."

31.

" Yellow without white in thy hair !
Long thy cheek ! thine eyelash slow !
Blue without rashness in thine eye !
Passion (e) and beauty behind thy curls !

32.

" Oh yesternight it was green the hillock,
Red is it this day with Yeearmaid's blood ;
And with the Een it had been wretched
Unless it had been ordered by Fiun."

33.

OISEAN.

" On this night's night though I be wretched,
There was once a time that I was not weak ;
Not lacking men, nor arms, nor feasting,
See each thing changes in the world !"

NOTES.—LETTERS.—J. F. C.

a The metre seems to require two lines here. I have not attempted to fill up the space, but I adhere to the division into verses of four lines, which the rhythm seems to indicate.

b Here there seems to be a break in the metre.

c Seud a jewel, an instrument. I understand it here to mean a warrior's jewels, his weapons, but it might mean some decoration. See Graidhne's answer. " A knife is the best jewel."

d Here three lines seem wanting to make up a stanza.

e CAISE, passion (Armstrong).

30

"Diarmaid, fear mhealladh nam ban,—
Mac righ Dhuibhn' a bu ghlan snuadh!
Suireadh cha tog a suil[25]
O chaidh uir air do ghnuis ghlain."

31

"Buidhe gun ghil' ann a'd' fhalt!
Fada do leac! mall do rasg!
Guirme gun bhrais' ann a'd' shuil!
Caise 's maise 'n cul nan cleachd!

32

"'S ann an raoir bu ghorm an tulach;
'S dearg an diugh e le fuil Dhiarmaid!
'S gur h-ann leis an Fhinn bu duilich,
Mar a bhithe Fionn 'ga iarraidh!"

33

OISEAN.

"Air an oidhche nochd gad tha mi truagh,
Bha mi uair nach robh mi faoin;
Gun easbhuidh dhaoin' arm na fleadh;
Faic gach ni mu seach 'san t-saogh'l!"

NOTES.—NUMBERS.—H. MacLean.

[1] Laoidh, lay, ode, lyric; it differs from dan a poem, in being more melodious, and capable of being sung. It narrates rapidly a few events ending tragically, almost invariably the death of a hero.

[2] Cli, weak, powerless. Duine gun chli, a man without strength. Airm chli, feeble weapons.

[3] Garg, fierce.

[4] Mala liath. The reciters pronounce this name Mala lith, but the Irish pronounce ia, ee, so that the name means gray eye-

brow, the old woman who owned the venomous boar and the swine, " aig sealbh mhuc," guarding her swine (herd of swine).

[5] Faghaid bhreige, a lying hunting party, that is got up to deceive and destroy him.

[6] Brave hero. Here the vocative is elegantly used.

[7] Euchdan, exploits.

[8] This is the death which you require to avoid.

[9] A monster (feminine in Gælic).

[10] Sgiath urla or urlaimh. Expert shield, a name for Diarmid, from his adroitness in the use of the shield.

[11] Tar, the belly.

[12] Eadar an crann. Here eadar is used in a sense not common now; between the shaft, that is in the shaft, not between the shaft and the head.

[13] Tèarainn, to come off without hurt.

[14] This stanza is not known to all the reciters, given by Donald M'Phie, Breubhaig, Barra.

> Gleann mo chridhe an gleann seo ri m' thaobh,
> Far am binn guth laoigh a's loin ;
> Far am bi farum nam Fiann,
> Air an t-sliabh an deigh nan con.
>
> My heart's glen, this glen by my side,
> Where sweet is the voice of calf and bird ;
> Where is the murmur of the Feean,
> On the mountain side after their hounds.

(This is almost the same as a verse of an old manuscript poem, now in course of publication by Messrs. Edmonston and Douglas, 1861.—J. F. C.)

[15] These are the lines according to Allan M'Phie, and Janet Currie, South Uist.

"Gu 'n d' shuidh e siar air a' chnoc," according to some ; That he sat west on the knoll.

[16] A chionn e bhith treis na thosd. After, or at the end of his being a while silent.

[17] Bu trom troidh, of heavy tread. This is the version used by most of them, and they explain it as referring to the warrior's strong firm step, and the largeness and strength of the leg ; how-

ever, I have inserted bu chruinn troidh, which implies a well formed or fine foot, which is Boyd's version.

[18] Fiadhain, more poetic than fiadhaich.

[19] This is Janet Currie's version of the line, which I think is best. Allan M'Phie gives,

"Urram nan slighne ghear goirt ;" a pretty line also, " The honour of the sharp keen spear."

A great many give, " Taghadh nan sleagh ruighinn, geur, goirt,"
Choice of the keen, tough, sharp spears,
which I think is inferior in poetic merit to the other two.

[20] Nach tlath 'san trod. That is, "not soft in fight." Here the poet very beautifully, in an abrupt manner, turns off to the present tense, so as to produce a vivid impression of the hero's great bravery on the mind of the hearer.

[21] " A dhealbhaich mo righ," Boyd.

[22] " Air son mo bheath' agus m' fhardoich," Boyd.

[23] This beautiful dying speech of Diarmid is not known so full as this to any of the reciters, except to Donald M'Phie, Breubhaig.

Cobhair is repeated here often, from the exasperated feeling at the ingratitude of the uncle. Such repetition is always the language of deep passion, as for instance in the case of Coriolanus in his reply, when called " thou boy of tears."

The repetition of this line, and the abruptness with which he turns off from other subjects, is very pathetic. Whoever has been in the company of the dying can feel the truth of this line, how they refer constantly to some of their favourite haunts. The ruling passion, the last, a favourite theme with modern philosophers and novelists, is here finely illustrated.

[24] " A dealbh-chuilean." This is the expression given by Janet Currie, who says it refers to the unborn child; Graidhne, according to her being with child to the Ciuthach. Boyd has da dhearbh chuilean. Macdonald gives the words inserted, who says they refer to the two best dogs of the Feen, after Bran, which were killed by the boar.

[25] Suireadh, a maid. Suireadh cha tog a suil, no maid will raise her eye ; that is with grief. The line is repeated no doubt in a corrupt manner, thus—

" Suireach cha tog a shuil," no lover will raise his eye, which would make no sense.

Leac, cheek. Rasg, eyelash, also the eye itself.

"Guirme gun ghlaise," and "guirme le ghlaise." Janet Currie gives the line inserted, which is prettier, and at the same time a contrast to the piercing blue eye ascribed by Tacitus to the ancient Germans. Bulwer, in one of his novels, describes the French dark eye as milder and softer than the Italian.

Cleachd, a ringlet.

Cùis a's mais' air chul nan gleachd. Boyd.

The poem is not the complete version of one reciter, but is built up and selected from several long versions, written from the dictation of the people named. If the evil spirit of the Ossianic controversy still cumbers the earth, the papers can be produced, and the authorities are alive. I will answer for the honest intention of the collector and the translator, and I can do no more.

J. F. C.

LAOIDH DHIARMAID.

NUAIR a bhiodh an Fhinn a' folbh a shealg bhiodh h-aon diu daonnan a' fantail aig an taigh a choimhead nam ban. Thuit e air Diarmaid an lath' ud gur h-e a dh' fhanadh. Bha rud ris an canadh iad sugh seirc an aodann an duine; 's bha clogad air nach fheumadh e thogail; chionn cha robh bean a chitheadh an sugh seirc nach tuiteadh ann an gaol air; 's bha fios aig Diarmaid gu 'n robh na buadhan seo air fhein. An latha a dh' fhan e aig an taigh bha duil aige nach robh neach 'ga fhaicinn, 's thug e togail air 'a chlogad, 's faicidh Graidhne nighean righ Choig' Ullainn aodann Dhiarmaid. Cha bhiodh an t-anam blath innte mar am falbhadh i le Diarmaid.

Arsa Diarmaid, "Cha fhreagair domhsa sin—falbh leatsa."

"O! falbhaidh sinn; airneo sracaidh mi m' aodach 's bheir mi suas thu do dh' Fhionn."

"Cha 'n 'eil aicheadh agam ort nach creid e thu; chionn gur tu a bhean dhileas fhein gu dearbh."

Dh' fhalbh iad, 's bha e comhla rithe tri lathan 's tri oidhchean; ach bha e saor a's i. Dh' fhalbh iad air an aghaidh. Bha iad a' dol a null air amhainn, 's thog ise a h' aodach suas ma 'm fliucht' i, 's dh' eirich breac beag an uair sin, 's bhuail e suas air a sliasaid.

"Mo laochan thu fhein a bhric bhig, bheadaidh, urad 's a thug dhomh de thoilinntinn cha d' thug Diarmaid domh o cheann nan tri lathan 's nan tri oidhchean a tha e leam; 's na 'm biodh tu air chomas falbh air tir leam bu choltach gur h-ann mar a bu lugha an duine a b' fhearr e."

" Mata," ars' esan, " na a dh' fhulaing mise air son geanmnuidh-
eachd de thamailt cha 'n fhulaing mi na 's fhaide e."

. . . . . .

" Tha Fionn a nis," ars' esan, " air tighinn dachaidh 's cha 'n
fhaigh iad sinn a staigh ; thig iad an sin air ar toir 's gheibh iad sin."
" Cha 'n fhaigh," ars' ise. " Co dhiu a gheibh no nach fhaigh bheir
sinn ionnsuidh air sinn fhein fhalach." Se 'n rud a ni sinn theid
sinn do 'n choill seo shuas 's falachaidh meanganan 's duilleach na
craoibhe sin." Dhirich iad do 'n chraoibh an sin, 's chaidh iad ann an
cridhe na craoibhe, 's tharruing iad meanglain 's duilleach na craoibhe
mu 'n cuairt orra.

Thainig an Fhinn 'ionnsuidh an taighe 's cha d' fhuair iad Diarmaid na Graidhne aig an taigh. " Seo, seo, Ghillean," arsa Fionn,
" tha mise gun bhean 's tha 'n Fhinn gun Dhiarmaid ; 's coir duinn
falbh gus am faigh sinn iad."

Dh' fhalbh iad air an torachd, 's chaidh iad a null air a cheart
amhainn. Nuair a chaidh iad a null arsa Fionn, " Tha sinn an deigh
treis choiseachd a dheanadh, 's o'n a tha, leigidh sinn anail bheag aig
bonn na craoibhe seo shuas." Ghabh iad comhairl' Fhinn 's shuidh
iad aig bonn na craoibhe.

Arsa Fionn, " 'S coir duinn teannadh ri cluiche, Ghillean."

" Tha sinn deonach," ars' iadsan.

B' abhaist do dh' Fhionn 's do dh' Osgar a bhith 'nan da cheann
stochd. 'Se Diarmaid daonnan a b' abhaist a bhith comhla ri Fionn.
Bha fios aig Fionn gu 'n robh buaidhean air Diarmaid aig cluichean.
Bha 'nis Osgar agus dh' fheumadh e duine a bhith leis, agus 's e
'athair fhein a 'b abhaist a bhith leis. Thoisich iad cur nan cluichean.
A' h-uile cluiche a bha' 'dol 's ann air Fionn a bha e 'dol, 's bha
Osgar a' buidhinn. Chuir iad tri chluichean. Arsa Fionn.

" Tha mi aig ionndrainn uam Dhiarmaid gu trom ; chionn b'
ainneamh leomsa cluich a dhol a m' aghaidh nuair a bhiodh Diarmaid leam ; ach tha iad a nis a' dol a m' aghaidh o'n a dhealaich e
rium ; ach theid mi uair eile riut."

Bha Diarmaid ag eisdeachd. Dh' fhalbh e 's chuir e ri thaobh
deas mar siud a lamh, 's rug e air té de na caora dearga a bh' air a'
chraoibh, 's leig e sios ris a chraoibh i, 's driom Fhinn ris a' chraoibh.
Dh' fhairich e rud a' bualadh air a dhriom, 's chuir e a lamh air a
chul-thaobh, 's rug e air a chaora, 's chuir e 'na phoca i. Thoisich
iad air cluiche 's chaidh an cluiche seo le Fionn. " Tha h-aon
agam," arsa Fionn. " Tha," ars' Osgar, " ach tha a dha gu
d' dhith." " An d' theid thu tuilleadh ann ?" ars' Osgar. " Theid,
theid," ars' Fionn. " Feuch a rithis e." Leig Diarmaid sios an
ath chaora 's bhuidhinn Fionn am fear seo. " An d' theid

thu ann tuilleadh?" ars' e.   "Theid," ars' Osgar, "ma tha a dha
agad tha fear gu d' dhith."   Leig Diarmaid a nuas an treas té
agus bhuidhinn Fionn an treas fear.   "Tha sinn a nis," ars' Osgar,
"cothrom a's cothrom; na 'bhuidhinn mi thug thu fhein air t' ais a
rithis e."   "An d' theid thu ann tuilleadh?" arsa Fionn.   "Theid,"
ars' Osgar, "bidh fios a mhath na 'uilc againn air an t-siubhal seo."
Chaidh iad ann a rithis; leig Diarmaid a nuas an ceathramh té, 's
bhuidhinn Fionn.   "Ge b'e air bith mar a bha fad 's a bha thusa
gun Diarmaid leat bha mise a' buidhinn. Ge b' e an bith mar a
tha a' chuis tha gnothaichean a bhoineas do Dhiarmaid mu'n cuart
ortsa an diugh ma 'm bheil thu air buinig a' cheathramh uair.
Ars' Oisean, "Cha do chuir m' athair oirnn, a mhic, le ceartas
idir."   "Chuir," arsa Fionn.   "Cha do chuir," ars' Oisean.   "Chuir;
a dhearbhadh gu 'n do chuir tha ceithir caoran ann a'm' phoca mu
choinneamh a' h-uile cluich a bhuidhinn mi."   Thug e mach na
ceithir caoran, 's nuair a thug e mach iad thubhairt e.

"Thig a nuas a sin a Dhiarmaid, thu fhein agus Graidhne,
nighean righ Choig' Ullainn; chionn tha sibh an sin comhla."

Thainig Diarmaid agus Graidhne a nuas; Roinneadh a' chuideachd as ur, 's chaidh Fionn a's Osgar thar a cheile. Thoisich na
h-airm, 's thoisich an sgath, 's bha iad a' deanadh moran coire air
a cheile.   Bha a' chuid eile de 'n Fhinn a' faicinn gu 'n robh
Osgar a' brath buinig air taobh a sheanar. Arsa Goll Mac Morna,
"Gad nach robh cuid againne de 'n aimhreit, 's coir dhuinn reite
's eadraiginn a dheanadh eadar clanna Treunmhor." Arsa Conan,
"Leig le Clann na Baoisge cuirp a cheile a ghearradh."   Thuirt
Fionn an sin ri Osgar, Casg a chur air armaibh, ma 'm biodh
Clanna Morna fhathasd 'nan deigh an Alba. Thug Fionn aire do
Dhiarmaid 's thuirt e,

"Tha mo ghrunnd, 's mo lamh, 's mo shuil
Deonach cuirt a dheanadh dhuit;
A Dhiarmaid O Duibhne, fhir threin!
Falbh le m' cheile gun fhios domh!!"

Bha boireannach ann ris an cainte Mala lith, 's bha speil mhuc
aice, 's bha torc nimhe air an ceann, 's chaidh iomadh gille math a
'shealg nach d' thainig riomh slan o'n torc. Arsa Fionn ri Diarmaid, "A Dhiarmaid theirig a shealg an tuirc aig Mala lith air
shealbh mhuc   'S iomadh fear a chaidh ann nach d' thainig as an
allt thar bhreac."

Dh' fhalbh Diarmaid a shealg an tuirc.

From Alexander M'Donald, Burgh, Barra.   September 20, 1860.

No. 4.

One more version carries the legend to the extreme northern and eastern Gaelic frontier. It varies somewhat from the others, but the main incidents are the same. The story is called the THE BOAR OF BEN LAIGHAL, and is thus told :—

There lived once upon a time a king in Sutherland, whose land was ravaged by a boar of great size and ferocity. This boar had a den or cave in Ben Laighal (Pr Loyal), full of the bones of men and cattle.

It came to pass that the king swore a great oath, saying he would give his only daughter to the man who should rid the country of this monster. Then came Fingal, Ossian, Oscar, and I know not who besides, and tried in vain to kill the boar, whose bristles were a foot long, his tusks great and white, and whose eyes glowed like beltain fires. But when Diarmid saw the king's daughter, whose robes were white, and beheld her blue eyes, and her long yellow hair, as she stood in the gateway, he said to himself, "that come what would he would win her." So he went out ere it was yet dawn, and when he came to the boar's lair he saw the monster lying, as large and black as a boat when its keel is turned up on the shore ; drawing a shot from his bow he killed it on the spot. All the king's men turned out and pulled the carcase home with shouts to the palace ; and the king's daughter stood in the gate, beautiful as the May morn. But the king's heart was evil when he saw that the boar was dead. He went back from his word secretly, saying to Diarmid that he should not have his daughter till he had measured (by paces) the body of his fallen foe, once from the head to the tail, and once

G

again backward from the tail to the snout. That would Diarmid gladly do, and the wedding should be the morrow's morning. He paced the beast from tip to tail without harm or hindrance, but on measuring it backwards the long poisonous bristles pierced his foot, and in the night Diarmid sickened and died. His grave and the den of the boar may be seen in Ben " Loyal " to this day.

This seems a different, and a sadder legend than the one which gives the Campbells their boar's head crest ; nearly as tragical as the fate of Adonis ; but it is common in the west of this county to call the Campbells MacDiarmid.—C. D., Sutherland.

It may be interesting to shew this legend of " Diarmaid," as the word is spelt now-a-days, in another shape.

The following is taken from a MS. which came from Cawdor Castle, and is now in my possession ; it is called,

" GENEALOGY ABRIDGEMENT OF THE VERY ANTIENT AND NOBLE FAMILY OF ARGYLL, 1779."

The writer explains that—

" In the following account we have had regard to the genealogical tree done by Niel MacEwen, as he received the same from Eachern MacEwen, his ffather, as he had the same from Art^r. MacEwen, his grandfather, and their ancestors and predecessors, senachies and pensioners to great ffamilys, who, for many ages were employed to make up and keep such Records in their accustomed way of Irish Rhymes ; and the account left by Mr. Alex^r. Colvin, who had access to the papers of the ffamily, and Pedro Mexva, a Spaniard, who wrote the origin of diverse and sundry nations, in his book entitled the Treasury of Antiquities."

The first statement is as follows :—

"The Campbells were of old, in the Irish language, called Clan Odinbhn or Oduimhn (bh and mh being pronounced as the Roman v), *id est*, the sons, children, or posterity of Duimhn, knights of the MacDuimhns ; particularly from Diarmid Mac-Duimhn, who makes such a figure in the Irish history, that from him they are sometimes called Siol Dirmed, *i.e.*, Diarmid's seed, or Sliochd Diarmid, *i.e.*, Diarmod's offspring."

In the next paragraph it is said—

"Yet to this day (1779), in the Irish language or Galic, they (the Campbells) are called both by the name of Campbell and O'Duimhn."

I may add that at this day, 1861, the name of Campbell is very rarely used in speaking Gaelic. A man is called *Kaim-bel-ach*, a Campbelite, or the Campbelltonian, but individually, he is Iain Ruagh, Russet John ; if he has the common burnt Sienna beard, Iain fada ; long John, if he be tall ; Iain na Airde bige, John of the little hill, if his farm be so called ; or John MacAllister, if his father's name be Alexander. In short, surnames are not yet in full use within the Highland bounds.

In the next paragraph the rhymes of the "Senachies" of the Argyll family are again called "Irish," and thus it appears that in the mind of this writer *Irish* and *Galic* meant one and the same language in 1779, as I hold that they are in fact now. The story goes on thus :—

"Although the common and ordinary method of reckoning the genealogy of the sirname of Campbell or Clan O'Duimhn is to begin at Arthur of the round table, king of the Britons, as a person very great and famous in history, yet we shall begin it some ages before him, by shewing the occasion of his accession to the crown of the Britons, as Boethius and Buchanan have it in their History of Scotland."

And accordingly the writer begins with Constantine, grandfather to King Arthur.

The half mythical heroes of Welsh and Breton tales, and of mediæval romances; and personages who still figure in Irish and Scotch Gaelic popular tales, as something more than mere mortals :—Arthur and Diarmaid, primeval Celtic worthies, whose very existence the historian ignores, are thus brought together by a family genealogist, and most of these west-country genealogies agree with him in claiming a descent from King Arthur for "Mac Callen Mor."

The fact proves nothing, and is of little interest in itself, but when brought to bear upon Celtic mythology it acquires an interest, for it shews that peasants' stories are sufficiently old to have found their way into family history in Scotland, as well as into what is called the Fenian literature of Ireland. The Irish theory crowds whole centuries of adventure into the lifetime of a single generation of one family, of which Fionn was the head, and which was exterminated, as it is said, about A.D. 277 or 294, at the battle of Gabhra in Ireland. The Scotch genealogist boldly asserts that

"It is plain that the family can trace their predecessors from father to son for upwards of 1360 years,"

and produces Diarmaid as one of a Scotch family all alive in 943. He goes on to shew how King Arthur brought Ireland under tribute, and received it at Cathair Ler-eon, now West Chester.

The next worthy is

"Smoroie Mor, or as others have it, Sir Moroie Mor, 'a son of King Arthur,' of whom great and strange things are told in the Irish traditions. He was born at Dumbarton Castle, on the south side of the fort, in the place called the Red Hall, or in Irish, Tour na-hella dheirg, i.e., the Tour of the Red Hall. He was called to his by-name, The fool of the Forest; he was a wild and undaunted person, and married a sister of King Andar's, the forty-ninth king of the Scots, and was contemporary with Columbus pius ; called in the Gaelic Colmkill, or Calum na-kill, because, when he retired from company they were always sure to find him in his cell at prayer."

Now there are a great many poems and stories still extant in Gaelic, some printed, others still as traditions, in which a "great fool" plays the chief part. I would refer to No. xxxv. vol. ii., and to the "Lay of the Great Fool" in this volume. A long version of the last has been printed already.

There is besides an Arthurian tradition in England of a buried army and a sleeping king, and a wizard who appears occasionally about Alderley edge, not far from Chester, and this has a counterpart in a story got from Islay, which localizes the very same legend in another shape at Dumbarton ; and that tradition of warriors sleeping a magic sleep in a cave is known in Barra and in the Isle of Man, in Spain and over nearly the whole of Europe ; and here again tradition and genealogy point to a common origin for Celtic tribes, and to a north-western route, and to a common mythology ; for to the best of my knowledge this legend is unknown beyond the Celts in the north. Having brought King Arthur to Dumbarton, the genealogist takes to dates (which I give as I found them), and goes on with a list of worthies, most of whom are unknown to fame.

" VI. Ferither-Our, i.e., Dun Ferither, A.D. 620.
" VII. Duimhn-Mor, who married a daughter of Duke Murdoch of Moraviæ, or Murray, or Elgin,"

and gave a name to the family, which has been variously explained.

" Odinbhin " and Mac-Oduimhn might suggest a Scandinavian descent, and some old sea-rover for an ancestor, who called himself a son of Odin. It has been suggested that the warriors of Fionn were fair Norsemen. Some Campbells are proud of the "ginger-hackle" which commonly adorns their chins, and claim to be Northmen; but if the name be Gaelic, as I believe it to be, I am compelled to translate Duimhn-Mor, as the Great Brown. The Browns are a nume-rous and respectable clan, and there is no cause to be ashamed of the connection, for Brown is synonymous with Don, and there are Browns and Dons of high degree.

"VIII. Arthur Oig MacDuimhn, *i.e.*, Young Arthur, son of Brown, 684,

"IX. Ferither eile MacDuimhn. The other Ferither, son of Brown, 730.

"X. Duimhn falt derig MacDuimhn. Brown of the red hair, son of Brown, 786, who married the grand-daughter of Con-nal Gulban, one of the sons of Neal na Nidgheallach, king of Ireland, who was so called because he had nine chains, fetters, or prisons, for confining captives taken in the wars. This Neal was father to Longirius, who reigned when St. Patrick came to Ireland."

So here comes in another hero of Gaelic romance, Connal Gulban, of whom there are more stories told in Gaelic at the present day than of any other indi-vidual, Fionn always excepted. As St. Patrick here makes his appearance on the stage with Diarmaid and Connal Gulban, and as he brought Christianity, and mayhap civilization to Ireland, it seems reasonable to suppose that such an event would stimulate the bards; and that about the name of St. Patrick all the floating legends of the old Pagan history and mythology would group themselves, as they are in fact found to do, in the Irish dialogues between St. Patrick and Osin. In these, the old blind poet tells the glories of his de-

parted race, and argues with the saint in a very dis-
contented and rebellious spirit, to say the least of it.
Osin, whose tribe was exterminated about 277, con-
verses with St. Patrick, who was born about 372,
flourished in 430, and, according to this genealogy, was
contemporary with Longirius and Connal Gulban.

"XI. Ferither finruo, *i.e.*, reddish white MacDuimhn, son of
Brown.

"XII. Duimhn dherig, *i.e.*, Brown the red, 860.

"XIII. Duimhn donn, *i.e.*, Brown Brown, 904, was cotem-
porary with Constantine, seventy-fifth king of the Scots."

"XIV. Dirmaid Mac Duimhn, 943."

And having arrived at this Dirmaid, to whom all
popular traditions trace the Campbell clan, the writer
breaks off into a digression on the origin of surnames.
Of Dirmaid he says :—

"This Dirmaid MacDuimhn, from whom the Campbells were
called Siol Diarmaid, *i.e.*, Diarmaid's seed, gained great reputation
in Ireland, and in all their traditions there is honourable mention
made of him for his conduct, valour, and loyalty. He was cotem-
porary with Malcolm the first, seventy-sixth king of the Scots. He
had to wife, Graine, niece to Cormac Vic Art Vic Chuin Cheud
Chathach, and thus his son was great-grandchild to that famous
Irish monarch, Conn Cheud Chathach, so called because he fought
one hundred battles.

Diarmaid, say the Irish writers, was one of the
Fenians, and they were exterminated A.D. 277; that
is, 666 years before the date of the Dirmaid and
Graine of the genealogy.

And then we are told how Dirmaid and Graine
had two sons—

"Arthur Armderig, 977 (red arms), and Duimhn Dedgheal,
Brown white tooth, who had to his son Gilcolm or Malcolm Mac-
Duimhn, who, after he had married a daughter of the lords of
Carrick, by whom he had three sons, of whom afterwards, and
after her death, in the reign of Kenneth the Third, the eightieth
king of the Scots, the said Malcolm MacDuimhn went to Nor-

mandy in France and married the heretrix of Beauchamp, *i.e.*, campus bellus, or pleasant field, sister's daughter to William the Conqueror, Duke of Normandy, afterwards King of England, of which lady he had three sons, who were called Campbells after the name of their lands in Normandy."

Further on we are told how the representative of the French branch came over and married the heiress of a knight of Lochawe, Evah, and how the clan took the name of Campus bellus; and how, centuries later, French worthies were entertained at Inverary, and acknowledged themselves to be of the same race and descent as their entertainer. And other genealogical incidents are related in the same quaint style down to the writer's time, and to John Duke of Argyll.

"44. John Campbell, XXVIII. Campbell, XX. MacCallen Mor, V. Duke, 1768; who (amongst other deeds) caused remove the old burgh of Inverary, but has reared up a much prettyer and more fashionable burgh royal, about a furlong south of the palace, upon the Gallow failean point."

So here are Diarmaid and Graidhne, the hero and heroine of so many Gaelic myths, stories, poems, and proverbs, the Venus and Adonis of Gaelic mythology, brought into juxtaposition with King Arthur and his knights, honestly married and planted in Scotland, A.D. 943, as Mr. and Mrs. Brown; a family tree grafted on their stock, and the growth of the tree itself all set forth as true family history in 1789.

There probably were people who bore these names. There are hundreds of Dermotts, and Dermids, and Donns, and Dons, and Guns, Mac-Dermotts and Mac-Diarmaids, still to be found in Ireland and in Scotland. There are Gwynnes in Wales, and there are many similar family names in France which have been hooked into the family tree, which springs from Oduimhn; but it is surely time to give up the attempt to convert

Celtic mythology into comparatively modern history, and to fix a time and place for the slaying of Diarmaid by the venomous boar of Beingulban.

In a learned note in the Transactions of the Ossianic Society (vol. v. p. 62, 1860), I find that the Celtic legends about magic boars which pervade Ireland, Wales, and Scotland, have already attracted the notice of Irish scholars, and that they are taking a wide view of their popular lore. The sacred swine of the ancient Celts are supposed to have given rise to this tradition. It is suggested that there was a "Porcine worship which was analogous to, if not identical with, the existing worship of the Hindoo deity Vishnoo, in his avatar as a boar." And that Diarmaid was a reformer who tried to abolish the worship of pigs, and died in the attempt.

To me it seems perfectly hopeless to attempt to explain a legend which is at least as old as the loves of Venus and Adonis, by referring it to any one time or place.

It is like making Hercules a doctor or a drainer, and the Hydra sulphuretted hydrogen embodied in an epidemic, and cured with steel.

Let this tale of Diarmaid rather be taken as one phase of a myth which pervades half the world, and which is still extant in the Highlands of Scotland, and in Ireland, amongst all classes of the Gaelic population. Let all that can be got concerning it be gathered from the most unsuspecting and the most unlearned witnesses; and when the traditions are compared with what is known to the learned, there is some chance of digging knowledge out of these old mines of fable. At all events, I have now shewn the same legend in a poem, a popular tale, a proverb, a family tradition, and a family history; I have shewn it in Ireland, Cantyre,

Islay, Lorn, Skye, the Long Island, and Sutherland ; and I believe it to be an ancient pagan myth, which belonged especially to a tribe of Celts who took possession of Argyll, and which has been transferred to the family of the chief of the most numerous clan, and perhaps to the real leader of the tribe, together with every thing else which a race of family historians thought likely to adorn their favourite topic.

There would seem to be two distinct forms of the myth; one the wildest and best known to the people, the other more rational and best known to the· educated classes.*

FABLES.

I am told on good authority, that stories in which beasts play a chief part are perhaps the most interesting of all in a scientific point of view. I accordingly give a few here, which should belong to No. XVII. in Vol. I. They will serve as a contrast to the heroic traditions with which I had intended to fill this third volume. Their value consists in their close resemblance to well-known stories, found elsewhere amongst peasants, and published in modern times, and in their possessing traits of their own, which seem to indicate that they are parallel traditions derived from a common source ; not stories derived from others, and following in their wake.

For example, the whole of the incidents in the story of the Fox and the Wolf are to be found in Grimm; but they are separated. Some of the incidents are also in the Norse tales ; but the Gaelic tale

* Since this was written I have seen two versions of the Lay of Diarmaid, one of 1786, the other written about 1530. I refer to them elsewhere.

fits Highland ways of life exactly, and the story is so widely spread in the Highlands, and can be traced so far back, that it seems almost impossible that the un-lettered men who tell it to their children should have got it from modern books which they could neither read nor understand.

LXII.

HOW THE FOX TOOK A TURN OUT OF THE GOAT.

From Hector Boyd, Barra.

THERE was a gray goat and she had kids, and if she had, the fox went on a day around them, and he caught them, and he killed them, and he ate them. Then the goat came home, and she was black melancholy and miserable when she came and was without them before her. She took on her way and she reached the house of the russet dog, and she went up on the top of the house, and the fox cried out—

" Who is that on top of my bothy, maiden my deary,
That will not leave my caldrons to boil,
That will not leave my bonnachs to bake,
And that will not let my little one go to the well?"

GOAT.
"There is me gray goat, harried out,
Seeking the three kindly kidlings,
And the gray-bellied buck,
And the buck lad."

FOX.
"Well then ; by the earth that is beneath,
By the aether over head,
By the sun that is gone down,
That I have never seen thy set of kids."

There was no bird in the flock that she did not go to ; and she returned home and she did not get them.

This story is known to that section of the poorer Gaelic population, which is, and which has been young ; but though everybody knows it, nobody will tell it. I persuaded an old woman on the banks of Loch Hourn, to tell it to me in part, and so far as it went her version was better.

> Chaidh a ghobhar ghlas don traigh
> Agus, bhrisd strabh a cas.

The gray goat went to the strand, and a straw broke her leg, and when she came home there were

> Na tri minneana mine-glas
> Taraigna taraghlas
> Driomana driomaghlas
> Agus am boc ceannaglas.

> The three kindly kidlings-gray,
> With bellies gray bellied,
> And with backs gray back-ed,
> And the buck gray-head.

And the ram (something, which I forget); and a whole party besides, whom my informant would not name; all gone away. And she went to the fox, and his clearing oath was :—

> Air an draigheann air an dreas
> Air an talamh fo mo chois
> Air a ghrian seachad siar
> Cha n fhaca mise riamh
>   Do chuid meann.

> By the blackthorn and the briar,
> By the earth beneath my foot,

By the sun that has gone west,
I have never never seen
Thy set of kids.

It is manifest that there is a great deal more of this, but I have not got it.*

LXIII.

HOW THE COCK TOOK A TURN OUT OF THE FOX,

AND NO CREATURE EVER TOOK A TURN OUT OF HIM BUT THAT COCK.

From Hector Boyd, Barra, Sept. 20, 1860.

THE russet dog came to a house, and he caught hold of a cock. He went away with the cock, and the people of the town-land went away after him.

"Are they not silly!" quoth the cock, "going after thee, and that they cannot catch thee at any rate."

The cock was for that he should open his mouth that he might spring out.

When he saw that the cock was so willing to go along with himself, he was so pleased.

"Oh! musician wilt thou not say—It is my own cock that is here, and they will turn back," said the cock.

The fox said, "Shê-mo-haolach-hay-n-a-han;" and when the fox opened his mouth the cock sprung away.

* May 1861.—I have received a much better version from Mr. Alexander Carmichael, from Carbost in Sky. The fox, disguised as the goat, after several trials gets in, and eats the kids. The goat goes to the houses of the gull, hoodie, and sheep, and at last to the fox. He lets her in, eats up a caldron of food, gives her none, and makes her scratch his paunch. The goat rips him up, out come the kids, and they go home. The rhymes are curious, and whole very original.

I have already given a version of this in vol. ii.; the main difference is, that the cock here calls the fox a musician, as the fox in the old story called the crow when he did him out of a cheese by the same stratagem. Ceolaire is used to express a silly fellow.

LXIV.

THE HEN.

From Hector Boyd. Learnt this story from Donald M'Kinnon, Laidhinnis, Barra, who died twelve years ago at the age of sixty. —Castle Bay, October 4, 1860.

THERE was a woman before now, and she bore a hen in rock by the shore, after she had been driven into banishment in some way or other.

The hen grew big, and she used to be going to the king's house every day to try if she could get something that she might give to her mother. The king came out on a day of these days, and he said to her,

" What, thou nasty little creature, art thou doing standing there upon my door ?"

" Well, then, though I be little, and even nasty, I can do a thing that the fine big queen thou hast cannot do," said she.

" What canst thou do ?" quoth the king.

" I can spring from spar to spar, with the tongs and the hook for hanging the pot trailing after me."

He went in and he told that to the queen. The hen was tried, and she did it ; they tied the pot-hook and the tongs to her, and she sprang over three spars (rafters), and she came down on the ground.

Then they tied the pot-hook and the tongs to the queen, and she went and she took a spring out of herself, and she cut the edge of her two shanks, and she fell, and the brain went out of her.

He had four queens, and the hen put them all out with this work.

" It would be better for you to marry my mother," quoth the hen ; " she is a very fine woman."

" Avoid me," said the king ; " thou hast caused me loss enough already, thou nasty creature."

" Well then, that is not what is best for thee, but to marry her," said the hen.

" Send down thy mother so that we may see her," said the king.

She went where her mother was, and she said to her, "The king is seeking you, mother ; I was asking him to marry you."

She went up, and she herself and the king married.

Then there was a Sunday, and they were going to sermon, the king and the queen ; and they left within but the hen and the son of the first wife. The hen went when they went away, and she went to a chamber, and she cast off her the husk that was upon her, and the lad went into the room, and he saw the husk that was upon her. He caught hold of it and he put it into the hot middle of the fire. She came down and she had no tale of the "cochall."

She came where the lad was, and she had a naked sword, and she said to him,

" Get for me my husk, or else I will take the head off thee, against the throat."

The lad took much fear, and he could not say a word to her.

" Thou nasty creature," said she, " it is much for me that thy death should be on my hands ; I don't know what I shall do now ; if I get another cochall they will think that I am a witch, and I had better stay as I am."

When the king came home he saw that fine woman within, going about the house, and he had no knowledge what had put her there, and the king must know what sort of a woman she was. She told every whit. She herself and the king's son married, and a great wedding was made for them.

I suspect this is a fragment of some much longer tale. I know nothing like it in any other language.

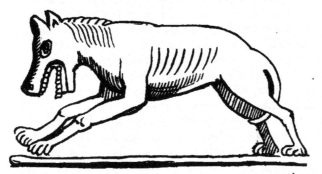

WOLF.—From a stone at St. Andrews.—*Sculptured Stones of Scotland*, Pl. lxi.

LXV.

THE KEG OF BUTTER.

From Hector Boyd, Barra, who learnt it from Neill M'Neill, Watersay; and from many other old men. Neill M'Neill died ten years ago, past eighty years of age.—Castle Bay, Sept. 20, 1860.

THE russet dog and the wild dog, the fox and the wolf, were going together; and they went round about the sea shore, and they found a keg of butter, and they buried it.

On the morrow the fox went out, and when he returned in he said that a man had come to ask him to a baptism. The fox went and he arrayed himself in excellent attire, and he went away, and where should he go but to the butter keg; and when he came home the wolf asked him what name was on the child; and he said that there was FOVEEAL (*under its mouth*).

On the morrow he said that a man had sent to ask him to a baptism, and he reached the keg and he took out about half. The wolf asked when he came home what name was on the child.

"Well," said he, "there is a queer name that I myself would not give to my man child, if I had him; there is MOOLAY MOOLAY (*about half and half*).

On the morrow he said that there was a man there came to ask him to a baptism again; and he went and he reached the keg, and he ate it all up. When he came home the wolf asked him what name was on the child, and he said that there was BOOILL EEMLICH (*tackling, licking, or licking all up*).

On the morrow he went and he said to the wolf that they ought to bring the keg home. They went, and when they reached the keg there was not a shadow of the butter in it.

"Well! thou wert not without coming to watch this, though I was without coming here," quoth the fox.

The other one swore that he had not come near it.

"Thou needst not be blessing that thou didst not come here; I know that thou didst come, and that it was thou that took it out; but I will know it from thee when thou goest home, if it was thou that ate the butter," said the fox.

He went, and when he went home he hung the wolf by his hind legs, with his head dangling below him, and he had a dab of the butter and he put it under his mouth, and if it was true, it was out of the wolf's belly that it came.

H

" Thou red thief !" said he, " I said before that it
was thou ate the butter."

They slept that night as they were, and on the
morrow when they rose the fox said,

" Well, then, it is silly for ourselves to be going
to death in this way with great excess of sloth ; we
will reach such and such a town-land, and we will
take a piece of land in it."

They reached the town-land, and the man to whom
it belonged gave them a piece of land the worth of
seven Saxon pounds.

It was oats that they set that year, and they
reaped it, and they began to divide it.

" Well, then," said the fox, " whether wouldst
thou rather have the root or the tip ? thou shalt have
thy two choices."

" I'd rather the root," said the wolf.

Then the fox had fine oaten bread all the year, and
the other one had fodder.

On the next year they set a crop ; and it was tata
root (potatoes) that they set, and the potatoes grew
well.

" Which wouldst thou like best, the root or the
crop this year ?" said the fox.

" Indeed, thou shalt not take the twist out of me
any more ; I will have the crop (top) this year," quoth
the wolf.

" Good enough, my hero," said the fox.

Then the wolf had the potato tops again, and the
fox the potatoes.   Then the wolf used to keep stealing
the potatoes from the fox.

" Thou hadst best go yonder, and read that name
that I have in the hoofs of the gray mare," quoth the
fox.

Away went the wolf, and he began to read the

name ; and on a time of these times the white mare
drew her leg, and she cast the head off the wolf.

"Oh !" said the fox, "it is long since I heard it.
I would rather be a clerk than be reading a book."

He went home, and the wolf was not putting
trouble upon him any more.

I heard this story often myself in boyhood. There
is some portion of dialogue that I remember, not in this
version. When the fox speaks to the wolf about the
christening, the conversation goes on in this manner :—

Madadh Ruadh. Och ! heun ! thall.
Madadh Alluidh. Dé tha thu 'faicinn ann.
Madadh Ruadh. Tha iad gam iarraidh gu gois-
deachd.
Madadh Alluidh. Och, och, ann d' theid thu ann.
Madadh Ruadh. Och, och, theid.

Fox. Och ! hein ! yonder.
Wolf. What seest thou there ?
Fox. They are asking me to sponsorship.
Wolf. Och ! och ! wilt thou go there ?
Fox. Och ! och ! I will.

H. MacLean.

See Norse Tales, p. 472, where the creatures are
fox and bear.

The Boor and the Fiend, Grimm, No. 189. The
notes in vol. iii., Grimm, shew that this is widely
spread. See also No. 2, Grimm, vol. iii., where the
creatures in company, in various versions, are cat and
mouse, cock and hen, cock and fox.

See also stories on Proverbs, 1854, London.

"Send not the cat for lard." The actors are a
kitten and a rat ; the scene, a belfry and a garret.

Fox, Huntsman, and Falcon.—From a stone at Shandwick.—
Sculptured Stones of Scotland, Pl. xxvi.

LXVI.

THE FOX AND THE LITTLE BONNACH.

From Hector Boyd, who learnt it from one John Campbell, who died three years ago, at the age of thirty.—Sept. 20, 1860.

THE fox was once going over a loch, and there met him a little bonnach, and the fox asked him where he was going. The little bonnach told him he was going to such a place.

" And whence camest thou ?" said the fox.

" I came from GEEOGAN, and I came from COOAIG-EAN, and I came from the slab of the bonnach stone, and I came from the eye of the quern, and I will come from thee if I may," quoth the little bonnach.

" Well, I myself will take thee over on my back," said the fox.

" Thou'lt eat me, thou'lt eat me," quoth the little bonnach.

" Come then on the tip of my tail," said the fox.

" Oh ! I will not ; thou wilt eat me," said the little bonnach.

" Come into my ear," said the fox.

" I will not go; thou wilt eat me," said the little bonnach.

" Come into my mouth," said the fox.

" Thou wilt eat me that time at all events," said the little bonnach.

" Oh, I will not eat thee," said the fox.　" At the time when I am swimming I cannot eat anything at all."

He went into his mouth.

" Oh! ho!" said the fox, " I may do my own pleasure to thee now.　It is long since it was heard that a hard morsel is good in the mouth of the stomach."

The fox ate the little bonnach.　Then he went to the house of a gentleman, and he went to a loch, and he caught hold of a duck that was in it, and he ate that.

He went up to a hill side, and he began to stroke his sides on the hill.

" Oh king! how finely the bullet would spank upon my belly just now."

Who was listening but a hunter.

" It will be tried upon thee directly," said the hunter.

" Bad luck to the place that is here," quoth the fox, " in which a creature dares not say a word in fun that is not taken in earnest."

The hunter put a bullet in his gun, and he fired at him and killed him.

See Chambers' Popular Rhymes of Scotland, 1858, 231.

See also Wolf's stories, where a wolf prays to Odin that an axe may fall on his head, and a man throws one.

LXII.

MAR a thug am Madadh ruadh an car as a' Ghobhair.

A' ghobhar ghlas.

Bha 'n siud ann gobhar ghlas, 's bha minn aice; s' ma bha chaidh am madadh ruadh latha timchioll orra, 's rug e e orra, 's mharbh e iad, 's dh' ith e iad. Thainig a ghobhar, an seo, dachaidh; 's bha i gu dubhach, bronach nuair a thainig i, 's gun iadsan air a coinneamh. Ghabh i air falbh, 's rainig i taigh a' mhadaidh ruaidh, 's chaidh i air mullach an taighe. Dh' eubh am madadh ruadh.

> " Co siud air mullach me bhothain ghruigich, ghraigich,
> Nach leig goil dho m' choireachan,
> 'S nach leig bruich dho m' bhonnachan,
> 'S nach leig mo leanabh beag dh' an tobar."

GOBHAR.

> " Tha mise 'ghobhar ghlas air a toirt as,
> Ag iarraidh nan tri minneana mine,
> 'S am boc tarraghlas,
> 'S an gille buic."

MADADH RUADH.

> " Mata, air an talamh a tha fodhad;
> S' air an athar as do chionn;
> 'S air a' ghrian a tha sios;
> Nach fhaca mise riamh do chiud meann."

Cha robh eun a bha 's an ealt nach deachaidh i a ionnsnidh; 's thill i dhachaidh, 's cha d' fhuair i iad.

LXIII.

MAR a thug an Coileach an car as a mhadadh ruadh; 's cha d' thug beathach riamh an car as ach an coileach a bha 'n siud.

Thainig am Madadh ruadh thun taighe, 's rug e air coileach Dh' fhalbh e leis a choileach 's dh' fhalbh muinntir a' bhaile as a dheigh.

"Nach iad a tha gorrach," urs' an coileach, "a falbh as do dheigh, 's nach urrainn iad breith ort co-dhiu." Bha 'n coileach, nuair a dh' fhosgladh e' bheul, gus leum as. Nuair a chunnaic e gu 'n robh an coileach cho deonach air falbh comhla ris fhein bha e cho toilichte.

"O," a cheolaire! nach abair thu, "'Se mo choileach fhein a th' ann', 's tillidh iad," ors' an Coileach.

Thuirt am Madadh ruadh.

"''Se mo choileach fhein a th' ann.''

'S nuair a dh' fhosgail am Madadh Ruadh a bheul leum an Coileach air falbh.

LXIV.

A CHEARC.

BHA boireannach ann roimhe seo agus rug i cearc ann an sgorr cladaich 's iad an deigh a cur air fuadach air doigh air chor-eigin. Dh' fhas a chearc mor, 's bhiodh i 'dol do thaigh an righ 'h-uile latha feuch ann faigheadh i rud a bheireadh i g' a mathair. Thainig an righ mach latha de na laithean, 's thuirt e rithe.

" De, a chreutair bhig, mhosaich, a tha thu deanadh a 't, sheasamh air mo dhorus an sin.''

"Mata gad a tha mi beag, mosach fhein, ni mi rud nach dean a bhanruinn mhor, bhreagh agadsa,'' urs' ise.

" Dé 'ni thu ? '' urs' an righ..

" Leumaidh mi o sparr gu sparr, 's an clobha, 's buthal na poite, slaodadh ruim.''

Dh' fhalbh e staigh 's dh' innis e siud do' n bhanruinn. Chaidh 'fheuchainn ris a' chirc 's rinn i e; Cheangail iad am buthal san clobha rithe, 's leum i thar tri sparrannan, 's thainig i air làr. Cheangail iad am buthal san clobha ris a bhanruinn an sin, 's dh fhalbh i 's thug i leum aisde, 's ghearr i faobhar an da lurga aice, 's thuit i, 's chaidh an t-ionachainn aisde. Bha ceithir banruinnean aige 's chuir a' chearc as doibh, air fad, leis an obair seo.

" 'S fhearra duibh,'' urs' a' chearc, "mo mhathair a phosadh; tha i 'na boireannach breagh.''

"Seachainn mi,'' urs' an righ; "rinn thu call na leoir domh cheana a chreutair mhosaich.''

" Mata cha 'n e sin a 's fhearra dhuit ach a posadh,'' urs' a' chearc.

" Cuir a nuas do mhathair 's gu 'm faiceamaid i,'' urs' an righ. Dh' fhalbh i far an robh a mathair, 's ars' i rithe, " Tha 'n righ 'gar n-iarr-aidh a mhathair; bha mise ag iarraidh air bhur posadh.''

Chaidh i suas 's phos i fhein san righ.

Bha 'n sin domhnach 's bha iad a' dol do 'n t-searmoin an righ 's a' bhanruinn, 's cha d' fhag iad a staigh ach a chearc, 's mac o 'n cheud mhnaoi. Dh' fhalbh a chearc nuair a dh' fhalbh iad, 's chaidh i do sheombar, 's thilg i dhi an cochall a bha orra, 's dh' fhalbh an gille staigh do 'n rum 's chunnaic e 'n cochall a bha orra. Rug e air

's chuir e'n teis meadhoin an teine e. Thainig ise nuas 's cha robh
sgeul aice air a chochall. Thainig i far an robh an gille 's claidheamh ruisgte aice 's thuirt i ris, " Faigh dhomhsa mo chochall
airneo bheir mi an ceann diot an aghaidh na braghad."

Ghabh an gille moran eagail 's cha b' urrainn e facal a radh rithe.

" A chreutair mhosaich," urs' ise, " 's mor leamsa do bhàs a bhith
air mo lamhan. Cha 'n eil fios 'am a nis dè 'ni mi ; ma gheibh mi
cochall 'eile saoilidh ,iadgur buitseach a th' annam ; agus 's fhearra
domh fantail mar a tha mi."

Nuair a thainig an righ dachaidh chuñnaic e 'm boireannach
breagh sin a staigh air feadh an taighe, 's cha robh fios aige dè 'chuir
ann i. B' fheudar gu 'm faigheadh an righ mach dè 'n seorsa
boireanniach a bh' innte. Dh' innis i' 'h-uile dad. Phos i' fhein 's
mac an righ 's rinneadh banais mhor daibh.

LXV.

AM BUIDEAL IME.

Bha 'm madadh ruadh 's am madadh alluidh a' falbh comhla, 's
chaidh iad timchioll a' chladaich, 's fhuair iad buideal ime, 's thiodh-
laic iad e.

An la 'r na mhaireach chaidh am madadh ruadh a mach, 's nuair
a thill e staigh, thuirt e gu 'n robh duine air tighinn a 'iarraidh gu
baisteadh. Dh' fhalbh am madadh ruadh a's sgeadaich e e fhein ann
an deagh thrusgan, 's ghabh e air falbh, 's cait an deachaidh e ach
'ionnsuidh a' bhuideil ime, 's thug e sios gu 'bheul gu math as a'
bhuideal, 's nuair a thanaig e dachaidh dh' fhoighnichd am madadh
alluidh dheth dé 'n t-ainm a bh' air a' phaisde, 's thuirt e gu 'n robh-
Fo bhial. An la 'r na mhaireach thuirt e gu 'n do chuir duine a
'iarraidh gu baisteadh, 's rainig e 'm buideal ; 's thug e as mu leith.
Dh' fhoighneachd am madadh alluidh, nuair a thainig e dhachaidh,
dé 'n t-ainm a bh' air a' phaisde.

" Mata," urs' esan, " tha ainm neonach nach d' thugainn fhein
air mo dhuine cloinne na 'm biodh e agam, tha Mu leith mu leith."

An la 'r na mhaireach thuirt e gu 'n robh duine, an siud, air
tighinn a 'iarraidh-san a rithis gu baisteadh. Dh' fhalbh e 's rainig
e 'm buideal 's dh' ith e air fad e. Nuair a thainig e dachaidh dh'
fhoighnichd am madadh alluidh dheth dé 'n t-ainm a bh' air a'
phaisde, 's thuirt gu 'n robh, " Buill' imlich. An la 'r na mhaireach
dh' fhalbh e 's thuirt e ris a' mhadhadh alluidh, gu 'm bu choir

dhaibh am buideal a thoirt dachaidh. Dh' fhalbh iad agus nuair a rainig iad am buideal cha robh sgath dh' an im ann.

"Mata cha robh thusa gu 'n tighinn a choimhead seo, gad a bha mise gun tighinn ann," urs' am madadh ruadh. Mhionnaich am fear eile nach' d' thainig e a choir. "Cha ruig thu leas a bhith a' mathachadh nach d' thainig thu ann; tha fios agamsa gu 'n d' thainig, 's gur tu thug as e; ach aithneachaidh mis' ort, nuair a theid thu dachaidh, ma 's tu dh' ith an t-im," ars' am madadh ruadh. Dh' fhalbh e, 's nuair e chaidh e dachaidh, chroeh e 'm madadh alluidh, air chasa deiridh, 's a cheann slaodadh ris, 's bha cnap de 'n im aige, 's chuir e fo a bheul e, 's ma b' fhior, gur h-ann a broinn a mhadadh alluidh a thainig e.

"A dhearg mheairlich," ars' esan, "thuirt mi roimhe gur tu dh' ith an t-im."

Chaidil iad an oidhche sin mar a bha iad, 's an la 'r na mhaireach, nuair a dh' eirich iad, thuirt am madadh ruadh.

"Mata 's gòrrach duinn fhein a bhith 'dol bàs mar seo le barrachd mor de 'n leisg; Ruigidh sin a leithid seo de bhaile 's gheibh sin piosa fearainn ann."

Rainig lad am baile, 's thug an duine leis am bu leis e piosa fearainn daibh—fiach sheachd puinnd Shasunnach. 'S e corc a chuir iad a bhliadhna sin agus bhuain iad e 's theisich iad ri 'roinn.

"Mata," ars' am madadh ruadh, "co-dhiu 's fhearr leat am bun na 'm barr? Gheibh thu do dha roighinn."

"'S fhearr leam am bun," ars' am madadh alluidh. Bha 'n sin aran breagh corc aig a' mhadadh ruadh fad na bliadhna; 's fodar aig an fhear eile !

An ath bhliadhna chuir iad barr; 's e buntàta a chuir iad agus dh' fhas am buntata gu math.

"Co-dhiu a 's docha leat am bun na 'm barr am bliadhna ?" ars' am madadh ruadh.

"Gu dearbh cha d' thoir thu 'n car tuilleadh asam! Bidh am barr am bliadhna agam," ars' am madadh alluidh.

"Gle mhath a laochain ;" ars' am madadh ruadh. Bha 'n sinn barr a bhuntata aig a' mhadadh alluidh a rithis; 's am buntata aig a' mhadadh ruadh.

Bhiodh, an seo, am madadh alluidh a' goid a bhuntata air a' mhadadh ruadh.

"'S fhearra dhuit a dholl a null 's an t' ainm sin agam ann an crodhan na laire baine a leubhadh," ars' am madadh ruadh.

Dh' fhalbh am madadh alluidh 's thoisich e air leubhadh an ainm, 's uair de na h-uairean tharruing an lair bhàn a cas, 's thilg i 'n ceann bhar a mhadadh alluidh.

"O!" ars' am madadh ruadh, "'S fhada o' n a chuala mi e. B' fhearr leam a bhith a' m' chleireach na 'bhith leubhadh leabhair."

Dh' fhalbh e dachaidh, 's cha robh am madadh alluidh a cur dragh air tuilleadh.

LXVI.

AM MADADH RUADH 'S AM BONNACH BEAG.

BHA 'm madadh ruadh uair a dol thar loch, 's choinnich bonnach beag e, 's dh' fhoighnichd am madadh ruadh dheth cait an robh e a' dol. Dh' innis am bonnach beag gu 'n robh e 'dol a leithid seo de dh' àite.

"'S co as thainig thu?" ars' am madadh ruadh.

"Thainig mi a Giogan 's thainig mi a Cuaigean, 's thanaig mi a leac nam bonnach, 's thainig mi a suil na brathan, 's thig mi uaitse ma dh' fhaodas mi." Ars' am bonnach beag.

"Mata bheir mi fhein a null air mo mhuin thu," ars' am madadh ruadh.

"Ithidh tu mi, ithidh tu mi," ars' am bonnach beag.

"Thalla air barr m' urbaill mata," ars' am madadh ruadh.

"O cha d' theid, ithidh tu mi," ars' am bonnach beag.

"Thalla nam chluais," ars' am madadh ruadh.

"Cha d' theid; ithidh tu mi," ars' am bonnach beag.

"Thalla nam' bheul," ars' am madadh ruadh.

"Ithidh tu mi n' uair sin co-dhiu," ars' am bonnach beag.

"Od cha 'n ith," ars' am madadh ruadh; "nuair a bhios mi a snamh cha n' urrainn mi rud sam bith itheadh." Dh' fhalbh e 'na bheul.

"O ho!" ars' am madadh ruadh, "faodaidh mi mo thoil fhein a dheanadh riut a nis. 'S fhada o 'n a chualas e. 'S math greim cruaidh am beul a ghoile."

Dh' ith am madadh ruadh am bonnach. Rainig e, 'n seo, taigh duine uasail, 's chaidh e gu loch, 's rug e air tunnag a bh' ann, s' dh' ith e.

Chaidh e suas air taobh cnoic, 's thoisich e air a bhlianadh fhein air a chnoc.

"A righ! 's gasda a sgailceadh am peilear air mo bhroinn an ceart' uir," ars' esan.

"Co a bha 'ga eisdeachd ach sealgair."

"Bidh e air fheuchainn riut an ceart' air," ars' an sealgair.

"An droch comhdhail air an àit a th' ann," ars' am madadh ruadh.

"Nach eil a chridhe aig neach facal a radh am beadradh nach b. air a ghabhail an d'ar righribh."

Chuir a sealgair peilear 's a' ghunna, 's loisg e air, 's mharbh e e,

The following two stories, LXVII. and LXVIII., were got in Islay from an old man, whose name has not been sent to me. They were written by Mr. Carmichael, an enthusiastic Highlander, and a good Gaelic scholar, who was stationed in Islay in July 1860, and is now, 1861, at Carbost in Skye.

The main incidents of these stories are quoted in the introduction, as known in the Isle of Man.

The Feinn (Fane) are here found in the spot where the Lay of Diarmaid left them, stationed near the old "Pictish towers," opposite to the Isle of Skye, and they next appear in Islay where the forging of Fionn's sword, "the Son of Luinne," is a well-known legend. The incidents are told in the Isle of Man of a baron, and the scene is partly Drontheim. Fionn's patronymic, by a change from the common spelling which hardly changes the sound, here becomes MacDugald, or the son of Black and White ; another slight change would make it MacDonald. And thus the most numerous clans of the West Highlands, the MacDonalds, MacDugalds, and Campbells, seem all to have something to do with MacCumhal and his men, who may have been Irish warriors, or Celtic gods, nevertheless ; for nearly all these West country traditions point back to Eirinn ; and the deeds of the Feinn are not always those of mortal men.

There is a curious poem of twenty-six verses about the smithy "Ceardach MhicLuin," in Gillie's Collection, 1787, p. 233. Several of the phrases in the story are in the poem, and the incidents are much the same. I have often heard that a number of poems were collected in Islay by a minister, and published, and verses about the forging of Fionn's sword are still repeated there. Probably the poem is the one of which I have heard.

LXVII.

CAOL REIDHINN.

WHY THE NAME WAS GIVEN TO IT.

From Mr. Carmichael (excise officer), Islay.

ON a certain time, when the Feinn had come home from the chase to the house of Farabhuil, at the foot of Farabhein in Ardnamurachan, they were much astonished to find their wives so lusty, fair, and comely; for the chase was very scarce at the time with the Feinn.

The Feinn determined that they would know what their wives were getting to make them thus; and when they went away again to the chase, they left Conan, one of themselves, at the house, so that he might find this out.

Conan kept a watch, and the meat that they had was the hazel top boiled, and they were drinking the bree. It is said besides that they used to wash themselves with this.

The women understood that it was to watch them that Conan had been left at the house, and they were in a great fury.

In the night when Conan laid down to sleep, they tied his hair to two stakes which they drove into the earth on either side of his head. Then the women went out to the front of the house, and they struck their palms with a great lament, till they awoke Conan.

Conan sprang on foot with great haste, but he left part of his hair and of the hide of his head fast to the stakes.

When Conan got the women within, he set fire to

heather and faggots in the front of the house, so that he might kill the women with the smoke.

The Feinn were at this time opposite to the house of Farabheil on the other side of Caol Readhin (Kyle Ray), and when they saw the fire and the smoke rising up, they cried out loudly, striking their left hands on the front of their faces with their eyes on the sky.

Then they ran to succour their set of wives, but the strait was between them; but with their blades they leaped the strait, (all) but one Mac an Reaidhinn (Ramsay). Mac an Reaidhinn fell in the strait and he was drowned; and since then to this day's day, (the name of) Reaidhinn's Strait has stuck to the narrows.

> Valour so swiftly for wives of the Feinn,
> And each one sprang on the point of his spear;
> And they left Mac an Reaidhinn in the strait.

By good fortune the women all came through it but one or two of them, for the Feinn made mighty running to succour them. The Feinn were in great fury against Conan for what he had done, and they seized him to put him to death. Conan asked as a favour that the head should be taken off him with MAC AN LUINNE that would not leave a shred behind, the sword of Fionn MacDhuil (MacDuguld), and that his own son Garbh should smite him on the thigh of Fionn.

> With earnest entreaty I would; ask it
> And my soul's privation to seek it;
> The son of Luinne to reap my soul
> Upon the thigh of the sense of the Feinn.

This was allowed him, but first seven gray hides and seven faggots of firewood, and seven "*tiruin*" of gray bark were laid about the thigh of Fionn.

Then the head of Conan was laid on that, and
GARBH, his son, struck the head off him with MAC AN
LUINNE—

And folds in the palm were not more plenteous
Than severed thews in the thigh of Fionn.

Then GARBH asked them where were the Feinn,
for he had gone mad ; and they said to him that they
were below beneath him. Then he went down till he
reached the sea, and he slashed at it till he drowned
himself.

LXVIII.

ON a day when Fionn and his set of men were out
hunting in Haslainn, in Gortean Taoit in Ile, they
saw coming to meet them an unhandsome man, with a
shaggy eye in the front of his face.* He was running
with might, and making right for Fionn MacDhuil.
When he met them he asked them to follow him to
the door of the smithy. Said Fionn, " Where, strip-
ling, is thy smithy ? or shall we be the better for seeing it ?"

" My smithy," said the Fairy Smith, " is not to be
found ; and if I may, ye shall not see it."

The Fairy Smith and Daor Ghlas stretched out
against the mountain breast ; and they would but give
the one step over each cold desert glen ; there could
but scarce be seen a glimpse of their clothes on their
hips.

On nearing the door of the smithy the heroes
neared each other.

" A little opening," said the Fairy Smith.

* He is one-legged in the poem, and his name Lun Mac-
Liobhain, and he has seven hands.

"Tear it before thee," said Daor Ghlas.

Then turned round the Fairy Smith and he said,

"Oh king! that thou hast earned the name oh Caoilte (slenderness), Daorglas shall not be thy name from this time."

It was then that they began at MAC AN LUINNE, and when they were at it the daughter of the Fairy Smith came in to the smithy, and she asked,

"Who is the slender grey fearless man?"

"A shineadh a' pinah cruach?"

The maiden fell into weighty questions with Daor Ghlas, and she gave him notice that her father would say to him when the sword was ready, "What did it want now?" and that he should say, "It wants one little thing yet;" then that he should seize the sword and thrust it through her father's body to temper it.

LXVII.

CAOL REIDHINN.

CARSON A THAINIG AN T'AINM AIR.

AIR am aridh, an do no Feinn tighinn dhachaidh fo'n t 'sealg, do thigh Fharbheil, aig bun Farabhein, ann an Ardnamurachan, bha ionghnadh mor orra, na mnathan aca fhaodinn, cho reambar, gheal bhoidheach, oir bha an t 'sealg fior ghann, air na Feinn aig an am so.

Chuir na Feinn rompa, gu'm bithidh fios aca gu de a bha na mnathan aca faodinn, ga 'n deanadh mar so; agus an nuair a dhalbh iad a rithisd, gus an t' sealg, 'dh fhag iad Conan, fear dhiubh fhein, aig an tigh, a chum so fhaodinn a mach. Rinn Conan faire; agus se am biadh a bha aca, barr a challtuin air a bhurich, agus iad a g' ol an t' suigh. Tha e air a ghrainn cuideachd, gu'n robh iad ga nighead fhein leis a so. Thuig na mnathan g'm h'an ga 'm faire a chai Conan fhageil, aige an tighe, agus bha fearg mhor orra.

Ann san oidhche, an nuair a luidh Conan a sis gu cadal, cheang, ail iad fhalt ri da stop a chuir iad san talamh, air gach taobh ga cheann. Chaidh na muathan a sinn a mach gu beul an tighe, agus bhuail iad am basan, le guileag mor, gus an do dhuisg iad Conan.

Leum Conan air a chois, le mor-chabhaig, ach fhag e pairt ga fhalt 'us do sheic a chinn ceangailt ris na stuip.

An nuair a fhuair Conan na mnathan 'stigh, chuir e teine ri fraoch agus connadh ann am beal an tighe, a chnm agus na mnathan a marthadh leis an toit.

Bha na Feinn aig an am so, mu-choinneamh tigh Fharabeil air taobh eile Chaol Readhinn, agus an nuair a chumaic iad an teine agus an toit, a g' eridh suas, ghlaodh iad gu ro-mhor a bualadh an lamh chli air clar-an aoduinn agus an suilean air an speur.

Ruith iad a sinn gu 'n, cuid mnathan a thearnadh, ach bha 'n 'caol eadar iad agus an tigh; ach le 'n lannan leum iad 'n caol, ach aon fhear—Macanreaidhinn, Thuit Macanredhinn sa chaol, agus chaidh a bhathadh; agus foidh sinn gus an latha n' duigh, lean Caol Readhinn air a chaol.

> · Fion ach as gu luath air ban traichd Fheinn,
> S' leum gach fear air barr a shleagh,
> 'Us fhag iad Macanreadhinn sa chaol.

Gu freasdalach thainig na mnathan uile roimhe, ach aon na dithis dhiu on rinn na Feinn a dean-ruith g 'n teasmiginn. Bha na Feinn ann an fearg mhor ri Conan, airson mar a rinn e', agus rug iad air a chum a chuir gu bas. Dh' iar Conan mar fhathor gun reacheadh, an ceann a thabhairt dheth le Mac an Luinne, nach fageadh fuigheall na dheigh, claidheamh Fhionn, Mhic Dhuil, agus a mhac fhinn, Garabh, ga bhualadh air sliasaid Fhion :—

> Achanidh gan' iarridh mi
> As eugmhais m' an am ri iaridh
> Mac an Luinne a bhuinte m' anam
> Air muin sleiste geile n' Fheinn.

Chaidh so a cheadachadh dha; ach chaidh an toiseach, seach seicheann glasa, seach cuailtean connaidh, agus seach tiruinn do riosga glas, a chuir air muin sliasaid Fhionn.

Chaidh ceann Chonan a leageadh (na leageil) air a sinn agus bhuail Garabh a mhac le Mac an Luinne an ceann deth agus.

> Cha bu lionmhoire crois san dearni,
> Na cuisle gearte an sliasoid Fhionn.

Dh' eoraich Garabh dhiu a sinn, caite am robh na Feinn, oir bha e

air dol air a chuthaeach, agus thubhairt iad ris gu'n robh iad gu h'
iseal foidh. Ghabh e sinn a sis gus an d' rainig e an fharige, agus
shlachdanich e.i gus an do bhath se e fhein.

LXVIII.

LATHA do Fhionn, agus ga chuid dhaoine, a bhi a mach a sealg ann
an Haslainn, ann an Gortean-taoid, ann an Ile, chunnic iad a tighinn
na 'n comhdhail, duine mi sgiamhach, agus suil mholach (?) na 'n
aodinn. Bha e dian-ruith, agus e sior-dheanadh air Fionn Mac-
Dhuil. An nuair a chonnich e iar gh, iar e orra, a bhi ga leantinn-
sa, gu doruisd a cheardeach. Arsa Fionn—" Caite a thrua a bheil do
cheardach, na n' fhearte sinne faicinn?" "Mo cheardach sa," arsa n
gobhainn, sith, " cha n'eil ri fhaodinn, 's ma g' fhaodas mise cha n'
fhaic sibh." *

Shin 'n gobhain-sibh agus Daorghlas, a mach ri uchd an t'
sleibh, 'us cha d' ugadh iad ach aon cheum, thar gach aon ghleann,
fuar, fasich. Cha n' fhaichte ach air eigin cearb gan' eideadh far am
masann.†

A tearnadh gu dorus na ceardach dhenich na laoich ri cheile.
Fosgla beag, arsa 'n gobhainn sith ; srac romhad e arsa Daorghlas.

Sinn thundeigh 'u gobhainn-sith agus thubhairt e. A righ gu
'm meal thu t' ainm a Chaoilte cha bhi Daorghlas ort fo 'n am sò.

San a sinn a thoisich iad air Mac-an-Luinne agus an nuair a bha
iad ris, thainig nighean a gobhainn-shith a stigh do'n cheardich agus
dh', eorich i " Co am fear caol, glas, gu'n tima a shineadh a' tinah
cruach?"‡ Thuit an oighe ann an trom cheiste air Caoilte (Daorglas)
agus thug i rathadh dha gu 'n abradh a n'athair ris an n'uair a
bhithadh 'n claidheamh deas gu dé bha dhi air an nis, agus easan a
ghrainn tha aon rud beag a dhi air fathast ; e sinn bheirsinn air a
chlaidheamh agus e ga chuir roimh chorp a h' athair ga faobhairt.

ALASDAIR, A. MAC 'ILLMHICHEIL.

I have followed the orthography of the MS.

* Faiceadh sibhse sin má dh' fhaodas
   Ach ma dh' fhaodas mise cha 'n fhaic sibh.—(*Gillies.*)

† Cha deanadh an Gobhain ach aon cheum
   Thar gach gleannan foin 'n robh fàsach
   Cha ruigeadh oirne ach air eigin
   Cearb d' ur n' aodach shuas ar masaibh.—(*Gillies.*)

‡ Here also come in several lines of the old poem, as given
by Gillies, 1786.

LXIX.

THOMAS OF THE THUMB.

From Catherine Macfarlane in 1809. John Dewar.

THERE was one before now whose name was Tómas na h òrdaig, and he was no bigger than the thumb of a stalwart man. Tómas went once to take a walk, and there came a coarse shower of hailstones, and Tómas went in under a dock leaf; and there came a great drove of cattle past, and there was a great brindled bull amongst them, and he was eating about the docken, and he ate Tómas of the Thumb. His mother and his father missed him, and they went to seek him. They were going past the brindled bull, and quoth Tómas na h òrdaig,

> " Ye are there a seeking me,
> Through smooth places, and moss places ;
> And here am I a lonely one,
> Within the brindled bull."

Then they killed the brindled bull, and they sought Tómas na h òrdaig amongst the paunches and entrails of the bull, but they threw away the great gut in which he was.

There came a carlin the way, and she took the great gut, and as she was going along she went over a bog.

Tómas said something to her, and the old wife threw away the great gut from her in a fright.

There came a fox the way, and he took with him the gut, and Tómas shouted

"Bies taileù! the fox. Bis taileù! the fox."

Then the dogs ran after the fox, and they caught him, and they ate him ; and though they ate the gut they did not touch Tòmas na h òrdaig.

Tómas went home, where his mother and his father were, and he it was indeed that had the queer story for them.

This varies from the book adventures of our old friend Tom Thumb, who is now supposed to have been the dwarf of King Arthur. The story comes from Glenfalloch, which is not far from Dumbarton, which was, according to family tradition, the birth-place of King Arthur's son. It was told to Dewar by a girl who took charge of him when a child, and it is known to one other man whom I know. I used to hear the adventures of "Comhaoise Ordaig" (Thumb's co-temporary), from my piper nurse myself, but I was so young at the time that I have forgotten all but the name.

The cry of "bis taileu" may still be heard in the mouths of herd laddies addressing their collies, and it may be the same as "tally-ho!" for which a French derivation has been sought and found—"tallis hors." I would rather imagine King Arthur, and his knights, and his dwarf, shouting an old Celtic hunting cry, and red-coated sportsmen keeping it up till now, than trace it to Norman-French ; but in any case, here is something like tally-ho in the mouth of Tom Thumb, and in a glen where tally-ho has never been heard.

LXIX.

TOMAS NA H-ORDAIG.

BHA fear ann a roimh so, do am b' ainn Tomas na h-òrdaig; agus cha bu mho e na òrdaig duine foghainteach, Chaidh Tòmas aon uair a ghabhail aràid, agus thainig fras gharbh chlachan meallain; agus chaidh Tòmas a stigh fo dhuilbeag chopaig, Agus Thainig dròbh mòr cruidh seachad, agus bha tarbh mòr riabhach na measg, agus bha e ag iche tiomchiol na copagaich. Agus dh'iche e Tomas na h-ordaic. Dhiondrain a mhathair s athair e, a's chaidh iad g'a iarraidh. Bha iad dol seachad air an tarbh riabhach, agus thubhairt Tomas na h-ordaig,

> " Tha sibhse an sin g' am iarraidhse,
> Feadh mhinegean, s mhonagan;
> S mise an so am aonarn,
> An ton an tairbh riobhaich."

An sin mharbh iad an tarbh riabhach, agus dh' iarr iad Tomas na h-ordaig, air feadh maodail s caolain an tairbh. Ach thilg iad uapa an caolan taomadh. Agus is-e sin an caolan ann san robh e.

Thainaig cailleach an rathad, agus thug i leatha an caolan taomadh, agus air dh i a bhith dol air a h-aghart, bhi a dol thair féith s leig . . s Thubhairt Tomas na h-ordaig, "tut . . . . . a chailleach," agus thilg a chailleach uaipe an caolan.

Thainig sionnach an rathad, s thug e leis an caolan, agus ghlaodh Tomas na h-ordaig "bìs-taileù ! an sionnach, bìs-taileù ! an sionnach."

An sin ruith na coin an déigh an t' shionnaich agus bheir iad air, agus mharbh is dh ith iad e, s ge-d dh ith iad an caolan, cha do bhuin iad do h-Thomas na h-òrdaig. Chaidh Tomas dachaidh far an robh a mhathair s athair, agus san aige a bha an sgeul neonnach doibh.

JOHN DEWAR.

This is the original spelling.

From a Stone at Inverness.—*Sculptured Stones of Scotland*, Pl. xxxviii.

The following is a very good gloss upon the language of bulls. The imitation can be made very close by any one who will repeat the Gaelic conversation of the champions, with the intention of imitating the sound of their angry bellowings. These go by the name of "Boor-eech" in Gaelic, and oo, ee, and r, express the prevailing sounds. I have tried to spell these sounds, but I have small hopes of conveying an idea of them by letters.

Whether this is a story founded on some old battle between tribes, which fought near the "Stone of the Bulls," or if so, who these may have been, I will not attempt to guess.

There are bulls and bulls' heads in the armorial bearings of several of the Highland clans; and the nickname of "John Bull" must have had some origin. There is a bull sculptured on an old stone near Inverness, which is figured in "The Sculptured Stones of Scotland," from which work the drawing above is copied. The story is certainly the invention of some one familiar with bulls, whatever it means.

LXX.

THE BULLS.

From John Dewar.   November 17, 1860.

THERE came before now a red bull from Sasunn (England), to put Albainn to shame. He stood on the shoulder of Bein Voorling, and he bellowed,

"Strooᴀh n dooaich! Strooᴀh n dooaich! The country is pitiable!"

There was a black Gaelic bull on the other side of Loch Loimein (Loch Lomond), opposite the top of Dun Polachròdh (Castlepool Castle), and he bellowed,

"Keeᴀ ᴀs ᴀ hᴀ oo? Keeᴀ ᴀs ᴀ hᴀ oo? Whence art thou?"

Quoth the red bull, "ᴀ tjeer do nᴀvaid. ᴀ tjeer do nᴀvaid. From thy foe's land."

Said the black bull, "Cud ê hêchd an tjeer. Cud ê hêchd an tjeer?" What is (the reason of) thy coming from the land?

"Kruinᴀchd s Feen. Kruinᴀchd s Feen. Wheat and wine," said the red bull.

"Hoorin oo n coir do hooil. Hoorin oo n coir do hooil. I'd drive thee backwards," said the black bull.

"Kᴀtche n do roogatoo? Kᴀtche n do roogatoo? Where wert thou born?" said the red bull.

"An craw an dooin. ᴀn craw an dooin. In the castle fold," said the black bull.

"Cud boo veeᴀ gooit on vᴀ oo d laogh? Cud boo veeᴀ gooit on vᴀ oo d laogh? What was thy food since thou wert a calf!" said the red bull.

"Bᴀine s bᴀr fraoich. Bᴀine s bᴀr fraoich. Milk and heather tops," said the black bull.

"An aorᴀchd chrom shaw am bêl do chlêv. An aorᴀchd chrom shaw am bêl do chlêv. This crooked horn in the front of thy chest," said the red bull.

"Hoogad mee! hʌn êgal do. Hoogad mee! hʌn êgal do. Shun me! no fear of me," said the black bull.

And the black bull went round about the upper end of Loch Lomond, and the two bulls met each other on the upper shoulder of beinn Voorluig, and they set heads to each other, and they struggled.

The black bull drove the red bull backwards as far as a great stone that was there, and they rolled the stone over, and the stone rolled down to a level place that is at the side of the road, about five miles on the upper side of the Lomond Tarbert, and three miles on the lower side of the upper end of the Loch of Lomond.

The black bull put his crooked horn into the front of the chest of the red bull, and he killed him; and "clach nan tarv." The stone of the bulls is the name that is on that stone till this day's day, and that is the greatest stone that is in the three realms.

LXX.

THE BULLS.

Thainig roimh so tarbh dèarg a Sasunn, a chum maslachadh a thoirt do Albainn, Sheas e air gualla beinn mhùrluig, s ghlaodh e "Is truagh an dùthaich, Is truagh an dùthaich."

Bha tarbh dubh gaidhealach, air taobh eile loch Loimeinn, ma coinneamh braigh Dùnn pholachròdh, agus ghloadh e, "Cia as a tha thu? Cia as a tha thu?

Ars an Tarbh Dearag "A tir do nàmhaid," A' tir do nàmhaid.

Ars an Tarbh Dubh "Ciod e do theachd an tir? Ciod e do theachd, etc.

An Tarbh dearg "Cruinneachd s fion, Cruinneachd s fion," etc.

An T Dubh, "Chuirinn thu an còir do chùil, etc.

An T Dearg, "C' aite an do rugadh tù? c' aite," etc.

T Dubh, "An crò an Dùinn, 'n crò an dùinn."

"T dearg, "Ciod bu bhiadh dhuit on bha thu ad làogh? Ciod bu bhiadh dhuit," etc.

T Dubh, "Bainne 's bàrr fraoich, Bainne," etc.

An T dearg, "An adhrac chrom so am beul do chléibh, an adhrac chrom s," etc.

An T dubh, "Chugad mi, cha 'n eagal domh. Chugad mi ! cha 'n eagal domh."

Agus chaidh an tarbh dubh, timchiol cheann shuas Loch-loimeainn agus choinnich an dà tharbh a cheile air gualla shuas beinn mhùr-luig agus. Chuir iad cinn ri cheile, s gleachd iad. Chuir an tarbh dubh an tarbh dearag iar ais an coinnimh a chuil, gu ruig Clach mhòr a bha an sin, 's chuir iad car de 'n clach, 's roil a chlach sios gu còmhnart, a ta aig taobh an rathaid mhòir, tuaiream air còige mìle, taobh shuas an Fairebeart loimeanach, agus trì mile an taobh shios do cheann shuas an loch-loimeainn. Chuir an tarbh dubh an adhrac chrom aige, am beul a chléibh aig an tarbh dhearag agus mharbh se e.

Agus is e clach nan tarbh, an t-ainm, a ta air a chlach gus an latha diugh, agus is i clach is momh a ta ann is na trì rioghachdan.

J. DEWAR.

This is the original spelling.

LXXI.

THE HOODIE CATECHISING THE YOUNG ONE.

THE hoodie fell to at catechising the gorrachan, and she said to him,—

"If thou seest one coming, and a slender stick in his oxter, and a broad end to it, flee—that will be a gun ; he will be going to kill thee. If thou seest one coming, and lifting a pebble, it is lifting it to kill thee, that he will be—flee. If thou seest one coming fair straight forward, and without anything in his oxter, and without stooping, thou needst not stir,·that one will not touch thee."

"What," said the croaker, "if the stone be in his pouch ?"

"Oh !" said the Hoodie, "I need not be instructing thee any longer."

AN FHEANNAG A' LEAGASG A' GHORBACHDAIN.

Thoìsich an fheannag air teagasg a' ghorrachdain 's thuirt i ris.
Ma chi thu fear a tighinn agus stichd chaol 'na asgaill agus ceann
leathann urra teich ; 's e gunna bhiòs ann ; bidh e dol a'd mharbhadh." Ma chi thu fear a' tighinn agus e togail doirnei'g, 's ann 'ga
togail a dhol a'd' mhorbhadhsa bhith eas e ; teich. "Ma chi thu
fear a tighinn lom, direach, 's gun ni 'sam bith 'na asgaill, 's gun e
cromadh, cha ruig thu leas carachadh ; cha bhoin am fear sin duit."
"Gu dé ars' an gorrachdan, ma bhios a' chlach 'na phoca." "O,"
ars' an fheannag, " cha ruig mise leas a bhi gad, ionnsachadh na' s
fhaide."

LXXII.
THE HOODIE AND THE FOX.

THE hoodie and the fox were good at early rising, and
they laid a wager with each other, for which should
soonest get up in the morning. The hoodie went into
a tree top, and she slept ; and the fox staid at the
foot of the tree, looking aloft (to see) when the day
would come. As soon as he perceived the day he
cried, "Sê-n-la-ban-ê." It is the bright day.

The hoodie had never stirred all the night, and
then she awoke with the cry, and she answered,
"Sad-o-bê-ê, sad-o-bê-ê." It's long since it was.
Then the fox lost the wager and the hoodie won.

AN FHEANNAG 'S AM MADADH RUADH.

Bha 'n fheannag 's am madadh ruadh math air moch-eirigh, agus
chuir iad geall ri 'cheile airson co a bu luaithe dh' eireadh 's a'
mhaidinn. Chaidh an fheannag ann am barr craoibhe agus
chaidil i, 's dh' fhan am madadh ruadh aig bonn na craoibhe, 's e 'g
amharc an aird cuin a thigeadh an latha, ach cha do chaidil e idir.
Co luath 's a mhothaich esan do 'n latha ghlaoidh e, "'S e 'n latha
bàn e." Bha 'n fheannag gun smoisleachadh fad na hoidhche gus
an sin ; dhuisg i le a ghlaodh san agus fhreagair ì, "'S fhad' o b' e e,
—'S fhad' o b' e e." Chaill am madadh ruadh an seo an geall 's
bhuidhinn an fheannag.

From John MacArthur (shepherd), Uchd nan Clach, who says
he learnt them from Donald MacGeachy, carding-miller, Walkmill,
a native of Kintyre ; and Dugald MacNiven in Cairnbui.—H. M'L.

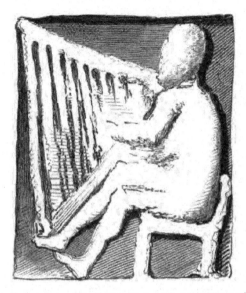

HARPER.—From a stone at Monifeith.—*Chalmers' Sculptured Stones of Angus.*

LXXIII.

THE YELLOW MUILEARTEACH.

1—BARD.

On a day when the Fhinn were on Oirill's mound,
A watching the Eireann all around,
There was seen coming on the tops of the wave,
The crooked, clamouring, shivering brave.

2

The name of that undaunted wraith
Was the bald russet-yellow Muilearteach ;
From Lochlann's bounds, coming on brine,
All in a day to cover Eirinn.

From a stone coffin at Govan.—*Sculptured Stones of Scotland*, Pl. cxxxiv.

A MHUILEARTACH BHUIDHE.*

1

Latha dh' an Fhinn, air Tulach Oirill,[1]
A' coimhead na h-Eireann mu timchill
Chunnacas a' tighinn, air barraibh thonn,
An eàrra, ghàireach, chraobhaidh, chrom.[2]

2

'Se b' ainm dh' an fuath nach bu thim
A' Mhuileartach mhaol, ruadh-bhuidhe,
O chriochan Lochlann 'tighinn air sàil
Gu h-Eïrinn a chomhdach a dh' aon là.

* In Gillies, this character is a man, and called a Mhuirearteach; perhaps muir iarteach,—sea western.

3

A rusted glaive was upon her belt,
Will give them a grim darkling pelt ;
When the time of the fury of battle shall come.

    .   .   .   .   .

4

There were two slender spears of battle,
Upon the other side of the carlin ;
Her face was blue-black, of the lustre of coal,
And her bone tufted tooth was like rusted bone.

5

In her head was one deep pool-like eye,
Swifter than a star in a winter sky ;
Upon her head gnarled brushwood,
Like the clawed old wood of the aspen root.

6

Her heart was merry for joy,
As she saw in the south the Fiantaidh ;
"Will ye not teach the wretch to her ruin,
Let not her's be a good gift without return."

7

And a hundred warriors she sportively slew,
And there was a grin on her rugged maw ;
A warrior exalted each warrior of these,
And that were raised up on slender trees.

8

A pouring of their blood amongst the hounds,
And the juice of the fruit of Oireal was threatened ;

    .   .   .   .   .
    .   .   .   .   .

3

Bha claidheamh meirgeach air a crios
Bheir dhaibh caisgeadh dùige, doite[3]
An am an d' thigeadh gairbhe catha,

. . . . .

4

Bha da shleagha chaola chatha
Air an taobh eile dh' an chaillich.
Bha 'h-aodann dubh-ghorm air dreach a' ghuail,
'S a deud cnábadach, cnàmh-ruadh.[4]

5

Bha aon suil ghlumach[5] 'na ceann
Bu luaithe na rionnag gheamhraidh ;
* Craohh mhìneach chas air a ceann
Mar' choill ìnich de 'n t-seana chrithinn.

6

Bha 'cridhe 'mire rì h-àdh,
'Si 'g amharc nam Fianntaidh fo dheas,
" Nach deachd[6] sibh a' bheist thun a h-aimhleis.
'S gu 'n tharladh leatha gean gun chomain ; "

7

'S gu 'n marbh i le 'h-abhachd ceud laoch ;
'S gu 'n robh càir[7] air a garbh chraos.
Laoch inbheach gach laoch a bh' ann,
'S a thogadh air chaola chrann.

8

Air sgath fala, 'measg nan con,
'S bha brigh mhios Oirill 'ga maoidheadh.

. . . . .
. . . . .

9—WITCH.

"Who are the warriors better than they?"
Out spoke the yellow Muilearteach;
"Terror or fear there is not upon me,
Before the king since I happened upon ye."

10—BARD.

To Fionn Prince of the Finne there came,
The ill-favoured goblin right valiant;
By her there were slaughtered nine in the plain,
As she sought for detestable combat.

11—WITCH.

"Now since I have come over the brine,
For the taking of all Eirinn;
Let yielding be given me without pain,
Or else a whole battle of hardy men."

12—BARD AND FIONN.

Mac Chumhail would give that without displeasure,
Ten hundred hounds, upon leashes of leather;
"Take the bribe, and besides (behold),
Ten hundred ruddy apples of gold."

13—WITCH.

"Although I should get all the value of Eirinn,
With her gold, and her silver, and her precious things;
I would rather have on board of my vessel,
The heads of Osgar, and Raonaidh, and Coiril."

14—BARD AND CONAN.

Spoke a hero that brooked no slur,
Son of great Morna, by name Conan;
"Thou shalt loose the bush of thy round head,
Because thou hast asked for the son of Oisein."

9

"Cia iad na laoich a 's fhearr na sin?"
Labhair a' Mhuileartach bhuidhe.
"Fiamh na eagal cha 'n 'eil orm
Roimh 'n righ, o'n tharladh mi thugaibh."*

10

Gu Fionn, flath na Finne, thainig
Am fuath dìth-mhaiseach,[10] deagh-dhana.
Mharbhadh leatha naonar 's a' mhagh,
'S i 'g iarraidh fuath'chadh na comhraig.

11

"Nis o'n thainig mi air sàil
Gu h-Eirinn uile do ghabhail,
Thugta geill gun doruinn domh,
Airneo comhrag cròdha churaidhean."

12

Bheireadh MacChumhail siud di gun diombadh,
Deich ceud cu air choimh-lion eille,
"Gabh 'an cumha, is e 'choir,"
"Deich ceud ubhlan dearg òir."

13

"Buaidh na h-Eirionn gad gheibhinn uile,
Le 'h-or, 's le 'h-airgiod, 's le 'h-ionmhas,
B' fhearr leam, air bord air mo luing,
Ceann Osgair, a's Raonaidh, a's Choiril."

14

Labhair laoch nach d' fhulaing tair,
Mac mor Morna d' am b' ainm Conan,
"Caillidh tu dos do chinn chruinn
Ann an dàil Mhic Oisein iarraidh."

* Another version is,—O'n ti a tharladh mi thugaibh.

15—BARD.

When they saw the wrath of the monster,
Up rose Fionn the Prince of the Finne ;
Up rose Oiséan, Prince of the men,
Up rose Osgar, and Iollainn.

16

Up rose Diarmaid o' Duibhne ;
Up rose they, and Iall o' Buidhne ;
Three sons of the dusky black king Dhuinne ;
Up rose they, and Cearbhal.

17

Up rose Glaisean o' Damhach ;
Up rose they, and Ard Amharc ;
Up rose Ciar Dhubh, Prince of Lomhann,
The doughtiest four that were in the Fhinn.

18

Went to do battle with the beast.

    .   .   .   .   .
    .   .   .   .   .
    .   .   .   .   .

19

She was serving them out in turn,
As a blade might run through flame ;
Until there met MacChumail the grand,
And the Muilearteach hand to hand.

20

Their equal was never yet seen,
Since the smithy of Lonn MacLiobhainn ; *
There was dew on the points of the spears,
Of MacChumhail of the sides so fair.

* See No. LXVIII.

15

Nuair chunnaic iad colg na beiste ;
Gu 'n d' eirich Fionn, flath na Fìnne ;
Dh' eirich Oisean, flath nam fear ;
Gu 'n d' eirich Osgar a's Iollainn.

16

Gu 'n d' eirich Diarmaid O Duibhne ;
Gu 'n d' eirich sin a's Iall O' Buidhne ;
Triuir mac an righ chiar-dhubh Dhùinne ;
Gu 'n d' eirich sin agus Cearbhall.

17

Dh' eirich Glaisean O Damhach ;
Dh' eirich sin agus Ard-amharc ;
Dh' eirich Ciar-dhubh, mac righ Lomhann.
A cheathrar a b' fhoghaintiche 'bha 'san Fhìnn,

18

Chaidh a chomhrag ris a' bheist.

.   .   .   .   .

.   .   .   .   .

.   .   .   .   .

19

Bha i 'gam frithealadh mu seach
Mar a ruitheadh lann roimh lasair,
Gus an do thachair Mac Chumhail an aidh
'S a' Mhuileartach lamh ri lamh.

20

An aicheadh cha 'n fhacas mar sin
O cheardach Lonn Mhic an Liobhann,
Bha dealt air bharraibh a shleagh
Aig Mac Chumhail an taoibh ghil.

K

21

Her side was pierced with sharp wounds,
There was rain of her blood on the heather;
The Muilearteach was slain by the king,
And if she was slain, it was no smooth slaying.

22—SMITH.

The smith took with him her bree*
To Tur Leoin of the high king
"My sorrow!" said the smith of the axes,
"If bald russet Muilearteach is slain."

23—KING.

The king said, "the people never stood,
That on the bald russet could bring blood;
Unless in a land of holes fell she,
Or was drowned upon the smooth bare sea."

24

"There never yet have come of any,
Those who the yellow Muilearteach could slay;
They did not slay her, but the Fhinn,
A band from whom tribute is not won."

25

"Great is the shame to the blossom of Phail,
To give under to the people of a single isle;
To the travelling, and to the west,
Travel we, and travel we in haste."

26

"That I would give my vow again,
If my mild Muilearteach has been slain;
That I with my people should never return,
Till Eirinn to a heap of ashes should burn.

* It seems that she was the wife of a superhuman Celtic sea
smith, who goes by the name of Balcan sometimes.

21

Bha 'taobh air a tholladh le guin;
Bha braon dh' a fuil air na fraochaibh.
Mharbhadh a' Mhuileartach leis an righ ;
Ma mharbhadh cha b' e 'm marbhadh min.

22

Thug an gobha leis an brigh
Gu tùr Leoin, an t-ard righ.
" Mo bheud," arsa gobha nan tuadh,
" Ma mharbhadh a' Mhuileartach mhaol ruadh."

23

Thuirt an righ, " nach d' fhas a shluagh
Na 'bheireadh fuil air a' mhaoil ruaidh.
Mar an deach i 'n talamh toll,
Na 'bathadh air muir sleamhuinn, lom."

24

" Cha d' thainig de dhaoine 'sam bith
Na 'mharbhadh a' Mhuileartach bhuidhe.
Cha do mharbh i ach an Fhinn,
Buidheann bhar nach buinigear cis."

25

" 'S mor an naire do Bhlaith Phàil
Geill a thoirt do luchd aon eilean.
Air an triallam, 's air an iar ;
Triallam, agus triallam mor."

26

" Gu 'n d' thugainn—sa mo bhòid a rìs,
Ma mharbhadh mo Mhuileartach mhìn,
A choidhch nach tillinn le m' shluagh
Gus am biodh Eirinn 'na torr luatha.

27

"In Eirinn let me not leave a stone,
In burn, or in moor, or in mountain lone;
Unlifted upon the beaks of my fleet,
Eirinn level of such great weight."

28

"I will bring my plungers upon the brine
To bring out of her sea bent all Eirinn."

     .   .   .   .   .

     .   .   .   .   .

29—BARD.

Great is the brag for the white ships
The whole of Eirinn to uplift,
And that there are not white ships in being
That could uplift one fifth of Eirinn.

30—KING.

"Gather to me my worthy race,
King of the Spaniards and his force,
The king of Greece and of Gallia clean,
King of Hispania and of the Inds."

31—BARD.

Gather of the whole world the clan,
The children of a king and of a single man,
Goblin or champion shall not get clear
From the beautiful Fhinn of the yellow hair.

32

Seven score ships, and one thousand
Gathered the king, what a heavy band
For the taking of all Eirinn,
Could it be brought to Fionn, prince of the Finne.

27

" An Eirinn na fagam clach,
An allt, na 'm monadh, na 'm fireach,
Gun thogail air chorraibh mo long ;
Eirinn chothromach, cho trom.

28

" Bheiream breabanaich air sàil
Toirt Eirinn uil' as a tan."

. . . .

. . . .

29

'S mor an spleadh do luingeas bàn
Eirinn uile do thogfàil ;
'S gun de luingeas bàn sam bith
Na thogadh, a dh' Eirinn, coigeamh.

30
Righ.

" Tionail thugam mo theaghlach còir,
Righ na h-Easpanaidh 's a shlogh,
Righ Greige, 's righ Gallia glan,
Righ na h-Easpainn a's na h-Inid."

31
Filidh.

Tionail sluagh an t-saoghail uile,
De chlann righ, 's de dh' aon duine ;
Fuath na eàrrachd cha d' thig as
O'n Fhinn aluinn fhalt-bhuidhe."

32.

Seachd fichead a's mile long
Thionail an righ, 's gu 'm b' fheachd trom,
Gu gabhail Eirinn air fad ;
Gu Fionn, fiath na Finne na 'n tàrt 'e.

33

There was not a port nor a half port within
The five-fifths of the Eireann
That of beaked barks was not full,
And of the barges of their lords all.

34

Though it was evil to be waiting for them,
'Twas no better for them that to us they came.

   .   .   .   .   .
   .   .   .   .   .

35

A messenger came from Blaith Phail,
To find for him the Muilearteach,
Or else the bold youth of all Eirinn,
The children of a single man or of a king.

That MacChumhail would give to the
King of Lochlann, and without a grudge.

   .   .   .   .   .
   .   .   .   .   .

36

Ten hundred helmets and fine mail,
Ten hundred shields and sheathed glaives,
Ten hundred collars of gold upon hounds,
Ten hundred slender stingers of battle.

37

Ten hundred fine coloured flags,
Ten hundred wise warriors whom he might choose,
Ten hundred bridles of gold and saddles.

33

Cha robh port na leith-phort ann,
An coig choigeamh na h-Eireann,
Nach robh lan de bharcaibh bheannach,
Agus bhirlinnibh o thighearnan.

34

Ge b' olc dhuinn a bhith air an cionn,
Cha 'n ann daibh-san a b' fhearr teachd thugainn.

. . . . .
. . . . .

35

Thainig teachdair o Bhlaith Phàil
A Mhuileartach fhaotainn da,
Airneo borbraidh Eirinn uile
Eadar clann righ 's aon duine.

Bheireadh MacChumhail siud do righ Lochlann
'S gun diomadh ;—

. . . . .
. . . . .

36

Deich ceud clogad a's caol luireach,
Deich ceud sgiath a's claidheamh comhdaicht,
Deich ceud lomhainn òir air chonaibh,
Deich ceud sallta chaola chatha,

37

Deich ceud bratach mhìne, dhaite,
Deich ceud saoidh, na 'm b' aille leis,
Deich ceud strian òir agus diollaid.

38.

Though he got all that, the king òf Lochlann
And the bold youth of the whole of Eirionn,
For ever with his people he would not be still
Till Errinn should become a ruddy hill.

39—LOCHLANNERS.

Then spoke an answerable true wise bard,
The lad that could answer with a knowing word ;
And he spoke timidly and like a seer
Unto the king that was too early.

40—BARD.

"Though you, like the whole of the Fhinn,
In the front of battle and combat
You must come as lions, weighty and gray,
Or else you will work out your own decay.

41.

" It were better to get us on a single place
Than from billow to billow to be on our trace."

42—KING.

"Thy counsel is lying, thou musical bard,"
Out spoke the king, wrathfully, hatingly,
"Because a third part of what is there (seen)
Thou hast never beheld in Eirinn."

43—FEENE.

* Then spoke Garaidh of the glens :(*)
"If you will take my counsel, Fhinn,
Let submission be given on the sea,
That for ever under his sway you may be."

* Here the action changes from one camp to the other.

38

Gad a gheibheadh righ Lochlann siud,
Agus borbraidh na h- Eirionn uile,
Choidhch' cha stadadh e le 'shluagh
Gus am biodh Eirinn 'na torr ruadh.

39

Thuirt filidh freagarrach, fior-ghlic,
An gille fhreagradh gu h-eolach—
'S labhair e gu fromhaidh, fàdh,
Ris an righ, gu 'n robh ro thrath.

40—Filidh.

"Ge math leibhs' an Fhinn uile
An tus cath agus comhraig ;
Thig sibh 'n 'ur Leomhana trom, ghlas,
Airneo ni sibh uil' 'ur n-aimhleas.

41

B' fhearr 'ur faighinn air aona bhall,
Na 'bhith 'g ur sireadh o thuinn gu tuinn."

. . . . .
. . . . .

42—Righ.

'S breugach do bheachd f hilidh bhinn,
Thuirt an righ gu fuathach, feargach ;
"Agus trian na 'bheil an sin
Nach fhaca tu riamh an Eirinn."

43

An sin labhair Garaidh nan Gleann,
"Ma ghabhas sibh comhairl, Fhinn,
Rachadh geill a thoirt air sàil,
'S gu 'm biodh sibh gu bràth fo iona."

44—BARD.

Up rose Iollain with a hero's tread,
And each one followed him side by side,
To give a leathering to Garaidh from the wild,
Who the service of man could not abide.

45—FIONN.

"Stay thou, Iollain, as thou mayest be,"
Said MacChumhail, the prince so high,
"Though evil the counsel of the man,
Stalwart his hand when the strife began."

46—OSGAR.

Said Osgar, as he felt the pain,
"Whatever ship is of loftiest sail,
Shall swim in blood beneath her keel,
If there be enough within her hull."

47—BARD.

Then raised they, and they were not scarce,
Their slender pennons on their slender shafts
The standard of MacChumhail of Victories,
"Sun's brightness," above the trees.

48.

There were nine chains from it downward fell
Of the yellow gold, of no lustre dull,
A hero at every chain of these,
That was holding them against the stays.

49.

In the camp there was many a thousand of men,
Many a one with blades and spears so keen, .
Many a trunkless head was there,
Many a neck there was swept bare.

From the first of the sun till the same evening.

44

Dh' eirich Iollainn, 's bu cheum laoich,
'S gach ti lean e taobh ri taobh,
Thoirt leadairt air Garaidh o 'n fhasach,
'S cha b' aill leis duine 'ga fhasdadh.

45—FIONN.

"Stad ort Iollainn mar a ta thu;"
Arsa Mac Chumhail an ard fhlatha,
"Ge b' olc impidh an fhir,
"Bu teom' a lamh anns an iorguill."

46—OSGAR.

Thuirt Osgar, 's e 'gabhail leon,
"Ge b' e long a 's airde seol,
Snamhaidh i 'm fuil fo' a driom,
Ma tha na h-urad 'na colainn."

47—FILIDH.

Thog iad an siud, 's cha bu ghann,
An caol shrolt, air an caol chroinn ;—
Bratach Mhic Chumhail an aidh,
Gile-ghreine, as cionn chrainnaibh.

48

Bha naoidh slabhraidhean aisde sios
De 'n òr bhuidhe gun dall-sgiamh ;
Laoch air gach slabhraidh dhiu sin
A bha 'gan cumail ris na slàithean.

49

Bu lionar 's a' chrò mìle fear ;
Bu lionar fear gheur lann 's sleagh ann ;
Bu lionar ceann ann gun chom iona ;
Bu lionar muineal ann air maoladh,

O thus greine gu con-fheasgar.

50

Those heroes the greatest of the tribe
That came to us with an army (of pride),
To them the camp was the narrowest
Ere their rough vapouring was dispersed.

51

In the thick of the people Osgar slew
One hundred spearmen for the first time,
Another hundred of the people by three,
Seeking a way to their Ard Righ.

52

Another hundred of the hosts of men
On the further side of the king of Lochlann,
Until he slew, in the thick of the host,
The king for all his great honour's boast.

53

When they saw that the king had fallen,
Their courage failed them, and in great swiftness,
They went all in ranks to the sea;
And the battle poet was driving them.

54

Amongst the warriors in turn,
It was the Osgar that was urging them.
After he had given the war
Came succour to the hero of bright arms.

55

For through the spear-holes there might go
The sickles (*) through the back of Osgar.

50

'An laoch sin bu mhò dhe 'n t-sliochd
A thainig thugainn le 'mhor fheachd ;
'Sann daibhsan bu chuing' an crò
Ma'n do sgaoileadh an garbh sgleo.

51

Mharbh Osgar, an tiugh an t-sluaigh,
Ceud fear sleagha mar cheud uair,
Ceud eil' as a' phobull a tri,
Ag iarraidh thun an ard righ.

52

Ceud eile de shluagh nam fear
An taobh thall de righ Lochlann,
Gus an do mharbh e, 'n tiugh an t-sluaigh,
An righ air mheud onarach.

53

Nuair chunnalc iad gun d' thuit an righ
Threig am meanmna iad 's am mor luathas :
Chaidh iad 'nan sreathan gu sàil,
'S a' chliar chatha 'gan iomain.

54

Eadar na saoidhean mu seach
'S e'n t-Osgar a bha 'gan iomain ;
An deis a bhith tabhairt a' bhlair,
'S ann thainig cobhair gu laoch arm-ghil.

55

Oir rachadh, roimh thollaibh nan sleagh,
Na còrran roimh dhriom Osgair.

56.

Whatever that day might hap to be
On the battle steep side of Beinn-Eudainn,
Such like great peril was not there found
From the first of the Finne till one day

On the day when the Fhinn were on Oirill's Mound.

Wrote down this poem from the recitation of Angus MacDonald, Staoine-breac, South Uist, September 1860, and again from that of Allan MacPhie, tailor.   MacDonald gives the same authority for it as for the "Great Fool," and MacPhie says he learnt it from one Donald MacIntyre, who has gone to America, and if living is now about 80 years of age.   In Barra, I heard it from Alexander MacDonald, Burgh ; and from Donald MacPhie, smith, Brembhaig, who learnt it from an uncle of his, Hector MacLaine, also a smith.   Some versions have lines which are wanting in others, and in some lines there are a few slight variations.   I have inserted those lines and words which I thought best when differences occurred.   H. M'L.

(¹) Maclean translates this brushwood, but the carlin was bald, and I have heard the word used to express a picture on a shield of some large bird, like an eagle, which is often mentioned in stories as "Creveenach."   The word may have something to do with Griffin, or Tree Lion.

(²) This warrior is said to have given the name to Glengarry. There are legends about him still current in that neighbourhood.

(³) Herons is the more evident meaning, but corr means any crooked instrument.   The line occurs elsewhere.

[In translating this, I have aimed at giving the meaning of each line, at imitating the rhythm of the original, as well as I could, and at giving the same amount of rhyme, where I was able to hit upon rhymes that would not alter the meaning.   MacLean's manuscript is not divided into quatrains, but I have heard this chanted, and the measure, and the music, and the meaning, all

56

Ge b' e bhitheadh an latha sin
Air taobh uchd-catha Bheinn Eudainn ;
A leithid de bhaoghal cha d' fhuaras ann,
O thus na Finne gus an aon latha,

'S latha dha 'n Fhinn air tulach Oirill.

---

point to a division into quatrains. I am indebted to
the collector for a literal translation, which has been of
the greatest assistance ; but I have here and there followed Armstrong's Dictionary, which contains many
rare words, avowedly taken from the Ossianic poems.
If there be errors in the translation, I hope they may
be overlooked.

MacDonald, who sang this and two other poems to
me in Barra, September 10, 1860, did it with only one
mistake. He forgot something near the beginning,
and stopped short, and uttering several expressions of
strong disgust at his own forgetfulness, he turned
back to the first line and began again, and got
over the difficulty with a rush that reminded me of a
man taking a running leap over a stiff hedge. With
that one mistake he recited a whole poem ; and so far
as I can judge, from hearing such crabbed Gaelic once,
it was the same poem which is here given, but we made
out that there were fourscore verses in it, whereas there
are but fifty-five incomplete in MacLean's manuscript.

I observed that, two or three times, in reciting this
and other poems, MacDonald repeated a couple of lines
to fill up the time and complete a quatrain.

The poem was attributed to Oisean, and whoever
composed it, clearly did so in the character of that old
half mythical bard, for he speaks like an eye-witness,
and dwells on the prowess of *his* son Osgar. I am

not sufficiently acquainted with early Norwegian and
Irish history, to be able to guess at the event which is
celebrated, or at a date, but I suspect the poem was
composed in remembrance of some real invasion of Ireland by the sea rovers of Lochlann, in which they got
the worst of the fight, and that it has been preserved
traditionally in the Hebrides ever since.   Could it
be Brian's famous battle, A.D. 1014.   MacLean has
named his authorities; one of them, MacDonald, is
referred to above.   He is a workman who cannot read,
and who speaks no language but Gaelic.   He is a fine
intelligent man, with a clear gray eye and smooth dark
hair, very fond of the old poetry of his native country,
and charmed to recite it to an audience able to take an
interest in it.   The audience was a numerous one on
the 10th of September, and we were highly attentive.
One woman was industriously weaving in a corner,
another was carding wool, and a girl was spinning dex-
terously with a distaff made of a rough forked birch-
branch, and a spindle which was little better than a
splinter of fir.   In the warm nook behind the fire sat a
girl with one of those strange foreign faces which are
occasionally to be seen in the Western Isles, and which
are often supposed by their neighbours to mark the
descendants of the Spanish crews of the wrecked
armada—a face which, at the time, reminded me of the
Nineveh sculptures, and of faces seen in St. Sebastian.
Her hair was as black as night, and her clear dark
eyes glittered through the peat smoke.   Her complexion was dark, and her features so unlike those who
sat about her, that I asked if she were a native of the
island, and learned that she was a Highland girl.   Old
men and young lads, newly returned from the eastern
fishing, sat about on benches fixed to the wall, and
smoked and listened; and MacDonald sat on a low

stool in the midst, and chanted forth his lays amidst suitable remarks and ejaculations of praise and sympathy. One of the poems was the Lay of Diarmaid, much the same as it appears here ; as I had got it from MacLean, who had written it from the dictation of another man elsewhere. " Och ! och !—aw! is not that sad ?" said the women when Diarmaid was expiring. One of the audience was a stranger from the south, a Campbell, who had come to Barra from some other place, and who, as usual, hailed me as a kinsman, claimed Diarmaid as our common ancestor, and MacCalain Mor as the head of his family. His hair was yellow, though tinged with white; and amongst the short, dark natives of Barra, he looked large, and gaunt, and bony. He gave me his prose version of the escape and pursuit of Diarmaid and Graidhne, and brought the fugitives from Ireland to the Isle of Skye. The main incidents were similar to those already given, but in detail they differed entirely, as all versions which I have, do from each other. The house where our meeting was held was one of those which are only to be found in the far west, and this may serve to give a notion of the people, who still preserve and delight in this old Gaelic poetic lore.

May 11, 1861.—Since this was printed, I have found a version of " Duan a Mhuirearteach" in a collection of Gaelic poetry, made by Hugh Gillies, and printed in 1786 at Perth. I am indebted to the Rev. Mr. MacLauchlan for a loan of the book, which is rare, and which I had sought in vain at the British Museum and elsewhere. There are 112 lines arranged in stanzas in the published version ; 213 in the traditional version here given.

The story, and some lines of the poetry, also appear in the proceedings of the antiquaries of Scotland (vol. iii., part ii. 1861), these are taken from a MS. collection made in Lewis. It appears that the heroine was wife of a superhuman Celtic sea smith, who is a kind of Neptune, and who had been maltreated by the Feen.

L

Another version of the poem was written from the dictation of a man at Gairloch ten years ago; and another has lately been written by Mr. Torrie in Benbecula, from the recitation of an old beggar wife.

LXXIV.

THE STORY OF THE LAY OF THE GREAT FOOL.

Written by Hector MacLean, September 13, 1860. Recited by Angus MacDonald (constable) at Stoney Bridge, South Uist, who styles himself Aonghas, Mac Iain, Mhic Aonghais, Mhic Dhomhnuill, Mhic Thormaid, Mhic Iain, Mhic Neill, Mhic Cha-lain, Mhic Eoghain, Mhic Aonghais oig, Mhic Aonghais Mhoir, Mhic Sheann Aonghais, a Ile 's tha iad ag radh nach robh e cli. That is to say, Angus, the son of John, and up to the thirteenth ancestor, "Old Angus from Islay; and they say he was not weak." MacDonald says he learnt this poem fifty-eight years ago from Aonghas, Raothaill bhàin, Mhic Iain, Mhic Dhomhnuill, Domh-nullaich, Mhic Ghilleaspaig, Mhic Iain, Mhic Uisdean, Mhic Aonghais, Mhic Raothaill, H. Earaich (that is to say, Angus of white Ronald, the son of John, and up to the tenth ancestor), who lived in North Uist, at Baile Ràthaill, and who died more than fifty years ago, about seventy years of age.

He could neither read nor write, and he learnt this and other stories from his mother, who died about seventy years ago, at the age of one hundred years.

He (MacDonald) says that the song—

A Nighean bhuidh bhàin nam falbhadh tu leom,
Gun ceannachain Gùnn de 'n sioda dhuit.

Thou fair yellow girl, if thou'dst go with me,
That I'd buy a gown of the silk for thee,

was composed by her.

The poem is, as usual, preceded by a short prose story, which is as follows :—

THERE were two brothers once in Eirinn, and one of them was a king and the other a " ridire." They were both married. On the knight there was a track (that

is, the knight had children), and there were no children at all to the king. It was a source of insult to
the knight and his lot of sons, that the king should
have the realm at all. The thing that happened was,
that they gathered armies, both of them, on each side.
On the day of the battle that they gave, the knight and
his three sons were slain.

The wife of the knight was heavy, and the king
sent word that if she were to have a babe son to slay
him, but that if it were a baby daughter to keep her
alive, and keep her. It was a lad that she had, and
there was a kitchen wench within who had a love son.
Braomall was her name, and Domhnull was the name
of her son.

When the son of the knight was born, this one
fled with the two, the knight's son and her own son.
They were being fed at the cost of the knight's wife.
She was there on a day, and for fear they should be
hungry, she went to a town land to seek food for them.
They were hungry, and she was not coming, and they
saw three deer coming towards the bothy. The
knight's son was where the other was, and he asked
what creatures were there. He told him there were
creatures on which there was meat and clothing.

"If we were the better for it I would catch them,"
said he.

He ran and he caught the three deer, and they
were before his "muime" when she came. She flayed
them, and they ate, and she made a dress for him of
the deer's hides.* Thus they were in a good way till
the deer failed, and hunger came upon them again,
and she went again to the town land. There came a
great horse that belonged to the king—a wild horse—

* I have several versions of a long very wild story called the
" Lad of the Skinny husks."

to the place where they were. He asked of Donald what beast was that.

"That is a beast on which sport is done, one is upon him riding him."

"If we were the better for him I would catch him," said he.

"Thou ill-conditioned tatterdemalion! to catch that beast! It would discomfit any man in the realm to catch him." He did not bear any more chatter, but he came round about, and he struck his fist on Donald, and he drove his brains out. He put an oaken skewer through his ear, and he hung him up against the door of the bothy. "Be there thou fifty beyond the worst," said he.

Then he stretched out after the horse, and the hides were trailing behind him. He caught the horse, and he mounted him; and the horse that had never borne to see a man, he betook himself to the stable for fear. His father's brother had got a son by another wife. When he saw the palace he went up with wonder to look at the palace of his father's brother.

His muime never had called him anything but "the great fool" and "Creud orm." When he perceived the son of his father's brother playing shinty, he went where he was, and, "Creud orm," said he.

"Who art thou," said the king's son—"of the gentles or ungentles of the realm, that has the like of that speech?"

"I am the great fool, the son of the knight's wife, the nursling of the nurse, and the foster-brother of Donald the nurse's son, going to do folly for myself, and if need were, it is I that could make a fool of thee also."

"Thou ill-conditioned tatterdemalion! make a fool of me?" said the king's son.

He put over the fist and he drove the brain out of him. "Be there, then, thou fifty over worse, as is Donald the nurse's son, with an oaken skewer through his ear."

He went in where the king was. "Creud orm," said he.

"Who art thou," said the king—"of the gentles or ungentles of the realm, that hast such a speech ?"

"I am the great fool, the son of the knight's wife, the nursling of the nurse, and the foster-brother of the nurse's son, going to make folly for myself, and if need were, it is I that could make a fool of thee also."

"Well, then, it is not thou that made me that, but my counsellor, on the day that I slew thy father, and did not slay thy mother."

Then the king went with him. Every one, then, that he fell in with in the town, they were going with him, and that was their blessing, "Creud orm."

There was a splendid woman in the realm, and there was a great "Fachach" that had taken her away. The people thought, if they could bring him to the presence of this woman, that he would set his head upon her, and that he would let the people away; that it was likely they would come between himself and the Fachach, and that the Fachach would kill him. That time he was an utter fool.

[Of the poem, MacLean remarks:—"Some of the phraseology and pronunciation is such as is considered Irish; for example, the particle ni for cha, dho for dhà, cos for cas; but these forms of expression were common in the Highlands; add to which, a cultivated dialect was probably common to both countries. The versification is exceedingly harmonious and varied. In some lines the number of syllables is shorter, to give room for the emphasis and slow utterance required by the sense. In reciting the poem, the pronunciation of the reciter was peculiar, and differed widely from that of his conversational dialect.

" It appears that this Lyric was considered by the Gael their
best, for it is said, 'Gach dàn gu dàn an Deirg;' 'Gach laoidh
gu laoidh an amadain mhoir;' 'Gach eachdraidh gu eachdraidh
Chonnail.' *Each poem to the poem of the Red ; each lay to the lay
of the great fool ; each history to the history of Connal (is to be referred as a standard).* In Dr. Smith's 'Sean Dàna,' there is a
laoidh an amadain mhoir quoted, entirely different from this
one."—H. MacL.]

The lay is in " Sean Dàna" as part of Cath
Mhanuis. Another long poem was published under
the name of " Laoidh an Amadain Mhoir," which I
have failed to get at the British Museum. The language of the version here given is difficult, and it differs
in construction and in sound from the spoken modern
Gaelic of the district. There seems every reason to
consider it as a fragment. It seems to describe a single
adventure only, and there must have been a prelude
and a sequel to it.

Perhaps Gillmhin (Fairfine) was the lady whom the
Fachach had taken away, and who made an entire fool
of the mighty simpleton.

There is something allegorical in the adventure.
There is a mystic valley in which the hero is tempted,
and yields to a cup of pleasure, but when he perseveres,
his punishment is lightened, and he gets to the golden
city. There he yields to sloth, but when he holds to
his promise, and resists temptation, and fights manfully,
he is delivered from all his woes. If this view be
correct, this may be part of the same tradition which is
interwoven with the romances of Arthur and his
knights, which were certainly founded on Celtic traditions, and which pervade all Europe.

The story of Peronnik L'Idiot, in the " Foyer
Breton," is of the same class. The hero is an orphan,
and a simpleton, and proves himself a hero with sharp

wits. He takes service as a herd at a farm, and there sees knights going to Kerglas to seek the golden basin, and the diamond lance. The one is filled with any food which the owner desires, cures diseases, and raises the dead; the other crushes all that it touches, and shines like a flame; both belong to a giant magician who lives at Kerglas. Now Kerglas might be Cathair Glas, the gray or mystic city. The golden basin, though it has more virtues, has the same properties as the Gaelic Ballan iochshlaint (vessel of balsam), and the shining lance is own brother to Claidheamh geal Soluis, the white glaive of light.

Kerglas was surrounded by an enchanted forest, in which rivulets seemed to be torrents, and shadowy rocks and vain shows terrified the wanderer. Beyond that, a dwarf korrigan guarded an apple tree, which was the same which grew in Eden; further on, a lion with vipers for a mane, guarded a magic flower, which dissolved enchantments; still further, a shoal of dragons watched the lake in which they swam; and lastly, a terrible black man, with many eyes, guarded a fearful valley. He was chained to a rock, and armed with an iron bullet, which returned to him when he had thrown it, and he at least is a common character in Gaelic tales (see page 15). When all these dangers were passed, temptation assailed the adventurer in the shape of delicious food, pleasant drinks, and fair women, and if he yielded he fell.

All these dangers Peronnik the Breton idiot overcomes by wily stratagems. The Gaelic Amadan Mor overcomes temptation also, but he conquers by valour and dogged perseverance, rather than by wiles.

Peronnik, the half-starved idiot, catches a colt of thirteen months, rides through the wood, and at last, by the help of a yellow lady who turns out to be the

plague, kills the magician, and acquires the magic
basin and lance.   He appears on the side of the Bretons
in a war with the French at Nantes, kills his foes with
the lance, brings his friends to life when killed, and
feeds them when alive with the magic basin; and
finally, he goes to Palestine, where he destroys armies,
forces the Emperor of the Saracens to be baptized, and
marries his daughter, "by whom he had one hundred
children."

By some accounts he still lives with all his family.
The great fool does not go to Palestine, but Connal
Guilbeinach does, and he there acquires a magic shining
sword, and a talisman, which brings the dead to life.
I am inclined to rank "the Great fool" with "Peronnik
the idiot," to place the golden city on the same magic
hill of the imagination as Kerglas, and to consider the
"lay" as one episode in the adventures of a Celtic
hero, who in the twelfth century became Perceval le
chercheur du basin.   He, too, was poor, and the son of
a widow, and half starved, and kept in ignorance by his
mother, but nevertheless he got a horse and venison,
and acquired knowledge from King Arthur's knights,
and joined them; and in the end he became possessed
of that sacred basin le Saint Graal, and the holy lance,
which, though christian in the story, are manifestly the
same as the Gaelic talismans which appear so often in
Gaelic tales, and which have relations in all popular
lore,—the glittering weapon which destroys, and the
sacred medicinal cup which cures.

May 18, 1861.—The fourteen verses numbered with an (*)
are inserted from a version written down for Sir Kenneth Mac- .
kenzie, in 1850, at Gairloch, chiefly from the recitation of John
MacPherson, then eighty-eight years old, and thus headed—"How
the might (neart) of the Great Fool got the victory over the
Glamour (druigheachd) of Mananan (mhananain), and how he

took his legs back again from him by his might." I am indebted to Mr. Nicholson of Edinburgh, who had the MSS.

The twelve verses numbered with (†) are not in the Gairloch version. The remaining thirty-seven verses are common to both. No two verses, hardly two lines are identical; but the variations are slight, and the phonetic value of the words is preserved in almost every instance. This seems a strong argument for the traditional preservation of these poems.

2 and 3, which are not in my version, and 4, which is not in the other, together lead me to suspect either that this was composed to imitate an older poem, and to teach a moral lesson; or that some one has tried to give an old poem a moral turn. The language of 2 and 3 is biblical; 4 is magical, and so is the bulk of the poem; and the rhythm of 3 and 4 is different from the rest. The bearing of this on Welsh tradition is referred to elsewhere.

DEER AND HOUND.—From a stone at Kirriemuir.—*Sculptured Stones of Scotland,* Pl. xlvi. *See Stanza* 15.

THE LAY OF THE GREAT FOOL.

1—BARD.

TALE of wonder that was heard without lie,
Of the idiot to whom hosts yield,
A haughty son who yields not to arms,
Whose name was the mighty fool.

2*

The might of the world he had seized
In his hands, and it was no rude deed.
It was not the strength of his blade or his shield,
But that the mightiest was in his grasp.

On his falling on a hidden glen,
Wherein he never before had staid,
Of loveliest strath and grass and plain,
And sound of the waves 'gainst each bright stone. (See 5.)

ELK.—From a stone in the churchyard of Meigle.—*Sculptured Stones of Scotland*, Pl. lxxii. *See note* (2).

LAOIDH AN AMADAIN MHOIR.—(1.)

1

Sgeul uamharr a chualas gun bhreug,
Air òinid dh'an geill na sloigh ;
Mac meanmnach nach dearg le airm,
D'am b'ainm an t-Amadàn mor.

2*

Neart an domhain gu'n ghlac e
'Na lamhaibh 's chu bu ghniomh borb.
Cha be neart a sgéith no lainn,
Ach an treine bh' ann a bhi na dhorn.

Air tachairt a'n gleann diomhair dhò
Anns nach robh e fos roimh riamh,
A b' ailte srath a's fear a's fonn,
Fuaim nan tonn ri slios gach leug.   (Gairloch 4.)

3*

Lasting long ere we had come,
Many a chief is beneath his sway ;
Another little tale I'd tell,
Be it there discerned, and it is strange.

4†

A day when the mighty fool
Was in Lochlan's bounds in a magic cloud,
Himself and one beauteous dame,
As a woman her beauty sufficed.

5

Meeting in a vast shore-glen,
As a rose ever growing through it,
Floods, and strife, and grass, and sound,
Roar of waves on shore of sea.

6—GILVEEN.

"There was seen," said Gilveen young,
" A gruagach of the yellowest cloak in the way,
A new coloured vessel in his grasp,*
Like to a cup in which was drink."

7†—FOOL.

It was then the great hero spoke,
" Is it an empty flower I see ?
It is, when greatest is my thirst,
That it's coming were best for health."

8—GILVEEN.

" An earnest entreaty I make to thee,
Drink not his draught, take not his food,
Till thou knowest what is the glen
Wherein thou wert never before."

* Of flaming gold.

3*

A leantuin fad air dhuine teachd
'S iomadh ceud a tha fu 'smachd;
Sgeul beag eile' dh' innsean ann
Tuigear thall 's gu bheil e ait.

4†

Latha do'n Amadan mhor,
An criochan Lochlann fo cheo draodh,—
E fhein agus aona mhaca mna;
Bu leoir a h-ailleachd mar mhnai.

5

Tachairt an gleann diomhair, ròdh,
Mar ròs fas roimhe riamh,
Sionan, streubh, a's feur, a's fonn,
Stoirm nan tonn ri stios na léi.

6

"Chunnacas," arsa Gilmhin og,
"Gruagach 'san ròd a's buidh brot,
Soitheach ur, daite 'na dorn*
Coltach ri corn am biodh deoch.

7†

Sin nuair labhair Macabh mor,
"An e ròs fòs(') tha mi a reir?
'San uair a's motha mo thart,
'S gu'm b' fhearr a theachd gu beatha."

8

"Achanaich a dh' iarrams' art,
Na ol a dheoch 's na gabh a bhiadh,
Gu fiosraich gu dé 'n gleann
Nach robh thu ann roimhe riamh."

* A dh' or laiste.

9†—GRUAGACH.

After that had been spoken to him,
Out spoke the Gruagach of the Cup,
" Be not downcast stalwart youth,
Be merry and quaff thy draught."

10—BARD.

In the like commune with him
Out spoke he, and it was no wise speech.
He gave a haughty clashing dart,
And there was no drop in the cup but he drank.

11

Away went the Gruagach of the Cup :
Unlucky was the cup to drink,
The two legs down from the knee
Were wanting to the mighty fool

12—GILVEEN.

Then it was young Gilveen spoke,
" Great is this woe has befallen thee,
Scarce are thy friends in the great world ;
Unliked by them is thy want of feet.*

13—FOOL.

" Hist ! now thou Gilveen young,
Cease thy woe and be thou still,
No leg shall be under one in the land,
Or I myself will get my two feet."

14†—BARD.

There they wended the pair,
The woman and the hero of heaviest tread,
Swifter was he on his two knees
Than six at their swiftness of foot.

* They'll not weep thy want of feet.

9†

An deigh sin f'hoclachadh dhò
Gu 'n do bheannaich gruagach a' chuirn,
" Na bi dubhach oglaich mhoir ;
Bi subhach a's ol do dheoch."

10

Air a' chomain chiadhna dhò,
Labhair esan 's cha b' e 'ghloir ghlic ;
Thug e sitheadh bruaisgneach borb,
'S cha robh braon 's a' chorn nach d' ibh.

11

Gu 'n d' imich gruagach a' chuirn,
Neo-bhuadhach a' chuirn ri ol ;
An da chois, fo'n ghluin-shios,
Bha 'dhith an Amadain mhoir.

12

'Sin nuair labhair Gilmhin og,
" 'S mor am bron seo thainig ort,
'S tearc do charaid 'san domhan mhor,
'S ni neo-oil leo thu 'bhith gun chois."*

13

" Uist a nis a Ghilmhin og,
Sguir ad' bhron, a's bi nad' thosd ;
Cha bhi cas fo fhear as tir
Neo gheibh mi fhin mo dha chois."

14†

Dh' imich iad an siud 'nan dis,
A bhean 'san laoch bu truime trosd ;
Bu luaithe esan air a dha ghluin
Na seisear air luathas an cos.

* S cha bhron leo thu bhi gun chos.

15

They heard the hunt in the glen,
The voice of the hound and music sweet,
Rapidly chasing the elk (*)
On the moorland that suited best.

16

On the moorland that suited best
Was seen the deer from the mountains wild,
The red eared and very white hound
Keenly baying upon his track.

17

Swiftly he gave a dart,
That sudden cast with his keen blade,
There was driven by force of the hero's hand
The spear through the deer's two sides.

18—Fool.

They caught hold of the white stag-hound,
And out of hand put him on leash.
" Be there making music by me,
Till one comes after thee from the chase."

19—Bard.

There was seen descending a glen
A Gruagach in full splendour of gold,
Hand on blade on his left side,
And his two spears and his shield in his grasp.

20

Certes they asked a tale from him,
Or what road the stranger used.
* They took an alternate tale about
* What was the land where they used to be.

15

Chual iad an fhaghaid 's a' ghleann ;
Guth gadhair ann a 's binn ceol
A' ruith na h-eilid gu dian
Air an fhireach a b' ihearr doigh.

16

Air an fhireach a b' fhearr doigh,
Chunnacas fiadh o bheannaibh borb,
'S gadhar cluas-dearg gle gheal
A' tabhann gu geur 'na lorg.

17

Thug esan sitheadh gu grad ;
An urchair chlis ud le lann geur ;
Thártadh, le neart lamh an laoich,
An t-sleagh roimh dha thaobh an Fheidh.

18

Bheir iad air a' ghadhar bhàn,
'S air a laimh gu 'n chuir air eill.
"Bi tu agam deanadh ciuil
Gu 'n d' thig fear o 'n iuil a' d' deigh."

19

Chunnacas a' tearnadh le gleann
Gruagach ann lan dearsadh òir,
Lamh air lann air a thaobh cli,
'S a dha shleagh 's a sgiath 'na dhorn.

20

Dh' fhoighneachd iad sgeul deth gu beachd,
Na co'n ròd a chleachd an aoidh ?
* Gabh iad sgeula dheth mu seach,
* Ciod i 'n tir a'n do chleachd a bhi.

M

21—GRUAGACH.

" Ridire Corcair is my name,
And on each spot I have victory won.
I am the Gruagach of the white stag-hound
That has fallen into thine hand."

22—FOOL.

" Thou Gruagach of the handsomest mien,
I will give thee assurance of this,
That Gruagach of the white stag-hound
Shall not henceforth be said to thee.

23

" Will't not suffice thee, mighty son,
A make-weight or two to be in the scale ?
As the whole of the hunt is beneath thy power
To leave the white stag hound with me.

24—GRUAGACH.

" It is I, indeed, who made the hunt,
As the idiot is wrathful and fierce,
Whichever one is of strongest hand,
His be the white stag-hound and the deer."

25*

" Since my stag-hound has fallen to thee,
And thy feet are awanting,
Food and clothing take thy desire ;
I would give that to thee and thy wife.

26—GILVEEN.

" Accept that, said Gilveen young,
And give the white stag-hound to him,"
" I'll give him, and a speckled hound,
And if it pleased thee, a greater thing."

* There seems to be some description of a fight wanting here,
unless the Gairloch version is right.

> " It is I myself who made the hunt,"
> So said the fool fiercely.

21

" Ridire Corcair b'e m' ainm,
'S air gach ball gu 'n d' thug mi buaidh.
'S mise gruagach a' ghadhair bhàin
A tharladh ann an laimh thu ; "

22

" A Gruagach ud a 's ailne dealbh
Bheir mise 'dhearbhadh sin duit,
Nach bi gruagach gadhair bain
As an seo ri ràdh riut."

23

" Nach fhoghainn leatsa 'Mhice mhoir
Leatrom no dha 'bhith 'san roinn,
'S an t-seilg uile 'bhith fo d' bhinn,
'S an gadhar bàn a leiginn leam."

24

" 'S mise sin a rinn an t-seilg ;
Mar tha'n t-Amadan garg, dian ;
'S ge b' e neach a's treise lamh
'S leis an gadhar bàn 's am fiadh."

25

" 'S o tharlladh mo ghadhar ort,
Agus do chosan gu d' dhìth,
Biadh a's aodach, gabh d'a reir,
Bheirinn dhuit fhein 's do d' mhnaoi

26

" Gabh siud," arsa Gilmhin og,
'S an gadhar bán a thoirt dhò."
" Bheiream agus gadhar breac,
'S na' b' aill leat na bu mhò."

27—BARD.

Then wended they on the three,
Under the guidance of the man.
He raised in the hollows of his shield
The sling-shaft (*), and the woman, and the deer.

28

Then was seen, appearing aside,
A still city filled with the glitter of gold,
And there was no hue that eye hath seen
That was not in plenty the court within.

29—FOOL.

Then asked the mighty fool,
"What was the city of gold by the way,
Of noblest form and most beauteous mien.
Shall I find out from whence it came?"

30—GRUAGACH.

"Gold Yellow City is its name,
From Mount Modest and glens of gloom,*
And there are in it of guileful men,
But I only and my single dame.

31†

"Yonder glen that thou camest through,
Full of glamour it is always,
But little it has taught to me
But to behold the worth of my dame.

32†

"A young wife that I found in the tower,
The sight of an eye no better was,
Whiter than very snow is her form,
Gentle her eye, and her teeth like a flower."

* Perhaps "Glannasmoil," in the county of Dublin, where
Fenian legends are localized.

27

Dh' imich iad, an sin 'nan triuir,
Anns an iuil a rinn am fear ;
Thog e 'n crannagaibh a sgiath
An crann-tabhuill, 's am fiadh, 's a' bhean.

28

Chunnacas a' tighinn ri taobh
Cathair chaomh 's lan dearsadh oir ;
'S cha robh dath a chunnaic suil
Nach robh anns a' chuirt na 's leoir.

29

Dh' fhoighneachd an t-Amadan mor,
" Co i 'chathair oir, ri 'h-iuil,
A's breagh cruth 's is ailne dreach ?
'S am faigh mi mach co dheth a tùs ?"

30

" 'Chathair orbhuidh gu 'm b' e 'h-ainm
O Dhun Tuirbh 's o ghleantna Smol,
'S cha 'n 'eil innt' a dh'fhearaibh fòil
Ach mise fòs a's m' aona bhean.*

31

" An gleann sin roimh d' thainig thu trid
Lan de dhraodhachd tha e 'ghnath ;
'S beag a dh' fhaoghluim e dhomh fhein
Ach 'bhith 'g amharc beus mo mhná.

32†

" Bean og a fhuair mi 'san tur
Nach robh amharc sùl na b' fhearr ;
'S gile na gach sneachd a corp,
'S mall a rosg, 's a deud mar bhlath."

---

* A chathair orruidh, and Dungarbh (Gairloch version), comain chrois ; a name incomprehensible.

33*—LADY.

The dame of exceeding beauty blessed
The Gruagach so lovely and brown.
" Who is the lady stately and young,
Or the big man thou hast yielded to?"

34*—GRUAGACH.

" The mighty Fool is his name,
And his wife is the young Fairfine;
The men of the world are at his beck,
And the yielding to him was mine."

35*—LADY.

" I think marvellous what thou say'st,"
So said the young Fairfine ;
" If the men of the world are at his beck,
That he'd let his legs go with them."

36*—GRUAGACH.

" I'll give thee my word, oh dame,
That the men of the world are at his beck ;
And were it not glamour of Comain cross,
He'd not let his legs go with them."

37

" And now that I may go to the chase,
To the ruddy mountains and glens of gloom,
Do thou watch, my brother of love,
My house, my wife, and my store of gold!

38

" So long as I am without,
Do thou nor slumber or droop thy head.
Let never a man within
Or a man out, if one come in."

33*

Bheannaich a bhean a b fhearr snuagh
Do na Gruagach aluinn donn.
" Co macan steudgheal og
No 'm fear mor d'an d' thug thu geill?"

34*

" An t amadan mor gur e ainm
'S a gheilbhinn og gur i 'bhean
Fir an domhain tha gu 'mhein
'S mise fein gu'n gheill da."

35*

" 'S ioghnadh leam na tha thu agradh,"
'Se labhair a Gheilbhinn og ;
" Fir an domhain gu bheil gu' mhein
S gu leigeadh e a chasan leo."

36*

" Bheir mise mo bhriathra' bhean
Fir an domhain gu bheil gu mhein ;
'S mar b' e druidheachd Chomain chrois
Cha leigeadh e a chasan leò."

37

Gu'n d' theid mise 'nis a shealg
A bheanntai dearg 's a ghleanntai smol ;
Mathaich thusa, 'bhrathair ghraidh,
Mo theach, 's mo mhnai, 's mo chuid oir.

38

Cho fad 's gu'm bi mise muigh
Na deansa lochd 's na crom do cheann ;
Na leig duin' idir a steach ;
Na duine 'mach ma thig ann."

39—BARD.

They went to the chase the three,
The dog, and the Gruagach, and the white stag-hound.
The two fair ones and the great son
Stayed waiting within the city of gold.

40—FOOL.

Then outspoke the hero large,
" Gilveen young, here at my head,
A heavy sleep is enticing me.
We did not yield up in the glen."

41*—BARD.

He was not long in his sleep
A Gruagach came in from the way,
And gave a kiss to the Gruagach's dame,
And the lady was not ill pleased that he came.

42†—BARD AND GILVEEN.

The young wife sat beneath his head ;
In her mien she pictured a sun,
And said she to the stalwart youth,
" Thou hast slumbered, but not for thy good.

43

" Thou hast slumbered, but not for thy good.
There came a mighty warrior in
And gave a kiss to the Gruagach dame ;
Unlucky it is that the stranger came."

44—BARD.

Up rose the mighty fool,
To the doorway went he,
Never struck blacksmith, tinker, or wright
A door more strongly than the angry wight.

39

Dh' imich iad a shealg 'nan triuir
An cu, 's an gruagach, 's an gadhar bán;
An dithis ban 's am macabh mor
Dh' fhan 's a' chathair oir ri h-iuil.

40

Sin do labhair Macabh mor,
" Ghilmhin og seo aig mo cheann
Tha 'n cadal trom 'gam bhuaireadh;
Ni 'n òbamaid suas 's a' ghleann."

41*

Cha b' fhada bha e na shuain
Thainig Gruagach a' ròd a steach
'S do bhean a Gruagaich thug e pog
'S cha b' fhuathach leis un oigh a theachd.

42†

Gu'n shuidh an og-bhean fo 'cheann;
Mac samhlaidh dealbha i ri grein;
'S thuirt i ris an oglach mhor,
" Rinn thu suaimhneas, 's cha b' e t' fheum.

43

" Rinn thu suaimhneas, 's cha b' e t' fheum;
Thainig gaisgeach treun a steach,
'S do 'n mhnaoi ghruagaich thug e pog;
'S neo-bhuadhach an aoidh a theachd."

44

Dh' eirich an t-Amadan mor; •
Thun an doruis a ghabh e.
Cha d' bhuail gobha, ceard, na saor,
Comhla, 's treise na 'n laoch borb.

45*—Fool.

" Unless I were sound enough
He had not come in from the road,
Till comes the Gruagach of the golden doon,
With my will he goes not out."

46—Gruagach.

Up rose the warrior straight and brown,
And the arms were seized by grasp.
" Leave the doorway, stalwart youth,
Thou art there instead of right."

47†—Fool.

Thus answered the warrior great
To the hero of the firm speech,
" Till he comes, the Gruagach who is out,
Thou shalt be in or thy head."

48*

" Still will I give my vows,
Though thou thinkest much of thy speech ;
When comes the Gruagach of the golden doon
He will repay thee for his wife's kiss."

49*—Gruagach.

" Wilt not suffice thee, thou mighty man,
Seven vats full of glittering gold,
Cattle and horses, and untaxed land,
Plain of the plains and the woman's doon ?"

50*

" Thou mayest get that, and to boot
My tissue vesture and horse,
Who's as ready on sea as on land,
If thou wilt but let me go out."

45*

" Mur bhithinn a' m' shuain gu leor
Cha tigeadh e a' rod a steach
'S gus an tig Gruagach dun an oir
Le mo dheoin cha teid e mach."

46

Dh' eirich an gaisgeach deas, donn,
S' ghlacadh leis na h-airm 'na dhorn,
" Fag an dorus oglaich mhoir ;
An àite coir a bhiodh tu ann."

47†

Air freagairt do Mhacabh mor,
Air a' ghaisgeach na gloir theann,
" Gu 'n d' thig an gruagach tha muigh
Bidh tusa steach no do cheann."

48*

" Bheir mise mo bhriathra fos
Ge mor leat na bheil thu ag' radh ;
Nuair thig Gruagach dun an oir
Gu'n diol e ort pog a mhna."

49*

" Nach foghnadh leatsa mhic a mhoir
Seachd lan dabhaich 'a dh'or glan
Crodh a's eich fearann saor
Raon nan raon a's dun nam ban."

50*

" Gheibheadh tu sin a's ni 's mò
Mo chulaidh shroil agus m' each
'S co deas leis muir agus tìr
A chionn mo ligeadh a mach "

51*—Fool.

"Still will I give my vows,
Though thou thinkest much of thy speech ;
When comes the Gruagach of the tissue cloak,
He will repay thee for his wife's kiss."

52—Gruagach.

"From the Gruagach of the Cup I got
Thy one foot to let me in ;
I'll blow it beneath thee with joy
If thou leave the way to go out."

53—Bard.

With his own magic he blew
His one foot beneath him as ever it was,
And said the Gruagach, who was wise,
"It is time for me now to depart."

54—Fool.

Thus answered the warrior great,
" A little stay yet for a slow space,
The other foot for a sturdy step,
I'll take from thee or thy head."

55—Gruagach.

When the hero was in hard straits,
He suddenly sprang to the breast of his dame ;
" My comeliness I throw upon thee,
Guard me my feet and my hand."

56†—Fool.

" If death be a terror to thee,
For the dear wife of most beauteous mien,
The other foot thou wouldst give away
A refuge in that hour for thy head."

51*

" Bheir mise mo bhriathra fos
Ge mor leat na bheil thu ag'radh
Gu'n tig Gruagach a bhrait shroil
'S gu'n diol e ort pog a mhna."

52

" Fhuair mi o ghruagach a' chuirn
Do leith chos a m' leig a steach ;
Seideam fodhad i' gu m' dheoin,
'S ma leigeas an ròd a mach."

53

Sheid esan le dhraodhachd fhein
A leith-chos foidh mar bha i riamh ;
'S thuirt an gruagach a bha glic,
"Gur tim dhomh bhith nis a triall."

54

Air freagairt do Mhacabh mor,
" Stad beag fathasd gu fòil mall ;
A chas eile gu ceum cruaidh
Bheir mise uait no do cheann."

55†

Nuair a bha 'n gaisgeach an càs cruaidh,
Duibh leum gu luath ri uchd na mnai,
"Tilgidh mi mo chuimrin (') ort ;
Dion domh mo chosan 's mo lamh."

56†

" Ma 's h-eagal leat am bàs,
Do 'n ghraidh-bhean a 's ailne dealbh
A' chas eile bheireadh tu uait ;—
Didean, air an uair, dho d' cheann."

57†—Bard.

He was not allowed to come to words,
When the great one was upon him,
And unless t' other foot was given him
Slice in two ! ere he could cry for Fionn.

58*—Gruagach.

Then with his own glamour he put
His two legs under him as they were,
And said the Gruagach, who was wise,
" It is time for me now to begone."

59—Fool.

" These feet I have now got below
I yield not to thee nor to them,
The day will not come that thou goest out,
Till comes the Gruagach of the golden doon."

60—Gruagach.

" I am the Gruagach of the golden doon,
And great is my boast of thy good will,
And (I am) the Gruagach of the white stag hound
That fell into thy hand, .

61†

" And that took these feet off thee
To try thy courage and thy force ;
I blow them beneath thee again,
Right as straight as thou wert."

62*

" Youth of most beauteous mein,
I esteem thee great in each thing ;
It was I took thy legs off thee
To try thy valour and mind."

57†

Cha d' leigeadh gu focail dhò
Nuair bha 'm fear mor as a chionn ;
'S gun a chos eile thoirt dhò,
Sgiol na dhò ma 'n goirear Fionn.

58*

Chuir e'n sin lè dhruidheachd fein
A dha chos fodha mar bha iad riamh
S thu' irt an Gruagach a bha glic.
"'S mithich a nis a bhi triall."

59

" Na casan seo fhuair mi fodham
Cha leig mi leat iad na leo.
Cha d' thig an la a theid thu mach
Gus an d' thig gruagach Dhun an oir."

60

" 'S mise gruagach Dhun an oir,
'S bu mhor mo bhosd os do riun,
Agus gruagach gadhair bhàin
A tharladh ann an lamh thu.

61†

"'S a thug na cosan ud diot
A dhearbhadh do ghniomh a's do lugh ;
Seideam fodhad iad a rìs
Cheart cho direach 's a bha thu."

62*

" Oganaich is ailte dreach
Gur mor mo bheach ort 's gach cuis ;
'S gur mi bhun do chasan d' iot
A dhearbhadh do ghniomh 's do thurn."

63—BARD.

Then they laid hold hand on hand,
Love on love, and good will on good will,
One little tale on the dames,*
A wondrous tale heard without a lie.

* Together, like the fellowship of the Fane.
And so the tale passed away.—(Gairloch.)

(¹) Fàs, empty. Ròs, a flower—probably the cup is called a
flower.

(²) The word is translated hind, roe, etc. It is the same word
as elk, but it means a stag here.

(³) Crann tabhail is translated " sling" in Armstrong; but
tabhail, according to the same authority, is "catapult;" "Crann"
is a tree. It seems, then, that the word means some instrument
made partly of wood, and used in the chase; and I suspect it
means cross-bow. Men are represented on the sculptured stones
of Scotland shooting with cross-bows. *See* p. 100.

(⁴) *Cuimeir,* neat, trim, well formed, elegance ; *cuimrin,* my
elegance, my elegant self.

63

Rug iad an sin lamh air lamh ;
Gaol air ghaol a's minn air mhìnn ;
Aona sgeul beag air na mnai,
Sgeul uamharr' a chualas gun bhreig.

* Araon mar chomunn na Feinne
'S dh imich an sgeul mar sin.

CAOGAD, fifty. IBH, to drink.

SIONAN, I do not know this word, unless it is a corruption of
sithean, a knoll. STREUBH, I do not know unless it is strath, a
strath. The line might be read this way—

Sithean, srath, a's feur a's fonn.
Knoll, strath, grass, and land.

STIOS na lei, I think is slios na lei. LIA, an old name for a
stream : on the side of the stream. RÒDH, I suspect, is " very
extensive." MACA MNA, is, I think, a superior woman.

SÒITHEACH UR DAITE na dorn, should be, I think, 'na dhorn.

H. M'L.

. On the authority of Armstrong, and taking similar words, I
have put a meaning on the doubtful line, but I am not sure that
it is correct. See various readings, footnote.   J. F. C.

LAOIDH AN AMADAIN MHOIR.

BHA dithis bhraithrean uair an Eirinn, 's fear dhiu 'na righ 's fear na ridire. Bha iad posda le cheile. Air an ridire bha aliochd, 's cha robh sliochd air an righ idir. Bu tamailteach leis an ridire 's le 'chuid mac an rioghachd a bhith aig an righ idir. 'Se an ni a bh' ann chruinnich iad arm le cheile air gach taobh. An latha blair a thug iad mharbhadh an ridire 's a thriuir mac.

Bha bean an ridire trom, 's chuir an righ fios na 'm bu leanabh mic a bhiodh aice a mharbhadh, ach na 'm bu leanabh nighinn a bhiodh ann a chumail beo 's a ghleidheadh. 'Se gille a bh' aice; 's bha searbhanta cidsin a staigh aig an robh mac diolain; 's e Braomall a b' ainn di, agus 's e Domhnull a bh' air a mac. Nuair a rugadh mac an ridire theich i seo leis an dithis, mac an ridire 's a mac fhein. Bha iad 'gam beathachadh air taillibh bean an ridire. Bha i 'n sin latha 's eagal gu 'm biodh acras orra dh' fhalbh i gu baile a dh' iar-raidh bìdh dhaibh. Bha 'n t-acras orra, 's cha robh ise a' tighinn, 's chunnaic iad tri feidh a' tighinn ionnsuidh na botha. Bha mac an ridire far an robh am fear eile 's dh' fhoighneachd a dé na creutairean a bha 'n siud. Dh' innis e dha gu'n robh creutairean air an robh biadh agus aodach.

" Na 'm b' fheairde sinne e bheirinn orra," ars' esan.

Ruith e 's rug e air na tri feidh, 's bha iad air coinneamh a mhuime nuair a thainig i. Dh' fheann i iad, 's dh' ith iad, 's rinn i deise dhasan de chraicinn nam fiadh. Bha iad mar seo gu doigheil gus an do theirig na feidh 's an d' thainig an t-acras orra a rithis, 's chaidh ise an sin thun a' bhaile. Thainig each mor a bheanadh do'n righ de dh dh' each fiadhail far an robh iad. Dh' foighneachd esan de Dhomhnull dé 'm beathach a bha 'n siud.

" Tha 'n siud beathach air am biotar a' deanadh spors; biotar air a mhiun ga mharcachd."

" Na'm b fheairde sinn e bheirinn air," ars esan.

" Thusa a luidealaich dhona a bbeireadh air a bheathach 'ud l dh, fhairtlich e air duine s' an rioghachd breith air." Cha d' fhulaing e tuilleadh seanachais, ach thainig e mu 'n cuairt 's bhuail e dorn air Domhnull, 's chuir e 'n t-eanchainn as. Chuir e stob daraich roimh a chluais 's chroch e ri dorns na botha e.

" Bi an sin caogad thar mhiosa," ars' esan.

Shin e air an each an seo 's na craicinn slaodadh ris. Rug e air an each 's chaidh e air a mhuin ; 's an t-each nach d' fhulaing duine riamh fhaicinn thug e'n stabull air leis an eagal. Bha brathair 'athar an deigh mac fhaotainn o mhnaoi eile. Nuair a chunnaic esan am paileas ghabh e suas le ioghnadh a choimhead paileas bhrathair 'athar.

Cha d' thubhairt a mhuime ris riamh ach an t-amadan mor agus ' Creud orm." Nuair a mhothaich esan mac bhrathair 'athar ag iomain chaidh e far an robh e 's, " Creud orm," urs' esan.

"Co thusa," arsa mac an righ, "de dh' uaislean na de dh' an-uaislean na rioghachd aig am bheil a leithid sin de chaint ? "

" Tha mise, an t-amadan mor, mac bean an ridire, dalta na banaltrum, 's comhdhalta Dhomhnuill, mac na banaltrum, a' falbh a' dean-adh amadanachd domh fhein, 's na b' fheudar e 's mi a dheanadh amadan diotsa cuideachd."

" Thusa a luidealaich dhona a dheanadh amadan dhiomsa," arsa Mac an Righ.

Chuir e thairis an dorn 's chuir e 'n t-eanchainn as.

" Bi thusa an sin caogad thar mhiosa mar a tha Domhnull mac na banaltrum agus stob daraich roimh a chluais."

Ghabh e staigh an sin far an robh an righ, " Creud orm ; ars' esan.

"Co thusa," ars' an righ, " de dh' uaislean na de dh' an-uaislean an rioghachd aig am bheil a leithid sin de chomhradh ? "

" 'Se mise an t-Amadan mor, mac bhean an ridire, dalta na banaltrum, 's comhdhalta Dhomhnuill, mac na banaltrum, air falbh a' deanadh amadanachd dhomh fhein, 's na 'm b' fheudar e 's mi a dheanadh amadan diotsa cuideachd."

" Mata cha tu a rinn diomsa e ach mo chomhairleach an lath, a mharbh mi t' athair nach do mharbh do mhathair."

Dh' fhalbh an righ an sin leis. A' h-uile h-aon an sin a bha ag amas air 's a bhaile bha iad a' falbh leis, 's b' e siud am beannachadh "Creud orm." Bha boireannach riomhach anns an rioghachd, 's bha fachach mor an deigh a toirt air falbh. Smaointich an sluagh na'n d' thugadh iad am fianuis a' bhoireannaich a bha 'n seo e, gu 'm gab-hadh e cean urra, s' gu 'n leigeadh e'n sluagh air falbh; gur docha gu 'n d' thigeadh iad eadar e fhein 's am fachach; 's gu 'm marbhadh am fachach e. Leig e a chead do 'n t-sluagh 's mharbh e am fachach. Bha e 'n uair sin 'na lan amadan.

An Ox "the Points of whose Horns were Backwards instead of being Forwards."—From a stone at Fowlis Wester, near Crieff.—*Sculptured Stones of Scotland*, Pl. lx. The sculpture probably represents a procession leading an ox to be sacrificed.

LXXV.

GUAIGEAN LADHRACH S' LOIREAN SPAGACH.

From Kate MacFarlane, as early as 1810, John Dewar, October 1860.

THERE was at some time a king in Albainn whose name was Cumhal, and he had a great dog that used to watch the herds. When the cattle were sent out the dog would lead them to a place where there might be good grass; and the dog would herd them there for the day, and in the evening he would bring them home.

There were certain people dwelling near to the

king's house, and they had one son, and they used to
send the son on matters to the king's house every evening. There was one beautiful sunny evening, and the
boy was going to the king's house on a matter, and he
had a ball and a shinny, and he was playing shinny
forwards on the way to the king's house.* A dog
met him, and the dog began to play with the ball ; he
would lift it in his mouth and run with it. At last
the boy struck a blow on the ball while it was in the
dog's mouth, and he drove the ball down the dog's
throat ; he stuffed it down with the shank of the
shinny, and he choked the dog ; and since he had
choked the dog, he himself had to go and keep the
king's cattle instead of the dog. He had to drive out
the cattle in the morning, to drive them to good grass,
and to stay and herd them all day, for fear they should
be stolen, and to bring them home in the evening as
the dog used to do. So since he killed the dog, and
since it was in the place of the king's dog that he was,
it was " Cu Chumhail " (Cual's dog) that they used to
say to him ; and afterwards they altered the name to
" Cuthullain."†

On a day of the days Cuchullin put out the cattle,
and he drove them to a plain that was there, and he
was herding them ; and he saw a giant who was so
big that he thought he could see the lift between his
legs, coming to the side where he was, and driving a
great ox before him ; and there were two great horns
on the ox, and their points were backwards instead of
being forwards. The giant came forward with the ox
where Cuchullin was, and he said,

* This is a common practice among Highland laddies now.

† The writer means the Ossianic hero, commonly called
Cuchullin ; so I have followed the usual spelling rather than
Dewar's, which is but another way of expressing the same sound.

"I am going to take a while of sleep here, and if thou seest any other man of the giants coming after me, awaken me. It may be that I will not easily be wakened, but waken thou me if thou canst."

"What is waking to thee?" said Cuchullin.

"It is," said the giant, "to take the biggest stone thou canst find and strike me on the chest with it, and that will wake me."

The giant lay and slept and his snoring was as loud as thunder. But sleep was not long for him, till Cuchullin saw another giant coming, who was so big that he thought he could see the lift between his legs.

Cuchullin ran and he began to awaken the first giant that came, but waken he would not. Cuchullin was shoving him, but his wakening could not be done; but at last he lifted a great stone, and he struck the giant in the chest with it. The giant awoke, and he rose up sitting, and he said, "Is there another giant coming?"

"There is; yonder he is," said Cuchullin, as he held his forefinger towards him.

The giant struck his two palms on each other, and he said, "Ach, he is!" and he sprang on his feet.

The other giant came forwards, and he said, "Yes! Ghuaigean làdhraich,* thou hast stolen my ox."

"I did not steal it, Loirean Spàgaich,† said he, "I took it with me in the sight of every man as my own."

Shamble Shanks seized one horn of the ox to take it with him, and Crumple Toes seized the other. Shamble Shanks gave a swift jerk at the horn which he had in his hand, and he took it off the bone; he threw it from him with all his strength, and he drove

* Crump-footed, toe-ish.

† Straddling tracker, or shambling shanks. A bandy-legged man is spágach.

it into the earth, point foremost, and it went down into the earth to the root. Then he seized the bone, and the two hauled at the ox to drag it from each other.

At last the head of the ox split, and the ox tore asunder down through his very middle to the root of the tail. Then they threw the ox from them, and they began at wrestling; and that was the wrestling! there was no knowing which of them was the stronger.

Cuchullin came to bring aid to Crumple Toes; he could not reach up aloft to give a blow to Shamble Shanks with a sword which he had, but he began to cut at the back of his legs to try to make a stair up the back of the giant's legs, up which he might climb to give him a blow of his sword.

Shamble Shanks felt something picking the back of his legs, and he put down his hand and he threw Cuchullin away; and where should Cuchullin go but foot foremost into the horn of the ox, and out of the horn he could not come. But at the time that Shamble Shanks was throwing Cuchullin away, Crumple Toes got a chance at him and Shamble Shanks was levelled, and Crumple Toes got him killed.

When that was done he looked about for Cuchullin, but he could not see him; and he shouted, "Where art thou now, thou little hero that wert helping me?"

Quoth Cuchullin, "I am here in the horn of the ox."

The giant went to try to take him out, but he could not put his hand far enough down into the horn; but at last he straddled his legs and he drove his hand down into the horn, and he got hold of Cuchullin between his two fingers, and he brought him up. Cuchullin went home with the cattle at the going down of the sun, and I heard no more of the tale.

JOHN DEWAR.

I have not given the Gaelic of this, because there is nothing peculiar in the language. It is curious as having a general resemblance to the adventures of Jack the Giant Killer and Tom Thumb, Thor, and other such worthies; and as showing two well-known Ossianic heroes in a nursery tale, as "early as 1810." Cumhal the father of Fionn; and Cuchullin.

I have another version of these incidents in a story dictated by Neil Macalister, Port Charlotte, Islay, and written by Mr. Carmichael at the request of my old friend, John MacLean, of Coulabus.

The Feinn were all in Islay to drive away the Lochlanners, and when they had succeeded, Cuchullin fell in with a fairy sweetheart, who had flocks and herds, and he staid, while the rest went north to fight the Lochlanners in Skye. The fairy sweetheart bore a son, and by desire of his father, called him Conlaoch. There was a neighbour called Garbh Mac Stairn, who was far stronger than Cuchullin, and one day he went to take his fine light-coloured bull. Cuchullin disguised himself as herd, met the giant, told him his mistress was ill in bed, and then ran round, and got into bed behind her. The wife said she had got a baby, and the giant poked his finger into his mouth, to see if he would make "fisean Cuin," a whelp of Conn, and the hero bit him to the bone. The wife complained of the draught from the door, lamenting her husband's absence, for he would turn the house away from the wind. The big man tried, but could not, so he made off to the cattle. The seeming herd got there before him, and they seized the bull by the horns, and tore him in two. Then they try the feats which Cuchullin could do. The giant carries a millstone which the herd cannot lift, to a hill top, and the herd rides it to the bottom. The giant tries, and gets many a hard fall. They go to a rock more than a hundred fathoms high, and perform a feat which used to be attributed to Islay boys; they "measure two feet and two fists" over the edge. The giant puts one heel on the edge, the other against his toe, stoops, and places his clenched hands on each other, on the other toe; and tumbles headlong into the "fierce black green sea."

Cuchullin gives a feast, and then goes to Skye to help Fionn, leaving a ring for his son. He grows up and follows, and his mother swears him never to tell his name till forced. Conlaoch finds the Feinn fighting at "Thaigh Mheile ann an Dura," Fionn sends to find out his name. Conan goes; they fight, and Conan is beat. Cuchullin goes, and the son keeps him off with his sword. They go out into the sea, to the bands of their kilts, to try "cath builg," and they cast their spears at each other, but the son casts shaft foremost. At last he is pierced by his father, and discovers himself; and they curse the fairy mother. The last few lines are fragments of a poem, and make six verses. "The death of Conlaoch" is told in an undated quarto MSS. in the Advocates' Library; the action is partly in Scythia, and there is much more incident. The poem of "Carthon," is founded on the incidents, but the names are different. This then is old, Ossianic, mythological, and Celtic; it is common to Scotland and Ireland; to MSS., print, and tradition.

See Carleton Irish stories, Dublin, 1846, p. 107, etc.

LXXVI.

CONALL GULBAN; OR GUILBEINACH, OR GULBAIRNEACH.

IN translating this I have departed from my first plan, which was to give in all cases exactly what I got from *one* man, and abstracts of other versions. In this case the longest version was translated; and to it passages and notes were added from three other written versions: and from two of which I took notes myself. Where the same incidents are given by two men in different words, the passage which seemed best has been selected. Where one version has an additional incident which the rest have not, it is inserted in its order. Where versions vary, the variation is given in a note. Thus many passages are substituted and inserted, but I have carefully avoided adding anything of my own invention.

At the earnest request of the publishers, the Gaelic of this long story is omitted, to make room for other matter; but the manuscript is preserved, and some few curious passages are given in foot notes.

The chief "author," as the scribe calls him, is John MacNair, who lives at Clachaig, near the powder mills at Dunoon. The scribe is John Dewar, a labourer now working in the woods at Rosneath, and their ver-

sion fills sixty foolscap pages. I find that there is a
tendency to change dialogue into narrative in writing
a story, as is the case here ; but when these men *tell*
stories, dialogue predominates.

MacNair, who is a shoemaker, got the story about
thirty-five years ago from an old man named Duncan
Livingston, who lived in Glendaruel, and was then
about sixty-five. Dewar says that he was a shoemaker,
and grandfather to another old shoemaker, James
Leitch, who lives at Eas klachain in Glendaruel, and
from whose dictation Dewar has taken down several
long and curious stories which I have. Leitch says
that his grandfather " had Ossian's Poems by heart,"
and many tales " sgeulachd ;" and a list of those who
still know the latter is given.

Of Livingston, MacNair says—

" I have an interesting story about that old man. In the time
of the American war, the laird was pressing the tenants to go,
and this old man seemed not willing ; so they pursued him
through a deep river or burn, as we call it ; and when he saw he
could not escape, he placed his leg between two stones and
snapped it in two, so they had to carry him home."

The second version was written by Hector Mac-
Lean, and fills twenty-five pages. The reciter was
Alexander MacNeill, who lives in Barra, and who
names as his authorities several old men. He also
recited No. XXXVI.

The third was also written by MacLean, from the
telling of John MacGilvray, labourer, Colonsay, in
July 1860. It fills fourteen pages, and has this tradition attached to it,—" Two ministers, long ago,
desirous of trying the powers of the Gaelic language,
composed this story and the Knight of the Red Shield
(No. LII.). MacLean suggests two Monks of Iona.

The fourth was written by Mr. Fraser of Mauld,

near Beaulay, Inverness-shire, and fills six pages. It
was told by Dugald Martin in Crochal.

I have heard the story told by various reciters,
particularly by Donald MacPhie in South Uist, and
Charles MacIntyre in Benbecula. The latter spoke
for an hour. I did not time the former, but he spoke
for a long time, and I thought his version the most
consistent and the most complete story which I had
then heard.

The story then is very widely spread in Scotland
—from Beaulay on the east, to Barra on the west, and
Dunoon and Paisley in the south. No two give it in
the same words, or give exactly the same incidents;
but MacNair's version written in Dunoon, and Mac-
Neill's in Barra, written independently by different
scribes, so far as they go together, closely resemble each
other.

Dewar, who is a very intelligent man, suggests
that the story is " purely Irish," and that " it was
composed about the time of the crusade, as it tells
about the Turks invading the king of Iubhar's country."
He thinks the Green Isle is one of the Orkneys.

" Innse torrain, the isles of noise. Ossian's poem
on Cathul," so called because covered with fir trees
and with large rocks facing the sea, against which the
waves make a great noise." (There are no trees in
Orkney.) Dewar does not think this tale so old as
many of the others which he has written for me.

My own opinion is that the story is mixed with the
adventures of the Norse sea rovers who frequented the
Western Isles; and that it is impossible to say whether
it was composed in Ireland or in Scotland; but it is
clear that it was composed a long time ago, and by some
one able to imagine and carry out an elaborate plot.
There are many old men in Scotland, widely separated,

and who cannot read, who know the story and can remember the plot, in whole or in part; so it must be old. It is also known in Ireland. I have traced the incidents amongst Irish labourers in London. One man, a bricklayer, had " seen Conall Gulban in an Irish manuscript;" and a story so called is mentioned in the transactions of the Ossianic Society of Dublin.

THE STORY OF CONALL GULBAN.

THERE was at some time a young king in Eirinn, and when he came to man's estate the high counsellors of the realm were counselling him to marry; but he himself was inclined to go to foreign countries first, so that he might get more knowledge, and that he might be more instructed how the realm should be regulated; and he put each thing in order for matters to be arranged till he should come back. He staid there a while till he had got every learning that he thought he could get in that realm. Then he left Greece and he went " do'n Fheadailte," to the Italy to get more learning. When he was in that country he made acquaintance with the young king of " an Iubhair," and they were good comrades together; and when they had got every learning that they had to get in Italy, they thought of going home.

The young king of the Iubhar gave an invitation to the young king of Eirinn that he should go to the realm of the Iubhar, and that he should stay a while there with him. The young king of Eirinn went with him, and they were together in the fortress of Iubhar for a while, at sports and hunting.

The king of Iubhar had a sister who was exceedingly handsome; she was " stuama beusach," modest and gentle in her ways, and she was right (well) instructed. The young king of Eirinn fell in love with her, and she fell in love with the young king of Eirinn, and he was willing to marry her, and she was willing to marry him, and the king of Iubhar was willing that the wedding should go on ; but the young king of Eirinn went home first, and he gathered together the high counsellors of the realm, and he told them what he desired to do ; and the high counsellors of the realm of Eirinn counselled their king to marry the sister of the king of Iubhar.*

The king of Eirinn went back and he married the king's sister ; and the king of the Iubhar and the king . of Eirinn made " co-cheanghal " a league together. If straits, or hardship, or extremity, or anything counter should come upon either, the other was to go to his aid.

When they had settled each thing as it should be, the two kings gave each other a blessing, and the king of Eirinn and his queen went home to Eirinn.

At the end of a little more than a year† after that they had a young son, and they gave him Eobhan as a name. Good care was taken of him, as should be of a king's son. At the end of a little more than a year after that they had another son, and they gave him Claidhean as a name. Care was taken of this one as had been taken of his brother ; and at more than a year after that they had another son, and they gave

---

* This seems to shew that Celtic kings did not act without the consent of their chiefs ; and this appears in other places, in this, and in many other stories. Iubhar is a name for Newry, but the story is not consistent with the supposition that Newry is meant. I suspect Jewry is the word, and that the Holy Land is meant.

† The island reciters always say, " at the end of three quarters," etc.

him Conall as a name, and care was taken of him as
had been taken of the two others.*

* The parentage and education of Conall are differently given,
in a very good though short version, written by Mr. Fraser of
Mauld. It is called the tale of Conall Guilbeanach, son of the
King of Eirinn, and Gealmhaiseach mhin (fair, beauteous, smooth)
daughter of the King of Lochlann.

A king of Eirinn was fond of the chase, and on a fine spring
day he chased the deer till he lost his dogs, and his people. In
the gray of the evening he sat on the side of a green knoll, behind the wind and before the sun, and he heard a voice beside
him say, "Hail to thee, King of Eirinn." "Hail to thyself thou
old gray man," said the king.

The old man took him into the mountain, and there he saw
what he had never seen before; such food and drink, meat and
music, and dancing, and the old man had a beautiful daughter.
He slept that night; and when he arose in the morning he heard
the cry of a child; and he had to stay for the christening of his
son, and he was named Conal Guilbeanach.

The king sent him venison from time to time, and he grew up
to be a stalwart youth, swift and strong.

Then war sprung up between the King of Eirinn and the King
of Lochlann; and the king sent Caoilte (one of the Feine), the
swiftest man in the realm, for Conall, and he could not keep up
with Conall on the way home.

The old gray man gave him a sword, and he said, "Here is
for thee, Conall, A Gheur Ghlas (the keen gray), that I got myself
from Ossean MacOscar na Feinne, etc.

An old man in Benbecula, Donald MacIntyre, told me this
story in 1859. It lasted about an hour, and I did not take notes,
but his version was the same as Mr. Fraser's, so far. A king of
Eirinn gets lost in a magic mist, is entertained by a gray old
man, stays in his house for a night, sees the man's daughter,
" and wheresoever the girl slept, it was there the king rose in the
morning." He had been there a year and a day. Conall was
born, and when the king went home he said nothing about his
adventures.

The man who was sent for Conall, when war broke out with

They were coming on well, and at the fitting time a teacher was got for them. When they had got about as much learning as the teacher could give them, they were one day out at play, and the king and the queen were going past them, and they were looking at their clann.

Said the queen, " This is well, and well enough, but more than this must be done for the children yet. I think that we ought to send them to Gruagach Bhein Eidinn to learn feats and heroes' activity (luth ghaisge), and that there is not in the sixteen realms another that is as good as the Gruagach of Beinn Eidinn.*

The king agreed with her, and word was sent for the Gruagach. He came, and Eobhan and Claidhean were sent with him to Bein Eidinn to learn feats and

the Turks, and the king's two sons refused to stay, was so swift that he could cover seven ridges at a stride ; but Conall beat him at all feats of agility, and when he came home with him he was seven ridges before him ; and as he went he kept a golden apple playing aloft with the points of his two spears, etc.

Old Donald MacPhie, in South Uist, also told me the story. Like all versions which I have heard, it was full of metrical prose passages, "runs" as they are called. His version agreed with MacIntyre's as to the parentage of Conall.

The correct reading then seems to be, that Conall's two brothers were the sons of the queen, but that the hero was the son of the daughter of Gruagach (? the Druid) of Beinn Eudain, an old gray man, who lived in the mountain, and who had been a comrade of Oisean and the Feine.

Conall had the blood of the ancient heroes in his veins, and they helped their descendant.

* Dewar says, " a master of arts and sciences, a title, old Gaelic ;" but he says so only on the authority of his stories. I suspect the word to be the same as Druidhach, a Druid or magician ; and that this relates to some real school of arms and warlike exercises. What the sixteen realms may mean I don't know.

activity, and what thing so ever besides the Gruagach could teach them.

They thought that Conall was too young to send him there at that time. When Eobhan and Claidhean were about a year by the Gruagach, he came with them to their father's house; they were sent back again, and the Gruagach was giving every learning to the king's children. He took them with him one day aloft up Beinn Eidinn, and when they were on high about half the mountain, the king's children saw a round brown stone, and as if it were set aside from other stones. They asked what was the reason of that stone being set aside so, rather than all the other stones on the mountain. The Gruagach said to them that the name of that stone was Clach nan gaisgeach, the stone of the heroes. Any one that could lift that stone till he could place the wind between it and earth, that he was a hero.

Eobhan went to try to lift the stone; he put his arms about it, and he lifted it up to his knees; Claidhean seized the stone, and he put the wind between it and earth.

Said the Gruagach to them, "Ye are but young and tender yet, be not spoiling yourselves with things that are too weighty for you. Stop till the end of a year after this and you will be stronger for it than you are now."

The Gruagach took them home and taught them feats and activity, and at the end of a year he took them again up the mountain. Eobhan and Claidhean went to the stone; Eobhan lifted it to his shoulder top, and set it down; Claidhean lifted the stone up to his lap, and the Gruagach said to them, "There is neither want of strength or learning with you; I will give you over to your father."

At the end of a few days after that, the Gruagach went home to the king's house, and he gave them to their father ; and he said that the king's sons were the strongest and the best taught that there were in the sixteen realms. The king gave thanks and reward to the Gruagach, and he sent Conall with him.

The Gruagach began to teach Conall to do tricks and feats, and Conall pleased him well ; and on a day he took Conall with him up the face of Beinn Eidinn, and they reached the place where the round brown stone was. Conall noticed it, and he asked as his brothers had done ; and the Gruagach said as he said before. Conall put his hands about the stone, and he put the wind between it and earth ; and they went home, and he was with the Gruagach getting more knowledge.

The next year after that they went up Beinn Eidinn where the round brown stone was. Conall thought that he would try if he was (na bu mhurraiche) stronger to lift the heroes' stone. He caught the stone and he raised it on the top of the shoulder, and on the faggot gathering place of his back, and he carried it aloft to the top of Beinn Eidinn, and down to the bottom of Beinn Eidinn, and back again ; and he left it where he found it.

And the Gruagach said to him, " Ach ! thou hast enough of strength, if thou hast enough of swiftness."

The Gruagach shewed Conall a black thorn bush that was a short way from them, and he said, " If thou canst give me a blow with that black thorn bush yonder, before I reach the top of the mountain, I may cease giving thee instructions," and the Gruagach ran up the hill.

Conall sprang to the bush ; he thought it would take too much time to cut it with his sword, and he pulled it out of the root, and he ran after the Gruagach with it; and before he was but a short way up the mountain, Conall was at his back striking him about the backs of his knees with the black thorn bush.

The Gruagach said, "I will stop giving thee instructions, and I will go home and I will give thee up to thy father."

The Gruagach wished to go home with Conall, but Conall was not willing till he should get every knowledge that the Gruagach could give him; and he was with him after that more than a year, and after that they went home.

The king asked the Gruagach how Conall had taken up his learning. "It is so," said the Gruagach, "that Conall is the man that is the strongest and best taught in the sixteen realms, and if he gets days he will increase that heroism yet."

The king gave full reward and thanks to the Gruagach for the care he had taken of his son. The Gruagach gave thanks to the king for the reward he had given him. They gave each other a blessing, and the Gruagach and the king's sons gave each other a blessing, and the Gruagach went home, and he was Mac-Nair. fully pleased.*]

The young King of Eirinn and the king of Laidheann were comrades, and fond of each other; and they used to go to the green mound to the

---

* So far, I have followed MacNair's version, which is the only one with this part. I have shortened it by striking out repetitions; but I have followed Dewar's spelling of the names. The next bit may be but another version of the education of the warrior, but it seems as if something were wanted to complete it. It is the beginning of the story as told in Barra, and I give it as part of the same thing. It agrees with the mysterious origin of Conall.

side of Beinn Eudain to seek pastime and pleasure of mind.

The King of Eirinn had three sons, and the King of Laidheann one daughter ; and the youngest son that the King of Eirinn had was Conall. On a day, as they were on the green mound at the side of Beinn Eudain, they saw the seeming of a shower gathering in the heart of the north-western airt, and a rider of a black filly coming from about the shower; and he took (his way) to the green mound where were the King of Eirinn and the King of Laidheann, and he blessed the men, and he inquired of them. The King of Eirinn asked what he came about ; and he said that he was going to make a request to the King of Eirinn, if it were so that he might get it. The King of Eirinn said that he should get it if it should be in his power to give it to him.

"Give me a loan of a day and a year of Conall thy son."

"I myself promised that to thee," said the King of Eirinn ; "and unless I had promised thou shouldst not get him."

He took Conall with him. Now the King of Eirinn went home ; he laid down music, and raised up woe, lamenting his son ; he laid vows on himself that he would not stand on the green mound till a day and a year should run out. There then he was at home, heavy and sad, till a day and a year had run.

At the end of a day and year he went to the green mound at the side of Beinn Eudain. There he was a while at the green mound, and he was not seeing a man coming, and he was not seeing a horseman coming, and he was under sorrow and under grief. In the same airt of the heaven, in the mouth of the evening, he saw the same shower coming, and a man upon a black filly in it, and a man behind him. He went to the green mound where the man was coming, and he saw the King of Laidheann.

"How dost thou find thyself, King of Eirinn?"

"I myself am but middling."

"What is it that lays trouble on thee, King of Eirinn?"

"There is enough that puts trouble upon me. There came a man a year from yesterday that took from me my son; he promised to be with me this day, and I cannot see his likeness coming, himself or my son."

"Wouldst thou know thy son if thou shouldst see him?"

"I think I should know him for all the time he has been away."

"There is thy son for thee then," said the lad who came.

"Oh, it is not; he is unlike my son; so great a change as might come over my son, such a change as that could not come over him since he went away."

"He is all thou hast for thy son."

"Oh, you are my father, surely," said Conall.

"Thanks be to thee, king of the chiefs and the mighty! that Conall has come," said the King of Eirinn; "I am pleased that my son has come. Any one thing that thou settest before me for bringing my son home, thou shalt get it, and my blessing."

"I will not take anything but thy blessing; and if I get thy blessing I am paid enough."

He got the blessing of the King of Eirinn, and they parted; and the King of Eirinn and his children went home.]

MacNeill.

After the sons of the King of Eirinn had gotten their learning, they themselves, and the king and the

queen, were in the fortress; and they were full of
rejoicing with music and joy, when there came a messenger to them from the King of Iubhar, telling that
the Turcaich were at war with him to take the land
from him; and that the realm of Iubhar was sore beset by the Turks; that they were (LIONAR NEARTMHOR
S' BORB) numerous, powerful, and proud (RA GHARG),
right fierce, merciless without kindliness, and that
there were things incomprehensible about them;
though they were slain to-day they would be alive to-
morrow, and they would come forward to hold battle
on the next day, as fierce and furious as they ever
were; and the messenger was entreating the King of
Eirinn to go to help the King of Iubhar, according to
his words and his covenants.*   The King of Eirinn
must .go to help the King of the Iubhar, because of
the heavy vows: if strife, danger, straits, or any hardship should come against the one king, that the other
king was to go to help him.†]   MacN:

They put on them for going; and when they had
put on them for going away, they sent away a ship
with provisions‡ and with arms.   There went away
right good ships loaded with each thing they might
require; noble ships indeed.   The King of Eirinn and
the King of Laidheann gave out an order that every
man in the kingdom should gather to go.

---

* All versions agree that there was war between Eirinn and
the Turks.

† This is the fullest version.   MacNeill gives the same incidents in a very few words.   The Colonsay man, MacGilvray,
begins here.   "The King of Eirinn thought that he would go to
put the Turks out of the realm of the Emperor — Impire.
Another version also says that the king had gone to put the
Turks out of the realm of the Emperor.

‡ The word provëëshon has been adopted by reciters.

The King of Eirinn asked, "Is there any man about to stay to keep the wives and sons of Eirinn, till the King of Eirinn come back? Oh thou, my eldest son, stay thou to keep the kingdom of Eirinn for thy father, and thine is the third part of it for his life, and at his death."

"Thou seemest light minded to me, my father," said the eldest son, "when thou speakest such idle talk; I would rather hold one day of battle and combat against the great Turk, than that I should have the kingdom of Eirinn altogether."

"There is no help for it," said the king. "But thou, middlemost son, stay thou to keep the kingdom of Eirinn for thy father, and thine is the half for his life, and at his death."

"Do not speak, my father, of such a silly thing! What strong love should you have yourself for going, that I might not have?"

"There is no help for it," said the King of Eirinn. "Oh, Conall," said the king, "thou that hast ever earned my blessing, and that never deserved my curse, stay thou to keep the wives and sons of Eirinn for thy father until he himself returns home again, and thou shalt have the realm of Eirinn altogether for thyself, for my life, and at my death."

"Well then, father, I will stay for thy blessing, and not for the realm of Eirinn, though the like of MacNeill. that might be."*]

The king thought that Conall was too young for the realm to be trusted to him; he gathered his high counsellors and he took their counsel about it. The coun-

* The Colonsay version and MacNair's give the same incidents; and Conall says that if the others get as much as Eirinn, they will be well off. "Thou art wise, Conall," said the king; and Conall was crowned King of Eirinn before they started.

sellors said that Conall was surely too young, but that
was (FAILLINN A BHA DAONAN A DOL AM FEOBHAS) a failing that was always bettering ; though he was young,
that he would always be growing older ; and that as
Eobhan and Claidhean would not stay, that it was best
to trust the realm to Conall.]   MacNair.

Then here went the great nobles of Eirinn, and
they put on them for going to sail to the realm of the
Tuirc, themselves and the company of the King of
Laidhean altogether.*]   MacNeill.

They went away, and Conall went along with them
to the shore ; he and his father and his brothers gave
a blessing to each other ; and the King of Eirinn and
his two sons, Eobhan and Claidhean, went on board of
a ship, and they hoisted the speckled flapping sails up
against the tall tough masts ; and they sailed the
ship fiulpandet† fiullandet‡. Sailing about the sandy
ocean, where the biggest beast eats the beast that is
least, and the beast that is least is fleeing and hiding
as best he may ; and the ship would split a hard oat
seed in the midst of the sea, so well would she steer ;
and so she was as long as she was in the sight of
Conall.

And Conall was heavy and dull when his father
and brothers left him, and he sat down on the shore
and he slept ; and the wakening he got was the one
wave sweeping him out, and the other wave washing
him in against the shore.

Conall got up swiftly, and he said to himself, " Is
this the first exploit I have done ! It is no wonder
my father should say I was too young to take care of
the realm, since I cannot take care of myself."

* The other versions do not say that the company of the King
of Laidhean went, but it is implied.
            † Bounding.   ‡ Seaworthy.

MacNair.

He went home and he took better care of himself after that.]

There was not a man left in the realm of Eirinn but Conall; and there was not left a man* in the realm of Laidheann, but the daughter of the King of Laidheann, and five hundred soldiers to *guard*† her.

Anna Diucalas, daughter of the King of Laidheann, was the name of that woman, the very drop of woman's blood that was the most beautiful of all that ever stood on leather of cow or horse. Her father left her in his castle, with five hundred soldiers to keep her; and she had no man with her in Laidheann but the soldiers, and Conall was by himself in the realm of Eirinn.

Then sorrow struck Conall, and melancholy that he should stay in the realm of Eirinn by himself; that he himself was better than the people altogether, though they had gone away. He thought that there was nothing that would take his care and his sorrow from off him better, than to go to the side of Beinn Eudainn to the green mound. He went, and he reached the green mound; he laid his face downwards on the hillock, and he thought that there was no one thing that would suit himself better, than that he should find his match of a woman. Then he gave a glance from him, and what should he see but a raven sitting on a heap of snow; ‡

* A man, DUINE, means a human being.

† GUARD, this is an English word which has crept into Gaelic stories; saighdair probably meant archer; it means soldier.

‡ This incident, with variations, is common. It is clear that the raven ought to have been eating something to suggest the blood; and so it is elsewhere.

Mr. Fraser of Mauld, Inverness, East Coast.

He had gone to see his grandfather, the mysterious old gray man.

" When he got up in the morning there was a young snow,

and he set it before him that he would not take a wife forever, but one whose head should be as black as the raven, and her face as fair as the snow, and her cheeks as red as blood.   Such a woman was not to be found, but the one that the King of Laidheann left within in his castle, and it would not be easy to get to her, for all the soldiers that her father left to keep her; but he thought that he could reach her.

He went away, and there went no stop on his foot nor rest on his head, till he reached the castle in which was the daughter of the King of Laidheann.]   MacNeill.

He took (his burden) upon him, and he went on board of a skiff, and he rowed till he came on shore on the land of the king of Laidheann.*   He did not know

and the raven was upon a spray near him, and a bit of flesh in his beak. The piece of flesh fell, and Conall went to lift it; and the raven said to him, that Fair Beauteous Smooth was as white as the snow upon the spray, her cheek as red as the flesh that was in his hand, and her hair as black as the feather that was in his wing."

MacPhie, Uist.

On a snowy day Conall saw a goat slaughtered, and a black raven came to drink the blood. "Oh," says he, "that I could marry the girl whose breast is as white as the snow, whose cheeks are red as the blood, and whose hair is as black as the raven;" and Conall fell sick for love.

(Benbecula) Macintyre gave the same incident.

The Colonsay version introduces an old nurse instead.

MacNair simply says that Conall heard of the lady.

* It seems hopeless to try to explain this topography. Laidheann should be Leinster, and Iubhar might be Newry, and Beinn Eudainn or Eideinn is like the Gaelic for Edinburgh, though the stories place the hill in Ireland; and here are the king of Eirinn and his son rowing and sailing about from realm to realm in Ireland, and the Turks at Newry a foreign land. If Iubhar mean Jewry, and this is a romance of the crusades, it is more reasonable.

the road, but he took a tale from every traveller and
walker that he fell in with, and when he came near to
the dun of the king of Laidheann, he came to a small
strait.   There was a ferry boat on the strait, but the
boat was on the further side of the narrows.   He stood
a little while looking at its breadth ; at last he put his
palm on the point of the spear, and the shaft in the
MacNair.   sea, he gave his rounded spring, and he was over.]
Then here he was on a great top that was there, and
he was looking below beneath him, and he saw the very
finest castle (luchairt) that ever was seen from the
beginning of the universe till the end of eternity, and
a great wall at the back of the fortress, and iron spikes
within a foot of each other, about and around it ; and
a man's head upon every spike but the one spike.
Fear struck him, and he fell a shaking.   He thought
that it was his own head that would go on the head-
MacGilvray, less spike.]   The dun was guarded by nine ranks of
Colonsay.
soldiers.   There were nine warriors (CURAIDHNEAN) at
the back of the soldiers that were as mighty as the nine
ranks of soldiers.   There were behind the warriors six
heroes (GASGAICH) that were as mighty as the nine warriors and the nine ranks of soldiers.   There were
behind these six heroes three full heroes (LANGASGAICH)
that were as mighty as all that were outside of them ;
and there was one great man behind these three, that
was as mighty as the whole of the people that there
were altogether, and many a man tried to take out Ann
Iuchdaris,* but no man of them went away alive.

     * This name is variously spelt :—1, as above ; 2, Anna Diu-
calas ; and 3, An Uchd Solais.   The first is like a common
French name, Eucharis, the second MacLean thinks has something to do with the raven black hair.   The third was used by
the Colonsay man and means bosom of light.   All three have a
MacNair.   similar sound, and I take Breast of Light as the most poetical.]

He came to near about the soldiers, and he asked
leave to go in, and that he would leave the woman as
she was before.

"I perceive," said one of them, "that thou art a
beggar that was in the land of Eirinn; what worth
would the king of Laidheann have if he should come
and find his daughter shamed by any one coward of
Eirinn."

"I will not be long asking a way from you," said
Conall.]   MacNeill.

Conall looked at the men who were guarding the
dun, he went a sweep round about with ears that were
sharp to hear, and eyes rolling to see. A glance that
he gave aloft to the dun he saw an open window, and
Breast of Light on the inner side of the window comb-
ing her hair. Conall stood a little while gazing at her,
but at last he put his palm on the point of his spear,
he gave his rounded spring, and he was in at the window beside Breast of Light.

"Who is he this youth that sprang so roundly in
at the window to see me?" said she.

"There is one that has come to take thee away,"
said Conall.

Breast of Light gave a laugh, and she said—
"Sawest thou the soldiers that were guarding the dun?"

"I saw them," said he; "but they let me in, and
they will let me out."

She gave another laugh, and she said—"Didst thou
see the warriors that are within the soldiers?"

"I saw them," said he; "they let me in, and they
will let me out."

She gave another laugh, and she said—"Many a
one has tried to take me out from this, but none has
done it yet, and they lost their luck at the end; my
counsel to thee is that thou try it not."

Conall put his hand about her very waist, he raised her in his oxter, he took her out to the rank of soldiers, he put his palm on the point of his spear, and he leaped over their heads; he ran so swiftly that they could not see that it was Breast of Light that he had, and when he was out of sight of the dun he set her on the ground.] (*Was not that the hero and the worthy wooer! that his like is not to be found to day!*)]

MacNair.

MacNeill, Barra.

Breast of Light heaved a heavy sigh from her breast. "What is the meaning of thy sigh?" said Conall.

"It is," said she, "that there came many a one to seek me, and that suffered death for my sake, and that it is (gealtair) the coward of the great world that took me away."

"I little thought that the very coward of Eirinn that should take me out who staid at home from cowardice in the realm of Eirinn, and that my own father should leave five hundred warriors to watch me without one drop of blood taken from one of them."]

MacNeill.

"How dost thou make that out?" said Conall.

"It is," said she, "that though there were many men about the dun, fear would not let thee tell the sorriest of them who took away Breast of Light, nor to what side she was taken."*

(*That's it—the women ever had a torturing tongue, teanga ghointe.*)]

MacNeill.

Said Conall—"Give me thy three royal words, and thy three baptismal vows, that thou wilt not move from that, and I will still go and tell it to them."

MacNair.

"I will do that," said she.]

Conall turned back to the dun, and nothing in the world, in the way of arms, did he fall in with but one

* Macgilvray also gives this incident, but omits the next. She kilted her gown and followed him.

horse's jaw which he found in the road ;] and when MacNeill.
he arrived he asked them what they would do to a
man that should take away Breast of Light.

"It is this," said they, "to drive off his head and
set it on a spike."

Conall looked under them, over them, through,
and before them, for the one of the biggest knob and
slenderest shanks, and he caught hold of the slenderest
shanked and biggest knobbed man, and with the head
of that one he drove the brains out of the rest, and the
brains of that one with the other's heads. Then he
drew his sword, and he began on the nine warriors, and
he slew them, and he killed the six heroes that were
at their back, and the three full heroes that were behind
these, and then he had but the big man. Conall struck
him a slap, and drove his eye out on his cheek, he
levelled him, and stripped his clothes off,] and he left MacNair.
no one to tell a tale or wear out bad news, but the one
to whom he played the clipping of a bird and a fool,
and though there should be ten tongues of a true wise
bard in that man's head, it is telling his own exploits,
and those of his men that he would be ; the plight
that the youth who had come to the town had made of
them.*] He asked him where was the king of Laid- MacNeill.
heann, and the big man said that he was in the hunting hill with his court and his following (dheadhachail)
of men and beasts.

Said Conall to him—" I lay it on thee as disgrace
and contempt (tair agus tailceas) that thou must go
stripped as thou art to tell to the king of Laidheann
that Conall Guilbeanach came, the son of the king of

---

* This is common to many stories. Beaarradh eoin us
amadain, means shaving and clipping and stripping one side of
a man, like a bird with one wing pinioned.

From a Stone in the Cemetery of Inch Brayoc, in the South Esk.
Sculptured Stones of Scotland, Pl. lxviii.

Eirinn, and that he has taken away his daughter Breast of Light.*

When the big man understood that he was to have his life along with him, he ran in great leaps, and in a rough trot, like a venomous snake, or a deadly dragon ;† he would catch the swift March wind that was before him, but the swift March wind that was after him could not catch him. The King of Laidheann saw him coming, and he said, "What evil has befallen the dun this day, when the big man is coming thus stark naked to us ?" They sat down, and he came.

Said the king, "Tell us thy tale, big man ?"

"That which I have is the tale of hate, that there came Conall Guilbeanach, son of the King of Eirinn, and slew all that there were of men to guard the dun, and it was not my own might or my own valour that rescued me rather than the sorriest that was there, but that he laid it on me as disgrace and reproach that I should go thus naked to tell it to my king, to tell him

* The spirit of this is like the Icelandic code of honour described in the Njal Saga. It was all fair to kill a man if it was done openly, or even unawares if the deed were not hidden, and here the lady was offended because the swain had not declared his name, and quite satisfied when he did.

† Na leumanan garbh 's na gharbh throte mar nathair nimh, na mar bheithir bhéumanach.

What the artist meant who sculptured the stone from which this woodcut is taken is not clear, but the three lower figures might mean Conall knocking out the big man's eye with a jaw bone, and the lady looking on. It might mean Samson slaying a Philistine. The upper part might represent the king hunting, but there is a nondescript figure which will not fit, unless it be the monster which was slain at the palace of the King of Light. The date and origin of stone and story are alike unknown, but they are both old and curious, and may serve as rude illustrations of past customs and dresses and of each other.

that there came Conall Guilbeanach, son of the King of Eirinn, and he has taken away Breast of Light thy daughter."

"Much good may it do him then," said the King of Laidheann. "If it is a hero like that who has taken her away he will keep her better than I could keep

MacNair. her, and my anger will not go after her."*]

Conall returned, and he reached the woman after he had finished the hosts.

"Come now," said he to Breast of Light, daughter of the King of Laidheann, "and walk with me ; and unless thou hadst given me the spiteful talk that thou gavest, the company would be alive before thy father, and since thou gavest it thou shalt walk thyself. Let thy foot be even with mine."

MacNeill. (*My fine fellow Conall, that's the way with her.*)]

She rose well pleased, and she went away with him ; they reached the narrows, they put out the ferry boat, and they crossed the strait. Conall had neither steed, horse, nor harness to take Breast of Light on, and she had to take to her feet.

When they reached where Conall had left the currach they put the boat on the brine, and they rowed over the ocean. They came to land at the lower side of Bein Eidin, in Eirinn. They came out of the boat,

MacNair. and they went on forward.]

They reached the green mound at the foot of Bein

MacNeill. Eidin.]

Conall told Breast of Light that he had a failing, every time that he did any deed of valour he must

MacNair. sleep before he could do brave deeds again.†]

---

* The king's company had started for the wars ; it is to be assumed the king followed.

† MacNair also gives the next passage in different words,

"There now, I will lay my head in thy lap."

"Thou shalt not, for fear thou should'st fall asleep."

"And if I do, wilt thou not waken me?"

"What manner of waking is thine?"

"Thou shalt cast me greatly hither and thither, and if that will not rouse me, thou shalt take the breadth of a penny piece of flesh and hide from the top of my head. If that will not wake me, thou shalt seize on yonder great slab of a stone, and thou shalt strike me between the mouth and nose, and if that will not rouse me thou mayest let me be."

He laid his head in her lap,* and in a little instant he fell asleep.

He was not long asleep when she saw a great

and with the variation, that a joint of his little finger was to be cut off.

Macgilvray, the same in different words. According to the introduction to Njal Saga, there were in Iceland long ago gifted men of prodigious strength, who, after performing feats of superhuman force, were weak and powerless for a time. While engaged in London about this story, an Irish bricklayer came to mend a fire-place, and I asked him if he had ever heard of Conall Gulban, "Yes sure," said the man with a grin, "he was one of the Finevanians, and when he slept they had to cut bits off him before he could be wakened. They were cutting his fingers off." And then he went away with his hod.

The incident is common in Gaelic stories, and Conall is mentioned in a list of Irish stories in the transactions of the Ossianic society.

* And he laid his head in her lap, and she—dressed—his hair. (MacPhie, Uist.) This is always the case in popular tales of all countries, and the practice is common from Naples to Lapland. I have seen it often. The top of his little finger was to be cut off to rouse him, and if that failed, a bit from his crown, and he was to be knocked about the ribs, and a stone placed on his chest.

vessel sailing in the ocean. Each path was crooked, and each road was level for her, till she came to the green mound at the side of Bein Eidin.

There was in the ship but one great man, and he would make rudder in her stern, cable in her prow, tackle in her middle, each rope that was loose he would

MacNeill. tie, and each rope that was fast he would loose,] and the front of each rope that was on board was towards

MacNair. him,*] till he came on shore at the shoulder of Bein

MacNeill Eidin.]   He came in with the ship at the foot of Bein
and Mac-
Nair. Eidin, and the big man leapt on shore ; he caught hold of the prow of the ship,† and he hauled her her own nine lengths and nine breadths up upon green grass, where the force of foes could not move her out without feet following behind them.

He came where Breast of Light was, and Conall asleep, with his head on her knee.   He gazed at Breast

MacNair. of Light, and she said,—]

" What side is before thee for choice ?   Or where art thou going ?"

" Well, they were telling me that Breast of Light, daughter of the King of Laidheann, was the finest woman in the world, and I was going to seek her for myself."

" That is hard enough to get," said she.   " She is in yonder castle, with five hundred soldiers for her guard, that her father left there."

" Well," said he, " though she were brighter than the sun, and more lovely than the moon, past thee I will not go."

" Well, thou seemest silly to me to think of taking me with thee instead of that woman, and that I am not worthy to go and untie her shoe."

MacNeill. " Be that as it will, thou shalt go with me.]   I

* MacGilvray gives the incident in different words.
† Long means a large ship.

know that it is thou by thy beauty, Breast of Light, daughter of the king of Laidheann."

"Thou hast the wishing knowledge of me," said she ; " I am not she, but a farmer's daughter, and this is my brother ; he lost the flock this day, and he was running after them backwards and forwards throughout Bein Eudain, and now he is tired and taking a while of sleep."]   MacNair.

"Be that as it will," said he, " there is a mirror in my ship, and the mirror will not rise up for any woman in the world, but for Uchd Soluisd, daughter of the King of Laidheann. If the mirror rises for thee, I will take thee with me, and if it does not I will leave thee there."

He went to the mirror, and fear would not let her cut off the little finger, and she could not awaken Conall. The man looked in the mirror, and the mirror rose up for her, and he went back where she was.]   Macgfilvray.

Said the big one, " I will be surer than that of my matter before I go further." He plucked the blade of Conall from the sheath, and it was full of blood. "Ha!" said he, "I am right enough in my guess, Waken thy champion, and we will try with swift wrestling, might of hands, and hardness of blades, which of us has best right to have thee."*

" Who art thou ?" said Breast of Light.

" I," said the big man, "am Mac-a-Moir MacRigh Sorcha (son of the mighty, son of the King of Light). It is in pursuit of thee I came."†]   MacNair.

---

* A good illustration of the law of the strongest, which seems to have been the law of the Court of Appeal in old times in Iceland, and probably in Ireland and Scotland also.

† Here, as it seems to me, the mythological character of the legend appears. Sorcha is *light*, in opposition to Dorcha, *dark ;* and further on a lady is found to match the king of Sorcha,

"Wilt thou not waken my companion," said she.

He went, and he felt him from the points of the thumbs of his feet till he went out at the top of his head. "I cannot rouse the man myself; I like him as well asleep as awake."]

MacNeill.

Breast of Light got up, and she began to rock (a chriothnachadh) Conall hither and thither, but he would not take waking.

Said Mac-a-Moir—"Unless thou wakest him thou must go with me and leave him in his sleep."

Said she—"Give thou to me before I go with thee thy three royal words and thy three baptismal vows that thou wilt not seek me as wife or as sweetheart till the end of a day and a year after this, to give Conall time to come in my pursuit."

Mac-a-Moir gave his three royal words and his three baptismal vows to Breast of Light, that she should be a maiden till the end of a day and a year, to give time to Conall to come in pursuit of her, if he had so much courage. Breast of Light took the sword of Conall from the sheath, and she wrote on the sword how it had fallen out. She took the ring from off the finger of Conall, and she put her own ring on his finger in its stead, and put Conall's ring on her own finger, and she went away with Mac-a-Moir, and they left

MacNair.

Conall in his sleep.] He took the woman with him on his shoulder and he went to the ship. He shoved out the ship and he gave her prow to sea, and her stern to shore; he hoisted the flapping white sails

who is in a lofty turret which no man could scale, but which the great warrior pulled down. So far as I know there is no place which now goes by the name of Sorcha, unless it be the island of Sark. According to Donald MacPhie (Uist), this was Righ-an-Domhain, the King of the Universe, which again indicates mythology.

against the mast, tall and enduring, that would not leave yard unbent, sail untorn, running the seas, ploochkanaiche plachkanaiche, blue clouds of Lochlanach, the little buckie that was seven years on the sea, clattering on her floor with the excellence of the lad's steering.

When Conall awoke on the green mound he had but himself, a shorn one and bare alone. Glance that he gave from him, what should he see but herds that the king of Eirinn and Laidheann had left, dancing for joy on the point of their spears. He thought that they were mocking him for what had befallen him. He went to kill the one with the other's head,] and MacNeill. there was such a (sgrann) grim look upon him that the little herds were fleeing out of his way.

He said to one of them—"What fleeing is on the little herds of Bein Eidin before me this day, as if they were mad ; are ye mocking me for what has befallen me ?" *]   MacNair.

"We are not," said they ; "it was grievous to us (to see) how it befell thee."

"What, my fine fellow, did you see happening to me ?"]   MacNeill.

Said the little herd—"Thou art more like one who is mad than any one of us. If thou hadst seen the rinsing, and the sifting, and the riddling (an Luasgadh, an cathadh, 'as an creanachadh) that they had at thee down at the foot of the hill, thou wouldst not have much esteem for thyself. I saw," said the little herd, "the one who was with thee putting a ring on thy finger."

Conall looked, and it was the ring of Breast of Light that was on his finger.

* Macgilvray awakens him by a troop of school-boys who were playing tricks to him.

Said the little herd—"I saw her writing something on thy sword, and putting it into the sheath."

Conall drew his sword, and he read—"There came Mac-a-Moir, the king of Sorcha, and took me away, Breast of Light; I am to be free for a year and a day in his house waiting for thee, if thou hast so much courage as to come in pursuit of me."

MacNair.

Conall put his sword into its sheath, and he gave three royal words.*]   "I lay it on myself as spells and as crosses, that stopping by night, and staying by day, is nót for me, till I find the woman.   Where I take my supper, that I will not take my dinner, and that there is no place into which I go that I will not leave the fruit of my hand there to boot, and the son that is unborn he shall hear of it, and the son that is

MacNeill.

unbegotten he shall hear tell of it."†]

Said the little herd to him—"There came a ship to shore at the port down there. The shipmen (sgiobe) went to the hostelry, and if thou be able enough thou mayest be away with the ship before they come back."§

Conall went away, and he went on board of the

---

* He also gives the following passage, but less fully.

† It was a common practice, according to the Njal Saga, for the old Icelanders to bind themselves by vows to perform certain deeds, and, according to Irish writers, a like practice prevailed in Ireland. It seems that the custom is remembered and preserved in these stories. The fruit, TORADH, rather means a harvest; he will leave a harvest of dead reaped by his hand.

§ Mr. Fraser, Invernesshire. "His grandfather took him to the side of the sea, and he struck a rod that was in his hand on a rock, and there rose up a long ship under sail. The old man put ' a gheur ghlas,' the keen gray (sword) on board, and at parting he said, in every strait in which thou art for ever remember me." —MacPhie. He wished for his grandfather, who came and said, "Bad! bad! thou hast wished too soon," and raised a ship with his magic rod.

ship, and he was out of sight with her before the mari-
ners missed him.] He gave her prow to sea, and her MacNair.
stern to shore, helm in her stern, rope in her prow,
that each road was smooth, and crooked each path, till
he went into the realm of Lochlann*] at a place which MacNeill.
was called Cath nam peileirn (Battle of bullets), but he
did not know himself where he was.

He leaped on shore, and he seized the prow of the
ship, and he pulled her up on dry land, her own nine
lengths and nine breadths, where the foeman's might
could not take her out without feet following behind.

The lads of the realm of Lochlann, were playing
shinny on a plain, and Gealbhan Greadhna, the son of
the King of Lochlann, working amongst them.†] He MacNeill.
did not know who they were, but he went to where
they were, and it was the Prince of Lochlann and his
two scholars, and ten over a score; and the Prince of
Lochlann was alone, driving the goals against the whole
of the two-and-thirty scholars.

Conall stood singing " iolla" to them, and the ball
came to the side where he was; Conall struck a kick
on the ball, and he drove it out on the goal boundary
against the Prince of Lochlann. The prince came
where he was, and he said, " Thou, man, that came
upon us from off the ocean, it were little enough that
would make me take the head off thee, that we might
have it as a ball to kick about the field, since thou
wert so impudent as to kick the ball. Thou must
hold a goal of shinny against me and against the two-
and-thirty scholars. If thou get the victory thou shalt

---

* The only variation here is the words.

† I have never seen the game of shinny played in Norway,
but there is mention of a game at " ball" in Icelandic sagas.

be free; if we conquer thee, every one of us will hit thee a blow on the head with his shinny."*]

MacNair.

"Well," said Conall, "I don't know who thou art, great man, but it seems to me that thy judgment is evil. If every one of you were to give me a knock on my head, you would leave my head a soft mass. I have no shinny that I can play with."

"Thou shalt have a shinny," said Gealbhan Greadhna.

Conall gave a look round about, and he saw a crooked stick of elder growing in the face of a bank. He gave a leap thither and plucked it out by the root, and he sliced it with his sword and made a shinny of it.†]

MacNair.

Then Conall had got a shinny, and he himself and Gealbhan Greadhna (cheery fire) went to play.

Two halves were made of the company, and the ball was let out in the midst. On a time of the times Conall got a chance at the ball; he struck it a stroke of his foot, and a blow of his palm and a blow of his shinny, and he drove it home.

"Thou wert impudent," said Gealbhan Greadhna, "to drive the game against me or against my share of the people."

"That is well said by thee, good lad! Thou shalt get two shares (earrann) of the band with thee, and I will take one share."

"And what wilt thou say if it goes against thee?"

---

* Iomhair Oaidh MacRigh na Hiribhi, Iver, son of the King of Bergen, is the person who plays this part in the Inverness-shire version. He was a suitor, and he was thrashed, but he afterwards plays the part of the King of Sorcha, and is killed. MacPhie makes him a young man, and a suitor for the Princess of Norway.

† According to MacPhie (Uist), he wished for his grandfather, who appeared with an iron shinny, and said, "Bad, bad, thou hast wished too soon."

" If it goes against me with fair play there is no help for it, but if it goes against me otherwise I may say what I choose."

Then divisions were made of the company, and Gealbhan Greadhna had two divisions and Conall one. The ball was let out in the midst, and if it was let out Conall got a chance at it, and he struck it a stroke of his foot, and a blow of his palm, and a blow of his shinny, and he drove it in.

" Thou wert impudent," said Gealbhan Greadhna a second time, " to go to drive the game against me."

" Good lad, that is well from thee ! but thou shalt get the whole company the third time, and what wilt thou say if it goes against thee ?"

" If it goes by fair play I cannot say a jot ; if not, I may say my pleasure."

The ball was let go, and if so, Conall got a chance at it, and he all alone ; and he struck it a stroke of his foot, and a blow of his palm, and a blow of his shinny, and he drove it in.

" Thou wert impudent," said Gealbhan Greadhna, " to go and drive it against me the third time."

" That is well from thee, good lad, but thou shalt not say that to me, nor to another man after me," and he struck him a blow of his shinny and knocked his brains out.*]　　　　　　　　　　　　　MacNeill.

He looked (taireal) contemptuously at them; he threw his shinny from him, and he went from them.

* This description of a game of shinny is characteristic, and the petulance of Prince Cheery Fire, with his two-and-thirty toadies, and the independence of the warrior who came over the sea, and who would stand no nonsense, are well described. MacNair's version is not so full, nor is the catastrophe so tragic, but otherwise the incidents are the same.

He was going on, and he saw a little man coming
laughing towards him.

"What is the meaning of thy laughing at me?"
said Conall.

Said the little man, "It is that I am in a cheery
mood at seeing a man of my country."

"Who art thou," said Conall, "that art a country-
man of mine?"

"I," said the little man, "am Duanach Mac-
Draodh (songster, son of magic), the son of a prophet
from Eirinn. "Wilt thou then take me as a servant
lad."*

"I will not take thee," said Conall. "I have no
way (of keeping) myself here without word of a gillie.
What realm is this in which I am, here?"

"Thou art," said Duanach, "in the realm of Lochlann."

Conall went on, and Duanach with him, and he
saw a great town before him.

"What town is there, Duanach?" said Connal.

"That, said Duanach, "is the great town of the
realm of Lochlann."

They went on and they saw a big house on a high
place.

"What big house is yonder, Duanach?"

"That," said Duanach, "is the big house of the
King of Lochlann;" and they went on.

They saw another house on a high place.

---

* From the Njal Saga it appears that the Northmen, in their
raids, carried off the people of IRELAND, and made slaves of them.
Macgilvray called this character Dubhan MacDraoth, blacky, or
perhaps crook, the son of magic, and he explained, that draoth
was one who brought messages from one enemy to another, and
whose person was sacred.

"What pointed house (biorach with points ? palli-sades or what) is there, Duanach ?" said Conall.

"That is the house of the Tamhasg, the best war-riors that are in the realm of Lochlann," said Duanach.

"I heard my grandfather speaking about the Tamhaisg, but I have never seen them ; I will go to see them," said Conall.

"It were not my counsel to thee," said Duanach.*] MacNair.

On he went to the palace of the King of Loch-lann (bhuail e beum sgeithe) and he clashed his shield, battle or else combat to be sent to him, or else Breast of Light, the daughter of the King of Laidheann.

That was the thing he should get, battle and com-bat ; and not Breast of Light, daughter of the King of Laidheann, for she was not there to give him ; but he should get no fighting at that time of night, but he should get (fardoch) lodging in the house of the amh-usg, where there were eighteen hundred amhusg, and eighteen score ; but he would get battle in the mor-row's morning, when the first of the day should come.

'Twas no run for the lad, but a spring, and he would take no better than the place he was to get. He went, and he went in, and there were none of the amhuish within that did not grin. When he saw that they had made a grin, he himself made two.] MacNeill.

"What was the meaning of your grinning at us?" said the amhusg.

"What was the meaning of your grinning at me?" said Conall.

Said they, "Our grinning at thee meant that thy

* Here my two chief authorities vary a little in the order of the incidents. MacNair sends him first to this house, the other takes him there later; they vary but little in the incidents. Macgilvray takes him at once to the palace, where he finds a great chain which he shakes to bring out the foe.

fresh royal blood will be ours to quench our thirst, and thy fresh royal flesh to polish our teeth."

And said Conall, "The meaning of my grinning is, that I will look out for the one with the biggest knob and slenderest shanks, and knock out the brains of the rest with that one, and his brains with the knobs of the rest.]

Every one of them arose, and he went to the door and he put a stake of wood against the door. He rose up and himself, and he put two against it so tightly, that the others fell.

"What reason had he to do that?" said they.

"What reason had you to go and do it?"" said he. "It were a sorry matter for me though I should put two there, when you yourselves put one there each, every one that is within."

"Well, we will tell thee," said they, "what reason we had for that: we have never seen coming here (one), a gulp of whose blood, or a morsel of whose flesh could reach us, but thou thyself, except one other man, and he fled from us; and now every one is doubting the other, in case thou shouldst flee."

"That was the thing that made me do it myself likewise, since I have got yourselves so close as you are." Then he went and he began upon them. "I feared to be chasing you from hole to hole, and from hill to hill, and I did that." Then he gazed at them, from one to two, and he seized on the one of the slenderest shanks and the fattest head; he drove upon the rest sliochd! slachd! till he had killed every one of them; and he had not a jot of the one with whom he was working at them, but what was in his hands of the shanks.*

---

* AMHAS, a madman, a wild ungovernable man; also, a dull stupid person (Armstrong). AMHASAN, a sentry (ditto); also, a

He killed every man of them, and though he was such a youth as he was, he was exhausted (enough-i-fied, if I might coin a word). Then he began redding up the dwelling (reitach na h araich) that was there, to clean it for himself that night. Then he put them out in a heap altogether, and he let himself (drop) stretched out on one of the beds that was within.*

There came a dream (Bruaduil)† to him then, and he said to him, " Rise, oh Conall, and the chase about to be upon thee."

He let .that pass, and he gave it no heed, for he was exhausted.

He came the second journey, and he said to him, " Conall, wilt thou not arise, and that the chase is about to be upon thee."

He let that pass, and he gave it no heed ; but the third time he came to him, he said, " Conall, art thou about to give heed to me at all ! and that thy life is about to be awanting to thee."

He arose and he looked out at the door, and he saw a hundred carts, and a hundred horses, and a hun-

wild beast, according to the Highland Society Dictionary. Perhaps these may have something to do with the Baresarks of the old Norsemen, who were " public pests," great warriors, half crazy, enormously strong, subject to fits of ungovernable fury, occasionally employed by saner men, and put to death when done with. The characters appear in many Highland tales ; and an Irish blind fiddler told me a long story in which they figured. I suspect this guardhouse of savage warriors has a foundation in fact. Macgilvray gives the incidents also.

* He made himself a bed of rushes at the side of the house.— Macgilvray.

† This word, thus written, is in no dictionary that I have, but it is the same as brudair ; and, the other version proves that a dream is meant. It is singular to find a dream thus personified in the mouth of a Barra peasant.

dred carters, coming with food to the amhusg ; supposing that they had done for the youth that went amongst them the night before ; and a piper playing music behind them, with joy and pleasure of mind.

They were coming past a single bridge, and the bridge was pretty large ; and when Conall saw that they were together (cruin round) on the bridge, he reached the bridge, and he put each cart, and each horse, and each carter, over the bridge into the river ; and he drowned the men.

There was one little bent crooked man here with them behind the rest.

"My heart is warming to thee with the thought that it is thou, Conall Gulban MacNiall Naonallaich ; the name of a hero was on his hand a hundred years ere he was born."

"Thou hast but what thou hast of knowledge, and the share that thou hast not, thou wilt not have this day," said Conall Gulban.

He went away, and he reached the palace of the King of Lochlann ; and he clashed his shield, battle or else combat to be given to him, or else Breast of Light, daughter of the King of Laidheann.

That was the thing which he should have, battle and combat ; and not Breast of Light, for she was not MacNeill   there to give him.*]

(So he went back and slept again.)

Word reached the young king of Lochlann, that the big man who came off the ocean had gone to the house of the "Tamhasg ;" that they had set a combat, and that the "Tamhasgan" had been slain. The young king of Lochlann ordered four of the best war-

* MacNair has not got this adventure of the carts ; and MacNeill has not the next adventure, unless it be the same considerably varied. I give both upon chance.

riors that were in his realm, that they should up to
the house of the Tamhasg, and take off the head of
the big man that had come off the ocean, and to
bring it up to him before he should sit down to his
dinner.

The warriors went, and they found Duanach there,
and they railed at him for going with the big man that
came out of the outer land,* for they did not know
who he was.

"And why," said Duanach, "should I not go with
the man of my own country? but if you knew it, I
am as tired of him as you are yourselves. He has
given me much to do ; see you I have just made a
heap of corpses, a heap of clothes, and a heap of the
arms of the "Tamhaisg ;" and you have for it but to
lift them along with you."

"It is not for that we came," said they, "but to
slay him, and to take his head to the young king of
Lochlann before he sits to dine. Who is he ?" said
they.

"He is," said Duanach, "one of the sons of the
king of Eirinn."

"The young King of Lochlann has sent us to take
his head off," said they.

"If you kill one of the children of the King of
Eirinn in his sleep you will regret it enough afterwards," said Duanach.

"What regret will there be ?" said they.

"There is this," said Duanach.   "There will be
no son to woman, there will be no calf to cow, no
grass nor braird shall grow in the realm of Lochlann,

* " AN FHOIRS TIR ;" this word is now commonly applied to
the furthest ground known, such as the outermost reef or even
fishing bank ; it is also written oirthir, edge-land.

till the end of seven years,* if ye kill one of the clan of the King of Eirinn in his sleep, and go and tell that to the young King of Lochlann."

They went back, and they told what Duanach had said.

The young King of Lochlann said that they should go back, and do as he had bidden them, and that they should not heed the lies of Duanach.

The four warriors went again to the house of the "Tamhasg," and they said to Duanach,—

"We have come again to take the head off the son of the King of Eirinn."

And Duanach said "He is yonder then, over there for you, in his sleep; but take good heed to yourselves, unless your swords are sharp enough to take off his head at the first blow, all that is in your bodies is to be pitied after that; he will not leave one of you alive, and he will bring (sgrios) ruin on the realm."

Each of them stretched his sword to Duanach, and Duanach said that their swords were not sharp enough, that they should go out to the Tamhasg stone to sharpen them. They went out, and they were sharpening their swords on the smooth grinding-stone of the Tamhasg, and Conall began to dream (again).

It seemed to him that he was going on a road that went through the midst of a gloomy wood,† and it seemed to him that he saw four lions before him, two on the upper side of the road, and two on the lower side, and they were gnashing their teeth, and switching

---

* Cha bhith mac aig bean; cha bhith laogh aig mart; 's cha chinn fear na fochan, ann an righachd Lochlann, gu ceann seachd Bliadhna, etc.

† Coille udlaidh, lonely, morose, churlish, gloomy. Pr. ood-lai. Compare outlaw, outlying.

their tails,* making ready to spring upon him, and it seemed to him that it was easier for the lions that were on the upper side of the road to leap down, than it was for the lions that were on the lower side to leap up ; and it was better for him to slay those that were on the upper side first, and he gave a cheery spring to be at them ; and he sprang aloft through his sleep, and he struck his head against a tie beam (sail shuimear) that was across above him in the house of the " Tamhasgan," and he drove as much as the breadth of a half-crown piece of the skin off the top of his head, and then he was aroused, and he said to Duanach,—

" I myself was dreaming, Duanach," and he told him his dream.

And Duanach said, " Thy dream is a dainty to read. Go thou out to the stone of the Tamhasg, and thou wilt see the four best warriors that the King of Lochlann has, two on each side of the stone round about it, sharpening their swords to take off thy head."

Conall went out with his blade in his hand, and he took off their heads, and he left two heads on each side of the stone of the Tamhasg, and he came in where Duanach was, and he said, " I am yet without food since I came to the realm of Lochlann, and I feel in myself that I am growing weak."

And Duanach said " I will get thee food if thou wilt take my counsel, and that is, that thou shouldst go to court the sister of the King of Lochlann, and I myself will go to redd the way for thee.†] MacNair.

There were three great warriors in the king's palace in search of the daughter of the king of Lochlann, and they sent word for the one who was the

* A casadh am fiacall s' a sguitse le n' earball.

† He has not got the next adventure, which I take from Mac-Neill.

most valiant of them to go to combat the youth that had• come to the town. This one came, and the Amhus Ormanach was his name,* and he and Conall were to try each other. They went and they began the battle, Conall and the Avas Ormanach. The daughter of the king of Lochlann came to the door, and she shouted for Duanachd Acha Draohd.†

"I am here," said Duanach.

"Well, then, if thou art, it is but little care thou hast for me. Many calving cattle and heifers gave my father to thy father, though thou art not going down, and standing behind the Avas Ormanach, and giving him the urging of a true wise bard‡ to hasten the head of the wretch to me for my dinner, for I have a great thirst for it."

"Faire! faire! watch oh queen," said Duanach; "if thou hadst quicker asked it, thou hadst not got it slower."

Away went Duanach down, and it was not on the side of the Avas Ormanach he began, but on the side of Conall. "Thou hast not told it to me for certain

---

* AMHUS, the savage, or wild man. ORMANACH is not so clear; written from ear it might be a word beginning with an aspirated silent letter, such as *th*, which would make the word "noisy," or it may be some compound of OR gold, such as OR-MHEINNEACH, gold-ore-ish, which would make him the wild man of the gold mines, or armour, or hair, or something else. Macgilvray called him an Amhas Orannach, the wild man of songs.

† Songstership of magic field, which is MacNeill's name for the character.

‡ Brosnachadh file fiorghlic. It is said that the bards from the earliest of times sang songs of encouragement to the warriors. The old Icelanders, as it is asserted in their sagas, sung themselves in the heat of the fight, and here is a tradition of something of the kind. In Stewart's collection, 1804, is the battle song of the Macdonalds for the battle of Harlaw.

yet if it be thou, when thou art not hastening thine hand, and making heavy thy blow! And to let slip that wretch that ought to be in a land of holes, or in crannies of rock, or in otter's cairns! Though thou shouldst fall here for slowness or slackness, there would neither be wife nor sweetheart crying for thee, and that is not the like of what would befall him."

Conall thought that it was in good purpose the man was for him, and not in evil purpose;[*] he put his sword under the sword of the Avas Ormanach, and he cast it to the skies, and then he himself gave a spring on his back, and he levelled him on the ground, and then he began to take his head off.

"Still be thy hand, O Conall," said Duanach Acha Draodh, "make him the binding of the three smalls there, until he gives thee his oaths under the edge of his set of arms, that there is no stroke he will strike for ever against thee."[†]

"I have not got strings enough to bind him," said Conall.

---

[*] Deogh run, droch run. *Rùn* has many meanings—love, etc.; purpose, etc.; a person beloved; a secret, a mystery; and, according to Armstrong, it is the origin of "runic." The man who told this story clearly meant "purpose" by run; but perhaps the original meaning of the passage which comes repeatedly in this story was that Songstership of Magic field sang "good *runes* for the victory of his countrymen." It must be remembered that Barra was in the way of Norsemen, and that their ways of life throw light on Gaelic traditions. According to Macgilvray—another islander—Dubhan MacDraoth was the Draoth (? herald) of the king of Eirinn when he went to put the Turk out of the realm of the emperor, and the king of Lochlann brought him home thence, and he was his draoth. As there was a guard of Norsemen in Constantinople this looks like a possible fact.

[†] "The d——l has sworn by the edge of his knife."—*Carle of Kellyburn Braes, Old Song.*

"That is not my case,"* said Duanach ; "I have of cords what will bind back to back all that are in the realm of Lochlann altogether."

Duanach gave the cords to Conall, and Conall bound the Avas Ormanach. He gave his oaths to Conall under the edge of his set of arms, that he was a loved comrade to him for ever ; and any one stroke he might strike that he would strike it with him, and that he would not strike a stroke for ever against him ; and MacNair. he left his life with the Avus Ormanach.]   "Thou shalt have that woman whom thou art courting and making love to (a suridh s a seircanachadh), the daughter of the king of Lochlann," said the Amhus Ormanach. "Thou shalt have that woman for thyself," said Conall ; MacGilvray. " It is not her that I am courting and making love to."]

The daughter of the king of Lochlann was right well pleased that he had left his life with the Avus Ormanach, so that it might be her own ; but what should she do but send for Conall.†

* Cha n e sin domh 's e.—It is not that to me it is.

† MacNair gives the following incidents more in detail, and more as matter of fact. The bard, to get food for the warrior, persuades the lady that he has come to court her, and with her consent, takes him food, and guides him to her chamber. He places a drawn sword between them, and never speaks. The bard sleeps on the stair outside ; the king's men seek in vain for Conall ; and in the morning the bard explains the mystery of the drawn sword to the lady, who is content. And so it happens thrice, when Conall feels able to fight the lady's brother, and the lady finds that the warrior is faithful to his first love, and the bard a cunning deceiver. This incident is very widely known in popular tales. See the " Arabian Nights," Grimm, etc. " Gu de am fath ma 'n do rinn se è mata?" orsa ise. " Tha," orsa Duanach, " tha e a los ma bhitheas leanabb gille eadar sibh gu am be e na fhear claidheamh cho math ris fein." Thuirt ise, " Ach na an saoillinn sin dheanainn a bheatha ciod air bhith doigh air an tigeadh e."

What should the daughter of the King of Lochlann do but send word for Conall to pass the evening together with the Queen and with herself, and if it were his will that she would not give him the trouble of taking a step with his foot, but that she would take him up in a creel to the top of the castle. Conall thought that much reproach should not belong to one that was in the realm of Lochlann, against one that was in the realm of Eirinn, that he should go to do that. He went and he gave a spring from the small of his foot to the point of his palm, and from the point of his palm to the top of the castle, and he reached the woman where she was.*

"If thou art now sore or hurt," said the daughter of the King of Lochlann, "there is a vessel of balsam (ballan fiochshlaint), wash thyself in it, and thou wilt be well after it."

He did not know that it was not bad stuff that was in the vessel. He put a little twig into the vessel, so that he might know what thing was in it. The twig came up full of sap (snodhach) as it went down. Then he thought that it was good stuff, and not bad stuff. He went and he washed himself in it, and he was as whole and healthy as he ever was. Then meat and drink went to them, that they might have pleasure of mind while passing the evening, and after that they went to rest ; but he drew his cold sword between himself and the woman. He passed the night so, and in the morning he rose and went out of the castle. He clashed his shield without, and he shouted battle or else combat to be sent to him, or else Breast of Light, daughter of the King of Laidheann. It was

* Thug e leum o chaol a choise go barr a bhoise, 's o barr a bhoise go mullach a chaisteil.

battle and combat he should get, and not Breast of
Light, for she was not there to give him.

Then the daughter of the King of Lochlann called
out, "Art thou there, my brother?*

"I am," said her brother.

"Well," said she, "it is but little count that thou
hadst of me. That man who has made me a woman
of harrying and hurrying, to whom I fell as a wedded
wife last night, not to bring me hither his head to my
breakfast, when I am greatly thirsting for it."

"Faire! faire! watch, oh queen," said he, "if
thou hadst asked it sooner thou hadst not got it slower.
There are none of men, small or great, in Christendom,
who will turn back my hand."

He went, and before he reached the door, he set
earthquaking seven miles from him. At the first
(mothar) growl he gave after he got out of the castle,
there was no cow in calf, or mare in foal, or woman
with child, but suffered for fear. He began himself
and Conall at each other, and if there were not gasgich
MacNeill. there at work it was a strange matter.]

They drew the slender gray swords, and they'd
kindle the tightening of grasp, from the rising of sun
till the evening, when she would be wending west;
and without knowing with which would be loss or
winning. Duanach was singing iolladh to them, and
when the sun was near about west.†

* According to MacNeill it was her father; and as the young
king goes away afterwards and is married, I follow MacNair.
MacNeill killed a brother at landing. MacNair left him alive to
be introduced further on, so I have altered one word in MacNeill's
account of the fight, and assume that Prince Cheery fire was a
younger brother of the young king.

† Tharruing iad an claidheamhaimn caola glas-adb a's dh
fhadadh iad teaneacha dorn, o na dh eiridh a ghrian gus am
feasgar tra bhithidh i a dol siar.

Then the daughter of the King of Lochlann cried out for Duanach acha Draodh that he should go down to give the urging of a truewise bard to her brother, to bring her the head of the wretch to her breakfast, that she was thirsting greatly for it.

BARD.—From a cross near Dupplin.

Duanach went, and if he did, it was not at the back of the King of Lochlann he went, but behind Conall.

"Oh, Conall," said he, "thou hast not told me yet if it be thou. When thou art not hastening thine hand, but making heavy thy blow! and level that wretch that ought to be in a land of holes, or in clefts of rock, or in otters' cairns! Though thou shouldst fall, there would be no wife or sweetheart crying for thee, and not so with him." *

Conall thought that it was in good purpose the man was for him, and that it was not in bad purpose.

* As this is a kind of chorus, and probably old, I give the original. Nur nach eil thu luaireachadh do laimh, ach a tromachadh do bhuille, agus a bhiast sin a bo choir a bhi 'n talamh toll, na 'n sgeilpidh chreag na 'n carn bhiasta dugha leagail! gad a thuiteadh tusa, cha bhiodh bean na leannan a glaoidheadh air do shon, cha b ionann sin a's esan.

He put his sword under the sword of the King of Lochlann, and he cast it to the skies ; and then he gave a spring himself on his back, and he levelled him on the ground, and he began to take off his head.

"Still thy hand, Conall," said Duanach achaidh Draodh," little is his little shambling head worth to

MacNeill.   thee.*] You are long enough at that game, throw away your swords and try another way. They threw away their swords, and they put the soft white fists in each other's breasts ; but they were not struggling long till Conall gave the panting of his heart to the young King of Lochlann on the hard stones of the cause- way.†

Said Conall to Duanach, "Reach hither to me my sword, that I may take off his head."

"Not I, indeed," said Duanach. "It is better for thee to have his head for thyself as it is, than five hundred heads that thou mightest take out with strife. Make him promise that he will be (diles duit) a friend to thee."

Conall made the young King of Lochlann promise with words and heavy vows, that he would be a friend to Conall Guilbeanach, the son of the King of Eirinn, in each strait or extremity that might come upon him, whether the matter should come with right or un- right; and that Conall should have the realm of Loch- lann under cess.‡

* MacNeill, who goes on to repeat the binding of this warrior in the same words. For variety, I substitute MacNair's descrip- tion of the same fight, which he, like the other, repeats several times as a kind of chorus.

† Chuir iad na duirn bhogadh ghealladh an cneasadh a cheile, ach cha bu fhada a gabh iad do an ghleachd gus an tug Conall cneadhaiseach a chridhe do righ og Lochlann air clach'n cruaidh a chausair. As written by Dewar.

‡ Fo chis, tribute or subjection. It seems almost a hopeless

When the King of Lochlann had given these promises, Conall let him up, and they caught each other by the hand, and they made peace and they ceased.

And the young King of Lochlann gave a bidding to Conall that he should come in with him to his great house, to dine with him ; and the young king set a double watch upon each place, so that none should come to disturb himself or the young son of the King of Eirinn, while they were at their feast.]   A MacNair. churchman was got, and the Amhas Ormanach was married to the daughter of the King of Laidheann.]   Macgilvray.

When each thing was ready the royal ones sat at the great board ; they laid down lament, and they raised up music, with rejoicing and great joy,] and they MacNair. were in great pleasure of mind.   Meat was set in the place for eating, drink in the drinking place, music in

task to make romance reasonable, and yet I am convinced that these are semi-historical romances.   When it is certain that Norse sea-rovers were actually settled in the Hebrides, and wandered from America to Constantinople, and levied tribute wherever they could ; when it appears from their sagas, which are believed to be almost true history, that these raids were often made in single ships, and when simple Icelanders fought with Orkney earls and Norse kings, and Norman adventurers conquered England ; it seems possible that one of the body guard from Constantinople might become "Emperor of the world" in the Hebrides, and a voyager from Greenland " king of the green isle that was about the heaps of the deep ;" and that such exploits as these men performed might be magnified, and applied to a Celtic warrior by celtic bards ; or that a Celtic warrior may have done as much.   It is admitted that Irish priests had found their way to Iceland before the Norsemen went there, and if so, perhaps Irish warriors may have been pirates or varangians, and successful in forays on the Vikings, as Vikings were in Irish forays.   We believe the Sagas, so far as they are reasonable ; why should not truth be sifted from these romances also.

the place for hearing; and they were plying the feast with great sport in *"an dining-room"* of the King of
MacNeill. Lochlann,] and they so liking and loving about each, taking their feast.

The soldiers were without watching, to guard the big house of the king, and they saw a great tasba-rltach* coming the way; they had such fear before him that they thought they could see the great world between his legs. As he was coming nearer, the watch were fleeing till they reached the great house, and into the passage, and from the passage into the room where were the young King of Lochlann and the young son of the King of Eirinn, at their feast; and the great raw bones that came began to fetter and bind the men, and to cast them behind him, till he had bound every one of them; and till he reached the young King of Lochlann, and he and the big man wrestled with each
MacNair. other.] He drew his fist and he struck the King of Lochlann between the mouth and nose, and he drove out three front teeth, and he caught them on the back
MacNeill. of his fist;†] but the end for them was, that the young King of Lochlann was bound and laid under fetters,
MacNair. and thrown behind together with the rest;] and the big man gave a dark leap and he seized the bride, and
Macgilvray. he took her with him.]

Conall gazed on all the company that was within, to try if he could see any man rising to stand by the king. When he saw no living man arising, he arose
MacNair. himself.] "Let that woman go," said he; "thou hast
Macgilvray. no business with her." That he would not do.] He gave a spring, he caught the slender black man between the two sides of the door (bhith), and he levelled

---

* Large, lean boned, savage and swarthy.—Dewar.

† MacNeill, who says he was a slender black man.

him; and when he had levelled him, he let the weight of his knee on his chest.

"Has death ever gone so near thee as that?" said Conall.

"It has gone nearer than that," said the slender black man.

He let the weight more on him. "Has he gone as near as that to thee?"

"Oh, he has not gone; let thy knee be lightened, and I will tell thee the time that he went nearest to me."

"I will let thee; stand up so long as thou art telling it," said Conall.*] MacNeill.

Conall loosed the young King of Lochlann and his men from their bonds and from their fetters, and he sat himself and the young King of Lochlann at the board, and they took their feast; and the big man was cast in under the board. Again when they were at supper the king's sister was with them, and every word she said she was trying to make the friendship greater and greater between her brother and Conall. The big man was lying under the board, and Conall said to him, "Thou man that art beneath, wert thou ever before in strait or extremity as great as to be lying under the great board, under the drippings of the waxen torches of the King of Lochlann and mine?"

Said he, "If I were above, a comrade of meat and cup to thee, I would tell thee a tale on that."

At the end of a while after that, when the drink was taking Conall a little, he was willing to hear the tale of the man who was beneath the board, and he

* MacNair's version is almost the same in different words. This has some resemblance to the story of Conall, Nos. V. VI. VII.; but the adventures of this man are quite different. Macgilvray gives the same story.

said to him, "Thou that art beneath the board, if I had thy name it is that I would call thee; wert thou ever in strait or extremity like that?"

And he answered as before.

Said Conall, "If thou wilt promise to be peaceable when thou gettest up, I will let thee come up; and if thou art not peaceable, the two hands that put thee down before, will put thee down again."

Conall loosed the man who was beneath, and he rose up aloft and he sat at the other side of the board, opposite to Conall; and Conall said,

"Aha! thou art on high now, thou man that wert beneath. If I had thy name it is that I would call thee. What strait or extremity wert thou ever in that was harder than to be laid under the board of the young king of Lochlann, and mine?"

STORY OF THE KING OF SPAIN.

MacNair.

Said he—"My name is Garna Sgiathlais Righ na Iospainde Garna Skeealace, king of Spain.* Let me tell you the hardest strait in which I ever was.] I was once a warrior, and the deeds of a warrior were on my hand well enough, and I was on my way to the dun of the king of Laidheann to take out Breast of Light with right strong hand; and I saw Mac-a-Mor, son of the king of the Sorcha, and the most beauteous drop of blood that I ever saw upon his shoulder. I never saw a woman that I would rather wish to have for myself than that woman. I was working with my

---

* It is not easy to put a meaning on these names; there are two Gaelic words which are like Sgiathlais, and which have appropriate meanings; one means winging about, the other story-telling. MacNeill gives neither name nor country. It might mean "Cut of the tale-telling," because the episode cuts the story in two. Old MacPhie did not give it.

own sword at him as high as the band of his kilt.
He had but the one duan (song) for me—'Wilt thou
not cease, and wilt thou not stop?' but I gave no heed
to him.*]   He fell upon me, and he bound me, and fet- MacNeill.
tered me, and set me on the horse before him, and he
took me to the top of a rock. The rock was high, and
he threw me down the rock, and if I had fallen to the
bottom I had gone to little morsels, but so it was that
I fell into the nest of a dreagan.† When I came to
myself I looked about me, and I saw three great birds
in the nest, and I held my hands and my feet to them
as they were bound, until they loosed them; the monsters! that they might tear me asunder.]   I saw a Macgilvray.
cave at the back of the nest, and I dragged myself into
the cave, and when the old dreagan would come and
leave food for the young ones, I would stay till the old
dreagan would go, and then I would come out and I'd
take the food from the young dreagans, that was all I
had to keep alive upon.   But at last the young dreagans
found death for want of food. The old dreagan understood that something was eating their food, and she ran-
sacked all about the nest, and she went into the cave.‡] MacNair.
She seized me then in her talons; she sailed to the
back of the ocean with me; and she sprang to the
clouds with me, and I was a while that I did not know
which was heaven or earth for me, nor whether she
would let me fall in the drowning sea, or on rocks of

* MacNair mounts him on a horse. Macgilvray makes him
the king of the universe.

† MacNeill says, Cro mhineach, which is a vast bird like an
eagle to be found in stories all over the world. Macgilvray says
Gbri Mhineach greeveen-each, and I have no doubt the word is
the same as Griffin.

‡ The other version is the same, less the cave, and there was
but one chick.

MacNair. hardness, or on cairns of stones ;] she was lifting me and letting me down, till she saw that I was soon dead, on the breast of the sea. Though I was not heavy, when I took the brine I was heavy indeed; and when she was lifting me she was spent. She lifted me with her from the surface of the sea as I was dead, and she sailed with me to an island, and the sun was so hot; and she put me myself on the sun side of the island. Sleep came upon herself, and she slept. The sun was enlivening me pretty well though I was

MacNeill. dead.] She had come down at the side of a well, and when she awoke she began at working herself about in the well. I understood that there was iocshlaint, healing in the well, because of how the side of me that was nearest to the well was healing with the splashes of water that the dreagan was putting from her. And I moved the other side of me towards the well, till that side was healed also. Then I felt for my sword; my sword had always stuck by me;* and I got it, and I rose up and I crept softly (eallaidh mi) to the back of the dreagan, and with the sword I struck off her head. But it was but simple to strike off her head, by keeping it off. The balsam that was in the well was so strong that though the head should be struck off her, it would spring on again, till at last I got the sword held between the head and neck, till the hag's-marrow froze, and then I got the head and neck driven

MacNair. asunder.] I did not leave a thong of her uncut, and that is the death that went nearest to me, till the blood

MacNeill. dried throughout the island,] and when the blood dried I put the dreagan into the well, and I went and I washed myself in it, and so it was that it seemed to myself that I grew stronger and more active than I had

* Claidheamh beag chorr na sgeithe, the little sword of the crook of the shield, according to MacNeill.

ever been before. And the first exploit (gaisge) that I tried to do after that, was to try to contend against the king of Lochlann ; and it would have gone with me hadst thou not been here. And my being cast into the nest of the dreagan, and what I bore before I got out, is a harder strait and a worse extremity, in my esteem, than to be under the board of the king of Lochlann and thine."

When Garna Sgiathlais had finished his tale, he said to Conall, "Now, thou man that art yonder, I should like to have thy tale, thy name, thy land, and what is the reason of thy journey to Lochlann." And Conall said—"My name is Conall Guilbeanach, son of the king of Eirinn." And he told his own tale.*

The sister of the king of Lochlann was listening ; she grew sorrowful, and the drops rained from her eyes when she understood that Conall had another sweetheart. She arose, and she left the room, and she was heavy and sad. Duanach followed her to console her, and put her in order as best he might. She took a ring from her finger, and she sent it to Conall by Duanach.

Conall turned Duanach back with it to herself again. He said that he had a ring from another on his finger already, since he had got no gift (tabhartas) to give it to her, as eiric.†

She sent Duanach back again with the ring to Conall, and she asked him to wear it for her. Conall took the ring and put it upon his finger.]

MacNair.

"Thou must go with me," said Conall to Garna Sgiathlais, " in search of that woman Breast of Light."

* Here the heads of all that has gone before are given in the original.

† This gives eiric the meaning of a forfeit or fine.

"It is easier for me to bear death than to go to meet that man any more."

"Thou wilt find death where thou art, then," said Conall.

"It is certain that if I am to suffer death where I am that I will go with thee," said the slender black

man."]

"The young king of Lochlann said that he would go too." Said Conall,

"Who will be a guide to us to take us the shortest way?"

Said Duanach—"I will make a guide for you (ni mise iull d' uibh).

Conall and his warriors made ready. The king of Lochlann's sister wished Duanach to stay with her till the rest should come back, but Duanach would not

stay.]

Away went Conall, and he rigged a ship, and when the ship was rigged he took with him the slender black man, Duanach acha Draodh, the king of Lochlann, and the Amhus Ormanach; they sailed, and crew enough

with them, and they reached the realm of the Sorcha.*]

When they reached, Duanach went in to the house of Mac-a-Moir, and he said—"Hospitality from thee, A Mhic-a-Mhoir."

"Thou shalt have that A Dhraoth aoith."

"Champions to fight from the great warrior."

"Thou shalt have that, thou Druid."

"A sight of Breast of Light," said Duanach.

"Thou shalt have that, Druid," said Mac-a-Moir.

Duanach got a sight of Breast of Light, and he told her that Conall had come with his warriors to take

---

* According to MacNair there were but two champions on board.

her from Mac-a-Moir, and Breast of Light was pleased, for she was tired of being kept there.

Duanach came out, and he told it to Conall, and the next day Conall came to the landmark of Mac-a-Moir. He clashed his shield—"Yielding or battle upon the field."

"Yielding thou gettest not in this town," said Mac-a-Moir; "Though it were but speech it was a mark to Mac-a-Moir to come out to try a combat with Conall."*] MacNair.

"I should go up to seek the thing I want," said Conall.

"Well, indeed, thou shalt not. There promised to fall first none but me," said the slender black man. I will go up before thee, and I will come to thee with word how the place is up before thee."

The slender black man went up, and he shouted battle or combat, or else Breast of Light, daughter of the King of Laidhean, to be sent out. That he should have battle and combat, but not Breast of Light, daughter of the King of Laidhean.†

* Geill na comhrag air an fhaiche Geill cha 'n fhaighe tu ann sa bhaille so orsa Mac-a-Moir Ga d' b' e bu chainnte s' a bu chomhra do Mhae-a-Moir a tighinn a mach dh feuchainn comhrag ri Conall; as written by Dewar.

† The Barra version (MacNeill's) here varies considerably from the Cowall version (MacNair's). There is more incident in the latter, which I have followed; but the language of the former is more curious. It is wilder altogether, and savours more of an old Bardic composition. It is, in fact, the version of a practised narrator, who cannot read. All the fights, are described by both the men in nearly the same words; but each has a different set of phrases, though sometimes they are very like each other. When these are rapidly given, the effect is that of a kind of chant; something which, with music, would almost be a rude chorus, and might be so uttered as to express the battle.

The Barra battles are thus arranged, and they have that

They stood, Conall, the young King of Lochlann, and Garna Sgiathlais, opposite to the house of Mac-a-Moir, and they clashed their shields for battle. Mac-a-

kind of symmetry which pervades Gaelic popular tales, as they exist in the islands.

1st, The slender, dark man, who, according to MacNair, is the King of Spain, says that he will not let Conall go first on shore, because he has promised to be the first to fall. He lands,

These strange figures may represent warriors of the period to which these romantic Gaelic stories chiefly belong. They are copied from plate lvii., *Sculptured Stones of Scotland*, which represents a curious cross near Dupplin Castle. They are consequently warriors who lived after the introduction of Christianity into Scotland, and beyond that I believe the date to be as uncertain as that of Conall. A great number of animals, knots, men, and monsters, are sculptured on the same cross, and it is manifestly very old.

Moir sent out the three best warriors that were in his realm to battle with them. They drew their slender gray swords, and they went to meet each other, but

and strikes his shield. Five hundred Lughghaisgeach, and as many Treanghasgeach are sent out ; he slays them all, and lies down amongst them.

2*d*, Conall, in the ship, says that he has fled, and offers again to go himself ; but the Amhas Ormanach has sworn to fall first, and he goes. He finds the dead hosts, and thinks the plague is in the place, and keeps to windward ; but his comrade is alive, and tells him that he must do as much as he has done ; so he clashes his shield, and there come 500 lughghaisgeach, 500 treanghaisgeach, and 500 langhaisgeach (a larger number, and the last of higher rank, full heroes)—these he slays, and lies down.

3*d*, The scene on board is repeated, and the King of Lochlann goes, and repeats the scene on shore ; slays 1500, and lies down. To complete the symmetry, the first should have killed 500; the second, 1000; and the third, 1500.

4*th*, Conall says he was wrong to trust his matter to any other, and goes himself, followed by Duanachd acha Draodh, repeats the scene on shore, and is told by his comrades that the King of Sorcha has none alive now, but his " beag chuideachd," small company, and that he will rather come out than send them. They will not interfere unless Conall flees.

So far, then, the whole goes on increasing to the grand climax—which is the drawing of the great foe, the victory of the hero, the death of the villain, and a happy wedding ; and this is no solitary instance of such an artificial arrangement, but is the principle on which a whole class of similar tales are arranged. From this symmetry, and the rhythmical jingle which pervades the language, I feel convinced that the island versions are the oldest, and that the mainland versions, though better preserved as to incident, have lost somewhat of their original shape. There is as much difference in the stories, as there is in the manners of mainlanders and islanders, and that difference is very much greater than is generally known.

Mac-a-Mor Mac Righ Sorcha comes out to answer Conall

the combat did not last long till the three heroes were slain.

On the next day Mac-a-Moir sent the Ridire Leidire,

"and the step of Conall was back, and not forwards;" but Duanach stands behind, and urges him with the words given above, perhaps words which have really been spoken by bards in real fights—and Conall casts up the sword of his foe to the skies. "he leaped on his back, and struck off his head." Then the head was aiming straight at the trunk; but Conall, by the advice of Duanach, put the iron on the neck, and the head played "gliong" on the sword, and sprang up again to the skies. Then Duanach shouted, "step on one side; the head is aiming at thee;" and he did so, and the head went seven feet into the earth with the force that it had; and here the narrator remarked, "was not that a head! did not Conall escape well!"

Then Conall took the lady from the castle, and the narrator exclaimed triumphantly, "Was he the dastard of Eirinn now!" The hero and his three comrades, and the rescued lady get into their ship, and reach an island called Na h Otolia.

Old MacPhie told this part better than I have ever heard a story told; it was exceedingly symmetrical, full of "ruithean" (runs), and very original.

Conall sails to the realm of the King of the Universe, and strikes his shield blow. Soldiers came out, and he slew them; nobles came out, and he knocked their brains out with one of their number; then came the king's son, and he bound his wrists and ankles to the small of his back. He promised to serve him, and they sailed on to some realm, and challenged. The house of the Tamhasg here came in, and Duanach appeared, but he was the son of the King of Lochlann, wounded, and a prisoner. He cured his wounds with white sugar, and another fight took place, nearly the same as the last. They go on with the new king and the half-starved wight, and sail to Sorcha.

Conall lands as a poor man, and learns that the lady is to be married to the king of Sorcha's son, so, on the morrow he challenges. He hears men coming, and he says, "Look out; who comes; is that himself?" There came a company in a particular dress (I think the dresses were red, green, and blue), but I

the knight, the mangler, his brother, out to try a combat with any one of Conall's warriors who had the
heart to try against him.

did not note it, and I forget. These, said he, are but the servants; go out and slay them. Then came the first of the nobles
in another dress, and the same was repeated; then the last of
the nobles in another dress. Then came the son of the King of
Light himself, and then a fight indeed. Conall conquers, and is
about to sail back to Eirinn, when an old man appears in a boat,
and challenges. The warriors go one by one, and are slain, all
but Conall; then he thinks for the third time of his grandfather,
who appears and says, that old man was with me a student of
the black art (then a lot of queer words, which I could not catch,
and have never heard since), but he could beat him at one art,
so they try, and the grandfather wins. After that Conall goes to
Turkey, and rescues the King of Eirinn; and by the help of a
magic ring he forces the queen-mother to confess that her two
sons are not the king's children, and Conall reigns. It will be
seen from these abstracts that the version which I have followed
is much more reasonable than the common versions. For
example—

The Colonsay version, which varies here from all the rest.

When they set off from Lochlann to take Breast of Light
from the King of the universe, Conall remembers that his father
told him that he might get aid in extremity from Righ na
Iorramhaich (the King of the Boat-songsters?). That personage
says, I have twelve sons, and thou shalt get them. I have
thirteen sons, but Cod is just married, and Cod has counsel himself. Reach Cod."

The Counsellor Son, whose name may be translated "What,"
agrees to go if he has two-thirds of his counsel, till they come
back, and away they go, with a kind of Rhyme-list, which is repeated several times.

Dh fholbh an seo Conall Gulbairneach
S 'an t Amhas Orannach Mac Righ bharragh nan sgiath.
S am Macabh Mor Mac Righ na Sorcha
S tri Mic dheag righ na h Iorramhaich
Cead a's Cod a's Michead.

" Who will go to battle with this hero of exploits to-day ?" said Conall.

Dubhan Mac Draodh a's Mac Righ Sigil
A dh iarraidh Uchd sbluisd nighean Righ Laidhean

Then went Conall Curlew,
And the Savage of Songs, son of the King of Splitting the
    Shields ;
And the great warrior, son of the King of the Light ;
And the thirteen sons of the King of the Boat-songsters ;
Leave, and What, and Refusal.
Hook, son of Herald, and the King of Seegeel,*

To seek Breast of Light, daughter of the King of Leinster ;
Going past a castle, there cried out
The great man whose the castle was,
Co sibh a dh haislean nan tri rann ?
Na ce ur n-ainmeanan ?
Na 'ur n eachdraidh a niotar ?

Who are ye of the gentles of the three divisions ?†
Or what are your names ?
Or (who) will your histories make ?

Conall Gulbeirneach gum be m ainms' e
Mac Righ Eirinn bu mhor airm
A cheile comhraig fo leon
A shleaghan cha d' fhuair an t-ath-bheo

Conall Curlew, it is my name,
Son of Eirinn's King of Great Arms ;
His battle spouse (adversary), under wounds
Of his spears, never got the next life.

---

    * Stripe making siogail means streaked, striped.
    † This would seem to indicate a date earlier that the discovery
of the 4th division, America.

" Myself," said Garna Sgiathlais, " because of how his brother threw me into the nest of the dreagan."

They went to meet each other ; they drew their slender gray swords, and the two battled with each

They reached the house of the King of the Universe, and the herald went in, and there he found the most beautiful woman that ever was seen from the beginning of the universe to the end of eternity, with two drops of blood on every eye, weeping for Conall.

The herald repeats the list, and she says, " Every Draoth I ever saw was telling lies ; if it were Conall he would come in." Accordingly Conall sprang in, and gave her na tri poga milisde blasda, the three sweet tasty kisses, and sprang out again.

The King of the Universe yields the lady without a struggle, comes home from his hunting, and asks them all to a feast ; a " minister " was got, and they were married.

In the midst of the festivities, a shout was raised that the King of the Universe had fallen in combat with a monster on the strand. Conall got up to help, but Cod bade him sit still ; and the king was seen in his chair.

This happened a second time ; and the third Cod had no share of the counsel, so Conall took his own, and went out.

He found the monster and the King of the Universe dead, sole to sole ; and there came a dove from the east, and she was stooping down to the monster with a *leig* (a pebble possessed of medicinal virtues, a chrystal, a talisman), which she had, and the creature was stirring, and opening its eyes. He sprang, and took hold of the leig, and took it from the dove.

" Give me my leig," said the dove, " and I will bring thy father and brothers alive in the Tuirk."

"If thou wilt do but that, I will do it myself," said Conall. He seized the dove, and pulled his head off ; and who came to meet him but Cod. Then Conall and Cod and Dubhan and the lady went to Turkey, and found out the graves of the king and the rest, and brought them alive, and took them home ; and the descendants of these people are yet in Eirinn—

Said John Macgilvray, labourer, Colonsay, July 9, 1860.

other; but long before the sun went west, the Ridire Leidire was slain.

Garna Sgiathlais took off his head, and he opened the mouth, and he cut the tongue out, and he split the tongue, and he struck it three slaps against himself; and he said to Mac-a-Moir—

"There, that is for thee, for how thou didst cast me into the dreagan's nest."

At night Duanach went into the house of Mac-a-Moir, and he said—

"Hospitality from thee, Vic-a-Voir."

"Thou shalt get that, thou Druid."

"Warriors to combat Conall to-morrow," Vic-a-voir.

"Thou shalt get, thou Druid."

"A sight of Breast of Light?" said Duanach.

"Thou shalt get that, thou Druid," said Mac-a-Moir.

Duanach got a sight of Breast of Light, and he told her each thing as it was going on outside of the dun, and she was sorrowful that so much blood was being spilt for her; and Duanach came out, and he gave the tale of Breast of Light to Conall.

On the next day Mac-a-Moir himself came out to try a combat with any one who had the heart to go to try him.

"Who will go to battle with the hero of exploits to-day?" said Conall.

"Myself," said Garna Sgiathlais, "for the day that he cast me down the rock to the dreagan's nest."

They came in front of each other; they drew their slender gray swords, and they kindled a fire of fists with their swords, from the rising of the sun till she was going west; but at last it went with Mac-a-Moir to level Garna Sgiathlais, to bind him and fetter him; and he took him with him, and he cast him into a den

of lions that he kept for pastime for himself, and
Mac-a-Moir would not come out again. till the end of
two days.

When the night came Duanach went into the
house of Mac-a-Moir, and he said—

"Hospitality from thee, Vic-a-Voir."

"Thou shalt get that, thou Druid."

"A sight of Breast of Light ?" said Duanach.

"Thou shalt not get that," said Mac-a-Moir; and
then Breast of Light was put into a dark chamber,
where she could not hear voice of friend, and where
she could not see light of sun.

When the battle-day of Mac-a-Moir came, he came
out, and he clashed his shield.*

"Who will go to battle with the hero of exploits
to-day ?" said Conall.

"Myself," said the Young King of Lochlann.†

They came in front of each other ; they drew their
hard thin swords, and they went to battle with each
other. But long before the sun went west, the young
King of Lochlann was levelled, bound, and fettered,
and taken away, and cast into the den of lions, where
Garna Sgiathlais was ; and Mac-a-Moir would not
come out any more to hold battle till the end of five
days.

Duanach went in every night of these to seek
food, and he got it ; and on a night of these nights he
asked for warriors to hold battle against Conall.

---

* There seems to be a regular system in this series of battles.
The victor in the last battle now comes out, and gives the chal-
lenge.

† Here there is a hole in the story. The King of Lochlann
ought clearly to have some quarrel to avenge, but he has none ;
and the King of Spain had two fights for the same quarrel, which
is entirely against regularity and order.

"Thou shalt get that, thou Druid," said Mac-a-Moir. A hundred full heroes were set in order before the great house on the next day.

It seemed strange to Conall to see the host going into order at the front of the big house ; and he asked if there was any knowing what was the meaning of that host going into order, in ranks, at the front of the big house this day.

Said Duanach, " I thought thou wert finding the time long here, not doing anything, and I asked for warriors to combat with thee."

" I have no wish myself to be slaying men without knowing why ; and, besides, how should I contend against a hundred full heroes, and I alone ?" said Conall.

" So many as thou dost not slay with thy sword I will kill with my tongue," said Duanach.*

MacNair.

They went to meet Conall]

The smooth lad looked from one to two ; and where they were thickest, there they were thinnest ; and where they were thinnest, there were none at all

MacNeill.

there.]

He struck them under, and over, through, and throughout ; and those who were thinnest, were most ill scattered ; and as many as were dead of them were lying down ; and as many as were hurt, they sat ; and the rest that were alive of them ran away.†

* This is like a sly allusion to the romantic and untrue side of the tale, and to the poetical license of bards such as Duanach.

† Sheall an gille min o h-aon go dha 's far am bo tiughe eud 's an a bo tainn' eud 's far am bo tainn' eud cha robh gin idir

MacNeill.

ann,] Bhuail e iad fodh-pa tharta trid us rompa s a chuid a bu tainne dhiubh gu am b ia bha a bu mhi-sgaoltiche, s' a mhead a marbh dhiubh bha iad nan luidh 's a mhead 's a bha leointe

MacNair.

dhiubh bha iad nan suidh agus an corr a bha beo dhiubh theich.]

And when the five days of delay that Mac-a-Moir had were gone past, Conall went to the fence of his house.

Mac-a-Moir had a bell on the top of his house, and he was a warrior, any one who could strike a blow on the bell ; and when a blow was struck on the bell, unless Mac-a-Moir should come out, then he was a dastard (cladhaire). Then when Mac-a-Moir was eating his breakfast, Conall went up upon the top of the house, and he struck a blow on the bell, and he drove the tongue out of the bell ; and the tongue fell down through the house, and down through the board at which Mac-a-Moir was taking his food ; and Mac-a-Moir said, "Ha, ha! comrade, it was easier to hold battle against thee on the day of Bein Eidinn than on this day."*

Mac-a-Moir came out to hold battle. Conall clashed his shield, and he said, " Yielding, or battle on the field."

" Yielding thou gettest not in this town," said Mac-a-Moir. Though it was but speech, it was a sign

Mr. Fraser, Inverness.—Thoisich è air an arm Lochlannach a sgathadh air an darna ceanu gus an deach e mach air a chean eille. Far am bu tiugh eud, san a bu tainn eud, s far am bu tainn eud san a bu luaidh shiulach eud ; far am bo luaidh shiul-ach eud, san bo luaidh a mharbhadh eud ; gus nach d' fhag e ceann air conn, ach aon fhear chloain ruaidh.

He began at slicing at one end of the army of Lochlann till he went out at the other end ; where they were thickest they were thinnest ; where they were thinnest they were swiftest ; where they were swiftest they were soonest slain, till he left no head upon hound, but on one gleed old man.

* Compare the battle chain of the giants in No. 58, vol. iii. In old romances there is always a horn, or some other instrument, for making a noise, hung up at the door of the castle, for the challenger's special convenience. Compare St. Patrick's bell.

for Mac-a-Moir to come out, to try a battle with Conall.

They drew their slender gray swords, and they kindled a fire of fists, from the rising of the sun till the evening, when she would be going west; without knowing with which of them the victory would be.

Duanach was singing "iolla" to them, and he said, "You are long enough at this play; throw from you your swords, and try it another way. They threw from them their swords, and they put their soft white fists in each other's breasts, and they wrestled, but they did not take long at the wrestling, till Conall give the panting of his heart to Mac-a-Moir on the hard stones of the causeway. "Stretch hither my sword," said Conall, "until I reap the head off him."

"I will not stretch it," said Duanach. It is better for thee that thou shouldst have his head for thyself as it is, than five hundred heads that thou mightest take out with strife," said Duanach; "take a pledge of him that he will be faithful to thee."

Conall made him promise that he would be faithful to Conall Guilbeanach, son of the King of Eirinn, whether the matter should come under right or unright; and that the realm of Sorcha should be under cess to the realm of Eirinn; and Mac-a-Moir gave these pledges to Conall, and he bound himself with words, and with weighty vows. Conall let him aloft; they caught hold of each other's hands, and they made peace with great friendship, and they were quiet.*

Then the first thing that Conall did was to go to the den of lions, to see if his two comrades were alive,

* According to the Barra version, the Amhas Ormanach here went home to his own country; and as he does not appear again, it is to be hoped that he went home to his wife, the Princess of Norway.

and they were ; for it is as left with the lions that they
will not touch, and that they will not do any hurt to
kings, or to the clan of kings.*

And Conall took Garna Sgiathlais and the young
King of Lochlann out of the lion's den, and he loosed
each bond and fetter that was upon them, and they
were free and whole.

The next thing that Conall did was to take Breast
of Light out of the dark place in which she was, and
she was pleased and joyful coming out.

Mac-a-Moir gave a bidding to Conall, and to Breast
of Light, to the King of Iospainde, and the young King
of Lochlann, to come into his house to take a feast. They
went there.   They raised music, and they hid sorrow ;
word was sent for a priest, and Conall was wedded to
Breast of Light, and they made a wedding that lasted
for the six days of the week, and the last day was no
worse than the first,] and that was the wedding that MacNair.
was cheery.   Meat was set in the place for using, and
drink in the drinking place, and music in the place for
hearing. They plied the feast and the company with
joy, and pleasure of mind, and long was there mind of
the wedding of Conall and Breast of Light.]   MacNeill.

But there was much envy (farnaite) with the
young King of Lochlann, Garna Sgiathlais, and Mac-
a-Moir at Conall, to see him married to one so beautiful,
modest, and learned, and that they themselves should
be wifeless, and they thought her like was not to be
found.   Each one of them was as anxious as the rest

* Oir tha e mar fhagail aig na leomhainn nach buin iad agus
nach deann iad dolaidh air bith air Righrean na air clan Righre.
(As written by Dewar.)

Here, according to Macgilvray, Conall acquired a talisman
from a mysterious pigeon, and fell in with a monster which slew
and was slain by the King of the Universe.   (See page 247).

that her like should be his as a wife, and they left it to Breast of Light to say who was the other one that would come nearest to herself in look, learning, and modesty. She said that there was Aillidh, daughter of the King of Greece, but it was by mighty deeds that she would be got (sar ghaisge).

The three kings made it up that they would go to seek Aillidh, daughter of the King of Greece. Breast of Light was unwilling that Conall should go with the rest, but the rest would not go without him, and when she saw that she consented.

It was left to Conall to say which of them was to get Aillidh, and Conall said, "Since the King of Lochlann was the first king who had come under cess to him, that he was the first for whom he would get a wife." Duanach wished to go with them, but Conall left him to be a king, and to take care of Breast of Light till he should come back.

Away went Conall, young son of the King of Eirinn, Mac-a-Moir, son of the King of Sorcha, and Garna Sgiathlais, King of the Hispainde, to get Aillee (Beauty), daughter of the King of the Grayke (Greece), for the young King of Lochlann to wife, and they reached Greece.*

* This, at first sight, appears utterly extravagant, if only from the distances, but the story is not more improbable than similar romances in other languages. It is far less improbable in Gaelic than it would be in French or German. A glance at the story of Burnt Njal will shew that in the eleventh century locomotion was not the difficulty for the Western Islanders; for example, Audun, an Icelander, before 1066, and within two years, sailed from Iceland to Norway, and thence to Greenland, back to Norway, and thence to Denmark, to give the king a white bear. He made a pilgrimage to Rome, and returned to Denmark and Norway again, and went home to Iceland with a big ship, having conversed on equal terms with the Kings of Denmark and Norway, and this

An old man met them that was their guide. He
gave them a tale about the realm of Greece, the desire
of the hosts, the battle ; the form of the arms, and the
customs of the country (miann sloidh, feachd ; s' rian
nan arm, agus cleachdanan na ducha), and he told
them the tale of the King of Greece, and how his
daughter was kept in the dun, and that no one at all
was to get Beauty, daughter of the King of Greece, to
marry, but one who could bring her out by great
valour ; and the old man told them about the wall that
was for a bulwark (daingneach) round about the dun,
how many heroes and soldiers there were in the inside
of the ramparts ; and besides, that there was no way to
get Beauty but by strong battle, brave deeds, and
ruse (feachd làdir, sàr ghaisge, agus seoltachd).
Conall went, and the three other kings, aloft up a
mountain that was above the dun of the big town of
the king, so that they might see what was going on
below beneath them. They lighted upon hunting
bothys (bothain sheilg) in the mountain, and they went
in into them, and they were there all night, and on
the next day they found old clothes in the hunting
huts.

Conall put on some of the old clothes which they
found, to go in the semblance of a poor lad, to try if he
could get to the inside of the gates (cachlaidhean) of

story is believed to be true. The countrymen of Audun fought
in Ireland in 1014, and got the worst of it, and one who was at
the battle went to Rome, and returned to Iceland. In short, supposing this to be a romance of that period, nothing is more in
accordance with probability than that a lot of warriors should set
out in search of kingdoms and princesses along the sea-coast of
Europe, and that their adventures should be woven in with the
romances of the Western Islands of Scotland, which the Norsemen possessed.

the dun of the king's town, and he said to the other
kings if they should hear on the third day a hunting
cry, or any terror (faoghaid na fuathas), that they
should run swiftly to help him. He went, and he
reached one of the gates (geata) of the dungeon (daingneach), and he was as a shy boy, ill-looking, without
the look of a man, without the port of a lad, or a dress
of armour (mar bhallach moitire mi sgiamhach, gun
aogosg duine gun dreach gille, na culaidh armachd).

He reached the gate-keeper (fear gleidh a gheata),
but that one would not let him in. He asked him
what he sought, and Conall said that he had come to
see if he could get teaching in feats of arms, nimbleness,
and soldier-craft (ionnsach ain iomairt arm, luth chleas,
's gaisge). The gate-keeper sent word for the ruler of
the fort (fear riaghladh an duin), and he came and he
asked Conall whence he was. Conall said that he had
come from the neighbourhood (iomal) that was furthest
off of the realm. The high ruler asked him what customs
the people of that place had, and if they tried to do
any feats ?

Conall said that they used to try casting the stone
of force (clach neart), and hurling the hammer.*

The high ruler asked Conall to come in, and he set
some to try putting the stone against Connal. Conall
could throw the stone further than any of them, and

---

* I myself once tried a match with a small Greek shepherd in
a sheep-skin capote, in a glen near the top of Mount Parnassus.
He had guided me there, and we were waiting in hopes a mist
would clear away. To keep ourselves warm we fell to at putting
the stone, leaping, and hop-skip-and-jump. Such games prevailed in ancient Greece long ago, as they still do in the Highlands and Lowlands of Scotland. The hitch in romances is in
the language. Heroes must have been great linguists, but even
that hitch is here met, for the old Irish king was educated in
Italy and Greece.

they saw that he had no want of strength if there were enough of courage in him.

A stick sword was given him, and they were teaching him swordsmanship, and Conall was coming on well. But it was little they knew about the teaching that Conall had got from the Gruagach of Beinn Eidinn before then. Conall made himself acquainted with the keeper of the arms, and he was exceedingly anxious to get a sight of their arms-house, but the armourer said that could not be done, for fear of the high ruler of the dun. But on the morning of the third day, when the governor was eating his breakfast, the armourer said to Conall, that if he were able enough now, that he might get a sight of the armoury before the high man who ruled the dun should come out from his morning meal.

Conall went with him swiftly, and the man who was keeping the arms opened the armoury (taisg airm). Conall went in and he looked amongst the arms, and he spied great glaives at the furthest off end of the armoury. He went where they were, and he began to try them, he would raise them in his hand, and brandish them, and some he would shake out of their hilts (ceana bhairt), and others he would break. The man who had the care of the arms began to shout to him that he should come out, but Conall was not pretending that he heard him. Conall would look at the swords, and some were rusted, and some were not. At last he found a sword that pleased him.*

He was going the way of the door of the arms-house with it, and the man who had the care of the

* This incident is told in Uist of a man whose grave is shewn there still. The "armoury" is a "barrel," but it is the same incident told as a fact. I believe it to be a bit of popular lore of unknown antiquity, for it is common in stories.

S

arms was begging him to put it from him, but Conall gave him no heed, and the man who had charge of the armoury said—

"If the high governor of the dun comes he will take the head off me for letting thee in."

When Conall was at the door the governor came in, and he desired Conall to put away that sword. If he knew the name of the man who had had that sword that he would not be long putting it from him ; that his name was Mor ghaisge na mor ghleadh. Great valour of the great tricks.

"You may give it that name still," said Conall.

The high governor said that he would drive the head off the man who had the care of the arms for letting Conall into the armoury, and off Conall for taking the sword out.

"Take thou care that it is not thine own head that will be down first, comrade."

The high governor called for his men. Conall struck the head off the high Governor, and he gave a hunting whistle (fead fhaoghaid), and the people gathered with their arms about Conall.

He struck them, under them, over them, through, and throughout them ; where they were thickest there they were thinnest ; where they were thinnest they were most scattered.

The king came out, and he said to Conall, " Thou man that came on us a-new ; hold on thy hand, and thy blade.*

The three other kings came to the gate, but they were not getting in. Conall ran to the gate, and he struck it a kick, and he drove it into splinters. Then came the King of Lochlann, and the King of Light,

* Fhir a thainaig oirn as uir cum air do laimh as do lann.

and the King of the Hispainde, in with their arms. The
people of Greece fled back, and the King of Greece
said—

"Oubh bhoubh ouv vouv!" "What a wonderful
turn has come on the matters! It was in the pro-
phecies that a son of a king of Eirinn would come, and
that he would lay the realm of Greece under cess, and
instead of that is an awkward fellow of an ill-looking
boy, that came and put the realm under cess."*

Said Conall, with a high voice, Thou King of
Greece, take not thou each man according to his seeming.† I am Conall Guilbeinach, son of the King of
Eirinn, but it is not to put the realm of Greece under
cess I am come, but to take out Beauty, thy daughter.

Said the King of Greece, "Thou shalt have Beauty,
my daughter, and two-thirds of my realm while I myself am alive, and the whole after my death."

Conall asked that Aillidh should be brought out,
and she came, and she was right willing to wed Conall,
but Conall told her he was married already to Breast
of Light, daughter of the King of Laidhean; and the
King of Greece said—

"If thou hast got Breast of Light, it is no wonder
though thou shouldst not take my daughter."

Conall told Beauty that she had her two choices, to
take the King of Lochlann, or be without a husband;
and she preferred to marry the young King of Lochlann.

And word was sent for a priest; and Aillidh,
daughter of the King of Greece, was wedded to the

* This is the idea which, in No. 58, has expanded into
another shape. The King of Greece and the first giant were
clearly once the same personages.

† This is the very foundation of all popular tales; the most
despised is the most worthy.

young King of Lochlann, and they made a wedding that lasted for the six days of the week, and the last day was no worse than the first day.

And when they were at the wedding, they asked Aillidh, the bride of Lochlann's King, who was the next one that was nearest to her in beauty and comeliness, virtue and learning. And she said that there was Cuimir,* daughter of the King of Na Frainge (the Franks, France).

Conall asked Garna Sgiathlais if he were willing to take that one as a wife, and he said that he was. Conall asked Aillidh where Cuimir was dwelling, and Beauty told that she was in the great royal house, and that there was a great fortress wall about the great house, and that there was a lion on either side of the gate, that was in through the wall, and that there was the house of the Tamhaisg, the best warriors that the King of France had, a little further on; and the Tamhaisg were proud and merciless to any over whom they might gain victory.†

The valiant kings made ready to go to France, but Aillidh was not willing to part with her new married husband, but the other warriors would not part from him; he must needs go with them, till they should put an end to all the valorous deeds they had to do, before they could get wives for Garna Sgiathlais, King of Hispania, and Mac-a-Moir, son of the King of Sorcha.

The four valorous kings put each matter in order in Greece as best they might, and they left Beauty in the care of her father till the King of Lochlann should come back. They went to France and when they reached

* Well formed, neat, trim. Carbad cuimeir Chuchullin.

† "Gu borb aniochdmhor ri feadbainn air bith air am faighe iad buaigh.

France they took a tale from each traveller that met them by the way, and so they got guidance to the great royal house, and when they reached the gate, that was without in the fortress wall, there was a great lion at either side of the gate, but that put neither fear nor sorrow upon them,* because it is as a charge left with lions that they will not injure kings, or the clan of kings. And Conall went on past the lions, and no one of them stirred his head at him. He reached on forward to where the Tamhasgan were, and they began gnashing their teeth,† making ready to spring upon him. He took sure notice of them, for the thick knobbiest one and the thinshankiest of them. He compassed them, under them, over them, through and throughout them; and he seized on the two shanks of the thinshankiest one amongst them, and he was driving out the brains of the rest, with the knob of that one, and the brains of that one with the knobs of the rest, till the part that was thickest of them was thinnest, and the lot that was thinnest they were the most ill-scattered.

The King of France came out, and he said to Conall.

"Thou man that hast come on us from a strange land, withhold thy blade and thine hand; slay not my warriors wholly; these are the Tamhaisg, the best warriors I have to guard the great royal house; but they are but as reeds in the front of a meadow before thee. How camest thou past the lions?"

"Thou and thy lions!" said Conall; "I will go down past thy lions, and I will come up past thy lions, and they will not touch me; and I will bring up three other warriors, that are down here, and the lions will not touch them."

* Eagal na smuairean.   † A càsadh am fiacall.

Garna Sgiathlais Mac-a-Moir and the King of Lochlann came up past the lions, kings were they, and a
clan from kings all together, and the lions did not stir
their tongues against them.

The King of France asked whence they were, and
Conall told that he was Conall Guilbeanach, son of the
King of Eirinn, and he shewed the young King of
Lochlann, and Mac-a-Moir, son of the King of Sorcha,
and Garna Sgiathlais, king of Hispania; and he told
him that it was not to disturb France they had come,*
but to take out Cuimir, daughter of the King of France,
to be wife to Garna Sgiathlais King of Hispania.

Said the King of France, "He shall get that."

Cuimir was brought out, and the matter was hidden,
and it was Conall she would rather take, for it was he
that had done the bravest deeds; but Conall told her
that he was wedded already to Breast of Light, daughter
of the King of Laidhean, and that the young King of
Lochlann was wedded to Aillidh, daughter of the King
of Greece, and that it was Garna Sgiathlais, King of
Hispania, she was to have. Cuimir was willing to
take the King of Hispania, so that she might be a
queen in a realm that was near the realm of her
father. Word was sent for a priest, and the wedding
was done, and they made a wedding that lasted for the
six days of the week, and the last day was no worse
than the first day.

When they were at the wedding they were talking
about who they should get for a wife for Mac-a-Moir;
and they left it to be said by Cuimir, the young Queen
of Spain. Who was the one that was fittest, in her
esteem, to be wife to Mac-a-Moir. And she said
that there was Deo Greine nighean righ an Eilean

---

* A chungais-each na Frainge.

Uaine.* They asked her if that one was to be got.
She said that she was not, but by exceeding valour;
that there was a fortress wall round about the dun of
the king, and that it discomfited the heroes; that
Deo Greine would be in a turret that was on the top
of the dun, and that none but a valiant warrior could
get her; but if Mac-a-Moir should get her, that he
had no cause to regret that he was the last of the kings
who had got a wife.

Mac-a-Moir was longing to begone in pursuit of
Deo Greine, and the rest were as willing and well
pleased as himself.† When they were at the feast,
the King of France was setting a ship in order for
them. Cuimir, daughter of the King of France, was
not willing to let her new married husband, Garna
Sgiathlais, away with the rest, but when the rest saw
that, they would not go without him. When Cuimir
understood that, she agreed to let him go with them.

The King of France set his slender ship in order
for them, with a crew of disciplined, active, strong,
hardy men, and the four honourable kings went on
board, and the Frenchmen sailed with them to the
shore of the Green Island.‡

* Sunbeam or breath, daughter of the King of the Green
Island. Who this mythical personage may be, I cannot make out.
The Green Island occurs continually, and is the land of wonders,
beyond the sea. I have surmised that it might mean America.
That the Son of Light should marry the daughter of the mythical
Green Isle in the west, where the sun sets, seems all right, and
the warriors are working westwards. I had imagined that Sorcha
might possibly be same as Sarkland of Icelandic Sagas, but that
is identified with Africa, Saracen land, and would not fit this
story, here, at all events.

† Togarach aighearach.

‡ Chuir Righ na Frainge a chaol loingeas air doigh air an
son, le sgioba do dhaoine foghluinte, easgaidh, ladir, cruadalach;
s chaidh na ceithir righrean uramach air bord.

They brought the ship to port,* and they put Mac-a-Moir and the three gallant kings who were with him on shore, and they themselves sailed back, home to France.

. They went on forwards to the dun of the town of the King of the Green Island, taking a tale from each traveller and journeyer that might fall in with them. They got on till they reached the fortress gate of the dun of the king's town. Conall struck at the gate, and the gate-keeper asked what they sought. Conall answered that they came to seek Sunbeam, daughter of the King of the Green Isle, to be wife to one of them. Word was sent for the high Governor of the dun, and he came, and he asked them who they were, and what they sought. Conall told him that they were kings, and they had come to seek Sunbeam as a wife for one of them. The high Governor said that they should not get her but by exceeding valour; that they must hold a battle against the warriors of the dun, and gain victory over them.

Conall asked who was the sturdy hero that would go first to battle against the warriors of the dun.

" Myself," said Mac-a-Moir. " If I am to get the daughter of the King of the Green Island as a wife, I will shew that I am worthy to have her."

They were asked in, and they went.

Warriors were got to combat Mac-a-Moir, son of the King of Sorcha. They drew their blades, and Conall, and Garna Sgiathlais, and the young King of Lochlann were singing iolla to them. But they had not taken long of the contest, when Mac-a-Moir struck the head off the champion of the King of the Green Isle.

Said Mac-a-Moir to the Governor, " Pick up the champion's head, and get me another one."

* Calla. Compare Calais.

Another was got ; but they had not taken long at the combat when Mac-a-Moir struck the head off that one too.   He asked for another, and another was got, but it was not long till the head went off that one in like manner.

The King of the Green Isle was taking sport at them, and he said—

" I see, my hero, that thou wouldst slay my men altogether, one after another, if thou hadst chance of arms.   I am not for spilling more blood ; I will try it another way.

My daughter is in a turret, that is at the top of the dun, and the man that can take her out shall get two-thirds of my realm while I live, and the whole of my realm when I die ; I am but an old man, and it is not likely that I will be long alive now, at all events.*

The way was shewn them to the turret, in which was the king's daughter, at the top of the dun.

" Who is the first man that will try to take the king's daughter out of the turret ?" said Conall.

" Myself," said Mac-a-Moir.

The turret was aloft, on the top of three carraghan ard, lofty pillars.

Mac-a-Moir went, and he did his very best, but he could not get aloft ; he thrust the pillars hither and thither ; he tried every way he knew, but it discomfited him.

" Who will try it again ?" said Conall.

" Myself," said the young King of Lochlann.   He went, and tried as well as he could, but he could not

* This is a very common saying amongst old Highlanders here put into the mouth of the king.   Cha neil anam ach sean duine an nis, s chu'n eil a coltach gu' m bi mi fada beo a nis co dhiubh.

level one of the posts that was beneath the turret, but it beat him.

Said the King of the Green Isle, "I perceive, my men, that it will not go with you to take my daughter out of the turret. Many a man has striven to take her out, but it went with none of them, and I see that it will not go with you any more; you may be off home."

"Well, then, if it does not go with us to bring her out, it is a great disgrace to us," said Conall.

He went and he struck a kick on one of the posts that was keeping the turret aloft, and the post broke, and the turret fell, but Conall caught it between his hands before it reached the ground. A door opened, and Sunbeam came out, the daughter of the King of the Green Isle, and she clasped her two arms about the neck of Conall, and Conall put his two arms about Sunbeam, and he bore her into the great house, and he said to the King of the Green Isle, "Thy daughter is won."

Sunbeam was very willing to stick to Conall, but Conall told her that he was married already to Breast of Light, daughter of the King of Laidheann, and the King of Lochlann was wedded to Beauty, daughter of the King of Greece, and that Garna Sgiathlais, King of Hispania, was married to Comely, daughter of the King of France, and that Great Hero, son of the King of the Light, was the only one of them that was unmarried. The King of the Green Isle was pleased when he understood that they were honourable kings altogether, and that his daughter had been taken out with honour; and he said that he would give two-thirds of his realm while he was alive, and the whole after his death, to the one that his daughter should have, and that he was an old man, and that he would not be long alive altogether. Every one of them was married but Mac-a-Moir, and he was the most unblemished amongst them. Sunbeam took a look around at each one of them. Though Mac-a-Moir was not so handsome as the rest, he was a stately, comely, personable man ; and Sunbeam said that he was the husband she would have, and word was sent for a priest, and Sunbeam, the daughter of the King of the Green Island, was wedded to Mac-a-Moir, son of the King of Light, and they made a wedding that lasted for the six days of the week, and the last day was no worse than the first day, and if there were better there were, and if not let them be.

When the other heroes found that Mac-a-Moir was married, they were in great haste to go home to see their own wives.*

The King of the Green Isle set in order a great high masted white-sailed ship. There was a pilot in her prow, and a steersman in the stern, and men managing the rigging-ropes in the middle. Each meat and each drink as was seemly for kings was put on board.†

When each thing was ready, and each matter arranged as it ought to be, Conall, son of the King of Eirinn, Garna Sgiathlais, King of Hispania, and the King of Lochlann left a blessing with the King of the Green Isle, with Mac-a-Moir, and Deo Greine, and they went on board of the ship. The shipmen sailed with the ship, and they sailed to realm of Sorcha, with

---

* Here I omit a recapitulation of the wives, and their countries.

† Long ard-chranach bhreidgheal air doigh. Bha iull na toiseach, fear-stiurr aig a deireadh, 's fir iomairt na' m ball beart na buillsgain. Chaidh, gach bidh, s dibh, mur bu chubhraidh do righre a chuir air bord.

Conall, the son of the King of Eirinn.* Conall reached the dun of the big town of Sorcha, came to Breast of Light and Duanach, without their having hopes of him, and they rejoiced with great joy to see him. Conall and Breast of Light were a while merry, and joyously, and fondly about each other, and Duanach was blithely and cheerily with them,† and when Conall had spent a while cheerily joyously with Breast of Light and Duanach, he began to think it long that he was not hearing from the realm of Iubhar how the fight was coming on between his mother's brother and the Turks,‡ or if his father or brothers were yet alive. He thought that he would go to the realm of the Iubhar to see. He wished to leave Duanach, as he was before, to take care of Breast of Light and the realm, but Duanach would not stay. If Conall would go to the realm of Iubhar, Duanach would go with him. Breast of Light wished Conall to go first to Eirinn to see if each thing were right in Eirinn, but his own counsel was best with Conall, and he wished Duanach to stay. But this is what Duanach said, "If thou goest, Conall, to the realm of Iubhar thou wilt fight, and I will be needful enough for thee."

And so it was agreed that Conall should take Duanach as a servant and counsellor.

Breast of Light, and Conall, and Duanach, went MacNair. away.§]

* MacNair here sends the two kings home, but, according to MacNeill and the rest, Conall and two comrades sailed to the realm of the Turk. So I leave out a paragraph.

† Gu aighearach aobhach speiseil ma cheile 's Duanach gu sundach sodanach comhla riu.

‡ If Iubhar were a corruption for Jewry, then the geography would be right, and this might be a romance founded on something to do with wars in the Mediterranean.

§ This is shortened.

Then he took with him the woman on board of the ship, and when he and his men were returning he was running out of provisions. There was an island here which they called Eilean na h Otolia. The man who was over the island was (so) that if he was for giving food it could be got for money, and if he were not he had three big dogs, and he would let them out, and they would kill them all.

Said the slender dark man to Conall, " I would rather myself thou wouldst stay out of it, than go into it."

" I myself would not rather stay than go, I will go and I will get it; but if you see that he is not willing to give it to me, you will leave me the front, and you will stay behind me, if so be that he hounds the dogs at us," said Conall.

He went up to the house, and he asked if he could get food. He said that they should not, that plenty were asking for it who were more likely to get it than he.

He let out the dogs. Every one of the company stood at the back of Conall, and he himself went to the front, he caught a napkin and put it about his fist. Each one as he came, he was seeing his liver down through his mouth, from the rage that he had towards the men. He thrust his hand into the mouths of the dogs, one after another, and he took the heart and the liver out of them, and he killed them.

" Come now and you shall get food," said the man who was over the island.

" Thou mayest give that now, but I will not give thee one ' sgillinn' for it; unless thou thyself hadst been a ' Trusdar,' a stingy filthy wretch, thou hadst got payment; but since thou wert so dirty, thou shalt not get payment, and we shall get meat in spite of thee."

"That is easy enough for you now," said he. "But hast thou heard how it has befallen the King of Eirinn and the King of Laidhean; they were fighting the Turk?"

"Well then I have heard how it has befallen these doubtless; the battle went with the Turk, and all the company that the King of Eirinn and the King of Laidhean had, have been slain; and the Great Turk has the King of Eirinn, and the King of Laidhean bound back to back, under cats, and dogs, and men's spittle, and with shame and insult on themselves and on their hosts, that came to give battle and could not do it."

"That story is sad for me to hear, but though it is, keep thou this woman for me till I come back from these men."

"Well, then," said he, "I will not keep her, I have no way of keeping her. The thing that I had myself for that, thou thyself hast put me in want of it."

"Unless thou hadst been such a Trusdar of a man as thou wert, I had not put thee in want of it, but thou must keep this woman, or else there will not be much of the world for thee, after letting her go," said Neill. Connal.]

He went and he left the woman, and when they reached the realm of Iubhar the fighting was going on, Conall and Duanach did not go to the house of the king but to a hostelry. They got their supper that night and they went to bed. On the next morning Conall's waking was to hear shouts of hosts and clash of armour;* heroes starting, commanders arraying soldiers to go to give a day of battle to the Turks. Conall arose and Duanach, they put on them their array

* Oighich sluaidh 's gleadhraich arm, clisg air gaisgich, cumandairean a cuir an ordugh shaighdearan, gu dol a thobhairt lathd blair do na Turcaich.

and their armour of battle, and they went to the fight
on the side of the people of the Iubhar. The fighting
began and Conall was mowing down the Turks as though
it were a man who was cutting down sow-thistles.
There was one big man amongst the Turks, and he was
mowing down the people of the Iubhar in the same
way. It was not going with any one to slay him, and
they thought that no arms could touch him. He and
Conall met each other in the fight. They tried their
nimble feats upon each other, and Conall slew the big
Turk. When the Turks saw that their champion was
slain they fled ; and the people of the Iubhar followed
the rout,* and they thought that they had not left many
of the Turks alive. In the night the people of Iubhar
returned back, and they thought they would have peace
on the next day ; and no one of them could understand
who he was, the hero that had slain the big Turk, that
had done them so much skaith.†

As on the other days Conall and Duanach went to
the hostelry where they were the former night, they got
food and bed, and they thought, by the number of
Turks that had been killed, that the war was at an end,
and they went to sleep.

The King of the Iubhar had never seen Conall
before ; but it seemed to him, by the look of his face,‡
that he was of the people of Eirinn. They went to
rest that night full of joy, thinking that the Turks
would not bring any more trouble upon them. But
no matter. What they got in the morning was, the
tale of horror that the Turks were coming forward as
numerous as they ever were. They had for it but that
they must arise, and put men in their harness, to go
to give a day of battle to the Turks again ; and

* An ruaig. † Dolaidh.
‡ Fiamh a gnuis might mean terror of his countenance.

Conall's morning waking was to hear the shout of the
chiefs calling out their soldiers to give a day of combat to the Turks.*

Conall sprang out of his bed and he put on his
array and armour,† and he went with the host of the
Iubhar to battle against the Turks. When the two
hosts met each other, Conall saw the big Turk that he
had slain the day before coming forward that day
again, and mowing down the people of the Iubhar as
he used to do.

Conall was mowing down the Turks till he and the
big Turk met each other, and tried their agile valour
upon each other that day again ; and the big Turk was
killed again that day by Conall. When the Turks saw
that their champion had been slain, they fled, and the
people of Iubhar followed the rout, and killed so many
of the Turks, that it seemed to them there were not
many of them to the fore, and they returned joyfully,
cheerily, thinking that there was an end of the war.
When Conall returned to the hostelry, he ate his supper
and lay down to sleep.

It seemed to the King of Iubhar, that the man
who had done the great feats of valour was his sister's
son Conall, and he went to inquire about him. He
heard that it was in the hostelry that the gallant man
was dwelling, and the king reached the inn.

Duanach knew him, and the king asked Duanach
if his master were in.

" He is," said Duanach, " but he is in his sleep,
and I will not wake him."

" I am anxious to see him," said the king.

" If thou choosest thyself to go to wake him,"

---

* Eigh nan ceannairdean, a gairm a mach na'n saighdearn, gus
latha comhra g a thoirt do na Turcaich.

† Eididh a' s armachd.

said Duanach, "thou mayest, but I will not wake him."

"What is thy country ?" said the king.

"It is," said Duanach, "the country from which my master came."

"What is the country * whence came thy master ?"

"That," said Duanach, "is the realm whence came the King of Eirinn."

"What is his name ?" said the king.

"It is," said Duanach, "Conall Guilbeanach Mac do Righ Eirinn."

"Tell Conall, when he wakes, that his mother's brother came to visit him, and that he wishes to see him at the house of the King of Iubhar tomorrow."

"I will do that," said Duanach. †

On the next day the Turks were coming on to drive the battle as they used, against the host of Iubhar ; and it was rustling of plumes, and shouting of hosts,‡ that awoke Conall. Then there were chiefs setting soldiers in order to go to hold battle against the Turks. Conall arose and put on his armour, and as soon as he could, and he went with the people of

* Co i an duthaich. Who she the country ?

† This is a good instance of the strange jumble of ideas which are found in popular tales. Here is Conall, the hero of romance, lodging at an inn, supping and going to bed like a Highland drover, while the king walks down in the evening, and calls and leaves a message with a gille, to invite the warrior to the palace, exactly as a hospitable Highland farmer often does when he hears of a stranger at the country inn, and asks him to his house. According to MacNair, this was the King of Eirinn, but as he was a prisoner or slain according to the others, I have substituted the uncle for the father.

‡ Is b'e fuaim dhos, is eidhich sluaigh.

T

Iubhar to the battle. Conall saw the big Turk coming opposite to him the third time ; they met, and Conall killed the big Turk the third time, and the rout went over the Turks. The people of Iubhar followed them, and they slew the Turks with a great battle ;* and when no more of the Turks were to be seen, the host of Iubhar returned.

It seemed to Conall that there was something that was to be understood going on in the field of battle in the night ; and he ordered Duanach to go to the hostelry to take his sleep, and that he himself would stay to watch the slain.† Duanach went a little way from Conall, and he stayed to watch Conall.

When the night grew dark there came a great Turkish Carlin, and she had a white glaive of light with which she could see seven miles behind her and seven miles before her ; and she had a flask of balsam ‡ carrying it.

And when she would reach a corpse, she would put three drops of the balsam in his mouth ; she would strike three slaps on their hurdies, and she would say, " Get up, and go home ; thy kail will be cold,"§ and they would rise and go.

She was going from one to one, and bringing them alive, and they would be ready to come to fight again on the next day. At last she came where Conall was himself ; she put three drops of balsam into his mouth, and hit him three slaps, and she said, " Get up, and go home, thy kail will be cold."

Conall sprang up suddenly, and she knew that he was not of the dead Turks, by his sudden rising, and she fled. Conal stretched out after her ; she threw away the flask of balsam that she had, and the white

* H-ar.   † Na āh-raice.   ‡ Buideal lan iocshlaint.
§ Eirich 's rach dachaidh bithidh do chal fuar.

glaive of light, but Conall ran till he was up with her ;
he gave a stroke of his sword, and he made two halves
of her. He turned back, and he found the white
glaive of light, but he could not find the flask of balsam. He was seeking it back and forwards, and
hither and thither, and at last he saw Duanach, and
he shouted.

"Is that thou ?" Duanach.

"It is I," said Duanach ; "and it is well for thee
that I am here."

"Hast thou got the flask of balsam ?" said
Conall.

"I have," said Duanach.

Duanach took the flask of balsam where Conall was,
and Conall gave the white glaive of light to Duanach
to lead the Turks who had been brought alive out of
the field, and Conall went to sleep since he could do
no more good till he should sleep ; and he put the flask
of balsam under his head, and he slept. Duanach
went away with the sword, and he led the Turks out
of the field ; he led them through mosses and bogs,
and when he found that they were in a dangerous
place he would put the sword out of sight, and the
Turks could not see, and they would fall into holes,
and they would go down into marshes (criathraichean),
and into well-eyes (suiltean cruthaich), and they would
be drowned. And again, he would bring the sword
in sight, and the sword would shine, and the Turks
that had not been drowned would follow, and Duanach
would lead them through places where there were many
scaurs, and Duanach would put a covering on the
white glaive of light, and darkness would come, and
many of the Turks would fall amongst the scaurs ; and
when they were out of that peril Duanach would bring
the white glaive of light into sight to let them see, and

he would lead them amongst crags ; and he would hide the sword, and the Turks would lose their way, and they would go over the crags. It was thus that Duanach followed on till he had put an end to all the Turks by leading them over crags, and through scaurs, and amongst bogs. Then Duanach turned back to where Conall was, and he staid near him till he had got his sleep over. When Conall awoke, Duanach told him how he had done with the Turks, and Conall was pleased that the war was over.*]

MacNair.

Then Conall brought the people that were slain to life with the balsam. He went about the field, and he found one of his brothers there levelled, and he said to Garna Sgiathlais, "Come thou and take this one with thee, and take care of him till I come back." He looked, and he searched about, and he found another of his brothers, and he put him on the back of the King of Lochlann, and he asked him to take him with him.†] He went in where his father was, and the Great Turk came out on his hands and knees.] He found his father and the King of Laidheann bound. He loosed his father and the King of Laidheann, and he seized nobles as honourable as there were within, and he bound them instead of his father and the King of Laidheann.

MacNeill.
MacPhie.

Then he asked what death the Great Turk was threatening for his father and the King of Laidheann. They said that he was threatening to hang them to an oaken beam that was within, and to thrust two iron darts through the bodies of each one of them. "The

* Here there is a hole in MacNair's version. No use is made of the balsam. It is evident that it ought to be used, and so I follow MacNeill and the Colonsay version.

† These were the Amhas Ormanach, and the slender black man, King of Spain, according to MacNeill.

very death with which he threatened you I will give to him," said Conall.

He seized the Great Turk and he hanged him, and he thrust the darts through his body, and he did the very same to another great noble.*] MacNeill.

The King of Eirinn was right well pleased, and that day they had peace. The King of Eirinn took Conall before the King of the Iubhar. The King made great rejoicings at seeing Conall, and because Conall had given peace to the realm of the Iubhar. No less would suffice the brother of Conall's mother than that Conall should be crowned King of the realm of Iubhar. The nobles of the realm (flathan na Rioghachd) were gathered, a great feast was made, and Conall was crowned King over the Iubhair; but though he was he did not stay in that realm. He was in haste to see Breast of Light.] He took his MacNair. father with him and the King of Laidheann and they sailed to the island (na h otolia). They took Breast of Light on board out of that realm and they put the young King of Lochlann on shore in a fitting place for going to Greece, and Garna Sgiathlais on shore in France.] They sailed to Eirinn,] and they sent a gille MacNair. on foot, and a gille upon the top of a horse, and MacNeill. another gille swifter than that, to tell the Queen of Eirinn that the king was coming home, and that Conall was married, and that he and his wife were coming home with the king. When the message came to the Queen of Eirinn, that was the joyful tale for her. She made a great preparation that she might have a feast ready for them, and a cheery company gathered to give them a royal welcome, and when the King of Eirinn, Conall, and Breast of Light came home, there were there to welcome them, Duncan MacBrian, Murdoch

* MacPhie's version agrees.

MacBrian, Frenzy, and Whitebelly, red men from
Mull, boatmen from Lorn, the brave blinding band of
the King of Eirinn, and the great gentles of the realm,
together as many as there were of them at the time.*

They had a hearty feast, with joy and solace ; they
raised music, and laid down lament, and each one was
content, they never saw such rejoicing before ; and
when the people thought the time fitting to go home,
each one went to his own place, and there was peace
and quiet in Eirinn.

Conall and Breast of Light thought that they
would go to the realm of Laidheann to see her father.
They made ready a ship, they went on board, and they
sailed ; they reached the realm of Laidheann, and the
king had no hope or expectation of them at the time,
but he saluted them, and made them welcome.]   Each
thing was set in order to make Conall and Breast of
Light happy and merry.†

MacNair.

And Conall and Breast of Light stayed in the realm
of Laidheann till they had their first son, and they were
happy and pleased together, but that she had had a cut
slicing tongue at odd times, as happed to many of the
women, and sure am I that Duanach Achaidh Draodh
stuck to Conall, and that his counsel was ever truly

* Donacha MacBhrian, Muracha MacBhrian Taoig a's Tarra-
gheal fir dherag o mhuile fir chronaig ea Latharna Buidheann
chròdhalanda a righ Eirinn. Agus mor maithean na rioghachd
gu leir mhead a's a bha leis diubh san am.

I am not sure of the whole of this translation; the spelling of
the scribes being somewhat independent of rules, these quaint old
passages are not easily rendered. Cronnag, means a kind of
basket. Crannag has the meaning of a boat, and this may mean
the corracle men of Lorne. Their passage from Eirinn was early
enough to have been made in such vessels, and the name may
have stuck to them.

† Gu sonadh aiteasach.

wise and truly moderate.]   And again, their son was MacNeill.
crowned Emperor of Eirinn, and King over the realm
of Laidheann, and over the realm of Iubhar, and he
had the realm of Lochlann, the realm of Sorcha, the
realm of Greece, France, and Hispania, under cess, and
so be they left.]   MacNair.

According to MacPhie and others, Conall was the king's
son, by a girl, who was daughter of a mysterious old man, and he
was a comrade of the Finne, and lived underground; he is a
magician always.   Conall, at the end, puts a ring on the Queen's
finger, it tightens, and forces her to confess that her sons are not
the king's children, and Conall reigns as the king's only son.
This incident ends several long Gaelic stories of the same stamp
as this long-winded history of Conall Gulban, which has the
name of being the best of its kind.

JUNE 1861.—MacNair tells me that his authority,
Livingston, was an old tailor, not the shoemaker mentioned by Dewar ; and he adds, that several passages
in which his story seems to vary from MacNeill's, are
mistakes made by the scribe.

There were three champions on board when they
sailed from Lochlann, and two sailed to the realm of
the Turk, so that all my authorities agree.

The Gaelic passage, page 278, is one of those which often give a
clue to other stories and traditions; which are clearly old, easily
remembered, and hard to explain.   Wishing to get all I could out of
it, I asked several men to translate the passage and the names, and
to give any reasons for the epithets.   The variety in these translations will perhaps be the best excuse which I can give for my own
shortcomings, so I give a few examples.

First, Scribe who wrote down *what he heard* according to my
special request :—" Duncan MacBrian and Murdoch MacBrian,
Passionate, and White Belly ; Dearg's men from Mull, and Fortress
men from Lorn; the King of Eirinn's valiant band, and the great
chieftains of the realm, altogether all that were with him at the time
(at the wars)."

This gives the sound " derag " as the proper name " Dearg,"

which "translators" made "Dergo," and which means Red; and it localizes an Ossianic hero in Mull. It gives "chrònaig" (genitive of cronag), the value of "fortress," and suggests the wattled forts found in lakes and mosses, which are, I believe, called cranogues by the learned in such matters. This·is the simple country translation of an intelligent man, and it throws light upon the traditions and antiquities of his country.

Second, from a gentleman who for a quarter of a century has been occupied about Gaelic books and translations; a native Highlander, who is an authority in Gaelic writings, and lives in a city, but who had nothing to guide him but the words before him:—" Duncan, son of Brian; Murdoch, son of Brian; Thadeus and Whitebelly, ruddy men from Mull, swarthy men from Lorn, a valiant band from the King of Ireland, and all the nobles of the kingdom, as many as were with (or adhered to) him at the time."

The same authority informs me that there is a place in Lorn called Cill a chronaig, and another in Mull called Derbhaig.

This simply translates the Gaelic names into their modern English equivalents; Taoig into Thadeus, Murcha into Murdoch, Donacha into Duncan, and so on. It gives the passage reasonably, and as it were historically or geographically; and it differs from the others in the meaning of "chronaig," which it renders "swarthy," from cron, brown; and this is the usual method of translating doubtful Gaelic into English:—freely. I also,had translated the passage freely. I was uncertain of the meaning of "Taoig," but as it is the genitive of Taog, a fit of passion, I gave it that meaning rather than assume that it meant Teague, Thaddy, or Thadeus; names which had some meaning once. It is established that a sound like Donacha shall mean Duncan; and Muracha Murdoch, so I too followed the stream; but I should have done better to translate the names, for every Gaelic proper name has a meaning, which may be dimly seen in Gaelic, but is utterly lost in its English equivalent. The passage fully translated, as I understand it by the help of my peasant authorities and Armstrong's dictionary, would run thus—"Donacha," * Brown of battle; "Mac," son of the judge (or ruler, or king; the man of words of authority. "Brian,"† Breean, Brethon, Bren). "Muracha,"‡ wall of battle; "Mac," son of Brian the ruler; Fury and Whitebelly; the men of the Red, from "Muile," the bluff; Wattle-

---

* Donn-a-chath. † Brian. ‡ Mur-a-chath.
The first might also mean Brownfield. The second might be Murrach-a-chath, able of battle; or Murcach, murky, gloomy. The third means "a word, a composition, a warrant, an author; and it is

fort, or boat-men from the grounds or settlements (from lar, a floor, the ground, etc. ; or lathar, an assembly, from Larne, a loch in Ireland ; or Latharna, a district of Argyll, now Englished "Lorne "). The camp-winnowing, or blind-valiant, or brave-blinding (chrò or chrodha-dhallan-da, from crò, a circle or fold, or enclosure, or cattle. Or from crodha, active, valiant, etc. ; and dallan, a blind man, also a large fan for winnowing ; from DALL, because of the blinding dust) band of the king of the western island or islands (of which Ireland is one, and Great Britain another), and the great good ones of the kingdom altogether, as much as were with him in the time.

Dewar understands " gabhail iolla " to mean, " taking notice of without joining in what was going on." The first word is the only one used for singing or reciting a tune, a song or story ; and it has the meaning of taking, and many other meanings besides. The second is not in dictionaries, and I did not know it ; but iuladh and ioladh have nearly the same sound as iolla, and mean fun, sport ; Iolach is a shout, mirth ; Iùlach, guiding, directing ; and from the context I believe the words to mean sometimes, that the lookers on were enjoying the fight, " taking sport ;" and at others, that they were shouting or singing to the combatants. Singing " iolla," a loud-directing or guiding song, such as the words of Duanach to Conall. If I am right, this is a new Gaelic word ; if I am wrong I cannot help it, but this will, I hope, excuse mistakes in my translations, for it shews that authorities may differ, and that dictionaries are bad guides. It will also shew the object which I had in view in generally translating as closely as I could, in utter disregard of English composition, rather than freely and according to precedent.

· Dewar translates "Dos, a sounding horn ;" and for "feet following," he gives " rapid pursuit, toir chas." He says, " There is an Irish poem about Conall Ghulbain coming to war against the Fiands ; he killed many of them, at last Oscar fought him, and it was doubtful for a long time which of them would have victory ; at last Oscar struck Connal's head off and threw it off the battle-field. Music was got to cheer Oscar from his weariness, but the music that was best with Fionn was what happened. It is evident that this tale was composed a long time after the Fiand's time." Dewar does not himself understand Irish of some kinds, for I tested him with an Irish blind fiddler whose dialect I could only partially understand myself. I know nothing more about this poem ; unless it be " Conull Ghulbuinn," published by MacCallum, 1816, which is Gaelic taken down in Scotland (162 lines). In this, " Conull " is slain by " Oscar."

---

close to Breith, a judge, to judge ; and to the word Brethon, which is applied to a code of Irish laws, and suggests Bren, holy, and our old school acquaintance Brennus.

LXXVII.

JOHN, SON OF THE KING OF BERGEN.

From Angus Mackinnon (tailor), South Uist.

1—COMHRAG.

" 'Tis the track of the youth beside the ford,
And the great impetuous stride.

2

" 'Tis not the daughter of Locha Luin,
And 'tis not Diarmaid of the clear eye.

3

" It is not one of the band of Fionn
That wended last night in the heavy glen.

4

" I gathered my garments, and wended forth ;
The gathering was hard throughout the moss.

5

" I was rushing and bounding,
And the big man hard striding.

6

" Then at the time I caught him,
And the precious woman between two scaurs.

7

" I asked so quietly of him,
Great man, whence comest thou thus ?"

8—SEATHAN.

" But little one, there, little man,
Though thou asked, it was not wise.

SEATHAN MAC RIGH BEIRBH.

1

'S lorg an oga seach an t-ath ;
'S an ceum rodh a tha ro dhian ;

2

Cha 'n i nighean Locha Luin ;
'S cha 'n e Diarmaid an ruisg ghlain ;

3

Cha 'n e h-aon a chuideachd·Fhinn ;
A dh' imich an raoir 'san troma ghleann.

4

Thruis mi m' aodach 's thar mi as ;
Feadh na mointich bu gharbh truis.

5

Bha mise nam' ruith 's nam' leum,
'S am fear mor 's e 'na chruaidh cheum.

6

An sin an uair a rug mi air,
'S a' bhean leig eadar da sgoir.

7

Gu 'n d' fhiosraich mi dheth gu foil,
" Fhir mhoir ciod as mar seo ?"

8

" Ach fhir bhig sin—ach fhir bhig,
Gad a dh' fharraid cha bu ghlic.

9.

" Thou hadst need bring the whole of the Een
To find out the race of a single man."

10—COMHRAG.

" If I should bring the whole of the Een,
A whole bone would n't be thy body within.

11.

" That which they would not crush with their hands,
Sure with their breath they would consume.

12.

" That was the time, when his weapon he cast,
The mighty spear that was in his grasp.

13.

" That he cast it beyond me, behind,
Seventeen feet into the ground."

14—SEATHAN.

" Thy trimmed shaft has touched my heart,
And the leech will not make my healing.

15.

" Farewell, and arise to thy house,
Yellow-haired youth of the curling locks."

16—COMHRAG.

" For thee, it is all the worse,
That thou didst not declare thy race.

17.

" That the head huntsman of Fionn
Gave thee battle in the heavy glen."

18—SEATHAN.

" I am John, son of Bergen's king,
Son of the fierce one of the sturdy tread."

9

" Cha b' uilear dhuit an Fhinn uile
'Thoirt gu sloinneadh an aon duine."

10

" An Fhinn uile na 'n d' thugainn ann
An cnaimh slan cha bhiodh a'd' cholainn ;

11

" A' chuid nach pronnadh iad le 'n lamhan,
'S dearbh gu 'n loisgeadh iad le 'n anail."

12

An sin an uair a thilg e arm,
An t-sleagh mhor a bha 'na dhorn.

13

Gu 'n d' chuir e i tharum siar
Seachd troidhe diag anns an talamh.

14

" Bhoin do chrann gleusta do m' chrì,
'S cha dean an lighich mo leigheas."

15

" Beannachd dhuit 's eirich gu teach,
Oganaich bhuidhe 'chuil chlannaich.

16

" Gur h-ann duitse 's measa sin,
Nach d' rinn thu do shloinneadh a dheanadh.

17

" Gu 'n d' thug gille cinn Choin Fhinn
Comhrag diots' anns an troma ghleann."

18

" Mise Seathan, Mac Righ Beirbh,
Mac an fhir ghairg bu mhor trosd.

19—COMHRAG.

" My name shall be, on coming home,
Combat of five hundred hounds."

I have not found this fragment anywhere else.
This seems to describe a raid made by the son of the
King of Bergen, who carried off a woman, and was
tracked and overtaken, and slain in a rift, by Comhrag
of the five hundred hounds, Fionn's head huntsman.
I am responsible for the division into stanzas of two
lines. Siar generally means west; here it means behind,
probably, for the same reason, that south and to the
right are synonymous. A man facing the rising sun
has his back to the west, and his right hand to the
south (deas). The left hand (lamh thosgail), to the
north, and the sun (air a Bheultaobh), on his mouth side,
on Baal's side. This may be fancy, but unless some
explanation is found, it does not appear how a man
can have a north and south hand, and a western back.

J. F. C.

From Angus MacKinnon, tailor, Dallabrog, South
Uist, who is a little dark-haired man, with quick-
moving grey eyes, and lively, kindly manner. He
wears neither shoes, nor stockings, nor bonnet, and
seemingly never has. He sings these pieces with considerable pathos, and has a tolerably good voice. He
appears to me to be about seventy years of age.

Beirbhe. Dictionaries translate Beirbhe, Copenhagen, but it
is more probably the Gaelic form of Bergen, which was formerly
the capital of Norway, which is part of the Gaelic Lochlann, as
well as Denmark. How Bergen may have passed into the Gaelic
Beirbhe, may be illustrated by the frequency with which bh passes
into g, or gh, and vice versa; thus, ubh or ugh, an egg; dubh,
or dugh, black, etc., *oov-oog, doo.*   H. M'L.

September 16, 1860.

19

"Gur h-e b' aimn dhomh tighinn gu teach
Comhrag nan coig ceudan con.

HOUNDS AND HUNTSMEN, ORNAMENTS AND CHARACTERISTIC SYMBOL.—
Copied from the "*Sculptured Stones of Scotland.*" At Kirriemuir, Pl. xliii.
and xlv.; near Dupplin, Pl. lviii.; Standing Stone of Sauchope, Crail,
Pl. lix.; Fowlis Wester, near Crieff, Pl. lx.; Crail, Pl. lxiv.; Largs,
Pl. lxvi.; Meigle, Pl. lxxii.; near Aberlemno, Pl. lxxx.

LXXVIII.

THE MASTER AND HIS MAN.

From John Dewar.

THERE were at some time ere now bad times, and there were many servants seeking places, and there were not many places for them.

There was a farmer there, and he would not take any servant but one who would stay with him till the end of seven years, and who would not ask for wages, but what he could catch in his mouth of the seed corn, when he should be thrashing corn in the barn.

None were taking (service) with him. At last he said that he would let them plant their seed in the best ground that he might have, and they should get his own horses and plough to make the thraive, and his own horses to harrow it.

There was a young lad there, and he said, " I will take wages with thee," and the farmer set wages on that lad, and the bargain that they made was that the wages which the lad was to have were to be as many grains of seed as he could catch in his mouth when they were beating sheaves in the barn, and he was to get (leave) to plant that seed in the best land that the farmer had, and he was to keep as much as grew on that seed, and to put with it what seed soever he might catch in his mouth when he was thrashing the corn, and to plant that in the best land which the farmer had on the next year. He was to have horses, and plough, or. any other " gairios "* he might want for planting or

* Apparatus ; also spelt goireas and gairaois.

reaping from his master, and so on to the end of the seven years. That he should have seven winters in the barn thrashing, seven springs to plant, seven summers of growth for the crop, and seven autumns of reaping, and whatsoever were the outcoming that might be in the lad's seed, that was the wage that he was to have when he should go away.

The lad went home to his master, and always when he was thrashing in the barn his master was thrashing with him, and he caught but three grains of seed in his mouth on that winter; and he kept these carefully till the spring came, and he planted them in the best land the carle had.

There grew out of these three ears, and there were on each ear threescore good grains of seed.

The lad kept these carefully, and what grains soever he caught he put them together with them.

He planted these again in the spring, and in the autumn again he had as good as he had the year before that.

The lad put his seed bye carefully, and anything he caught in his mouth when he was thrashing in the next winter he put it with the other lot; and so with the lad from year to year, till at last, to make a long story short, the lad planted on the last year every (bit of) ploughing land that the carle had, and he had more seed to set, and the carle was almost harried. He had to pay rent to the farmer who was nearest to him, for land in which the lad might set the excess of seed which he had, and to sell part of his cattle for want of ground on which they might browse, and he would not make a bargain in the same way with a servant for ever after.

U

This story only wants a moral to be a regular fable, and the meaning is so clear that to express it by a moral would be waste of words. Scotchmen, all over the world, are noted for frugality, and here is the lesson taught by a Celtic peasant to his son. I suspect there has been a numerical puzzle upon the numbers 3, 7, and 20, which is lost. Words relating to agriculture are interesting, and this gives a number of them. I subjoin an attempt at phonetic spelling.

Siol, *sheel;* seed, the young of fish, oats, etc. etc.

Crann, *krʌn;* a tree, a plough, a mast, etc. etc.

Cliathadh, *Kleeʌug;* harrowing, from cliath, basket work of any kind, a bush harrow, from which it follows that ploughs and harrows were made of wood.

Treabh, *Treo;* to till, plough, probably from troimh, through, a thraive, a furrow. Sanscrit root, TRA, an instrument of any kind, a plough.

Biceannan, Beeganan; grains, beag, small, diminutive, Bigan.

Bualadh, Booʌlug; thrashing, beating, striking, hitting.

Sabhal, *Sʌvul* or *Sʌ-ul;* a barn.

Arbhar, *Arʌr;* corn as reaped, standing corn. Sanscrit root, Ar, to plough, to cut open; to plough the sea. Gaelic, Eithir, a boat.

Ire, *Eere;* land, also produce. Sanscrit, Ira, earth.

Earrach, *Yarach;* spring, earing time.

Cur, *Coor;* to plant, to put, to set.

Cinneas, *Keenyas;* growth, also kin.

Bar, *Bʌr;* top, point, crop.

Buain, *Booain;* to gather, pluck, reap.

Toradh, *Tawrug;* increase, probably from tor, a heap, a heaping.

Màl, *Mʌl;* mail, rent.

Tuathannach, *Tooʌnʌch;* a farmer.

AM MAIGHISTIR AGUS AN GILLE.

Bha uaireiginn roimh so 'droch thimannan ann agus bha mòran de sheirbhisich ag iarraidh aiteachann, agus cha robh meran de aite- achann ann d' aibh. Bha tuathannach an sin, agus cha gabhadh e gille sam bith, ach gille a dh' fhuireadh leis gu ceaun seachd bliadhna, agus nach iarradh de thuarasdal ach na ghlacadh e na bheul de'n t-sìol, tra bhiodh e a bualadh an arbhair anns an t- sabhal.

Cha robh gin a gabhail aige. Ma dheireadh thubhairt e, gu'n leigeadh e leo an sìol a chur anns an ìre a b fhearr a bhiodh aige, agus gum faigheadh iad na h-eich, s an crann aige fein a dhean- amh an treabh, agus na h-eich aige fein thun a chliathadh.

Bha gille òg an sin, agus thubhairt e, " Gabhaidh mise tuarasdal agad "   S chuir an tuathanach tuarasdal air a ghille sin.   Agus se am bargan a rinn iad, gu'm b'e an tuarasdal bha gu bhith aig a ghille, na ghlacadh e de bhiceannan sìol na bheul, tra bhitheadh e a bualadh an arbhair, anos an t-sabhal.   Agus bha e gus faotuinn an siol sin, a chur anns an ìre a b' fhearr a bh' aig an tuathanach, agus bha e gus na chinneadh air an t-siol sin a ghleidh, agus ciod ar-bhith an sìol a ghlacadh e na bheul, tra bhitheadh e a bualadh an arbhair, a chuir comhla ris, agus sin a chur anns an ìre a b' fhearra bh' aig an tuathanach an ath bhliadhna.   Bha e gu eich 's crann, na gairaois air bith eile a bhiodh feumail d'a air son cur na buain, fhaotninn o mhaighistir ; agus mar sin gu ceann nan seachd bliadh- na.   Gu 'm bitheadh aige, seachd geamhraidhean san t-sabhal a bualadh, seachd earraich gu cur, seachd samhraidhean cinneas do'n bharr, agus seachd fogharadh'n buain, agus ciod air bhith an tighinn a mach a bhiodh an siol a ghille 's na seachd bliadhna, b'e sin an duais a bha gu bhith aige tra dh' fhalbhadh e.

Chaidh an gille dachaidh thun a mhaighistir agus daonnan tra bhiodh e a bualadh anns an t-shabhal, bhitheadh a mhaighistir a bhualadh leis.   Agus cha do bheir e na bheul, ach air trì bìgeannan sìl, rè a gheamhraidh sin.   Agus ghleidh e iad sin gu cùramach, gus gu'n d' thainig an t-earrach, agus chuir e iad anns an ìre b' fhearr a bh' aig a bhodach.

Chinn asda sin trì diasan, agus bha air gach dias, trì-fichead bigeannan matha sìl.

Ghleidh an gille iad sin gu cùramach, agus ciod air bhith bigeannan sìl air an do bheir e, chuir e còmhla riu iad.

Chuir e iad sin a rithis aig an earrach. Agus aigh an fhogharadh a rithis'd bha toradh aige, cho math is a bh' aige a bhliadhna roimh sin.

Chuir an gille seachad a shiol gu cùramach, agus ciod air bhith a ghlac e na bheul, tra bha e a' bualadh san ath gheamhradh, chuir e leis a chuid eile a.

Agus mas sin do'n ghille, o bhliadhna gu bliadhna gus ma dheireadh, a dheanamh sgeul fada goirid ga'n do chuir an' gille, air a bhliadhna ma dheireadh na h-uile ìre threabhaidh a bh' aig a bhodach. Agus bha corr sìl aige ri chuir agus cha bu mhòr nach robh am bodach air a chreachadh. B' fheudar d'a màl a phaidh do'n tuathanach b' fhaigse dha, air son ìre sa 'n cuireadh an gille an corr sìl a bh' aige, agus pairt de 'n spreidh aig a chreic, a chion gruinnde air an ionaltraidh iad; agus cha deanadh e baraga air a cheart doigh ri gille gu bràth tuille.

From my father more than forty years ago.—JOHN DEWAR.

LXXIX.

THE PRAISE OF GOLL.

From Donald MacPhie, Breubhaig, Barra.

There came a stranger the way of the Finne, and
he asked what sort of man Goll was, and Fionn said—

1 High mind of Goll, Fionn's man of war,

2 Broad, burly* hero, dauntless and hardy ;

3 Fair generous hero, of sweetest speech.

4 His mildness mild, harmless his grace.

5 Of brightest mood,† teacher of schools.

6 King-like is Goll, hide it not Fionn.

7 Might of the waves, by valour bright.‡

8 Lion like hind, valiant in deed.

9 Powerful his hand, choice of the kings.

10 Man friendly kind, forsakes not his friend.

11 In strife of kings, not slack his hand.

12 Crushing his shout, hound-like‖ his might.

13 Youthful and soft, warlike and great.

MOLADH GHUILL.

Thainig coigreach an rathad na Finne a dh' fheoraich de 'n saeorsa duine a bha ann an Goll 's thuirt Fionn.

1530	1787	1860	
MS.	Gillies.	Oral.	
71 lines	18 lines	13 lines	
1	1	1	Ard aigne Ghuill fear cogaidh Fhinn ;
2	2	2	Laoch leothar, lonn,* fulangach nach tim ;
9	3	3	Laoch fionn, fial, a 's misle gloir ;
	5	4	A-mhìne mìn; sgèimh gun chron.
12	6	5	'S c 's glaine gean,† oide na sgoil.
26	7	6	Amhuil righ a's Goll na ceil ort Fhinn ;
27	8	7	Treise nan tonn ; air ghaisge grinn.‡
36	9	8	Leomham mar agh ; crodha 'na ghniomh ;
37	10	9	Neartar a lamh ; rogha nan righ.
55½	15	10	Fear daimheil, caomh, nach treig a dhaimh ;
56	11	11	An cogadh righ nach lag a lamh.

* Lonn, strong.

† Perhaps GEIN, a sword, of brightest sword, or of purest kin.

‡ Grinn, means excellent and beautiful, and is the superlative of praise, applicable to anything.

| 30 | 17 | 12 | Pronntach a ghair ; conach *·a threoir ; |
| 31 | 18 | 13 | Fiuranta min ; mileanta mor. |

From Donald MacPhie, Breubhaig, Barra, who says he learnt it from his uncle, Hector MacLaine, Breubhaig, Barra.   October 1, 1860.—H. M'L.

This is a traditional fragment of the poem given at page 29 of the selections from the Dean of Lismore's, MSS. 1530.   Of the thirteen lines here given, nine are almost identical with the Gaelic, as given by Mr. MacLauchlan.   There are seventy-one lines in the oldest version.   The corresponding numbers are here placed opposite to the lines for reference.   Another version is printed in Gillies' collection, 1784.   Page 34, there are eighteen lines, of which thirteen appear here slightly modified, and in a different order.   There are considerable variations in several of the lines, for example, damhail, friendly, is deud-gheal, white-toothed. A fourth version, eighteen lines, was published by MacCallum, 1816, and has five lines which I have not.

LXXX.

OSGAR, THE SON OF OISEIN.

WHEN Osgar was a boy he was sent to a school. When they used to get out at the mid-day, they used to go to play shinny on to a strand that was there.   At the time when he was sixteen years of age,

* Conach, canine.   The old stag-hounds were powerful, large active animals, and they are constantly represented on old stones in Scotland.   (See page 287.)

there would be a like number of the lads working on each side, and the side on which Osgar might be, that was the side which would hold.

He became exceedingly big, so that there was no one of his cotemporaries that he was not twice as much as he. At last there used to be two divisions against him, and one division with him. At last there would be no man with him but himself, and the rest altogether against him.

They were there on a day of these days playing shinny, and they saw a boat coming in, and one man in her, and they never saw a man equal to him. The scholars took great fear before the man when they saw him coming, and they gathered about Osgar, every begotten one of them, to make a protector of him, and this wild man that was here came down where they were, and not a bit of him to be seen but the eyes, with blue-green scales of hardening upon him.*

He came towards them, and every one on whom he would strike his palm he would level him on the strand. He struck Osgar and put him in a faint. It was but scarcely that he could rise ; but he thought that it was best for him to lie still ; if he should get up again that he would slay him utterly.

Then he seized on Osgar, and he put him on the end of a withy, and sixteen of the scholars on top of him. He put the withy on his shoulder, and he betook himself to the boat with it. He put in the withy, "and it's I that was under altogether," said Osgar.†

---

* Probably "tempered scale armour;" here a scaly monster. The phrase is not in Gaelic dictionaries, but it occurs pretty often sligneach chruadhach.

† This idea is taken from the common method of carrying fish, viz., on "gad," a withy. A hook is left at the large end of a supple stick, and the small end is run through the gills of

"I am saying to you," said Osgar, "that was as sore a blow as I have had, when he struck my ribs against the boat's floor, and the rest on top of me." Then he rowed the boat away for the length of a time, and he reached an island, and then he caught hold of the withy again, and he put it out. Then he took with him the withy on his shoulder, and I below. He reached a castle, and he went in. He left the withy there, and he went up to the end of the house, and there was a fine woman there. He said to her that he was going to take a nap, and when he should wake that the best hero who was there should be cooked before him."*

"She went where the withy was, and she began to feel them. And I was the biggest there. I caught her by the hand, and said to her to let me be for the present. She went and she took with her the best one she found of the others. She put the roasting stake through him, and she roasted him on the fire. Then he got up, and he asked if she had got him cooked. She said that he was. Then he said, "There was a better boy than this there ; I am going to sleep, and unless thou hast him cooked when I awake, I will have thyself in his place."†

a lot of cuddies or trouts. Consequently, the first has all the others upon him, and he often has a rough time of it, for the boys do not trouble themselves to kill their prizes.

* That is to say, the castle was in the mind of the narrator a building like his own dwelling ; a long room, with the wife at the end of it, beside the fire ; and the fine lady was to cook a warrior as his wife would roast a herring.

† With proper audience and emphasis, with fish broiling on a peat fire, and a string of cuddies in a corner ; with a ruddy light within, and a winter's night outside, this must be a thrilling passage.

She went down then again and said, " I must take thee with me now."

" That is not best for thee, but leave me alive. Art thou his wife ?"

" Not I. It is (so) that he stole me here seven years ago, and I in dread that he will slay me every day. Do thou help me, and I will help thee, and may be that we might put an end to the monster. Put thou the poker in the fire, and when it is red give me notice."

She did this, and when it was red she gave him notice.* Osgar went up then when she loosed him, and he took the poker with him to where he was in his sleep. There was no part of his face bare, with scales of hardness, but his two eyes. He put the poker down through his eye to the ground ; and she caught hold of his sword, and she struck off his head.

They went away then, and they took with them silver and gold enough, and Osgar hit upon the spot where they had left the little boat. He did not know to what side he should turn her prow, but they began to row, and they reached the very spot from which they had gone, on the strand. Then he reached the king of the Finne. They took exceeding good care of the woman that was there.†

The heroes of the Finne went one day to the hunt-

---

* It is curious how often in this and in other cases the narrator identifies himself for a time with his hero. A story so told becomes a kind of dramatic representation, and the more untutored the narrators the more dramatic they are.

† This first adventure is like part of Nos. V. VI. VII. and of a vast number of other stories which I have. It is at least as old as Homer ; but as the Gaelic versions invariably introduce a woman. I do not believe that the stories come from Homer. See notes, Vol. I. 154.

ing-hill, and they parted from each other. They went
to a glen that was there, and they did not know that
they had ever been in the glen before. They hit upon
a kind of burgh there, and a great wild savage of a
giant in the upper end of the house.

"What's the news of the warriors of the Finne?"
said he.

"Well, then, we have the news that we had no
knowledge of ever having been in this place before."

He arose, and he put a cauldron on the fire, and
a stag of a deer in it.

"Sit," said he, "and burn (fuel) beneath that
cauldron, but unless the deer be cooked when I awake,
you shall have but what you can take off his head,
and by all you have ever seen do not take out the
head."

They were tormented by hunger, and they did not
know what they should do. They saw a little shaggy
man coming down from the mountain. "Ye are in
extremity," said he, himself; "why are ye not tasting
what is in the cauldron?"

"We are not," said they; "fear will not let us."

They took the lid out of the end of the cauldron,
when they thought it was boiled, and so it was that
there was frozen ice came upon it.

The old carl got up so wildly, and when he saw
the little shaggy man, he laid the one great grasp upon
him.

The carle went down, and he asked battle or combat
from them. Caoilte rose in front of him, and they
began upon each other. He was about to have got
Caoilte under him now, and the little shaggy man got
up, and he shook himself.

"Take notice that I am here," said he to the giant.
He took to the tuft of (fell upon) the giant, and he kept

back Caoilte. They arose against each other now, and
the little shaggy man slew the giant.

"Go now, and be going home." They went, and
they were going before them, but they were not hitting
upon the proper road. They saw the very finest man
they had ever seen coming to meet them, and he met
them, and he asked what was their wish.

They told him that they were seeking (to get) home
to the Finne.

"It were right for me, Osgar, son of Fionn," said
he, "to tell the way to thee. I am the ugly man
whom ye saw coming through the mountain, and that
slew the giant. He has had me under spells for eight
years there, and I should have been there for ever,
unless thou hadst come to help me to kill him. I am
the son of the King of Greece, and it was a sister of
mine that thou tookest from the other giant in the
island."

They reached the Fhinn, and the son of the King
of Greece and his sister knew each other. He kissed
her, and he himself and she herself went, and Fionn,
and Osgar, to Greece ; and before they came back,
Osgar married her.

The Gaelic is omitted to make room.

This then gives part of the early adventures of
Osgar. If any reliance is to be placed on early Irish
history, he was a real personage ; and if so, this,
stripped of the marvellous element, would seem to
shew that he was carried off by a mail-clad warrior ;
that he escaped, and made his way to Greece. The
reasonable explanation would be that this is part of
the history of a sea rover, who wandered, as the Icelanders did in the ninth century, from Labrador to

Constantinople. The caldron that froze, the more it was boiled, indicates a cold climate. But while there is a reasonable explanation for the story, there is a mythical element which cannot be reasonably explained; and probably the name of Osgar has attracted a lot of floating myths whose origin cannot be discovered.

The following poem relates the death of Osgar, and is more reasonable; it certainly relates to some real event in Irish history. The first volume of the transactions of the Ossianic Society of Dublin (1853) contains an Irish poem on the "Battle of Gabhra," which embodies the main incidents, such as :—War between Cairbre, the red-haired, and the Feen; the death of Cairbre and his son, by the hand of Osgar; the wounding of Osgar by a spear-thrust from the hand of Cairbre; the arrival of Fionn on the field after the battle; the placing of Osgar on a mound; the examination and nature of the wound, which had been foretold; the weeping of Fionn, who never wept but for Osgar and for Brann; the death of Osgar, and the lament for him. There is enough resemblance to shew clearly that the two poems relate to the same events. There are several stanzas which seem to indicate a common origin, but there the resemblance ends. The two poems are wholly distinct, and probably separated from one another by centuries; and yet they must have had a common origin, unless they are independent accounts of a real event. At page 75 is this stanza,—

When we marched from Binn Eadair.

" The bands of the Fians of Alba,
  And the supreme King of Britain,
  Belonging to the order of the Fian of Alba,
  Joined us in that battle."

Beinn Eadair, say the Irish authorities, is the Hill of Howth. It is the haunt of the Feen and of Conal Gulban, according to Gaelic stories, if it be Beinn Eudain or Eidain. In the introduction to the Irish poem, which was taken as it appears from a comparatively modern MS., a fragment is quoted, taken from an *ancient* Irish MS., now preserved in the College Library, and supposed by good authority to have been written prior to A.D. 1150. This contains the incidents of the death of "Oscar" by the hand of "Cairpre," the grandson of "Conn," and the death of Cairpre by the hand of Oscar, "by a mighty spear, on a white horse's back."

It seems, then, that this traditional poem, written from the dictation of a peasant in Barra in 1860, relates to a battle fought prior to 1150, near the Hill of Howth, at which the "Fenians" of Alba were present, and that the battle was called the battle of Gabhra in Ireland. The Scotch Gaelic word used means corpses. The Irish explain Gabhra to mean Garrystown, near Dublin.

At page 25 of the selections from the Lismore MSS., a Scotch poem on the same subject is given. It is attributed to Allan MacRuaraidh, and was written at least three centuries ago. The incidents are much the same, and several lines are common to this traditional version. Another version is quoted as written down in 1856, from the dictation of an old woman in Caithness. It is therefore beyond a doubt that this is one of many poems relating to the same ancient event, some of which are orally preserved and still recited, and others are found in MSS. of various ages.

A poem, almost identical, was printed in 1787, at page 313 of Gillies' collection; another version of 120 lines is given at page 167 of the same book; another version, 247 lines, is at page 154 of MacCallum,

1816. The incidents are the opening of Macpherson's
Temora, and I have heard of several other versions
orally collected. Here, then, are seven Scotch versions
—one orally collected in 1860, one in 1856, one in
1816, two before 1786—Macpherson's versions, of
doubtful authority, 1760, and Dean MacGregor's MS.
version of 1530, besides an Irish book of 1853, and an
Irish fragment of some date before 1100 ; nine Gaelic
poems, all different, yet all telling the same story, and
there are many other versions.

The conclusion which I would draw is, that this was
a Celtic popular ballad, composed to celebrate a real
battle between an Irish usurper named Cairbre, and a
band of warriors who spoke Gaelic, who were headed
by the Osgar (the bounding warrior), who went from
Scotland to Ireland on this occasion, whatever his
native country may have been ; who was the grandson
of Fionn, the chief of the Finne, who on this occasion
came from Scotland after the battle ; and the son of
Oisein, in whose person the poet speaks, and who is
supposed to be addressing " Padruig."   He would
be an illiberal Celt who claimed this for Scotland
or for Ireland alone, and a very prejudiced critic who
could now attribute Témora wholly to Macpherson.
This ballad is later than St. Patrick and earlier than
1530.   The battle was earlier than 1100 ; I will not
attempt to fix the date of either.

LXXXI.

THE LAY OF OSGAR.

From Donald MacPhie, Smith, Breubhaig, Barra; and others.

IT was said at that time that Eirinn was the better chase than Albainn; that there were many great beamed deer in it, rather than in this Albainn. It was this which used to cause the Fhinn to be so often in Eirinn; but true Albanian Gaul (Scotch highlanders) they were.

The red-haired Cairbre came in as king over the fifth part of Eirinn, at the southern end. The Fhinn were now over in Eirinn, and Fionn had dwelling-houses in every place in which it was most usual for them to stay.

The ord Fhiann (hammer of Fionn) was a bell. It was not to be struck but in time of great rejoicing, and in time of hard straits, and it could be heard in the five-fifths of Eirinn.

They had a house on the land of the red-haired Cairbre, and they came on the northern side of Eirinn to hunt.

Padruig was asking Oisean—

"Would their set of arms be on them when they went to hunt?"

Oisean said to him—

"Without our armour and our arms;
We would not go to hunt like that.
There would be arms, and stout headgear,
And in each man's grasp were two great spears."

When the Fhinn went to hunt to the northward, they left Osgar to keep the house, and three hundred of the old warriors with him, for they were heavy for walking. Said Oisean, when he was going to tell the old story to Padruig (a).

LAOIDH OSGAIR.

Bha e air a radh 'san am ud gu 'm b'e Eirinn a b'
fhearr sealg na Albainn ; gu 'n robh moran de dh'
fheidh chabrach mhor innte seach an Albainn seo. 'Se
sin a bhiodh a' toirt do 'n Fhinn gu 'm biodh iad cho
tric an Eirinn ; ach 'se fior Ghaidheil Albannach a bha
annta.

Thainig an Cairbre ruadh a stigh 'na righ air a'
choigeamh cuid de dh' Eirinn air a' cheann deas. Bha
'n Fhinn 'san am seo thall an Eirinn, 's bha tighean
comhnuidh aig Fionn anns a' h-uile h-àite a bu tric
leo a bhith stad ann.

Clag a bha anns an ord Fhiann ta. Cha robh e ri
'bhualadh ach an am toil-inntinn mhoir, 'san am eigin
chruaidh, 's chluinnt' ann an coig choigeamh na h-
Eirionn e.

Bha tigh aca air fearann a' Chairbre ruaidh, 's
thainig iad air an taobh mu thuath de dh' Eirinn a
shealgaireachd.

Bha Padruig a foighneachd de dh' Oisean,

" Am biodh an cuid arm orr' uile nuair a rachadh
iad a shealgaireachd ?"

Thuirt Oisean ris,

" Gun ar n-eideadh, 's gun ar n-airm,
   Cha rachamaid a shealg mar siud ;
   Bhiodh airm, agus ceannabheart chorr,
   'S da shleagh mhor an dorn gach fir."

Nuair a chaidh an Fhinn a shealgaireachd do'n taobh
tuath dh' fhag iad Osgar a' gleidheadh an tighe 's tri
cheud de na seann laoich comhla ris, o bha iad trom
gu coiseachd.

Thuirt Oisean nuair a bha e 'dol a dh' innseadh an
t-seanachais do Phadruig. (a)

1—OISEAN.

" I will not style my strain, ' my Prince,'
How sad is Oisean to-night.
Osgar and the Cairbre stalwart
Ebb away in strife of corses. (¹)

2

" The venomous spear in the hand of Cairbre,
In anger's hour, how baneful was it ;
The raven would utter with fear,
That with it should be slain the Osgar."

3 —RAVEN.

" It is worse," to himself he'd say
That black raven in his craze,
" These five to be washing about a trough,
Than blood of men to be gorging us."

4—OSGAR.

" Why should our own blood choke us ?
What weakness is on our eyelids ?
That we for such small cause should weep."

5—WASHERWOMAN.

" The raven will croak to-morrow early
Upon thy cheek in the field of battle ;
From the socket thine eye shall be forced ;
Out of this thus much will come."

Said one of the old warriors, as he saw the hue of
the blood on the water that she had washing the clothes
of Osgar.

1

" Cha 'n abair mi, mo thriath, ri m' cheol,
Cia b' oil le Oisean e nochd ;
Osgar agus Cairbre calma,
Traghar iad ann an cath cairbhre. (¹)

2

" An t-sleagh nimhe, 's i'n laimh Chairbre,
Gu'n craidhteach i ri uair feirge ;
Theireadh am fitheach ri 'ghiomh,
Gur h-ann leatha 'mharbht' an t-Osgar."

3

" 'S miosa theireadh e ris fhein,—
Am fitheach dubh 'na mhi-cheill ;
A' choigear a' taiseadh mu (b) 'n chlar,
Ach fuil fir a bhith 'gar tacadh.

4

" Com' an tacadh ar fuil fhein,
De ghiamh a th' air ar rasgabh ;
Nuair a chaoineamaid chaol reachdaibh.

5—Bean Nighidh.

" Gairidh am fitheach, moch a maireach,
Air do ghruaidh-sa anns an araich.
Cuireadar do shuil a gluchd ;
As an sin a thig na h-uiread."

Arsa fear de na seann laoich, 's e 'faicinn dath na
fala air an uisge a bh' aice a' nigheadh aodach Osgair.(²)

6

" Surely it is a shroud thou washest,
Red is the look that is upon it,
But until this day had come,
That shroud's spaeing was not evil."

7—OSGAR.

" Thou witch there thy clothes that washest,
Make for us a sure soothsaying ;
By us shall a man of them fall,
Ere that we all go to nothing ?"

8—SHE.

" Five hundred by thee shall die ;
Wounded by thee the king's self ;
Thus much, and a man of law (cut) off,
Off the world all that came (c)."

9—OSGAR.

" Let him not hear thee, Rasg MacRuaidh,
Nor one that belongs to his people ;
Let not the Een hear thee this night,
Lest we be spiritless all."

10—OISEAN.

" Heard ye of the raid of Een,
The time he wended to Eirinn ;
There came the fierce Carbre of spears,
And grasped all Eirinn under sway.

11

" Away went we with eager hurry,
As many Feen as were of us ;
We laid our army and our people
On the northern side of Eirinn.

6

" ' S dearbh gur n-aobh sin tha thu nigheadh,
'S dearg an t-aogasg a tha orra ;
Ach gus an d' thainig an diugh
An aobh sin cha b' olc a h-inneal.

7—Osgar.

" A bhaobh sin, a nigheas t' aodach,
Dean-sa dhuinne faisneachd chinnteach ;
An tuit aon duine dhiu leinn
Ma'n d' theid sinn uile do neo-ni ?

8—Ise.

" Marbhar leatsa coig ceud,
A's gonar leat an righ f hein ;
Mar sin a's fear Lagha dheth(²)
Bhar saoghail uile gu 'n d' thainig.(³)

9—Osgar.

" Na cluinneadh e thu, Rasg MacRuaidh,
Na duine 'bheanas dh' a shluagh ;
Na cluinneadh an Fhinn thu nochd,
Ma 'm bi sinn uile gun mhisneach.(⁴)

10—Oisean.

" An cuala sibhse turas Fhinn
An uair a ghluais e gu h-Eirinn ?
Thainig an Cairbre sleaghach, garg,
A's ghlac e Eirinn fo aon smachd.

11

" Dh' f halbh sinne le dian damhair,—(⁵)
A lion de'n Fhinn 's a bha dhinn ;
Leagalh leinn ar feachd, 's ar sluagh,
Air an taobh mu thuath de dh' Eirinn.

12

" There was sent down by Cairbre
Word for Feene's hardy Osgar,
To go down to the Feen's carousal,
And he would get his cess according.

13

" He rose who never baulked a foeman,
The beauteous Osgar to the king's hearth,
Three hundred stalwart men with him,
To answer his will and need.

14

" We found honour, we found food,
As we ever before had found ;
We were merrily within,
With Cairbre in the house of the king."

15—CAIRBRE.

" Upon the last drinking day,"
Said the Cairbre with a voice so high,
" An exchange of spear-shafts I'd like from thee,
Thou brown Osgar of the Alba."

16—OSGAR.

" What shaft's exchange wouldst thou wish,
Thou red-haired Cairbre of the ports of ships ?
Oft were my spear and myself with thee,
In the day of battle and combat (free)."

17—CAIRBRE.

" I'd need no less than cess and kain
From any warrior your shores within,
And I'd need no less for my life's term,
Than to get as I ask for it every arm."

12

" Chuireadh le Cairbre 'nuas
Fios air Osgar cruaidh na Finne,
A dhol a dh' ionnsuidh fleadh na Finne,
'S gu'm faigheadh e cis a reir sin.

13

" Dh' eirich, o nach d' ob e namhaid,
An t-Osgar aluinn gu Leac Righ ;
Tri cheud fear treun dh' imich leis
A fhreasdal dh' a thoil 's dh' a fheum.

14

" Fhuair sinn onair, fhuair sinn biadh,
Mar a fhuair sinn roimhe riamh ;
Bha sinn gu subhach a steach
Maille ri Cairbre 'san Teamhraidh." (*)

15—Cairbre.

" An latha mu dheireadh dh' an ol"
Thuirt an Cairbre le guth mor.
" Iomlaid croinn sleagh b' aill leam uait
Osgair dhuinn na h-Albann."

16—Osgar.

" Gu de an iomlaid croinn a bhiodh ort,
A Chairbre ruaidh nan long-phort ?
A's tric 'bu leat mi fhein 's mo shleagh
An latha cath agus comhraig."

17—Cairbre.

" Cha b' uilear leamsa cis a's cain
Bhar aon seoid a bhiodh 'nar tir ;
'S cha b' uilear leam ri m' linn a bhos,
Gach seud a dh' iarrainn gu 'm faighinn."

18—Osgar.

"In sooth, there's nor gold, nor precious thing,
That might be asked from us by the king,
Without dishonour or disgrace,
That were not thine, oh Tjeearnai's."

19

"But exchange of shafts without head's exchange,
That were unjust to demand from us ;
The reason thou hast asked it is,
That I am without Een and father."

20—Cairbre.

"Although the Feene and thy father
Were as good as they were ever ;
I'd need no less for my life's term,
Then to get as I ask for it every arm."

21—Osgar.

"Were but the Feene and my father
As well in life as they were ever ;
That thou scarcely shouldest win
Thy dwelling's breadth in Eirinn."

22—Oisean.

"Coldness fell on the warrior's keen,
At hearing the skirmishing ;
There were rough vows bandied there,
Between the Cairbre and the Osgar."

23—Cairbre.

"I will give a lasting vow,"
So would say the red-haired Cairbre,
That he'd plant the seven-edged spear (d)
Between his reins and his navel.

18—Osgar.

"Cha n-'eil or, na earras, gu fior,
A dh' iarradh oirnn an righ,
Gun tair, na tailceas dhuinn e,
Nach bu leatsa 'thighearnais."(')

19

"Ach malairt croinn, gun mhalairt cinn,
B' eucorach sind iarraidh oirnn ;
'S e'm fath mu 'n iarradh tu oirnn e
Mise bhith gun Fhinn, gun athair."

20—Cairbre.

"Gad a bhiodh an Fhinn a's t' athair
Co math 's a bha iad riamh 'nam beatha,
Cha b' uilear leamsa ri m' linn,
Gach seud a dh' iarrainn gu'm faighinn."

21—Osgar.

"Na 'm biodh an Fhinn agus m' athair
Cho math 's a bha iad riamh 'nam beatha,
'S teann air am faigheadh tu sin,—
Leud do thaigh ann an Eirinn."

22—Oisean.

"Lion fuarrachd na laoich loin
Ri claistinn na h-iomarbhaidh :—
Bha briathran garbha, leith mar leith,
Eadar an Cairbre 's an t-Osgar."

23—Cairbre.

"Bheireamsa briathar buan,"
'Se 'theireadh an Cairbre ruadh ;
Gu'n cuireadh e sleagh nan seachd seang (d)
Eadar 'airnean agus 'imleag.

24

"Another vow against that,"
So would say the Osgar valiant,
That he'd plant the nine-edged spear
About the shaping of face and hair.

RECITER.

The Cairbre had a place made in a pillar of rock,
and there would not be a bit of him out but his face.

25

"That lasting vow, then ; that lasting vow,"
So would say the red-haired Cairbre,
That he would bring chase and sorrow
To Albainn upon the morrow.

26

"Another vow against that,"
So would say the Osgar valiant,
That he'd plant the nine-edged spear
About the shaping of face and hair.

27

"That night we were without aid,
Hither and thither about the river ;
There was an isthmus in the midst ; (f)
There was a great isthmus betwixt us.

28

"An olla was heard with a soft voice,
On a sweet-toned harp, bewailing death ;
Up rose Osgar in heavy wrath,
And seized his arms in his mighty grasp.

24

" Briathar eile 'n aghaidh sin,"
'Se 'theireadh an t-Osgar calma ;
Gu'n cuireadh e sleagh nan naoi seang
Mu chumadh fhuilt agus aodainn.

Bha àit aig a' Chairbre, air a dheanadh ann an
carragh creige, 's cha bhiodh mir a mach deth ach an
t-aodenn.

25

" Briathar buan sin,—briathar buan,"
'Se 'theireadh an Cairbre ruadh ;
Gu 'n d' thugadh e sealg agus creach,
Do dh' Albainn an la'r na mhaireach.

26

" Briathar eile 'n aghaidh sin,"
'Se 'theireadh an t-Osgar calma ;
Gu 'n cuireadh e sleagh nan naoi seang,
Mu chumadh fhuilt agus aodainn.

27

" An oidhche sin duinne gun chobhair
Thall agus a bhos mu 'n amhainn ;
Bha doirlinn leith mar leith,—(f)
Bha doirlinn mhor eadaruinn.

28

" Chualas Olla, le guth tim,
Air chlarsaich bhinn a' tuireadh bàis.
Dh' eirich Osgar ann am feirg,—
'S ghlac e 'airm 'na dhornaibh aidh.

29

" Uprose we upon the morrow,
The whole of our people, as many as we were ;
We raised a raid upon Sliabh Goill,
So swiftly, actively, strongly.

30

" When we arrived there within
The pass of combat of the narrow glen ;
Then warmed the Cairbre high,
Brandishing, and coming to meet us.

31

" Fivescore of Gaidheal fierce,
That came to land in time of storm ;
These fell yonder by the hand of Osgar,
'Tis a rousing for the King of Eirinn.

32

" Fivescore of men of bows
That came to Cairbre's succour ;
These fell yonder by the hand of Osgar,
'Tis a rousing for the King of Eirinn.

33

" Seven score of men of war,
That came from the snowy shore ;
These fell yonder by the hand of Osgar,
The shame is for the king of Eirinn.

34

" Seven score men of gray glaives,
That never went backwards a single pace,
There fell yonder, by the hand of Osgar—
The shame is for the King of Eirinn.

29

" Dh' eirich sinn an la'r na mhaireach,—
Ar sluagh uile,—sin na 'bha dhinn,
Thog sinn creach air Sliabh Goill
Gu luath, lasgara, lughar.

30

" Nuair a rainig sinn ann,—
Bealach comhraig nan caol ghleann,
'S ann a bhlath an Cairbre ard,
A' lannaireachd a' tighinn 'nar comhdhail.

31

" Coig ficheud Ghaidheal garg([8])
A thainig do 'n tir an uair gharbh ;—
Thuit siud le laimh Osgair thall,
'Se 'mosgladh gu righ Eirionn.

32

" Coig fichead de dh' fhearaibh bogha
Thainig air Cairbre g' a chobhair ;—
Thuit siud le laimh Osgair thall,
([9])'Se mosgladh gu righ Eiroinn.

33

" Seachd fichead de dh' fhearaibh feachd([10])
A thainig a tir an t-sneachd ;—
Thuit siud le laimh Osgair thall,
Tha 'mhasladh gu righ na h-Eirionn.

34

" Seachd fichead fear claidheamh glas
Nach deach aon troidh riamh air 'n ais,
Thuit siud le laimh Osgair thall ;
Tha 'mhasladh gu righ na h-Eirionn.

35

" Four hundred of mighty men,
That came to us from the Lion's land,
These fell yonder, by the hand of Osgar—
The shame is for the King of Eirinn.

36

" Five score of a royal breed,
Whose birthright was valour and great deeds,
These fell yonder, by the hand of Osgar—
The shame is for the King of Eirinn.

37

" Mangan MacSeirc,([11]) who was a foe
That could combat a hundred gray glaives,
That one fell yonder, by the hand of Osgar—
The shame is for the King of Eirinn.

38

" The five who were nearest the king
Of great valour and deeds,
These fell yonder, by the hand of Osgar—
The shame is for the King of Eirinn.

39

" When the red-haired Cairbre saw
Osgar a-hewing the people,
The envenomed dart in his hand
He let it off to meet him.

40

" Osgar fell on his right knee,
And the deadly spear through his waist ;
He gave another cast thither,
And the King of Eirinn was slain by him.

35

" Ceither cheud de dh' fhearaibh mora,([12])
Thainig airnn o thir nan leomhan ; ([13])
Thuit siud le laimh Osgair thall,
Tha 'mhasladh gu righ na h-Eirionn.

36

" Coig fichead de chlannaibh righ
D' am bu dual gaisge 's mor ghniomh ;
Thuit siud le laimh Osgair thall,
Tha 'mhasladh gu righ na h-Eirionn.

37

" Mungan MacSeirc a bu namh,
A chomhraigeadh ceud claidheamh glas ;
Thuit siud le laimh Osgair thall,
Tha 'mhasladh gu righ na h-Eirionn.

38

" An coigear a b' fhaisge do 'n righ,
Bu mhor gaisge' agus gniomh ;
Thuit siud le laimh Osgair thall,
Tha 'mhasladh gu righ na h-Eirionn.

39

" An uair a chunnaic an Cairbre ruadh,
Osgar a snaidheadh an t-sluaigh ;
A' chraosach nimhe 'bha 'na laimh,
Gu 'n do leig e i 'na chomhdhail.

40

" Thuit Osgar air a ghluin deis,
'S an t-sleagh nimhe roimh a chneas ;
Thug e urchair eile null,
'S mharbhadh leis righ na h-Eirionn.

41—Cairbre.

" Arise Art, and grasp thy glaive,
And stand in the place of thy father ;
And if thou get'st thy due of the world,
I 'll think that thou art a king's son."

42—Oisean.

" He gave another cast aloft,
Its height appeared to us sufficient ;
There fell by him, by his aim's greatness,
Art MacCairbre at the next spear cast."

Reciter.

The Cairbre was dead, and Osgar was upon his
knees, and the spear through him. Cairbre had a
ceap made against the rock, and they put the ceap
(helmet) on the crag, so that Osgar might think he
was alive.

43—Oisean.

" They set about the king his ceap,
Cairbre's people, rough in fight,
That they might reap the fruit of the field,
When they saw that Osgar was wounded.

44

" He lifted a slab from a hard plain,
From off the earth of the ruddy side ;
He broke the pillar on which was the ceap,
The last deed of my worthy son."

45—Osgar.

" Raise me now with you, Eeanna,
Never before have you lifted me ;
Take me now to a clear mound,
That you may strip off me my armour."

41—CAIRBRE.

"Eirich Art a's glac do chlaidheamh,
A's seas ann an àite t' athar ;
'S ma gheibh thu do dhiol saoghail,
Saoilidh mi gur mac righ thu."

42

"Thug e urchair eile 'n airde ;—
Air leinne gu 'm bu leoir a h-airde,
Leagadh leis, aig meud a chuimse,
Art MacChairbre air an ath urchair."

Bha Cairbre marbh, 's bha Osgar air a ghluinean.
'san t-sleagh roimhe. Bha *ceap* aig Cairbre air a
dheanadh ris a' chreig, 's chuir iad an ceap air a chreig,
air dhoigh 's gu 'n saoileadh Osgar gu 'n robh esan
beo.

43

" Chuir a chum an righ mu cheap .
Sluagh Chairbre bu gharbh gleachd,
An los gu 'n buinte leo buaidh larach,
Air faicinn daibh Osgair gu craidhteach."

44

"Thog e leac a comhnard cruaidh,
Bhar na talmhuinne taobh-ruaidh ;
Bhrisd e 'n carragh air an robh 'n ceap,
Gniomh mu dheireadh mo dheagh mhic."

45—OSGAR.

"Togaibh leibh mi nis Fhianna,
Nior thog sibh mi roimhe riamh ;
Thugaibh mi gu tulaich ghlain,
Ach gu 'm buin sibh dhiom an t-aodach."

Y

46—OISEAN.

"There was heard at the northern strand,
Shouts of people and edge of arms ;
Our warriors suddenly started,
Before that Osgar was yet dead."

47—OSGAR.

"Death's shrouds be about thee, thou victory's son,
A second time wilt thou lie to us ;
These are my grandsire's ships,
And they are coming with succour to us."

48—OISEAN.

"We all gave blessing to Fionn ;
What though he saluted not us
Until we reached the hillock of tears,
Where was Osgar of the keen arms."

•   RECITER.

Fionn could heal any wound that might be on any
being in the Een, unless there should be poison in it.

49—FIONN.

"Worse, my son, wert thou for it,
The battle day of Bein Eidinn ;
The sickles might float through thy waist,
It was my hand that made thy healing."

50—OSGAR.

"My healing does not increase,
No more shall it be done for ever ;
The Cairbre planted the seven-edged spear
Between my reins and my navel. (⁴)

46—OISEAN.

" Chualas aig an traigh mu thuath
Eibheach sluaigh a's faobhar arm,
Chlisg ar gaisgich gu luath
Ma 'n robh Osgar fhathasd marbh."

47—OSGAR.

" Marbhphaisg ort a mhic na buadha,
Ni thu breug an darna uair dhuinn ;
Luingeas mo sheanar a th' ann,
'S iad a' teachd le cobhair thugainn."

48—OISEAN.

" Bheannaich sinn uile do dh' Fhionn,
Gad tha cha do bheannaich dhuinn ;
Gus an do rainig sinn tulach nan deur,
Far an robh Osgar nan arm geur."

Leighseadh Fionn creuchd sam bith a bhiodh air
neach san Fhinn, ach gun puinsean a bhith ann.

49—FIONN.

" 'S miosa 'mhic a bhiodh tu dheth,
An latha catha air Beinn Eudainn ;
Shnamhadh na corran roimh d' chneas,
'S i mo lamhsa rinn do leigheas."

50—OSGAR.

" Mo leighas cha n 'eile e 'fas,
'S cha mhò a niotar e gu bràch ;
Chuir an Cairbre sleagh nan seachd seang
Edar m' imleag agus m' airnean.

51

" I planted the nine-edged spear
About the shaping of his face and hair ;
The deep sting in my right side,
The leech has no skill to heal it."

52—FIONN.

" Worse, my son, wert thou for it,
On the battle day of Dun Dealgan ;
The geese might float through thy waist, ([15])
It was my hand that made thy healing." (g)

53—OSGAR.

" My healing does not increase,
No more shall it be done for ever ;
The Cairbre planted the seven-edged spear
Between my reins and my navel.

54

" I planted the nine-edged spear
About the shaping of his face and hair ;
The deep sting in my right side,
The leech has no skill to heal it."

55—OISEAN.

" That was the time that Fionn went
Up to the mound above him ;
The tears streamed down from his eyelids,
And he turned his back to us."

56—FIONN.

" My own calf, thou calf of my calf,
Thou child of my fair tender child,
My heart is bounding like an elk,
Not till the last day, rises Osgar.

51

" Chuir mise sleagh nan naoi seang
Mu chumadh fhuilt-san agus aodainn ;
An gath domhainn am' thaobh deas
Cha dual do'n leigh a leigheas."

52—Fionn.

"'S miosa 'mhic a bhiodh tu dheth,
Latha catha sin Dhun Dealgain ;
Shnamhadh na geoidh roimh d' chneas,
'Si mo lamhsa rinn do leigheas."

53—Osgar.

" Mo leigheas cha n-'eil e 'fas,
'S cha mho a dh' eireas mi gu bràch ;
Chuir an Cairbre sleagh nan seachd seang
Eadar m' imleag agus m' airnean.

54

" Chuir mise sleagh nan naoi seang
Mu chumadh fhuilt-san agus aodainn ;
An gath domhainn a' m' thaobh deas
Cha dual do 'n leigh a leigheas." ([16])

55—Oisean.

" 'Sin an uair a chaidh Fionn,
Air an tulaich as a chionn ;
Shruthadh na deoir sios o 'rasgaibh,
'S thionndaidh e ruinn a chul."

56—Fionn.

" Mo laogh fhein thu—'laoigh mo laoigh,
A leinibh mo leinibh ghil chaoimh
Mo chridhe 'leumraich mar lon ;
([17])Gu lath bhràch cha 'n eirich Osgar !

57

"The whining of the hounds by my side,
And the wailing of the ancient warriors,
The crying of the women in turns—
These were the things that pierced my heart-strings.

58

"So it was that I ever thought
No fleshly heart was in my breast;
But a heart of the holly spikes,
All over-clad with steel.

59

"Pity it was not I that fell
In the battle of Corses, not scarce in deeds;
And thou in the east and the west ward,
Thou'dst be before the Fiantan Osgair."

60—CONAN.

"Although it had been thou that fell
In the battle of Corses, not scarce in deeds;
Alas! in the east or the west ward,
Groaning for thee would not be Osgar."

61—OISEAN.

"We raised with us lovely Osgar,
On shoulders and on lofty spear-shafts;
We had a glorious carrying
Until we reached the house of Fionn.

62

"No wife would weep her own son,
No man bewail his brother kind;
As many as we were about around the house,
We were all bewailing Osgar."

57

"Donnalaich nan con ri m' thaobh,
Agus buirich nan seann laoch ;
Gairich nam ban mu seach ;([18])
Siud an rud a ghon mo chridhe.

58

"'S ann a shaoil mi roimhe riamh,([19])
Nach cridhe feola 'bha'nn a' m' chliabh ;
Ach cridhe de ghuin na cuilinn
Air a chomhdachadh le stailinn.

59

"'S truagh nach mise thuiteadh ann
An cath Cairbhre, an gniomh nach gann ;
A's tusa, 'n ear agus an iar
A bhiodh roimh na Fianntan Osgair."

60—CONAN.

"Gad a bu tusa 'thuiteadh ann
An cath Cairbhre an gniomh nach gann,
Ochon ! an ear na 'n iar
A' t' iargain cha bhiodh Osgar."

61—OISEAN.

"Thog sinn leinn an t-Osgar aluinn
Air ghuaillibh 't air shleaghaibh arda ;
Thug sinn as iomchar ghrinn
Gus an do rainig sinn taigh Fhinn.

62

"Cha chaoineadh bean a mac fhein,
'S cha chaoineadh fear a bhrathair caomh,
'S cia lion 's a bha sinn mu 'n teach ;
Bha sinn uile caoineadh Osgair."

63—Fionn.

" Death of Osgar that tortured my heart,
Eirinn's men's lord, our mighty loss ;
Where in thy time was ever seen,
One so hardy behind a blade."

64—Oisean.

" Fionn never gave over trembling and woe,
From that day till the day of for ever ;
He would not take, and he would not desire,
A third of his life though I should say. ([20])

([1]) Cairbhre, abounding in carcases, producing carcases ; from cairbh, a carcase. H. M'L.   Gabhra, in Gillies.   J. F. C.

([2]) Araon 's am fear a (laghadh Laoidheadh) dh'e.   J. F. C.

([3]) Together, and one who would sing of it (a reading in Gillies).   J. F. C.

([4]) This introduction is given in Gillies; it varies somewhat from this, but it is not a whit more comprehensible.   J. F. C.

([5]) Damhair, hurry.

([6]) Teamhradh, a royal residence ; from tàmh righ, king's dwelling, or rest, " Temora."

([7]) Tighearn, a lord, or proprietor of land ; from ti fhearann, person of lands.   In this line tighearnas is used in the same sense as majesty.   Tighearn was evidently synonymous with Righ, king, at one time, and is no doubt the same word as the Greek, turannos, a king,   H. M'L.

([8]) From this line it might be inferred that the Gaels at some period were not the native race in the south of Ireland. H. M'L.

([9]) Tha mhasladh gu righ na h-Eirionn.—Patrick Smith. This seems to me to be the better line, as the one inserted hardly makes sense.   H. M'L.

([10]) The Scandinavian race.   H. M'L.

([11]) Bear, son of Love.

([12]) This stanza is from Patrick Smith, who, in the enumeration of the heroes, invariably uses ceithir ceud, four hundred.   H. M'L.

63—FIONN.

" Bàs Osgair a chraidh mo chrì,
Triath fear Eirionn 's mor g' ar dith ;
Cait am facas riamh ri d' linn,
Aon cho cruaidh riut air cul lainn.

64—OISEAN.

" Nior chuir Fionn deth crith a's grain
O'n latha sin gu la bhràch ;
Cha ghabhadh, 's cha b' fheairde leis
Trian de 'n bheatha gad dh' abruinn.

(13) The Phœnician or Carthaginian race.   H. M'L.

(14) Here Osgar exults in having given the nobler wound.
                                                  H. M'L.

(15) (?) The winds.

(16) Na 'n ruigeadh mo dhuirn a chneas,
     Cha deanadh an leigh a leigheas.

(17) 'Se mo chreach nach eirich Osgar.—Patrick Smith.

(18) Gul a' bhannail 'caoidh mu seach.—Donald MacPhie.

(19) These lines are put in the mouth of Oscar by some reciters, and in the version published by MacCallum, which would
imply that Oscar's fortitude gave way from the pain of his wounds ;
but this is altogether inconsistent with the character ascribed to
Oscar in all Fenian tales and poems, while, on the contrary, when
uttered by Fionn, the loftiest heroism that can be conceived is
represented ; the steel-encased holly heart overpowered by deep
feeling ; the stern, indomitable old captain completely subdued
by the tears of warm and generous affection.   H. M'L.

Part of this poem was recited to me by Patrick Smith, South
Boisdale, South Uist, September 17, 1860.   The whole of it as
written here, excepting a few lines peculiar to Smith's version,
was got from Donald MacPhie, smith, Breubhaig, Barra, October
1, 1860. It seems to be a fragment of a much larger poem, some
peculiar ancient drama. The commencement is rather obscure,
and it is not easy to make sense of some of the lines. H. M'L.

(20) This abrupt termination seems to indicate more to follow,
or a repetition of the first line, which seems to be the usual termination of these poems.   J. F. C.

(a) This introduction is curious. The Irish tradition is, that Scotland was the hunting ground of Fionn. The lay is part of a dialogue between the old poet and St. Patrick, which savours of Irish extraction ; but Barra is a Roman Catholic district.

(b) Moistening, Taiseadh. This seems to refer to some ancient method of soothsaying connected with washing clothes. In broad Scots it is mentioned in an old song, which I quote from memory—

> "My droukit sark sleeve I was waulking,
>   His likeness cam ben the house stalkin'."
>   The verra grey breeks o' Tam Glen."

In Britany (Foyer Breton, vol. i., 144), the night washerwomen (kannérez-noz) were a troop of ghosts, which appeared on a certain night in November. They washed, they dried, and they sewed the shroud of the dead who yet walk and talk, singing,—

> "Till there come Christians' saviour,
>   We must bleach our shrouds,
>   Under the snow and the wind."

They asked passengers to help to wring the wet sheets, and if a man turned the clothes with them it was well, if he turned against them he was crushed, and died.

Taisbean, s.m., means a vision, an apparition.

Taisbein, v.a., to reveal.

Taisgeal, s.m., the finding of something lost, and I have heard " an Taistear " used as a term of opprobrium. The collector is unable to explain the passage, but this seems to be an imperfect explanation of it. The raven has been a soothsayer time out of mind.

(c) This 8th stanza seems imperfect, and it is very hard to make any sense of it as it stands, but supposing that I am right in my explanation, this might be an exclamation of the mystic washerwomen previous to their disappearance. See note (2), page 328.

(d) 'Seang probably refers to the slender, sharp, tough, qualities of a spear. Three slender points and three thin edges make a barbed head, and a tough springy shaft makes a spear of seven " seang," add to that a couple of slender cords for throwing the weapon, of which there are traces in Irish stories; and we have a spear of nine "seang," slenders, and a phrase similar to the "binding of the three smalls."

(*f*) This line is given in Armstrong's dictionary under the word doirlinn.

(*g*) The geese might float. This, taken literally, is absurd, and is at variance with the spirit of the rest of the poem. I suspect, therefore, that the word which now means geese, and nothing else must have had some other meaning, as the word which means herons in verse 49 also means any crooked cutting instrument. It might be gaoithe, winds, and suggest the idea of the breath escaping from the wound.

LXXXII.

HOW THE EEN WAS SET UP.

From Angus MacDonald, Stoneybridge, South Uist.

THERE was a king on a time over Eirinn, to whom the cess which the Lochlanners had laid on Alba and on Eirinn was grievous. They were coming on his own realm, in harvest and summer, to feed themselves on his goods ; and they were brave strong men, eating and spoiling as much as the Scotch and Irish (Albannaich and Eirionnaich ; Alban-ians Eirin-ians) were making ready for another year.

He sent word for a counsellor that he had, and he told him all what was in his thought, that he wanted to find a way to keep the Scandinavians (Lochlannaich ; Lochlan-ians) back. The counsellor said to him that this would not grow with him in a moment ; but if he would take his counsel, that it would grow with him in time.

"Marry," said he, "the hundred biggest men and women in Eirinn to each other; marry that race to each other; marry the second race to each other again; and let the third kindred (ginealach) go to face the Lochlaners."

This was done, and when the third kindred came to man's estate they came over to Albainn, and Cumhal at their head.[*]

It grew with them to rout the Lochlaners, and to drive them back. Cumhal made a king of himself in Alba that time with these men, and he would not let Lochlaner or Irelander to Alba but himself. This was a grief to the King of Lochlann, and he made up to the King of Alba that there should be friendship between them, here and yonder, at that time. They settled together the three kings—the King of Lochlann, and the King of Alba, and the King of Eirinn—that they would have a great "ball" of dancing, and there should be friendship and truce amongst them.

There was a "schame" between the King of Eirinn and the King of Lochlann, to put the King of Scotland to death. Cumhal was so mighty that there was no contrivance for putting him to death, unless he was slain with his own sword when he was spoilt with drink, and love making, and asleep.

---

[*] This seems to have a trace of probability about it. There must have been more spoil on the more fertile and accessible east coasts of Ireland and Scotland to tempt invaders; and the Celts might well assemble amongst the mountains and wild islands of the western coasts of Ireland and Scotland to make head against the Norsemen, who certainly were settled in Ireland, about Dublin and elsewhere, in historical times. Cumhal and a warlike tribe might well have risen and set up in Scotland, and this story gives more standing ground for MacPherson's story of a king in Morven than anything which I have. This also explains one meaning of Cumhal, subjection.

He had his choice of a sweetheart amongst any of the women in the company; and it was the daughter of the King of Lochlann whom he chose.

When they went to rest, there was a man in the company, whose name was Black Arcan, whom they set apart to do the murder when they should be asleep. When they slept Black Arcan got the sword of Cumhal, and he slew him with it. The murder was done, and everything was right. Alba was under the Lochlaners, and the Irelanders and Black Arcan had the sword of Cumhal.*

, The King of Lochlann left his sister with the King of Eirinn, with an order that if she should have a babe son to slay him; but if it were a baby daughter, to keep her alive. A prophet had told that Fionn Mac-Chumhail would come; and the sign that was for this was a river in Eirinn; that no trout should be killed on it till Fionn should come. That which came as the fruit of the wedding that was there, was that the daughter of the King of Lochlann bore a son and daughter to Cumhall. Fionn had no sister but this one, and she was the mother of Diarmaid. On the night they were born his muime (nurse) fled with the son, and she went to a desert place with him, and she was keeping him up there till she raised him as a stalwart goodly child.†

She thought that it was sorry for her that he should be nameless with her. The thing which she did was to go with him to the town, to try if she could find means to give him a name. She saw the school-boys of the town swimming on a fresh water loch.

* Supposing this to refer to an early attack on Ireland and Scotland by Scandinavians, the story is probable enough.

† This is manifestly the same story as that of the Great Fool (See No. 75), and it is in Irish also.

"Go out together with these," said she to him, "and if thou gettest hold of one, put him under and drown him ; and if thou gettest hold of two, put them under and drown them."

He went out on the loch, and he began drowning the children, and it happened that one of the bishops of the place was looking on.[*]

"Who," said he, "is that bluff fair son, with the eye of a king in his head, who is drowning the school-boys ?"

"May he steal his name !" said his muime.

"Fionn, son of Cumhall, son of Finn, son of every eloquence, son of Art, son of Eirinn's high king, and it is my part to take myself away."

Then he came on shore, and she snatched him with her.

When the following were about to catch them, he leapt off his muime's back, and he seized her by the two ankles, and he put her about his neck. He went in through a wood with her, and when he came out of the wood he had but the two shanks. He met with a loch after he had come out of the wood, and he threw the two legs out on the loch, and it is Loch nan Lurgan, the lake of the shanks, that the loch was called after this. Two great monsters grew from the shanks of Fionn's muime. That is the kindred that he had with the two monsters of Loch nan Lurgan.[†]

Then he went, and without meat or drink, to the great town. He met Black Arcan fishing on the river,

---

[*] This makes the date of Fionn later than the establishment of Christianity in Ireland.

[†] This gives the clue to another story which I have not yet got hold of, and seems to be a bit of mythology grafted on a tra-dition of some historical event.

and a hound in company with him.   Bran MacBuidheig (black, or raven, son of the little yellow).

"Put out the rod for me," said he to the fisherman, " for I am hungry, to try if thou canst get a trout
for me." The trout laid to him, and he killed the
trout. He asked the trout from Black Arcan.

"Thou art the man!" said Black Arcan; "when
thou wouldst ask a trout, and that I am fishing for years
for the king, and that I am as yet without a trout for
him."

He knew that it was Fionn he had. To put the
tale on the short cut, he killed a trout for the king,
and for his wife, and for his son, and for his daughter,
before he gave any to Fionn. Then he gave him a
trout.*

Thou must, said Black Arcan, broil the trout on
the further side of the river, and the fire on this side
of it, before thou gettest a bit of it to eat; and thou
shalt not have leave to set a stick that is in the wood
to broil it. He did not know here what he should do.
The thing that he fell in with was a mound of sawdust,
and he set it on fire beyond the river. A wave of the
flame came over, and it burned a spot on the trout,
the thing that was on the crook.† Then he put his

---

* I have heard a similar story told of a saint who came to a
fisherman, and got the promise of the first fish he should catch.
The first was a large one, so he promised the next; but that was
larger, so he promised the next; and so on till the thirteenth,
which was a toad. He gave that to the saint, who cursed him
and the river, saying that no more salmon should ever be caught
there. The story was told of a small river which runs out of
Loch Guirm in Islay, up which salmon cannot get for natural
obstacles, but where salmon are often seen leaping in the sea.
A similar story is told of rivers in Ireland, and I think there is some
such legend about Kent.

† This word is used for a crozier and a shepherd's crook.

finger on the black spot that came on the trout, and it burnt him, and then he put it into his mouth. Then he got knowledge that it was this Black Arcan who had slain his father, and unless he should slay Black Arcan in his sleep, that Black Arcan would slay him when he should awake. The thing that happened was that he killed the carle, and then he got a glaive and a hound, and the name of the hound was Bran MacBuidheig.

Then he thought that he would not stay any longer in Eirinn, but that he would come to Alba, to get the soldiers of his father. He came on shore in Farbaine. There he found a great clump of giants, men of stature. He understood that these were the soldiers that his father had, and they (were) as poor captives by the Lochlaners hunting for them, and not getting (aught) but the remnants of the land's increase for themselves. The Lochlaners took from them the arms when war or anything should come, for fear they should rise with the foes. They had one special man for taking their arms, whose name was Ullamh Lamh fhada (Pr. oolav lav ada oólav long hand). He gathered the arms and he took them with him altogether, and it fell out that the sword of Fionn was amongst them. Fionn went after him,

Bachal? Baculum. Here it seems to mean the method of roasting fish, which I learned from Lapps, and have practised scores of times. Wooden skewers are stuck through slices of fish, and a long rod is spitted through these, and one end is planted in the ground to windward of a fire of sticks.

The incident of saw-dust, as wood that grew and is neither crooked nor straight, is proverbial in the Highlands, and common to many stories. So is the fish which gives knowledge when eaten. (See No. 47. Vol. II. 362). This, then, is clearly some wide-spread myth about a fish attached to a Celtic hero. It is given in the transactions of the Ossianic Society of Dublin in another shape, and has very old Irish manuscript authority.

asking for his own sword. When they came within sight of the armies of Lochlann, he said—

"Blood on man and man bloodless,
  Wind over hosts, 'tis pity without the son
    of Luin.

"To what may that belong?" said Ulamh lamh fhada.

"It is to a little bit of a knife of a sword that I had," said Fionn. "You took it with you amongst the rest, and I am the worse for wanting it, and you are no better for having it."

"What is the best exploit thou wouldst do if thou hadst it?"

"I would quell the third part of the hosts that I see before me."

Oolav Longhand laid his hand on the arms. The most likely sword and the best that he found there he gave it to him. He seized it, and he shook it, and he cast it out of the wooden handle, and said he—

It is one of the black-edged glaives,
It was not Mac an Luin my blade ;
It was no hurt to draw from sheath,
It would not take off the head of a lamb.

Then he said the second time the same words.
He said the third time—

"Blood on man, and bloodless man,
  Wind o'er the people, 'tis pity without the son
    of Luin."

"What wouldst thou do with it if thou shouldst get it?"

"I would do this, that I would quell utterly all I see."

z

He threw down the arms altogether on the ground. Then Fionn got his sword, and said he then—

"This is the one of my right hand."

Then he returned to the people he had left. He got the t-ord fiannta (? Dord) of the Fian, and he sounded it. (See illustration, page 287, for an ancient horn, sculptured on a stone in the east of Scotland.)

There gathered all that were in the southern end of Alba of the Fiantaichean to where he was. He went with these men, and they went to attack the Loch-laners, and those which he did not kill he swept them out of Alba.*

* This, then, seems to be popular history, interlarded with Celtic mythology. History of a successful rising of Celts in Scotland, headed by a leader who was a Scandinavian by the mother's side; against the Scandinavians who had beaten them twice before. Once and for a long time in Ireland, whence they retired to Scotland, and again long afterwards, treacherously and by the help of Irish allies in Scotland.

The mythology has to do with fish; so has that of the two stories which follow; so, as an illustration, I have copied all the fish which are figured in the "sculptured stones of Scotland," together with some of the characteristic ornaments which accompany them.

It is remarkable that, with the exception of two, all these are swimming from the left to the right of an observer, and that a nondescript creature which is often figured on the same stones with fish, heads the same way. I take the monster to be a representation of a water animal, a walrus, by an artist who had never seen one.

As no explanation has yet been found for the symbols, as fish clearly have to do with Celtic mythology, and as Celtic mythology appears to have been mixed with solar and well worship, it seems worth considering whether these symbols may not have an astronomical meaning. One of the signs of the Zodiac is and has been for many a day Pisces; and the symbol is $\mathcal{H}$. The sun passes northwards through the constellation in

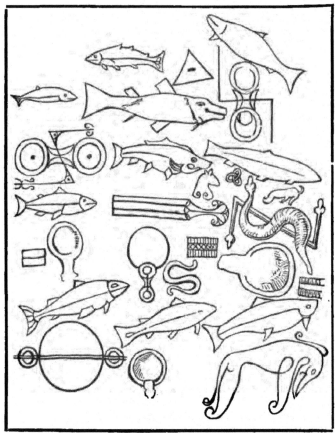

the spring, and when the sun is travelling north "the fish" are swimming south. South and to the right are expressed by the same word in Gaelic—" deas." Fish swimming to the right are swimming south (deas). The sun crosses the equator at the vernal equinox ; and one of the emblems here associated with fish consists of circles, which still stand for the sun in our almanacks ; joined by two crescents which in like manner stand for moons or months, and separated by a line. Another consists of a circle

MAR A CHUIREADH SUAS AN FHINN.

BHA righ aon uair air Eirinn leis am bu duilich cis a leag na Lochlannaich air Alba 's air Eirinn. Bha iad a' tighinn air a rioghachd
fhein an am fobhair agus samhraidh 'gam beathachadh fhein air a
chuid, 's iad 'nan daoine calma, laidir; ag itheadh 's a' milleadh 'na
'bha na h-Albannaich 's na h-Eirionnaich a' deanadh ri bliadhna eile.
Chuir e fios air comhairleach a bh' aige 's dh' innis e dha na 'bha 'na
bheachd; gu 'n robh toil aige air doigh fhaotann air na Lochlannaich a chumail air an ais. Thuirt an comhairleach ris nach cinneadh
siud leis an gradaig, ach na'n gabhadh e chomhairle-san gu 'n cinneadh e leis ri uine.

" Pos," ars' an comhairleach, " an ceud fear agus an ceud bean a's
mò an Eirinn air a' cheile; pos an sliochd air a cheile a rithis; leig
an treas ginealach an coinneamh nan Lochlannach." Chaidh seo a
dheanadh, 's nuair a thainig an treas ginealach gu h-inbhe dhaoine
thainig iad a nall a dh' Albainn agus Cumhal air an ceann. Chinn-
ich leo na Lochlannaich a sgrios 's a chur air an ais. Rinn Cumhal
righ deth fhein an Alba an uair sin leis na daoine seo, 's cha leigeadh

---

bisected by a double line, which also cuts two smaller circles,
touching it on either side. May not all these symbols refer to the
sun of winter and the summer sun; to the sun crossing the line at
the vernal equinox; and may not these rude sculptured stones be
erected to mark spots for celebrating festivals. A sword, a mirror,
and a comb, or things like them, accompany the fish; and at
first sight they would appear to have nothing to do with this
supposition.

But the sword may be the bright shining mystic Sword of
Light of Gaelic stories, and an emblem of the sun, and it points to
the left or north. The sun is the God of the long yellow bright
hair everywhere, and the comb may be another of his emblems;
and the looking-glass, if it be one, might be a third emblem for
its brightness.

This is but conjecture thrown out for the consideration of the
learned. I am quite prepared to believe that the emblems repre
sent the frying pans, gridirons, cauldrons, and spits on which
ancient North-Britons cooked the fish whose portraits they drew
so well.

e Lochlannach na Eirionnach a dh' Albainn ach e fhein. Bha seo
'na dhoilgheas le righ Lochlann, 's rinn e suas ri righ Albann gu 'm
biodh cairdeas eatorra thall 's a bhos an uair sin. Chuir iad ri cheile,
na tri righean, righ Lochlann, 's righ Albann, 's righ Eirionn, gu 'm
biodh bàil mor damhsaidh aca, 's gu 'm biodh cairdeas agus reite
eatorra.

Bha sgeim eadar righ Eirionn agus righ Lochlann righ Alba a
chur gu bàs. Bha Chumhal cho treun 's nach robh innleachd air a
chur gu bàs, mar am marbhta le a chlaidheimh fhein e, nuair a
bhiodh e dìolta òil agus mnatha, 'na chadal. Bha 'roghainn aige de
dh' aona bhoireannach a bha 's a' chuideachd, agus 's i nighean righ
Lochlann a ghabh e mar roghainn. Nuair chaidh iad a luidhe bha
duine anns a' chuideachd d' am b' ainm Arcann dubh a shonraich
iad airson am mort a dheanadh nuair a bhiodh iad 'nan cadal. Nuair
a chaidil iad fhuair Arcan dubh claidheamh Chumhail 's mharbh e
leis e. Bha 'm mort deanta 's bha 'h-uile cuis ceart. Bha Alba fo
na Lochlannaich 's fo na h-Eirionnaich, 's bha claidheamh Chumhail
aig Arcan dubh.

Dh' fhag righ Lochlann a phinthar aig righ Eirionn, 's ordan aige
na 'm bu leanabh mic a bhiodh aice a mharbhadh, ach na 'm bu
leanabh nighinn a bhiodh ann a cumail beo. Bha faidheachd ag
innseadh gu 'n d' thigeadh Fionn Mac Chumhail, 's gur h-e 'n comh-
arra a bha air seo, amhainn a bha an Eirinn, nach marbhta breac
urra gus an d' thigeadh Fionn. 'S e a thionndaidh a mach a thoradh na ceud oidhche a bha 'n sin gu 'n d' rug nighean righ Lochlann
mac agus nighean do Chumhal. Cha robh pinthar aig Fionn ach i
seo, 's b' i mathair Dhiarmaid. An oidhche a rugadh iad theich a
mhuime leis a' mhac, 's chaidh i do dh' àite fasail leis, 's bha i 'ga
bheathachadh 's 'ga chumail suas an sìn gus an do thog i 'na leanabh
foghainteach, tlachdar e.

Smaointich i gu 'm bu duilich leatha e 'bhith gun ainm aice. 'S
e 'n ni a rinn i dh' fhalbh i leis thun a' bhaile feuch am faigheadh i
innleachd air ainm a thoirt air. Chunnaic i sgoilearan a' bhaile a'
snamh air loch uisge.

" Falbh a mach cuide riutha siud," ars' ise ris, " 's ma gheibh thu
greim air h-aon cuir fodha e 's bath e, 's ma gheibh thu greim air
dithis cuir fodha iad 's bath iad."

Ghabh esan a mach air an loch 's thoisich e air bathadh na
cloinne. Thuit gu 'n robh fear de dh' easbuigean an àite 'ga
choimhead.

" Co," ars' esan, " am Mac Maol Fionn 'ud, s rasg righ 'na cheann
a tha a' bathadh nan sgoilearan ? "

" Gu meal e ainm," ars' a mhuime,
Fionn Mac Chumhail Mhic Fhinn Mhic Uile-bheurais,
Mhic h-Art, Mhic Ard-righ Eirionn,
'S tha uams' a bhith 'gam thoirt fhein as."

Thainig esan, an sin, air tir agus sgriob ise leatha e. Nuair a bha
'n toir gu breith orra leum e bhar muin a mhuime, 's rug e air chaol
da chois urra, 's chuir e mu amhaich i. Chaidh e staigh roimh
choille leatha, 's nuair a thainig e mach as a' choille cha robh aige
ach an da lurga. Thachair loch ris an deigh tighinn a mach as a'
choille 's thilg e 'n da chois a mach air an loch. 'S e Loch nan Lurgann a theirte ris an loch as a dheigh seo. Dh' fhas da bheist mhoir
a da lurgann muime Fhinn. 'S e siud an cairdeas a bh' aige ri da
bheist Loch an lurgann.

Dh'fhalbh e 'n seo, 's e gun bhiadh gun dibh, 'ionnsuidh a' bhaile
mhoir. Choinnich Arcan dubh, ag iasgach air an amhainn, e, agus
cu air cuideachd ris, Bran Mac Buidheig.

"Cuir a mach an t-slat air mo shonsa," ars' e ris an iasgair, " 's
an t-acras orm, feuch am faigh thu breac dhomh.

Luidh am breac ris, 's mharbh e 'm breac. Dh' iarr e 'm breac
air Arcan dubh.

" 'S tusa 'm fear," ars' Arcan dubh, "nuair a dh' iarradh tu 'm
breac, 's mise 'g iasgach o cheann bhliadhnaichean do 'n righ, 's gun
breac agam da fhathasd."

Dh' aithnich e gur h-e Fionn a bh' aige. Gus an sgeul a chur an
aithghearr mharbh e breac do 'n righ, 's d'a mhnaoi, 's d'a mhac, 's
d'a nighinn, ma 'n d' thug e gin do dh' Fhionn. Thug e 'n sin
breac da.

"Feumaidh tu," ars' Arcan dubh, " am breac a bhruich an taobh
thall de 'n amhainn, 'san teine 'n taobh seo di, ma 'm faigh thu mir
deth ri 'itheadh ; 's cha 'n fhaigh thu cead maide 'tha 's a' choille a
chur a 'bhruich."

Cha robh fios aige 'n seo dé a dheanadh e. 'S e an ni a thachair
air torr min shaibh, 's chuir e 'na teine i thar na h-amhann. Thainig
tonn de 'n lasair a nall 's loisg i ball air a' bhreac, ni a bha air a
bhacail. Chuir e 'n seo a mheur air a' bhall dubh a thainig air a
bhreac, 's loisg e i, 's chuir e 'n sin 'na bheul i. Fhuair e 'n seo fios
gur h-e Arcan dubh seo a mharbh 'athair ; 's mar am marbhadh esan
Arcan dubh, 's e 'na chadal, gu 'm marbhadh Arcan dubh esan an
uair a dhuisgeadh e. 'Se 'n ni a bha ann mharbh e 'm bodach.
Fhuair e 'n sin cu 's claidheamh ; 's e b' ainm do 'n chu Bran Mac
Buidheig.

Smaointich e 'n sin nach d' thoireadh e 'n Eirinn na 'b' fhaide, ach gu 'n d' thigeadh e dh' Alba airson saighdearan 'athar fhaotainn. Thainig e air tir am Farbaine. Fhuair e 'n sin meall mor a dh' Ataich, daoine gnathasda. Thuig e gu 'm b' e na saighdearan a bha aig 'athair a bha ann, 's iad 'nan ciomaich bhochd aig na Lochlann-aich, a' sealg daibh, 's gun iad a' faotainn ach an t-iomall 'na theachd-an-tir dhaibh fhein. Thug na Lochlannaich uatha na h-airm nuair thigeadh cogadh na ni sam bith eagal eiridh leis na naimhdean. Bha aon duine sonraicht, aca airson togail nan arm sin d' am b' ainm Ullamh Lamh-fhada. Chruinnich esan na h-airm 's thug e leis iad uile, 's thuit gu 'n robh claidheamh Fhinn 'nam measg. Dh' fhalbh Fionn as a dheigh 's e 'g iarraidh a chlaidheimh fhein. Nuair a thainig iad an sealladh an airm Lochlannaich thubhairt e.

> Fuil air fear 's fear gun fhuil,
> Gaoth thar sluaigh, 's truagh gun Mac an Luin.

" Dé a bhith g' am buin sin?" arsa Ullamh Lamh-fhada. " A' chorcag chlaidheimh a bha agam," arsa Fionn, " thug sibh leibh a measg chaich i; 's misde mise gum' dhìth i 's cha 'n fheairde sibhse agaibh i."

" Dé 'n t-euchd a b' fhearr a dheanadh tu leatha na 'm biodh i agad?"

" Cheannsaichinn an treas cuid de 'na chi mi mu m' choinneamh de shluagh."

Thug Ullamh Lamh-fhada lamh air na h-airm. An claidheamh a bu choltaiche 's a b' fhearr a fhuair e ann thug e dha e. Rug e air 's chrath e e, 's thilg e as a mhaide feadain e, 's ars' e,

> 'S e fear dh' an ealtuinn dhuigh a th' ann;
> Cha b' e, Mac an Luin—mo lann;
> Cha bu lochd a thoirt a truaill,
> Bhar uain cha d' thugadh e 'n ceann.

Thuirt e 'n dara uair na briathra ciadhna, Thuirt e 'n treas uair, Fuil air fear agus fear gun fhuil, Gaoth thar sluaigh 's truagh gun Mac an Luin.

" De a dheanadh tu leis na 'm faigheadh tu e?"

" Dheanadh gu 'n ceannsaichinn uile na' chi mi."

Thilg e air lar na h-airm uile. Fhuair Fionn a chlaidheamh, 's ars' e 'n sin, " 'Se seo fear mo laimhe deise-sa."

Thill e 'n sin 'ionnsuidh nan daoine a dh' fhag e. Fhuair e 'n t-ord fiannta 's sheinn e e. Chruinnich na bha 'n taobh deas de dh' Alba de na Fianntaichean far an robh e. Dh' fhalbh e leis na daoine seo, 's chaidh iad am bad nan Lochlannach, 's a' chuid nach do mharbh iad diu sgiurs iad a Alba iad.

From Angus MacDonald, Staoine-breac, South Uist, September 14, 1860.

This story is very popular in South Uist and Barra, and is known to the most of old people in these islands.—H. M'L.

LXXXIII.

THE REASON WHY THE DALLAG (DOG-FISH) IS CALLED THE KING'S FISH.

From Angus MacKinnon, South Uist.

WHAT but that the King of Lochlann should come to the King of Eirinn to be a while along with him.

The King of Lochlann and Fionn went on a day to fish, and they had a little boat, and they had no man but themselves.

They spent the greatest part of the day fishing, and they did not get a thing.

Then there laid a beast on (the hook of) Fionn, and he fell to fishing, so that he put the hook into him.*   He took in the fish; and what fish was it but a dog-fish.   The hook of the King of Lochlann was in her maw, under the hook of Fionn, and the hook of Fionn was in the outer mouth.   Then the King of Lochlann fell to at taking out the dog-fish, since it was his hook that was farthest down in her.   They

---

* This is peculiarly descriptive of handline fishing, when a "beast" takes, it feels as if a weight had *laid* quietly on the line, and a green hand often loses a fish by neglecting to strike, not knowing that the fish is there.

fell to arguing with each other, and Fionn would not yield a bit till they should go to law.

Then they went to land with the boat, and they went to law, and the law made (over) the fish to Fionn ; and that there should be a fine laid upon the King of Lochlann, since he had not felt the fish when first it struck him.

With the rage that the King of Lochlann took he went home to Lochlann, and he told to his muime and his oide (his foster parents) how it had happened.

The Muilearteach was his muime, and the Smith of Songs, who was married to her, was his foster-father.

She said that it was she who would bring out the recompense for that.

Then she came till she reached Eirinn, and the King of Lochlann with her, and the Smith of Songs.

The Dallag was never said after that but the king's fish *

* A creature something like a king-fish, which is a sort of diminutive shark, is figured on the sculptured stones of Scotland. A version of this is already referred to, page 145. It is a kind of introduction to the Muilearteach, and explains who that personage was.

The Smith of Songs is probably the same as Loan Mac Libhinn, the maker of Fionn's sword, about whom there is a long poem, and I suspect them to be mythological, perhaps Thor and his wife. Thor and a giant once rowed out together in a small boat to fish, and Thor hooked, and lost the sea-serpent. Perhaps the giant was Fionn.

The coming of the Muilearteach to Islay with the smith and the smithy on her back, is told in another story. See No. 85.

THE LAY OF MAGNUS.

A poem so called is known in Ireland, and is preserved in MSS. in Dublin, according to writers in the transactions of the Ossianic Society.

A poem of 172 lines, "comhrag Fhein agus Mhannis" was published in 1786, in Gillies' Scotch collection. An Irish version was published by Miss Brooke, 1789. I have compared my version with the poem in Gillies. I find that they vary from each other; in words, in lines, and even in whole stanzas; but the two might be fused so as to produce a third, perfectly genuine, and more complete than either. The version orally collected in 1860 goes a step beyond the other, printed in 1786, and I feel certain that it is historical. This story is in substance the same as "Fingal," and might be the germ of that poem. Irish writers claim it as Irish, and assert that the Lay of Magnus was MacPherson's original for part of Fingal. It first appeared in print in Scotland, and it is still repeated there, wherever it was composed. Irish collectors have copies taken down orally in Scotland long ago.

Now, if Magnus can be identified, it would fix the earliest possible date for the poem, and a later date for the poet than is usually given to Oisein, by Scotch and Irish writers; and this opinion agrees with Miss Brooke's.

The prose tale is also about Magnus; it was written by MacLean. I heard it recited by old MacPhie in 1860. He is failing fast, and cannot dictate slowly; I miss several of the measured prose passages, which I heard him repeat with the utmost fluency, when he was allowed to go his own pace. The story is manifestly incomplete; and it reminds me of one which old MacPhie repeated a second time for me. He then gave disjointed incidents, and broken sentences, instead of a connected story in very good language, with few repetitions, with curious rythmical passages interspersed, which he gave the first time.

It is hard to say what this story means, unless it is Celtic mythology engrafted upon a bit of Norwegian history.

I give it with all its shortcomings, because, if Celtic mythology is ever to be discovered, it will be found in some such shape.

We have here, at all events—

The King of the World, whose life is in that of a horned, deadly or hurtful or venomous animal; and his son Brodram.

The King of Light, who is conquered by a lion; and his son, the white long-haired one, whose life is in that of three fish; who has twelve bald ruddy daughters; who marry twelve men, the foster-brothers of Manus the hero.

Balcan, the smith, who has twelve apprentices; and his son, who is a sailor, and has a wonderful spotted ship, and twelve sailors.

In short, there are many things which suggest solar worship and mythology—Aries, Taurus, Leo, Pisces—12 hours of day, 12 of night, 12 months, 12 signs of the zodiac, Light, the Smith or artificer Balcan; the sailor, his son:—Vulcan and Neptune, &c. But while there is much to suggest inquiry, there is nothing definite.

The poem, on the contrary, is definite enough, and in that respect it resembles other poems which I have collected, and differs from the prose romances.

MANUS.

I have endeavoured to restore this dress from various authorities. From grave stones; two in Iona, and two in Islay, of which I happened to have very rough sketches; and from tradition.

I leave the legs bare, because there is no indication of any covering on the legs of the sculptured figures, and because Magnus the Great was called "barelegs" when he adopted the dress of the islands, and because there is no mention of any covering for the legs in the traditional descriptions of dress. On the contrary, at page 442, vol. ii., it appears that the warriors had shoes, but that their legs were bare.

Some stones indicate that the arms were clothed in some material, with longitudinal folds; others indicate no covering.

The shape of the shield is from a stone at Iona. On some there are traces of armorial bearings.

The lion, snake, and griffin, are from the story as repeated to me by old MacPhie, " His boss-covered, hindering, sharp-pointed shield on his left arm, with many a picture to be seen thereon. Lion and Creveenach, and deadly Serpent." A lion and a serpent appear in the Welsh romance of the Lady of the Fountain, which this story resembles in some degree.

The helmet and sword are copied from stones, some of which are roughly carved in relief nearly six inches above the surface.

The tippet and shirt are very like the dress commonly worn by the Lapps of the Luleo river, and by little Scotch children at the present day.

The Lapps wear a loose deer-skin shirt, and a belt round the waist, and a tall conical cap. In rainy weather they slip a tippet over their heads, which is tied round the forehead, and protects the chin, throat, and shoulders, covering all but the face.

Scotch children wear a kilt and sleeve-waistcoat in one, into which they slip, and which, with a shirt, often constitutes their whole attire.

The warrior's outer dress was probably some such garment made of leather, with iron scales. The same Gaelic word means patched cloak, and coat of mail, and such a dress seems to be meant at page 205, vol. ii. The virgin and child are from the stone in Kilnaughton church, Islay, and the symbol indicates a Christian warrior and a date.

LXXXIV.

MANUS.

From Donald MacPhie, Iochdar, South Uist.

THERE was a King of Lochlann, and he married, and two sons were born to him. Oireal was the name of one, and Iarlaid of the other. Their father and mother died. A "Parlamaid" sat to put "Cilead-earachd," a regency on the realm, till the children should come to age, and till they should take the vows of the realm on themselves. They sent word for the lads, and Oireal was a feeble man, and Iarlaid was the bigger. Oireal said to the "Parlamaid" that he would not have anything to do with the realm as yet.

"Clod of it you shall not have," said the Parliament, "unless you take it this day."

Said Iarlaid to Oireal, "take thou the one half, and I will take the other half."

"Well, then," said Oireal; "I will do that."

The realm was written upon the lads. In a few years Iarlaid married the daughter of the King of Greece, and Oireal married the daughter of King Sgiath Sgial, King of the Arcuinn.*

Sgiath Sgial gave six maids of honour with his daughter, and the King of Greece gave the very like with his own daughter.

Three quarters from that night the ailment of children struck the daughter of the King of Greece; and, besides, the ailment of children struck the daughter of

---

* I have no notion what monarch or realm is meant, but the Orkney would be appropriate.

Sgiath Sgial, and sons were born to them, and twelve
sons were born to maids of honour. Manus was given
(as a name) to the son of Oireal, and Eochaidh to the
son of Iarlaid. The sons began to come on; Manus
was growing big, and Eochaidh was but little. They
were sent to school, and his own foster brethren were
together with each one of them.

They were playing shinny on the field, coming
from school, and Manus drove the ball against Eochaidh.

"I will have my own father's realm," said Manus.

Said the daughter of the King of Greece, "It were
my wish to put an end to Manus, of murdering and
spoiling and slaying."

"Well, then, that were the great pity to put that
(end) to the son of our brother," said the king.

"If thou wilt not do it, I will do it," said she.

She went in, and gave a slight box on the ear
(Leideag) to her own son, and she drove him out of the
house.

"Begone," said she, "and betake thyself to the
four brown boundaries of the world, and let me not
see thy sole on the same land as long as the world is
set. I will take Manus with me, and he shall be a
son for myself."

She took Manus in with herself, and she set her
own son on a beautiful sunny single-stemmed hill,
where he could see every man, and no man him.

Manus was within with her, and he was not getting to see his mother at all. Then his mother said
that she would go where her muime was, and that she
would take her counsel.

At the end of a year she sent word for Manus.
And in a few years the wife of his father's brother
sent word for Manus.

"What, oh Manus ! said the daughter of the King
of Greece, "art thou thinking of doing this day ? If
thou wilt marry, thou wilt get the third part of the
realm ; land, corn-land, and treasure."

"Well, then, I am not of age to marry at all,"
said he.

"Thou needst not (say) that," said she.   "There
is one man on my own land that will suit thee.   Thou
shalt go to ask his daughter, and thou shalt marry her.
He is the Earl of Fiughaidh ; thou shalt marry the
daughter of the Earl of the Fiughaidh."*

She went away, and she took with her high families, and she would take with her five hundred men.
She reached the house of the Earl of Fiughaidh, to
give her to Manus to marry.

Said the wife of the Earl of the Fiughaidh to her,
"My daughter is not of age to marry yet, and Manus
is not of age to marry."

"Well," said the daughter of the King of Greece,
"house or heap thou shalt not have upon my land
unless thou givest thy daughter to him."

The man thought that there was no good for him
to refuse her, and Manus and the daughter of the Earl
of the Fiudhaidh were married to each other.

They lay that night in the house of his father's
brother.

"Is it thou that art here, Manus, mighty son, and
bad man ? dost thou know what wife yonder one gave
to her own son, Eochaidh ?   She gave him the swift
march wind.   It was not to a worldly wife she married him, so that he might take the head off thee.
Thou with a wife on thy bed at this time of night !

* Here, again, I am at fault. This probably is a real name,
but corrupted by transfer to another language, and by the lapse
of time.

Thou wilt be going back every day, and thou wilt not hold battle against him."

" Is it thus it is ? " said Manus.

He went where she was.

" Be leaving the realm," said the wife of his father's brother to him, " or else thou wilt have but what thou takest to its end."

" It was," said he, " the third part of the realm that thou didst promise me."

" Clod thou shalt not have here," said she. " Thy share is under stones and rough mountains in the old Bergen."

" Well, then, since thou art putting me away, give me the six foster brothers of Eochaidh, that I may have twelve."

He got that ; he went away, and he betook himself to the old Bergen.

When he reached the old Bergen, no man dared to come near his castle. There were sheep in the old Bergen, and sheep of Corrachar, is what they were called.

They fell to making pits in the earth ; the sheep were going into the pits, and they were catching them, and they were killing them, and keeping themselves in flesh thus in the old Bergen.*

" Be it from me ! be it from me !" said Manus ; " it is a year since I saw my muime ; I had better go and see her."

" It were not my advice to thee to go there," said they; " but if thou art going, thou hast twelve foster brothers, and take them with thee."

---

* I am not aware that there are, or ever were, wild sheep in Bergen ; but a wilder hunter's land does not exist, and wild reindeer, and, I believe, wild goats, may yet be found in the high mountains.

"They were no sorry company for me to be with me," said he.

He went. The daughter of the King of Greece was looking out of a window, and she perceived Manus coming. She went down to where his father's brother was.

"The son of thy brother is coming here," said she, "with costly coloured belts on his left side, with which might be got the love of a young woman, and the liking of maidens;" that it were for her pleasure to put an end to him, of murdering, and misusing, and slaying.

His father's brother said that were a great pity, and that he would not be to the fore to do that to him.

"If thou wilt not do it, I will do it," said she.

She went out of the house, and she took his twelve foster brethren from him, and she swore them to herself. He went back to the Old Bergen by himself, gloomy, tearful, sorrowful, and it was late. What should he see but a man in a red vesture.

"It is thou that art here Manus?" said he.

"It is I," said Manus.

"I think if thou hadst bad or good arms that thou would'st get to be King over Lochlann."

"I have not that," said he.

"Well," said he of the red vesture, "if thou would'st give me a promise I would give thee arms."

"What promise shall I give thee? I have not a jot to give thee."

"Well, I will not ask thee much. I was the armourer of thy grandfather, and thy great-grandfather, if thou wouldst give me a promise that I should be armourer with thee I would give thee arms this night."

"I will give thee that (promise), if so be that I am ever a king."

They went, and they reached the house. The man of the red vesture took out a key, and he opened a door, and when he had opened it the house was full of arms, and not a jot in it but arms.

"Begin now and choose arms," said the man of the red vesture.

Manus seized a sword, and he broke it, and every one he caught he was breaking it.

"Don't do that Manus, don't be breaking the arms, in case thou mightest have need of them yet. When I was a young man thy grandsire had a war, and I had an old sword, an old helmet, and an old mail shirt on, try them," said the man of the red vesture.

Manus seized the sword, and it beat him to break it. He put the sword and the helmet on. What should he see but a cloth (hanging) down from the ridge of the house. "What is the use of that cloth?" said Manus. "It is," said he "that when thou spreadest it, to seek food and drink, thou wilt get as thou usest. There is another virtue in it. If a foe should meet thee, he would give a kiss to the back of thy fist."

He gave the cloth to Manus, and he folded the cloth in his oxter. What should he see but an iron chain (hanging) down from the ridge of the house.

"What is the good of that chain?" said Manus.

"There is no creature in the world that if yonder thing should be put about his neck the battle of a hundred men would not be upon him," said the man of the red vesture.

Manus took the chain with him. When he was going, what should he see but two lions, and a whelp with them. The lions came in front of him to eat him, and to put him to skaith. He spread the cloth, and the lions came, and they kissed the back of his fist, and they went past him. The lion whelp got in amongst the folds of the cloth, and he wrapped the cloth about him, and he lifted him with him to the old Bergen.*

When he reached the old Bergen the daughter of the Earl of the Fiughaidh was within. He put the chain about the neck of the lion whelp. The lion whelp went, and he cleared the castle ; he did not leave a creature or a monster alive in it. He set fire to the castle.† He was there a year, and he had no want.

He went out one day, and he said he would go to see his muime.

He took the lion whelp with him, and he went away. She perceived him coming. There was a sword at his side that day. She came out to meet him, and she had a brown lap-dog. He went to meet Manus with his mouth open, to put Manus to skaith, and to eat him. Away went the lion whelp, and he went before Manus, and he set his paw at the back of the throat of her " measan," and he let out his entrails on the earth.

" There, Manus," said she, " but put thy whelp in at the ridge of the lion's house."

He put the lion whelp in at the ridge of the house, and he put the chain about his neck, and he did not

* When the old man told me the story, he described devices on the shield of Manus, and a lion was one of them. This probably is founded on some lion on a flag. According to Gaelic poems Fionn's people had banners with devices on them, and Icelandic warriors had devices on their armour in the ninth century, according to the Njal Saga. Some of the articles are amongst the gear of King Arthur in the Mabinogion.

† It is manifest that something is wanting here. There is nothing before said about an enchanted castle, beset by monsters, and an imprisoned lady ; but there must have been monsters to clear out.

leave a lion under the ridge of the house unslain, and laid himself (down) stretched for dead along with them.*

Manus went home without whelp, without man, that night. What work should his twelve foster brethren be set to, but to clear out the lion's house. When they were put out there was not a lion under the ridge of the house that had not his throat cut. The lion whelp was without a drop of sweat upon him, and the iron chain that Manus had put on him (was) about his neck. One of them said that the lion which was yonder seemed strange to him, without a drop of sweat upon him, unlike the rest.

"That is the lion whelp of the man of my love," said one of the company. "The lion whelp of Manus."

"Well, then," said one of them, "though we are sworn not to go out of the town, before he rises we might go, and give a message."

"There is no man who goes out of this town," said the rest, "after the coming of night that there is not the pain of seven years upon him afterwards."

They went to the window, and when they went to the window the lion's whelp opened his eyes, and he came alive.

She went where her husband was, and she said to him to put the rough traveller† in order, and five hundred men in it.

He said that there would be the pain of seven years on any being who should go out after the falling of the night.

* This is like a bit of the story of Conall, and the house of the Tamhasg.

† Another possible meaning for this word may be the corpse buryer. It is often impossible to translate these names, the reciters do not understand them, and the context gives no help.

She said though there should be the pain of seventeen years in it, that they should go to seek the head of Manus.

The deaf haltman was what they used to call the man who was guarding the realm at that time, and he could not hear a jot till there should be nine nines shouting in his ear. He could kill nine nines backwards, and nine nines forwards with his sword. What should awake him but the stormy sound of the rough traveller coming, and he thought that it was a foe that was there. He arose upon the rough traveller, and he did not leave a mother's son of the five hundred alive, himself and the lion's whelp, and the twelve foster brothers of Manus went to the Old Bergen.

"Never thou mind," said she. "Though Manus did that to me. There is the Red Gruagach, son of the King of Greece, and he will take the head of Manus out of the Old Bergen."

Then went his mother here, and she sent a ship to Manus to the Old Bergen to take him away before the Red Gruagach should take the head off him. What should his muime do but put a sea thickening on the ocean, so that Manus might not get away. His mother sent a pilot in the ship, and what should the ship do but stop in the sea thickening.

"Is there a ship in the world that will take us out of this?" said Manus to the pilot.

"Indeed there is the speckled ship of the son of Valcan Smith," said the pilot.*

They were on board, and they could not stir.

---

* Bhalcan. There seems to have been some Celtic divinity, who was a smith, and a sea god—a kind of Neptune and Vulcan in one. Bhalcan occurs in Irish poems, and modern Gaelic poets have introduced Venus, Cupid, and other classical names into their modern songs. See note, Gaelic below, page 377.

At the mouth of the night the lion whelp thrust his head under the arm of Manus, and he went out off the ship, and Manus on his back. He went, and he reached a scaur. He left Manus on the scaur, and he himself made a spring down the other side of it. Manus fell asleep, and he would like as well to find death with the rest, rather than be left by himself on a rock. There came a voice to him, and it said to him "Arise." He rose, and he saw a ship.

Who was here but the ship of MacBhalcan Smith, and the lion whelp in the shape of pilot at the helm, and Mac-Vic-Valcan Smith and his twelve sailors dead on her deck. He reached the ship, and he put his twelve foster brethren and the daughter of the Earl of the Fiughaidh in the ship of MacBhalcan Smith. He fell to at sailing amongst the thickening. What should he see but land, and when he saw the land he saw the very finest castle he ever saw. He went on shore, and he put MacBhalcan Smith and his twelve sailors on shore on a point. He reached the castle, and he went in, and there was a fine woman there within, and twelve bald ruddy maidens. His twelve foster brothers sat beside the bald ruddy maidens,* and they said that they would never go for ever till they should get them to marry.

It was not long till there came home the White Gruagach, son of the King of the Light, and a great auburn clumsy woman, his mother.

"Who is here," said he, "looking my twelve brown ruddy daughters in the front of the face? and that I never saw a man that might look at them that I would not take his head off against his throat."

"These are my twelve foster brothers, and they

* Or cropped auburn maidens.

have taken love for thy bald ruddy daughters, and thou must give them to them to marry," said Manus.

"Well," said the White Gruagach, "the covenant on which I would do that, I am sure that thou wouldst not do it for me, that is, to put me in against my father, and that I am out from him for seven years."

"I will do that," said Manus, "but that thou thyself shouldst go with me."

On the morrow they went away, and they reached the King of the Light. The King of the Light came out, and he gave his right hand to his own son, and his left hand to Manus.* The lion whelp went, and he seized him, and he levelled him.

"Choke off me the monster before he takes my life from off me," said the King of the Light.

"I will do that," said Manus, "but write with a drop of thy blood that thy son is thy beloved heir."

"Well, it's long since I would have done that, if he had come himself to ask it."

Then he went and he wrote, and they went away to come home. When they were coming the daughter of the Earl of the Fiughaidh was in a burn.

"O," said the White Gruagach, "I am dead."

"What ails thee?" said Manus.

"There is a stone," said he, "in the burn, and there are three trouts under the stone, and they are in thy wife's apron. As long as the trouts should be alive I would be alive, and thy wife has one of them now in the fire."†

---

* His south hand, and his northern hand.

† The word which now means trout in Gaelic means speckled, and is sometimes translated salmon. It appears that there were sacred salmon in Irish mythology. Fish appear on the sculptured stones of Scotland, and salmon commonly appear as something magical in other Gaelic stories.

"Is there anything in the world," said Manus, "that would do thee good?"

"The King of the Great World has a horned venomous (creature), and if I could get his blood I would be as well as I ever was."

From a Stone in the Churchyard of St. Vigeans.—*Sculptured Stones of Scotland*, Pl. lxx. The stone has Christian symbols, but this would seem to represent the sacrifice of some fabulous animal. The people who sculptured the cross, the monks, and this figure, may have intended to represent the myths or ceremonies connected with the stone in Pagan and in Christian times.

They reached the house, and the White Gruagach was dead.

Then Manus went, and the speckled ship was stolen from him, and there was no knowing who in the world had taken it from him.

One of his foster brothers said that Brodram, son of the King of the Great World, had taken it with him.

He went away to Brodram. He asked him what made him take that ship from him. He said that he had stolen her himself before, and that he had no right to her. He said that his father had a venomous horned (creature), and that while the Beannach Nimhe was alive that his father would be alive, and that if the Beannach Nimhe was slain that he would have the realm.

He went with Brodram, and the venomous horned beast was in a park. The lion whelp went into the park, and he put his paw into the hollow of the throat of the venomous horned beast. The venomous horned beast fell dead, and the king fell dead within.

Then Brodram was King over the Great World, and Manus got the blood, and he returned back, and with it he brought the White Gruagach to life.

" It may not be that thou wilt not go thyself with me now to put me in on the realm," said he to the White Gruagach.

The White Gruagach said that he would go. He reached Brodram, and he said that he would go with him.

Balcan and his twelve apprentices were working in the smithy, and he revived his twelve sailors. He asked him to go with him, and Balcan said that he would.

There went Balcan, and the White Gruagach, and Brodram, and the Gruagach of the Tower, son of the King of Siginn, with him.

They reached Lochlann,
There met them a man in a red vesture ;
The White Gruagach, and the Red Gruagach began
Fearfully, hatefully proudly,
Three destructions they would drive off them.
To the cloud flakes of æther and heaven.

There gathered stag hounds, savage hounds,
To take pleasure in the monsters.
They would make the sea dry up,
And the earth burst,
And the stars fall.

The Red Gruagach* was slain, and his head stuck
on a stake, and Manus was crowned King over Lochlann, and he did not leave a living man in Lochlann.

Here I had intended to give the "orally collected"
version of the poem of Magnus as the fitting sequel and
contrast to this story, but as there is scant room within
my limits, I give the prose stories which go with it.
The lay of Magnus has often been translated. I hope
to be believed when I say that Magnus as I found him
in 1860 resembles Gillies, 1786, very closely.

This is the opening story of Magnus.

"When the Lochlannaich came on shore, Fionn said
to the lads that they should go to hunt; that he wished
to give them a feast that night, because it was not
likely that they themselves had much. They went to
hunt, and when the hunt was over, Caoilte was sent to
gather the game since he was the swiftest. It was
three hundred deer they killed, and twenty boars.

"Now when Caoilte had gathered the game there
went two hundred to gather heather to cook them,
a hundred and a half went to set in order the stones
under the caldron, and it was ten (deichnar) who were
burning (the fuel) beneath it. Three hundred went to
flay. Then Fionn sent Fearghus down to give a bidding to the Lochlannaich, and they did not deign to
answer him. Fionn took much proud anger because
the feast had been made and they had not answered."

* The Greek personage.

Then follows the poem as repeated by Donald MacPhie (smith), Breubhaig, Barra, October 1860, who learned it from his mother, and traces it up, for six generations, to an ancestor who came from Kintyre.

The poet, supposed to be Oisein, speaks as one who was present at "Uisge Laoire nan sruth séimh," where the scene is laid. They see a thousand barks coming to shore. The Feinn gather from every place, and converse. Conan, as usual, is cross grained throughout. Feargus, the son of Fionn, the brother of the poet, goes, and finds that it is

> " Mànus fuileach am fear fial
> Mac righ Beìth nan sgiath dearg
> Ard righ Lochlann ceann nan cliar," etc.

Blood spilling Manus, the generous one,
Beithe's king's son, of the red shields (? Bergen).
High King of Lochlann, chief of the brave, etc.

Come to seek Fionn's wife, and his famous hound Bran. A battle ensues, Manus is bound, and allowed to go home, and so it goes on for 164 lines of very smooth good Gaelic verse.

In Gillies there are 172 lines, or 43 verses, I have a verse which is not in Gillies, and the variations only amount to different readings, and to variations in language and orthography. After the poem comes the sequel of the story, also taken down from Donald MacPhie, which is not in Gillies.

"After the battle that was here, the Lochlanners were three years in disgrace with their wives. Fionn had been before this in Lochlann, and the daughter of the King of Lochlann had taken love for him. The thing which they did was to send Athach (a monstrous warrior or giant) to ask him to a feast in Lochlann, to make the arrangement of a league between them, that there might not be disputes for ever."

"In the Athach there was but one eye, and what was the very day that he reached the house of Fionn but a day that Fionn had a great feast for his set of lads. It was late that they had the feast, and when the Athach came in they had just sat at the feast. The Athach took (his way) up without leave or bidding, and he sat at the right shoulder of Fionn. When Conan saw how bold he was, he arose and he smote him, and he levelled him. Fionn got up on the instant, and he seized his shoulder, and he raised him, and he set him sitting where he was before. Then Fionn asked the Athach what man he was, and he told who he himself was. He said that he was a herald (teachdair) from the King of Lochlann, that came to give a bidding to themselves to a feast in Lochlann; that the daughter of the King of Lochlann was in great grief with the love she had taken for himself, and, though he had another wife, if he himself should lay bare one sight of her, there was no knowing but that she would be the better of it."

"When Fionn heard that it was a herald from the King of Lochlann, he desired Conan to be seized, and the binding of the three smalls to be laid on him, and that he should be cast into a dark hole, where he should see neither night nor day till the feast should be finished. Conan was there but half an hour when Caoilte said,—

"I never saw a herald coming from the King of Lochlann, for whose sake I would leave Conan bound, and that there is no knowing but he did the better deed."

"He let Conan loose, and he brought him in to the feast. They took well and right well to the Athach

that night, and on the morrow they made (ready) for
going with him. Said Fionn to Goll,—

"It is a shame for us to carry arms to a feast. It
will not be fitting to see them, but we will take with
us knives, that we may hide under our cloaks, and do
not uncover them for ever till I give you warning."

"Then here they went, and they reached Lochlann."

(And here let me point out how exceedingly inconsistent all this is with the common meaning of Lochlann, Scandinavia, and how simply is it all explained,
by supposing Lochlann to be the possessions of the
Lochlanners, the Scandinavians in Ireland, or in Scotland, or in any one of the islands.)

"When they arrived, the Athach steered them to a
great long house, with a door at its end. There was a
board there, from the door till it reached the upper end
of the house. The way of sitting they had was, one of
the company of Fionn was set about the board, and
two Lochlanners at his side. When the house was
filled, on each side there were two Lochlanners on each
side of the Fiantan. The feast was on the board, but
it was not to be touched till the King of Lochlann and
the Queen should come in. The king came, and the
queen, and their daughter. When the king came in,
Fionn rose up standing to salute and welcome him
(cuir failte air), and he would not take his hand. It
seems that he would not take his hand till every one
who had slain any of his lot of sons should tell in what
place he had left him. Every man was telling where
he left the son he had slain. It was from Osgar that
he asked the last one, and said Osgar,—

Mharbh mis e air truigh Chliabhain mu thuath,
Far an do thuit do mhor shluagh

Gun taing do dhuin agaibh d'a chionn,
A dh' fhas riamh an rioghachd Lochlann.
I slew him on the strand of Cliabhain in the north,
Where fell thy mighty host,
In spite of a man of you of any kin,
That ever waxed in the realm of Lochlann.

An seo nuair dh' aithnich Fionn,
Gun robh miothlachd ri bhith ann ;
Thoisich Fionn an sin,
Air deanadh rann.

Here now when Fionn perceived,
That ill blood was to be,
Then Fionn began
At making rymes.

" Na'm bithinns' um' ghobha,
'S math a dheanainn sgeanan,
Chuirin cruaidh 'non saidhean,*
S' chuirin siom† 'nan roinnean.‡
Chuirinn casan fraoich,
Le 'n cinn bhuidhe,
Ann an cuil thiugha,
Nam faobhar tana."

If I were a smith,
Well I'd make knives,
I'd put temper in handles,
I'd put shimmer on points.
I'd put hafts of heather,
With their ends of yellow,
In the thick backs
Of the keen edges.

* SAIDHEAN. The part of a knife or sword which goes into
the haft. There is no equivalent in English, so far as I know.
† SIOM. An image reflected by a blade from high polish.
‡ Roinn. The point of a sword, dagger, or knife.

Then they arose and they fell upon each other. They had but their knives, and the Lochlanners were under full arms.

Said Fionn—

" Where are they great vows, Manus ?
They were left where they were found said Manus."
" Cáite am bheil na mionnan mor a Mhanuis ?
Dh fhagas far an d' fhuaras thar Manus."

While the rest were at work, Fionn was in a dark corner making love to the daughter. The Fhinn beat the Lochlanners with the knives, and Manus was slain. Fionn took the daughter with him, and she was a year with him as a wife.

MacLean truly says, " this description of the manufacture of knives is wonderfully vivid and vigorous, and shews the richness of the language in such terms, while it appears to prove that the construction of warlike weapons was well understood in past times in the Highlands ;" but the next story seems to shew that the smith's art was not known in the days of *the* mythical Fionn, who got his sword from the fairy smith of Lochlann. Archæology seems to prove that the ancient inhabitants of Britain were once armed with bronze weapons, poor in iron, and rich in gold, and the Feinn were armed with pointed sticks, hardened in the fire, when they put gold rings on the fingers of warriors whom they had slain, and wished to honour. Icelandic sagas speak of abundance of gold amongst the Irish ; Gaelic stories mention gold frequently, and abundance of gold ornaments are dug up all over the United Kingdom : but iron swords are always mythical, and iron swords are rarely found, and their pattern is often Scandinavian on the sculptured stones, and when they are dug up.

May not the Scandinavians have been better blacksmiths than the Western Islanders, and the Celts better goldsmiths, richer, and more civilized than the Norsemen when they first met?

MANUS.

BHA righ Lochlann ann, 's phos e, 's rugadh dithis mac da. 'S e Oireal a bha air an darna fear agus Iarlaid air an fhear eile. Dh' eug an athair 's am mathair. Shuidh Parlamaid arson cileadaireachd a chur air an rioghachd gus an d' thigeadh a' chlann gu h-aois, 's gus an gabhadh iad bòidean na rioghachd orra fhein. Chuir iad fios air na gillean; 's bha Oireal 'na dhuine meata; 's e Iarlaid a bu mhotha. Thuirt Oireal ris a' pharlamaid nach gabhadh e gnothach fhathasd ris an rioghachd.

"Plochd cha bhi agaibh di," arsa a' pharlamaid, "mar an gabh sibh an diugh i."

Ars' Iarlaid ri Oireal, "Gabh thusa an dara leith 's gabhaidh mise an leith eile."

"Mata," ars' Oireal, "ni mi sin."

Sgriobhadh an rioghachd air na gillean. An am beagan bhliadhnachan phos Iarlainn nighean righ na Greige, 's phos Oireal nighean righ Sgiath sgial, righ na h-Arcuinn. Thug Sgiath sgial seisear mhnathan coimhideachd le a niginn 's thug righ na Greige 'leithid eile le a nighinn fhein. Tri raithean o'n oidhche sin bhuail anacair cloinne nighean righ na Greige, 's cuideachd bhuail anacair chloinne nighean Sgiath sgial, 's rugadh mic dhaibh, 's rugadh da mhacdheug do na mnathan coimhideachd. Thugadh Manus air mac Oireil, 's Eochaidh air mac Iarlainn. Thoisich na mic air tighinn air an aghaidh. Bha Manus a' fas mor, 's cha robh Eochaidh ach beag. Chuireadh do 'n sgoil iad, 's bha a chomhdhaltan fhein comhla ris a' h-uile fear aca.

Bha iad ag iomain air an fhaiche 'tighinn as an sgoil, 's chuir Manus am ball air Eochaidh.

"Bidh rioghachd m' athar fhein agamsa," arsa Manus.

Thuirt nighean righ na Greige, "B'e mo thoil crioch mhoirt, agus mhillidh, agus mharbhaidh, a chur air Manus."

"Mata b' e' sin a bu mhor am beud a chur air mac mo bhrathar fhein," ars' an righ.

2 B

"Mar an dean thusa e, ni mise e," ars' ise.

Dh' fhalbh i staigh 's bhuail i leideag air a mac fhein, 's chuir i mach as an taigh e.

"Falbh." ars' ise, " 's thoir ceithir ranna ruadha an t-saoghail ort, 's na faiceam air do bhonn air an fhonn(a) chiadhna thu fhad 's a bhitheas an saoghal air suidheachadh. Bheir mise leam Manus 's bidh e 'na mhac agam fhein."

Thug i Manus a staigh leatha fhein agus chuir i 'mac fhein air grianan aluinn, aon chasach, far am faiceadh e a' h-uile duine, 's nach fhaiceadh duine e. Bha Manus a staigh aice 's cha robh e a' faighinn dol a dh' amharc a mhathar idir. Thuirt a mhathair, an siud, gu 'n rachadh i far an robh a mhuime 's gu'n gabhadh i a comhairle. Ann an ceann bliadhna chuir i fios air Manus. Ann am beagan bhliadhnachan chuir bean bhrathar 'athar fios air Manus.

"Dé a Mhanuis," arsa nighean righ na Greige, " a tha thu a' smaointeachadh a dheanadh an diugh? Ma phosas thu gheibh thu an treas cuid de 'n rioghachd; fonn,(a) a's fearann, agus ionmhas."

" Mata cha 'n 'eil aois posaidh agams' ann," ars' esan.

" Cha ruig thu leas sin," ars' ise, " tha aon fhear air an fhearann agam fhein a fhreagras duit. Theid thu a dh' iarraidh a nighinn agus posaidh tu i. 'Se Iarla na Fiughaidh a th' ann. Posaidh tu nighean Iarla na Fiughaidh."

Dh' fhalbh i 's thug i leatha corr-theaghlach, 's bheireadh i leatha coig ceud fear. Rainig i taigh iarla na Fiughaidh a 'toirt do Mhanus a 'posadh. Thuirt bean iarla na Fiughaidh ritbe, " Cha 'n 'eil aois posaidh aig mo nighinnsa fhathasd, 's cha 'n 'eil aois posaidh aig Manus."

" Mata," arsa nighean righ na Greige, "taigh na tulach cha bhi agad air an fhearann agamsa mar an d' thoir thu do nighean da."

Smaointich an duine nach robh math dha a diultainn, 's phosadh Manus agus nighean Iarla na Fiughaidh ri 'cheile. Chaidh iad a luidhe an oidche sin an taigh bhrathar 'athar.

" An tu seo a Mhanuis, a mhic àidh agus a dhuine dhona? Am bheil fios agad dé a' bhean a thug i siud do dh' Eochaidh, a mac fhein? Thug a' gaoth luimneach Mhairt. Cha 'n ann ri mnaoi shaoghalta a phos i e; gus an d' thugadh e 'n ceann diotsa. Thusa agus bean agad air do leabaidh trath oidhche!(b) bidh thu 'dol as a' h-uile latha, 's cha chum thu cath risean."

"An ann mor seo a tha?" arsa Manus.

Chaidh e far an robh ise.

" Bi 'fagail na rioghachd," arsa bean bhrathar 'athar ris, "airneo cha bhi agad ach na 'bheir thu g' a chionn."

"B' e," ars' esan, "an treas cuid a gheall thu domh de 'n riogh-achd."

"Plochd cha bhi agad an seo," ars' ise; "tha do chuid fo chlachan agus fo gharbhlach anns an t-seana Bheirbhe."(c)

"Mata, o'n a tha thu 'gam chur air falbh, thoir dhomh seisear chomhdhaltan Eochaidh, 's gu 'm biodh a dha dheug agam."

Fhuair e siud. Dh' fhalbh e 's thug e air an t-seana Bheirbhe.†
Nuair rainig e 'n t-seana Bheirbhe cha robh a chridhe aig duine dol a choir a' chaisteil; Bha caoraich anns an t-seana Bheirbhe agus 'se na caoraich chorrachar a theirte riutha. Bhuail iad air deanadh sluichd 'san talamh. Bha na caoraich a' dol 'san t-slochd 's iad a' breith orra; 's bha iad 'gam marbhadh 's a' cumail feola riutha fhein. Bha iad bliadhna mar seo 's an t-seana Bheirbhe.

"Bhuais e! Bhuais e!" arsa Manus, "tha bliadhna o'n a chunnaic mi mo muime. 'S fhearra dhomh dol a 'faicinn."

"Cha b' e mo chomhairle duit dol ann," ars' iadson; "ach ma tha thu a' falbh tha da chomhdhalta dheug agad, 's thoir leat iad."

"Cha chuideachadh suarach dhomh fhein iad a bhith leam," ars esan.

Ghabh e air falbh agus bha nighean righ na Greige ag amharc a mach air uinneig 's mhothaich i do Mhanus a' tighinn. Chaidh i sios far an robh brathair 'athair.

"Tha mac do bhrathar a' tighinn an seo," ars' ise "le criosan duinte, daite, air a thaobh cli, air am faighte gaol ban og agus gradh mhaighdeannan."

Gu 'm b' ann g' a toilse crioch mhoirt, agus mharbhaidh, agus mhillidh a chur air. Thuirt brathair 'athar gu 'm bu mhor am beud siud; 's nach biodh esan an lathair siud a chur air.

"Mar a dean thusa e ni mise e," ars' ise.

Chaidh i mach as an taigh 's thug i a dha chomhdhalta dheug uaidh 's mhionnaich i iad di fhein. Dh' fhalbh esan air ais gus an t-seana Bheirbhe leis fhein gu dubhach, deurach bronach; 's bha 'n t-anmoch ann. De a chunnaic e ach fear earraidh dheirg. (d)

"An tu seo a Mhanuis?" ars' esan.

"'S mi," arsa Manus.

"Tha mi 'smaointeachadh, na 'm biodh olc na mhath de dh' airm agad, gu 'm faigheadh th 'd' righ air Lochlainn."

"Cn 'n 'eil sin agam," ars' esan.

"Mata," arsa fear an earraidh dheirg, "na 'n d' thugadh tu gealltanas domhsa bheirinn airm dhuit."

"De 'n gealltanas a bheir mise dhuit? Cha 'n 'eil dad agam ri 'thoirt duit."

"Mata cha 'n iarr mi moran ort; bha mi ann a' ni fhear pasgaidh arm aig do sheanair 's aig do shionseanair; na 'n d' thugadh tusa gealltanas domh gu 'm bithinn ann a' m' fhear pasgaidh arm agad bheirinn airm duit a nochd."

"Bheir mise sin duit ma 's e gu 'm bi mi gu brach a' m' righ."

Dh, fhalbh iad 's rainig iad an taigh. Thug fear an earraidh dheirg iuchair a mach 's dh' fhosgail e 'n dorus, 's nuair a dh' fhosgail e e bha 'n taigh sin lan arm; 's gun bìdeag ann ach airm.

"Siùd a nis 's tagh airm," arsa fear an earraidh dheirg. Rug Manus air claidheamh 's bhrisd e, 's a' h-uile fear a bha e 'breith air bha e 'ga bhrisdeadh.

"Na dean a Mhanuis,—na bi a' brisdeadh nan arm, 's gun fhios nach bi feum agad orra fhathasd. Nuair a bha mise ann a' m' dhuine og bha cogadh aig do sheanair, 's bha seana chlogad, agus seann luireach orm. Feuch iad." Arsa fear an Earraidh dheirg. Rug Manus air a' chlaidheamh 's dh' fhairtlich air a bhrisdeadh. Chuir e 'n clogadh 's an claidheamh uime. Dé a chunnaic e 'n sin ach brot(e) a nuas a driom an taighe. "Dé air am math am brot ud?" arsa Manus.

"Tha," ars' esan, "nuair a sgaoileas tu oirean air seilbh bidh agus dibhe, gheibh thu e mar a chosgas tu. Tha buaidh eile air; na 'n coinneachadh namhaid thu, a' gabhail seachad, bheireadh e pog do chul do dhuirn."

Thug e 'm brot do Mhanus, 's phaisg e'm brot na achlais. Dé a chunnaic e ach slabhraidh iaruinn a nuas a driom an taighe.

"Dé air am math an t-slabhraidh ud?" arsa Manus.

"Cha 'n 'eil creutair, air an t-saoghal, a chuirte siud mu amhaich nach biodh comhrag ceud fear air." Arsa fear an earraidh dheirg.

Thug Manus leis an t-slabhraidh. Nuair a bha e a' falbh dé a chunnaic e ach da leomhan agus cuilean aca. Thainig na leomhain mu choinneamh, 's iad gus itheadh, 's gus a sgath. Sgaoil e 'm brat, 's thainig na leomhain 's phog iad cul a dhuirn, 's ghabh iad seachad air. Dh' fhalbh an cuilean leomhain feadh a' bhruit 's phaisg e 'm brot mu 'n cuairt air. Phaisg e 'm brot mu 'n cuairt air 's thug e leis gus an t-seana Bheirbhe e. Nuair a rainig e 'n t-seana Bheirbhe bha nighean Iarla na Fiughaidh a staigh. Chuir e 'n t-slabhraidh mu amhaich a' chuilean leomhain. Dh' fhalbh an cuilean leomhain 's ghlan e 'n caisteal, 's cha d' fhag e creutair na uile bheist beo ann. Chuir e teine anns a' chaisteal. Bha e bliadhna an seo ann 's cha robh dith air. Chaidh e mach latha 's thuirt e gu 'n rachadh e dh' amharc a mhuime.

Thug e leis an cuilean leomhain 's dh' fhalbh e. Mhothaich ise

dha a' tighinn. Bha claidheamh air a thaobh an latha sin. Thainig
i mach 'na choinneamh 's bha measan donn aice. Ghabh e 'n
coinneamh Mhanuis, 's a bheul fosgailte, gus Manus a sgath agus
itheadh. Dh' fhalbh an cuilean leomhain 's ghabh e air thoiseach air Manus, 's chuir e 'spog ann an cul a' bhraghaid aig a
mheasan aice-se, 's leig e 'mhionach a mach gu talamh.

"Siud a Mhanuis," ars' ise, "ach cuir do chuilean a staigh air
driom taigh nan leomhan."

Chuir e 'n cuilean leomhain a staigh air driom an taighe, 's chuir
e 'n t-slabhraidh mu 'mhuineal, 's cha d' fhag e leomhan fo dhriom
an taighe gun mharbhadh, 's leig e e fhein 'na shineadh marbh
comhla riu. Chaidh Manus dachaidh, gun chuilean gun duine, an
oidhche sin. Dé 'n obair gus an do chuireadh a dha chomhdhalta
dheug ach a chartadh taigh nan leomhan. Nuair a chuireadh a mach
iad cha robh leomhan fo dhriom an taighe nach robh 'sgornan air a
ghearradh. Bha 'n cuilean leomhain agus gun bhoinne falais air, 's
an t-slabhraidh iaruinn, a chuir Manus air, mu 'amhaich. Thuirt
fear diu gu 'm bu neonach leis an leomhan a bha 'n siud; gun
bhoinne falais air, seach cach.

"Sin cuilean leomhain fìr mo ghaoil," arsa fear de 'n chuideachd,
"cuilean leomhain Mhanuis!"

"Mata," arsa fear diu, "gad a tha mionnan oirnn gun falbh as a'
bhaile; ma 'n eireadh esan dh' fhalbhamaid agus bheiremaid brath
seachad."

"Cha 'n 'eil duine a theid a mach as a' bhaile seo," arsa cach,
"an deigh do 'n oidhche tighinn, nach 'eil goirteas sheachd bliadhna
air as a dheigh."

Chaidh iadsan thun na h-uinneig; 's nuair a chaidh thun iad na
h-uinneig dh' fhosgail an cuilean leomhain a shuilean, 's thainig e
beo. Dh' fhalbh ise far an robh a fear 's thuirt i ris, an garbh-
theaghlach (ʃ) a chur air doigh agus coig ceud fear ann. Thuirt esan
gu 'm biodh goirteas sheachd bliadhna air neach a rachadh a mach
an deigh thuiteam na na h-oidhche. Thuirt ise gad a bhiodh goirteas
sheachd bhadhna deug ann gu 'm falbhadh iad a dh' iarraidh ceann
Mhanuis.

'Se 'm Bodhar Bacach a theireadh iad ris an fhear a bha a' dion
na rioghachd anns an am sin, 's cha chluinneadh e smid gus am
biodh naoidh naonar ag eubhach 'na chluais. Mharbhadh e naoidh
naonar air ais, 's naoidh naonar air adhart, leis a' chlaidhimh. Dé a
dhuisg e ach stoirm a' gharbh theaghlaich a' tighinn, agus shaoil e
gur h-e namhaid a bha ann. Dh' eirich e air a' gharbh-theaghlach,
's cha d' fhag e mac mathar de 'n choig ceud beo; e fhein agus an .

cuilean leomhain. Dh' fhalbh an cuilean leomhain, 's da chomhdhalta dheug Mhanuis, do 'n t-seana Bheirbhe.

"Coma leat," ars' ise, "gad a rinn Manus siud ormsa tha 'n
Gruagach dearg, mac righ na Greige ann, 's bheir e ceann Mhanuis
as an t-seana Bheirme."

Dh' fhalbh a mhathair, an seo, 's chuir i soitheach thun Mhanuis
gus an t-seana Bheirm, g'a thoirt air falbh, ma 'n d' thugadh an
gruagach dearg an ceann deth. Dé a rinn a mhuime ach muir-
tìothachd (g) a chur air a' chuan air alt 's nach faigheadh Manus falbh.
Chuir a mathair mairnealaiche (h) anns an t-soitheach. Dé a rinn an
soitheach ach stad anns a' mhuir tìothachd.

"Am bheil soitheach air an t-saoghal a bheir as an seo sinn ?" arsa
Manus ris a' mhairnealaiche.

"An leobhra tha; long bhreac Mhic Bhalcain (i) ghobha," ars'
am mairnealach.

Bha iad air bord 's cha b' urrainn iad gluasad.

Am beul na h-oidhche sparr an cuilean leomhain a cheann fo
achlais Mhanuis, 's ghabh e mach bhar na luinge, 's Manus air a
mhuin. Dh' fhalbh e 's rainig e sgeir. Dh' fhag e Manus air an
sgeir 's ghearr e fhein leum leis an taobh eile di. Thuit Manus 'na
chadal; agus bu mhath leis am bàs fhaighinn le cach, seach fhagail
leis fhein air sgeir. Thainig guth g'a ionnsuidh 's thuirt e ris,
"Eirich." Dh' eirich e 's chunnaic e soitheach.

Co a bha 'n seo ach long Mhic Bhalcain gobha, agus an cuilean
leomhain 'na riochd air an stiuir, 's Mac Mhic Bhalcain gobha, 's a
dha sheoladair deug, marbh air a h-urlar. Rainig e 'n soitheach, 's
chuir e 'dha chomhdhalta dheug, 's nighean Iarla na Fiughaidh ann
an long Mhic Bhalcain gobha. Bhuail e air seoladh air feadh na
tìothachd. Dé a chunnaic e ach fearann; 's nuair a chunnaic e 'm
fearann chunnaic e 'n aona chaisteal a bu bhreagha a chunnaic e
riamh. Ghabh e air tir 's chuir e Mac Bhalcain gobha 's a dha
sheoladair dheug air tir air rugha. Rainig e 'n caisteal, 's chaidh
e staigh, 's bha boireannach breagha staigh an sin 's a dha dheug
de nigheana maola, ruadha. Shuidh a dha chomhdhalta dheug
lamh ris na nigheana maola, ruadha, 's thuirt iad, nach fhalbhadh
iad gu bràch gus am faigheadh iad ri 'm posadh iad.

Cha b' fhada gus an d' thainig an gruagach bàn mac righ na
Sorcha dachaidh 's buinnseach (k) ruadh 'na mathair dha.

"Co seo ag amharc," ars' esan, "air mo dha dheug de nigheana
maola, ruadha an clar an aodainn ? 's nach fhaca mi duine riamh a
bhiodh ag amharc orra nach d' thugainn an ceann an aghaidh na
braghad deth."

" Tha da chomhdhalta dheug agamsa 's tha iad an deigh gaol a ghabhail air do nigheana maola, ruadha, 's feumaidh tu 'n toirt daibh a 'm posadh," arsa Manus.

" Mata," ars' an Gruagach bàn, " an cumhnant air an dean-ainnsa sin, tha mi cinnteach nach deanadh tusa rium e; sin mise a chur a staigh air m' athair, 's mi muigh air o cheann seachd bliadhna."

" Ni mi sin," arsa Manus, " ach thu fhein a dhol comhla rium." An la 'r na mhaireach dh' fhalbh iad. Rainig iad righ na Sorcha. Thainig righ na Sorcha mach, 's thug e 'lamh dheas d'a mhac fhein, 's a lamh thoisgeal do Mhanus. Dh' fhalbh an cuilean leomhain 's rug e air, 's leag e e.

" Caisg diom a' bhiasd ma 'n d' thoir e mo bheatha diom," arsa righ na Sorcha.

" Ni mi sin," arsa Manus, " ach sgriobh le boinne de t' fhuil gur h-e do mhac t' oighre dligheach."

" Mata 's fhada o'n a dheanainnsa sin na 'n d' thigeadh e fhein g'a iarraidh."

Dh' fhalbh e 'n seo agus sgriobh e e 's dh fhalbh iadsan an seo gu tighinn dachaidh. Nuair a bha iad a tighinn an seo bha nighean Iarla na Fiughaidh ann an allt.

" O," ars' an gruagach bàn, " tha mise marbh."

" Dé a th' ort ?" arsa Manus.

" Tha clach," ars' esan, " anns an allt, 's tha tri bric fo 'n chloich, 's tha iad ann an apran na mnatha agad. Fad 's a bhiodh na bric beo bhithinn-sa beo. Tha fear aca 's an teine, an drasd aig do mhnaoi-sa."

" Am bheil dad air an t-saoghal," arsa Manus, " a dheanadh feum dhuit ? "

" Tha," ars' esan, " beannach nimhe aig righ an domhain mhoir 's na 'm faighinn fhuil bhithinn cho math 's a bha mi riamh."

Rainig iad an taigh 's bha 'n gruagach bàn marbh. Dh' fhalbh Manus an seo, 's bha 'n long bhreac an deigh a goid air, 's cha robh fios, air an t-saoghal, co a thug uaidh i. Thuirt fear d'a chomhdh-altan gu 'n d' thug Brodram, mac righ an domhain mhoir, leis i. Ghabh e air falbh gu Brodram. Dh' fhoighneachd e dheth dé a thug dha an soitheach a thoirt uaidh. Thuirt esan gur h-e goid a rinn e fhein roimhe, 's nach robh coir aig urra. Thuirt e gu 'n robh beann-ach nimhe aig 'athair, agus fhad 's a bhiodh am beannach nimhe beo gu 'm biodh 'athair beo, 's na 'm marbht am beannach nimhe gu 'm biodh an rioghachd aigesan.

Dh' fhalbh e le Brodram, 's bha 'm beannach nimhe a staigh ann

am pairc. Chaidh an cuilean leomhain a staigh do 'n phairc, 's chuir
e a spog ann an lag a bhraghad aig a bheannach nimhe.   Thuit am
beannach nimhe marbh 's thuit an righ marbh a staigh.   Bha Brodram an seo 'na righ air an domhain mhor, 's fhuair Manus an fhuil,
's thill e, 's thug e beo leatha an gruagach ban.   " Cha 'n fhaod e
'bhith nach d' theid thu fhein leam a nis a m' chur a staigh air an
rioghachd," ars' e ris a' ghruagach bhan.

Thuirt an gruagach ban gu 'n rachadh.

Rainig e Brodram 's thuirt Brodram gu 'n rachadh e leis.   Bha
Balcan 's a dha fhaolainn (*l*) deug ag obair 'sa' cheardaich 's dh' ath
bheothaich e a dha sheoladair deug.   Dh' iarr e air dol leis 's thuirt
Balcan gu 'n rachadh.

Dh' falbh Balcan, 's an gruag ch ban, a's Brodram, 's gruagach
an tuir, mac righ Siginn leis. Rainig iad Lochlainn.   Choinnich
fear an earraidh dheirg iad.

> Thoisich an gruagach ban agus an gruagach dearg (*m*)
> Gu fiachach, fuachach, meanmnach.
> Chuireadh iad tri dithean diu
> Ann an cleidibh (*n*) athair agus iarmailt.
> Chruinnich mialchoin Fialchoim (*o*) (J. F. C.)
> A ghabhail aighir air na biastan.
> Bheireadh iad air an fhairge traoghadh;
> Air an talamh sgaineadh; .
> Air na rionnagan tuiteam.

Mharbhadh an gruagach dearg, 's chuireadh a cheann air stob,
's chrunadh Manus na righ air Lochlainn, 's cha d' fhag iad duine
beo ann an Lochlainn.

From Donald MacPhie, Iochdar, South Uist, who learnt it from
Iain MacDhomhnuill Ic Thormaid Domhnullach, Aird a mhachair,
who died sixty years ago at the age of sixty.   H. M'L.

I heard the man tell part of the story myself.   J. F. C.

Notes for Gaelic.

(*a*) Fonn, land generally on a larger scale than fearann. Probably
fearann may be arfhonn, arable land, the f slipping in as frequently
happens in Gaelic words.

(*b*) Trath oidhche, the time of night; different in meaning from
trath 'san oidhche, early in the night.

(c) A Bheirbhe, sometimes the old man said Bheirm. This word is translated Copenhagen by some scholars, I don't know why. The sound is nearer to Bergen, for b and g frequently replace each other in Gaelic; *e.g.* ubh, ugh, dubh, dugh, etc.

(d) Earradh, a dress, costume. Aodach trusgan, eideadh earradh. Aodach is any clothes good or bad; Trusgan is a good dress; Eideadh is a distinguishing dress or uniform; Earradh is a dress rather distinguishing an individual from others. Eideadh gaidheal-ach, we could never say an t-earradh Gaidhealach.

(e) Brot, same as brat.

(f) Garbh-theaghlach, this seems to have been some large kind of vehicle. It is spelt as it was pronounced. It might have been garbh-shinbhlach or carr-shiuhlach.

(g) Muir-tiothach, some curious thickening of the ocean so as to prevent the ship from moving. Muir-teachd may be the same word as this differently pronounced; and if so, it means gelly fish.

(h) Mairnealaiche, a pilot.

(i) Balcan. Is this the same as Vulcan? Bailc means a plunge, a flood. The smith constantly plunging his iron or steel in water might receive this name in consequence; falc is to bathe.

(k) Buinnseach, a big, strong, clumsy woman.

(l) Faolainn, same as foghlainte or foghlainteach, an apprentice.

(m) An gruagach dearg, a different person from the other fear earr-aidh dheirg.

(n) Cleid, a flake. Cleidean athair, sky flakes, clouds; probably the fine white clouds called cirri. May not this word be the root of cloud. H. M'L.

(o) Fialchoin, so pronounced; probably Fiadh-choin, deer-dogs, or wild-dogs, wolves, probably the last. J. F. C.

LXXXV.

THE SONG OF THE SMITHY.

From Donald MacPhie, Breubhaig, Barra.

1—OISEIN.

On a day as were on wide spread Rushes,
A valiant four of the company,
Myself, and Bound, and Grey Earth,
Fair's self was there, he was Bondage's son.

2

There was seen a coming from the plain
The big young lad on a single foot,
In his black, dusky black skin mantle,
With his dusky head-gear so rusty red.

3

Grim was the look of the young lad,
Hideous it was, and disfigured,
With his largeheaded mighty helmet,
With his blunt ploughshare (a) that grew russet red.

4—FIONN.

Then spoke to him Fionn MacChumail,
As a man who was like to faint,
" At what place is thy dwelling,
Thou lad with thy dress of skins ? "

5—SMITH.

" Blade, son of Furbishing, 's my right name,*
If you had the knowledge of a tale of me ;
I was a while at the smith's mystery,
With the King of Lochlann at Upsala. (b)

* Gillies,   1786 . . Lun MacLiobhainn.
  MacCallum, 1816 . . Luinn MacLiobhuinn.
  MacPherson   . . . . Luno.

DUAN NA CEARDACH.

1

Latha dhuinn air Luachair leothair,
Do cheathrar chrodha de 'n bhuidhinn ;
Mi fhein, a's Osgar, a's Daorghlas ;
Bha Fionn fhein ann, 's b' e Mac Chumhail.

2

Chunnacas a' tighinn o'n mhagh
An t-olach mor 's e air aona chois,
'Na mhanndal dubh, ciar-dhubh craicinn,
Le cheanna-bheairt lachdann 's i ruadh-mheirg.

3

Bu ghruamach coslas an olaich ;
Bu ghrannda sin agus bu duaichnidh ;
Le 'chlogada ceann-mhor, ceutach ;
Le 'mhaoil éitidh a dh' fhas ruadh dhearg.

4

Labhair ris Fionn MacChumhail,
Mar dhuine 'bhiodh a' dol seachad,
" Co 'm ball am bheil do thuinidh,
'Ille le d' chulaidh chraicinn ?"

5

" Lon* MacLiobhann, b'e m' ainm ceart e,
Na 'm biodh agaibhs' orm beachd sgeula ;
Bha mi treis ri uallach gobhainn
Aig righ Lochlann ann an Spaoili.'

* Lonn, a sword, a blade, a bar, a stake of wood, a bier pole,
anger ; a surge, a sea swell ; strong, powerful. Lonnrach, bright,
etc., a blaze, a gleam. Lunn, a smooth rolling swell, an oar
handle. Manks, *Lhun*, or *Lhunn*.

6

"I am laying you under enchantments,
Since you are a people in need of arms ;"
That you shall follow me, a band of quietness,
Westward to my smithy doors."

7—FIONN.

" Upon what place is thy workshop,
Or shall we profit by seeing it ?"

SMITH.

" Do you see it, if it may be,
But see it you shall not, if I can."

8—OISEIN.

Then they set them to their travel,
O'er the fifth of Munster in their hurrying speed,
And on yellow glens about birch trees,
Then went they into four bands. (c)

9

One band of these was the blacksmith,
Another band of them Daorghlas ;
Fionn was behind them at that time,
And a few of the chiefs of the Finne.

10

The blacksmith would cut but the one step,
On each lonely glen through the desert,
But scarcely his arms would reach to
A tuck of his clothes on his haunches.

11

Ascending the ground of the corrie,
Descending the pass of the edges ;
" A little delay," said the blacksmith,
" Shut not before me," quoth Daorghlas.

6

"Tha mise 'gur cur-sa fo gheasaibh,
O 's luchd sibh 'tha 'm freasdal armaibh,
Sibh gum' leantail, buidheann shocrach,
Siar gu dorsan mo cheardach."

7—FIONN.

"Co 'm ball am bheil do cheardach?
Na 'm feairde sinne g'a faicinn?"

GOBHA.

"Faiceadh sibhs' i ma dh' fhaodar;
Ach ma dh' fhoadas mise cha 'n fhaic sibh."

8

Gu 'n d' thug iad an sin 'nan siubhal
Air Choige Mhumha 'nan luath dhearg;
'S air Ghleannan buidhe mu bheithe
Gu 'n deach iad 'nan ceithir buidhnibh.

9

Bu bhuidheann diu sin an gobha;
Bu bhuidheann eile dhiu Daorghlas;
Bha Fionn 'nan deaghainn an uair sin
A's beagan de dh' uaislean na Finne.

10

Cha ghearradh an gobha ach aona cheum
Air gach gleannan faoin roimh fhasach,
'S cha ruigeadh airm ach air eigin
Cearbh dh' an aodlach shuas air mhasan.

11

A' direadh ri urlar a' choire,
A' tearnadh ri bealach nam faobhar,
"Fosadh beag ort" ars' an gobha;
"Na druid romham," arsa Daorghlas.

12—SMITH.

" Thou d'st not be in the door of my workshop,
In a strait place, were I alone." (*d*)

    .   .   .   .   .

    .   .   .   .   .

13—OISEIN.

Then they got bags for blowing,
The workshop was scarcely found out;
Four men were found of the king of Bergen,
Of crossgrained men and unshapely.

14

To every smith there were seven hands,
Seven pincers light and substantial;
And the seven hammers that crushed them,
And no worse would it suit with Daorghlas.

15

Daorghlas who watched at the workshop,
'Tis a certain tale that they fell out;
He was red as a coal of the oaktree,
And his hue like the fruit of the working.

16

Out spoke one of the blacksmiths
So gruffly, and eke so grimly,
" Who is that dauntless slender man
That would stretch out a bar of temper?"

17

Out spoke Fionn, who was standing,
The man of good answer at that time,
" That nickname shall not be scattered,
His name was Daorghlas till this hour."

12

" Cha bhiodh tu 'n dorus mo cheardach
An àite teann 's mi 'nam aonar."

. . . . .

. . . .

13

Fhuair iad an sin builg ri sheideadh ;
Fhuaradh air eigin a' cheardach ;
Fhuaras ceathrar dhaoine righ Meirbhe,'
De dhaoine doirbhe, mi-dhealbhach.

14*

Bha seachd lamhan air gach gobha ;
Seachd teanchairean leothair,' aotrom,
'S na seachd uird a bha 'gan spreigeadh ;
'S cha bu mhiosa 'fhreagradh Daorghlas.

15

Daorghlas, fear aire na ceardach,
'S sgeula dearbha gu 'n do throid iad,
'S e cho dearg ri gual an daraich,
'S a shnuadh a thoradh na h-oibre.

16

Labhair fear de na goibhnean
Gu grìmach agus gu gruamach ;
" Co e 'm fear caol gun tioma
A thairneadh a mach teinne (²) cruadhach ?"

17

Labhair Fionn a bha 'na sheasamh,
Fear a bu mhath freagairt 'san uair sin,
" Cha bhi 'n t-ainm sin sgaoilte,
Bha Daorghlas air gus an uair seo."

* This verse is not in MacCallum's version.

18

Then they got there stretched out
The arms that were straight and coloured,
The completed work that was finished,
Of finished arms for the battle.

19*

" Hiss " and " Fye " and " Make sure,"
And the " Like blade's daughter the smith's shop,"
And the long blade of Diarmaid—
Many was the day that he tried it.

20

I had " the Tinker of striplings,"
Of loud rattle in the battle keen ;
And "the son of the surge," that was MacChumail's,
Which never left a shred of the flesh of man.

21

Then we took to our travel,
To take a tale from the king of Lochlann ;
Then out spoke the king so high born
With force of sweet words as became him well.

22

We would not give, by your fear,
A tale of six of our party ;
We lifted up the spears,
And it was in front of the banners.

* The following verse from MacCallum gives the names of
some more of the swords :—

The " Magic bladed " was the blade of Oscar,
And the " Hard Massacrer " the blade of Caoilte,
And the " Polisher" the blade of Diarmaid,
Many a wild man killed she.

18

Thuair iad an sin 'nan sineadh
Na h-airm a bha direach daite,
'S an coimhlionadh a bh' air a dheanadh
De dh' armaibh deanta na faiche.

19*

" Fead " agus " Fuidh," agus " Fasdail,"
'S a' " Chomhlann" 'Ic na Ceardaich,
'S an lann fhada 'bh' aig Diarmaid,
'S iomadh latha riamh a dhearbh i.

20

'S agam fhein bha " Ceard⁵ nan gallan"
A b' ard farum 'n am nan garbh chath ;
" 'S Mac an Luin" a bh' aig Mac Chumhail †
Nach d fhag fuigheall riamh dh' fheoil dhaoine.

21

Gu 'n do ghabh sinne mu shiubhal
A ghabhail sgeula de righ Lochlann ;
Sin nuair labhair an righ uasal
Le neart suairce mar bu chubhaidh.

22

Cha d' thugamaid, air bhur n-eagal,
Sgeula do sheisear dh' ur buidhinn,
Gu 'n do thog sinne na sleaghan ;
'S gu 'm b' ann ri aghaidh nam bratoch.

* The following verse is from MacCallum :—

    Bi n Druidh lannach lann Oscair
    'S b' i Chruaidh Cosgaireach lann Chaoilte
    'S gu' m b' i n Liobhanach lann Dhiarmaid
    'S iomadh fear fiadhaich a mharbh i.

† Irish, Mac an Loin.

23

They were in seven battalions, (e)
And no warrior thought of fleeing ;
But on the ground of the field of Fine
We were there but six.

24

Two of these were myself and Caoilte,
Three of them was wily Faolan,
Four of them was Fionn the foremost,
And five of them was Osgar valiant.

25

Six of them was Goll MacMorna
That brooked no slur that I can mind ;
Now will I cease from the numbering,
Since the Fhinn have gone to decay.

26

We were good in the day of the Teavrai,
In the workshop of Lon MacLiobhain ;
This day how frail is my strength,
After having numbered the band.

(a) Eite is a piece added to a ploughshare when worn, a peri-
phrasis for an old sword ? Eite is the word in Gillies.

(b) I am indebted to MacLean for this clever suggestion. The
grave of Thor is shewn at Old Upsala. The same Gaelic word
is used in Gillies.

(c) In Gillies this varies considerably.

(d) Here there is a break in Gillies also, and the meaning is
obscure.   MacCallum makes it, Leave me not alone in a strait
place.

(e) This is so in Gillies also. Irish writers say that the Feinne
were a standing army of Irish warriors divided into seven battalions ; this makes the men of Lochlann to be so divided. One
Irish author says that the Feinne were Norsemen who guarded
Dublin.

23

Bha iadsan ann 'nan seachd cathan,
'S cha do smaointich flath air teicheadh ;
Ach air lar na Faiche fine
Cha robh sinne ann ach seisar.

24

Bu dithis diu sin mis' agus Caoilte ;
Bu triuir diu Faolan feall ;⁵
Bu cheathrar dhiu Fionn air thoiseach ;
'S bu choigear diu 'n t-Osgar calma.

25

Bu sheisar Goll MacMorna
Nach d' fhulaing tair ri m' chuimhne ;
Sguiridh mi mis dh' an aireamh
O chaidh an Fhinn gu sodradh.

26

Bu mhath sinn latha na Teamhruidh
Ann an ceardach Lonn 'Ic Liobhann ;
An diugh is anmhunn mo chàil
An deis a bhith 'g aireamh na buidhne.

¹ Spaoili, probably Upsala.
² Teinne, a mass, or bar of metal.
³ Meirbhe, same as Beirbhe, Bergen?
⁴ Leothair, substantial, from leoir.
⁵ Ceard, any kind of smith ; or-cheard, a goldsmith ; ceard
airgid, a silversmith ; ceard copair, a coppersmith ; ceard stavin,
a tinsmith, tinker ; ceard spainean, a spoonsmith. Gipsies and
travelling tinkers are pre-eminently ceardan or smiths, because
they work in a great variety of metals. Ceard nan Gallan, the
smith of the branches or youths, so called from being well
adapted to cut down the young and strong.
⁶ *Feall* here is probably *fial* mispronounced.

From Donald MacPhie, smith, Breubhaig, Barra, who learnt
it from his uncle Hector MacLaine.—H. M'Lean.
Breubhaig, Barra, October 1, 1860.

So far this is almost the very same as the version given in Gillies, published 1786. The number of verses is the same, and the number of lines, and the order of the story the same; but there are considerable variations in a small way. In the 8th verse they set off to travel "as chuige mugha na luimedheirg," on a yellow mountain, as Beither, a dragon, which may mean, like the fifth of Munster of Limerick, but which I suspect refers to some other legend, for it does not appear how Munster should run like a dragon. In the 16th verse only one smith, he who spoke, has seven hands. In the 20th verse Ossian's sword is "Deire na 'n colg," the end of anger. In the 26th, the word is teann ruith, hard running, instead of the word pronounced teavrai; and there are many slight verbal differences and changes in orthography. The piece is without doubt the very same which is in Gillies, and if the book is in the Long Island it might have been learned from it. But, on the other hand, the book professes to be a collection made in the Highlands, its genuineness has never been questioned, and I believe that this is but a proof of the tenacity of popular memory for things which suit popular taste.

Another version was taken down for MacCallum, and published in 1816; I have indicated the chief differences in the footnotes. There is an Irish prose version of the story lately published (Ossianic Society's 2d vol.), which differs materially; it reduces the whole to a race; Fionn carried his sword with him; the smith is a giant with one leg, one arm, and one eye, who is bound by Fionn; his name is Roc, son of Diocan. As the Manks tradition (see introduction, vol. i. liii.) agrees with these Gaelic poems, I suspect the Irish story is the tradition more fallen to decay.

Now as an example of the way in which these poems pervade the whole traditions of the country and are interwoven with each other, let me give the following account of a visit to pick up a version of the poem in Islay. MacLean's letter seems worth preservation.

Ballygrant, May 27, 1861.

Sir—I called on old MacPhail at Scanlistle last Friday; it was the first time I had spoken to him for at least twenty years, for it is but lately that he has come to this parish. He left it fully more than twenty-five years ago, and was for a long time a workman with Doctor MacTavish. There the poor fellow got hurt, and the result was that he lost his leg. It may be well to state that he was a skilful and industrious workman, as there is a current opinion that these storytellers are found among the worthless and lazy. Before he left this parish he was a workman with old Rounsfell at Pearsabas, and he was the person that was always sent to kiln-dry and mill the corn at Ballygrant. It was then, while kiln-drying corn, that he amused me with these Fenian stories. I regret to say that the verses are not so complete as I used to hear them from him. I reminded him of Sinsearrachd Fhinn, of which he was wont to give me a long list, but of this he could remember nothing the other day. I remember it went this way :—Fionn MacChumhail, 'Ic Trathuil, 'Ic treun-moir, 'Ic Cham laora, but I cannot remember any other name beyond cam laora, or crooked toes.

When I entered the house he was sitting by the fireside with his wooden leg. The old fellow's eye brightened when he saw me, and I told him I wished to hear some of his old lore again. "O," said he, "b' abhaist domh 'bhith 'gan gabhail sin a chumail toil inntinn riut" (I used to be reciting these to thee to keep thee pleased). "Cha bhiodh esan ach 'na phaisde an sin" (he would be but a child then), said his brother's wife. "Bha e 'na bhalach caol, luirgneach 'san am" (he was a slender leggy boy at the time), a description which is not altogether inappropriate yet. I inquired of him about the old people whom he was wont to hear reciting these stories in his youth, and he enumerated several, and said that the poems were long and beautiful, and that to listen to them was the delight of all. He quotes something

here and there of almost all I have got. "Bas Gharuidh;" he related to me, "The Incident of the Pigeons;" but with respect to
Fionn, he says his thigh was cut through, and that he was worthless ever afterwards.

"O bu lurach an eachdraidh i nuuir a bhiodh i air ah-innseadh
gu ceart" (Oh that history was one of price when it was rightly
told), exclaimed he with enthusiasm.   During the conversation I
gave him three glasses of good strong whisky, and you would not
know that he had tasted it, further than being in good spirits.
Verily alcohol is not always poison, as total abstainers pronounce
it to be.—I am, Sir, yours sincerely,

                                        HECTOR MACLEAN.

The conversation is written in Gaelic, but a translation is sufficient.

I give the verses as an example of the way in
which scraps may be picked up,. which might be used
in mending other versions.

DUAN NA CEARDACH, ETC.

From   Malcolm MacPhail, Scanlistle, aged eighty years.
Learnt it from Alexander MacQueen, Persabas, sixty years ago.
MacQueen was past eighty years of age at that time.

                          2

          Chunnacas a teachd ar coir,
          Fear mor agus air aona chois ;
          Le a mhantal dubh ciardhabh craicinn ;
          Le 'ionnar lachduinn 's le ruadh bheairt.

                    2—New verse.

Aon suil mholach an clar sodainn
'Se sior dheanadh air MacChumhail,
" Ce thu fhein ? " arsa MacChumhail;
" Na cia as duit ? "

3—GOBHA. New.

" Thainig mis' 'ur cur fo gheasaibh,—
Seisear de mhaithibh na Feinne,
A bhith 'gam ruith gun easraich
Siar gu dorus mo cheardach."

4—New.

Thug e as mar ghaoth an earraich
Mach ri beannaibh dubha 'n t-sleibhe.

10

Cha d' thugadh e ach an aona cheum
Thar gach aon ghleann fuarraidh, fasaidh ;
'S cha 'n fhaiceadh tu ach air eigin
Cearb d' a eideadh thar a mhasan.

FIONN RI CAOILTE.

" Freagair agus sin do chasan,
'S gabh sgeula de'n rugha." *

11

A' tearnadh aig Alltan a' chuinir,
Fosgladh gu 'n d' thug an gobha,
" Na druid romham," arsa Doorghlas.

7

CAOILTE.

" A rugha cait am bheil do cheardach ?
Na 'm b' fheairde sinne g' a faicinn ? "

GOBHA.

" Mo cheardach cha 'n 'eil ri fhaotainn,
'S ma dh' fhaodas mise cha 'n fhaic sibh."

14

Labhair gobha de na goibhnean,
Lo curam mor agus le gruaim ;
" A righ co 'm fear caol gun tioma,†
A shineas an sineadh cruadhach ?"

* Rugha, a smith. Reciter.
† Sineadh, a bar of metal. Reciter.

15—Fionn.

"A righ gu meal thu t' ainm a Chaoilte !
Cha bhi Daorghlas ort o'n uair seo."

New.

A' Chruaidh Chosgarrach lann Osgair,
An Leadarnach mhor lann Chaoilte,
Mac an Luin aig Fionn MacChumhail,
Nach fag fuigheall de dh' fheail dhaoise.

2—Various.

There was seen nearing us
A big man upon one foot,
With his black dusky black skin mantle,
With his hammering tools, and his " steel lathe."

New verse—follows the 3d.

One shaggy eye in his forehead,
Making ever for MacChumhail,
" Who is thyself," said MacChumhail,
" Or whence art thou ?"

New verse—follows the 4th.

" I came to lay you under enchantments,
Six of the chiefs of the Feinne,
To be chasing me without hurry,
West to the door of my workshop."

7—Half new verse ; follows 7th.

He set off like the wind of the spring time,
Out to the dark mountains of the high grounds.

10

He would take but a single step,
O'er each single cold glen of the desert ;
Thou could'st have seen but hardly
A tuck of his clothing o'er his hurdies.

FIONN TO CAOILTE. New—follows 10.
Answer and stretch thy legs,
And take a tale of the blacksmith.

Rugha is a smith according to the reciter. Raute
is a Lapp nickname for a smith, as I learned on the
Tana, where I took the sketch of the skin-clad smith,
whose portrait I give as an illustration.

Here the old man forgot his poem, but remembered
a bit of his story.

" When Caoilte was at full speed, thou might'st see
three heads on him. His two shoulders would be
rising aloft, as though there were two heads, and his
head would be crouching down, he would be going as
it seems half bent." At vol. ii., 416, this occurs
in the tale of the white chief, and this explains what
I did not understand.

Then he went on with a few lines of verse.

11
Descending by the streamlet of the Shaper,

.   .   .   .   .

At the opening that the smith made,
" Shut not before me," said Daorghlas.

7—CAOILTE.
" Oh, Rugha, where is thy workshop,
Or should we profit to see it ? "

SMITH.
" My smithy is not to be found out ;
And if I may, see it you shall not."

14—Various.
Out spoke a smith of the blacksmiths,
With great care and a grim frown,
" King ! who is the slender fearless man,
That will stretch the tempered bar."

15—FIONN

"King ! mayst thou snatch the name,
Thou shalt not be Daorghlas from this hour."

19—Partly new ; follows 19.

"Victorious hardness," Osgar's blade,
"The big slasher," the blade of Caoilte,
"Mac-an-Luin" was Fionn MacChumhail's,
That never left a shred of the flesh of man.

Here this poem ends, so far as this old man is concerned ; but enough remains to prove that he did not borrow from Gillies or MacCallum, for there are several lines and some verses which are not to be found in the books.

It is also manifest that there is a great deal missing. In the Lay of Diarmaid, he says that he was one of the party ; his sword is mentioned here, but he is not.

MacLean writes :—"At the end of this verse Mac-Phail relates that the arms required to be tempered in the blood of a living person ; that the smith's daughter took a fancy to Fionn, who had a love spot (which was Diarmaid's property), and that she told him, unless he killed her father with the sword, that her father would kill him. This Fionn accordingly did. This is different from the usual story, according to which the sword is tempered in the blood of the old woman, the smith's mother. Probably the variation may be owing to forgetfulness on the part of Mac-Phail, caused by old age and by having had a paralytic stroke last winter."

"This was when they got the arms they had before ; but 'Tunnachan,' they were sticks with sharp ends made on them, and these ends burned and hardened in the fire. They used to throw them from them, and they could aim exceedingly with them, and they could drive them through a man. They used to have a bundle with them on their shoulders, and a bundle in their oxters. I myself have seen one of them that was found in a moss, that was as though it had been hardened in the fire."

This then gives the popular notion of the heroes, and throws them back beyond the iron period.

"There was a great day of battle between themselves and the Lochlanners, which was called Latha nan Tunnachan, the day of the stakes. I have heard old men speaking of it, and it was down thereabouts, about Chnoc angail that they gave it. They had a great day there."

This then fixes the period; at the time of the wars with Lochlann in Islay.

" It was in the side of a knoll at Alltan a chuirin that the fairy smith had his smithy."

" There was a great carlin once in Lochlann. It is Muirearteach maol ruadh that they used to say to her. She came from Lochlann, and she brought a smithy and the smith (ceardach agus an Gobha) with her on her back to sharpen the spears; she was but a witch, but the Fheinn slew her. Said the King of Lochlann when he heard this"—here comes in verse 23 of the poem given already, page 130, with the English word sink introduced, and a few variations; and this joins the lay of the witch to the lay of the smithy.

" The Lochlanners were difficult (that is, cross and fierce); and they had so much iodramanach and witchcraft that it is thus they used to do much of their valour."

" Goll was the strongest man that was in the Fheinn, and he could eat seven stags at his dinner. Fionn was a patient worthy man, and they used always to take his counsel. Fionn and Osgar, Goll and Oisean, four 'postaichean' of the Feinne, the high law people, Luchd ladh."

This would seem to explain how three generations fill such a large space in Celtic popular tradition. If the names of the original warriors became the names of offices or officers they may have been Celtic gods at first and commanders of Irish, Scotch Scandinavian, and British Feinne afterwards, in the third century and in the twelfth. There were many Osgars at the battle of Gaura, and Fionn, who is killed in one century, is all alive in the next.

"Fionn was not a king over land, he was but a chief over the men."

"Was there any other name said to him but Righ na Feinne, king of the Fane?"

"There was not."

"It is Conan who was the weakest man that was in the Fheinn, because they used to keep him maol (cropped). He had but the strength of a man, but if the hair should get leave to grow there was the strength of a man in him for every hair that was in his head; but he was so cross that if the hair should grow he would kill them all. He was so short-tempered (athghoirid) that he used to be always fighting with them."

So all accounts agree; and Kai, Arthur's attendant, was of the same disposition.

"When Goll would be in great rage the one eye would come 'dorn gulban' out, and the other eye would go 'dorn gulban' in. I think myself that his appearance would not be beautiful then."

Neither narrator, scribe, nor translator knows what "dorn gulban" means, but Conall *Gulban* struck *dorn* a fist on a man, and knocked his eye out on his cheek.

" Did you ever hear," Righ Mhor bheinn (king of
Morven, of great hills), said to Fionn ?

" I have heard it" (chual). This was put as an
experiment to try the effect of a leading question, and
it produced a contradiction ; but he might have heard
the name and have forgotten it till reminded.

" They would be always staying over at Eas Laigheann, at Goirtean taoid, when they were in this island
(Islay), and the place for the caldron is there yet, and ·
they say that the caldron is buried there. It is Eas
Laigheann nan sruth seimh that they used to call it—
lin of Laigheann of the still streams—they were so
fond of it. They had no house at all there."

This joins Gaelic to Welsh and Irish traditions,
for this caldron is often mentioned, and it upsets Scotch
and Irish topography altogether.

" There came a woman on them there once from
the westward, and they said to her—

> Tha sinne 'cur mar choran 's mar gheasan ort,
> Gu 'n innis thu, co thu fhein na co do mhiunntir ?
> 'S mise nighean righ na Sorchann,
> Sgiàth an airm ;
> 'S gur h-e 's ainin dha 'm Baoidhre borb ;
> 'S gu 'n d' thoir e mise leis,
> Cià mor bhur treis as an Fhéinn.
> Cia b' fhada 'n oidhche gu latha,
> Cha bu ghna leinn 'bhith jun oheol.

We lay it as a circuit and as spells on thee,
That thou tell us who thou art, or thy people.

" I am the daughter of the king of Sorchann,*

---

* Sorchann, MacLean suggests, may be Drontheim or Trond-
jem. Sorachan used to mean an elevation on which a shinny
ball was played to be " hit off," and it meant any other hillock.

Baoidhre, from Beithir, a large serpent or dragon, and Righ,
a king, so called probably from having a serpent as part of his
armorial bearings.—H. M'L.

Shield of armies,
And that his name is Baoidhre borb,
And that he will take me with him.
Though great our time from the Fane,
Though long be the night to day,
It was not our wont to be without music.

"They were in such a great (Iomagain) trouble about the man who was coming that they did not set up any music."

" 'We will rise out in the morning,' said they, ' to see who is coming upon us.' "

Chunnucas a' teachd ar coir fear mor air steud chiar-dhubh, rionna-gheal, a' coiseachd air an fhairge, staigh as an aird an iar.

Cuireamaid ar comihairle ri cheile,
Feuch co 'ghabhas sgeula de 'n oigear.
Labhair Goll le curam mor as le gruaim,
Co 'theid fo m' sgéith-sa chumail diom nam buillean
    cruadhach.

Bhuail am fear a thainig beum sgéithe 's dh' iarr e comhrag coig ceud laoch. Leum an deo as a' mhnaoi an an taobh eile dhiu leis an eagal.

" There was seen coming near us a great man on his dun black, white-haired steed, walking on the sea, in from the western airt.

' Let us lay our counsel together,
  See who will take a tale from the youth,'
Spoke Goll, with great care, and a frown,
' Who will go under my shield to ward off the
    tempered strokes.'

" The man who came struck a shield blow, and he asked for a battle of five hundred heroes. The life leaped out of the women on the other side of them for fear.

" They killed him at last.

> Thiodhlaicear aig braigh an eas,
> Fear mor bu mhor meas agus miadh ;
> Chuir Fionn MacChumhail fainn oir,
> Air gach meur aig an onair an righ.

They buried at the top of the lin
The great man of great honour and esteem.
Fionn MacChumail put a golden ring
On each of his fingers in honour of the 'king.

" I saw a man in Goirtean taoid (in Islay), and he found one of the rings on the point of his sock when he was ploughing—Murchadh MacNeacail. It was one of the old Highland ploughs he had. There were great long beaks on them. The carle got much money for the ring."

Now this is the story of the well-known poem of Fainesoluis, localized in Islay, and the finding of a gold ring assumed to be proof positive of its exact truth by the old man who tells it. I also have a gold ring which was found in Islay with a lot of others. It is said that the finder made handles for a chest of drawers of these gold rings, and that a pedlar gave him a fine new *brass* set in exchange for the old ones, which he carried off and sold. Some of them are said to be in the museum at Glasgow, one I have, and the rest were probably melted. I know of several discoveries of gold rings, chains, etc., made in Islay. Now it is possible that this tradition of the Feinne may be true. The story is in Dean MacGregor's MS. as a poem of 161 lines, attributed to Ossian in 1530. It is an episode in the 3d book of Fingal, 1790. It is claimed by Irish writers as Moira Borb, 1789, in vol. v. of the Ossianic Society's transactions, 1860.

I have three traditionary version as poems, one

written down in September 1860, in Barra, called
MacOighre Righ na Ior-smàil ; eighty-four lines from
Donald MacPhie, Breubhaig, who says he learned it
from Hector MacLaine (smith), an uncle of his who
could neither read nor write, and who died aged about
eighty some twenty years ago.   In this, Padruig and
Oisean, and Fionn, and Fionn's four sons, and Osgar,
and the daughter of the king under the waves, and a
big man who comes in a ship, are the actors.   The
language is curious, and the poetry good.   I regret
extremely that I have no room for it.

The other is from Patrick Smith, South Boisdale,
South Uist ; an old man who learned it in his youth
from Roderick MacVicar, North Uist, seventy-three
lines, Macabh Mor MacRigh na Sorcha.   The story
is the same, but Padruig does not appear.   The burial
of the hero at the top of a lin with rings on his fingers
is given, which is in the Dean's version.   The last line,

Tha sgeul beag agum air Fionn,

is the first and last line in the Dean's, and generally
my versions and this fragment and the Dean's might
be fused so as to make a more complete story, and a
longer and perfectly genuine poem in Scotch Gaelic.
The third version is called dan na H ighean, and has
eighty-four lines, written by Mr. Torrie in Benbecula,
from the dictation of Donald Macintyre, who learned
it some fifty years ago from an old man who afterwards
went to America, John MacInnes or Iain og Mac-
Fhionlai.   This joins Scotch and Irish traditions, Mac-
Pherson's Ossian, with genuine traditions and old MSS.,
and joins poetry to prose tales.

"There was a young lad in the Fheinn, who was
called Coireall, and he used always to be in the house
of the women, because he had not come to the age of a

man. It is Goll that had Mir morra na Feinne, the great morsel of the Fane, that was every bit of marrow that was in every bone to be gathered together and brought to him. Coireall came in, and he took with him some of the marrow, and he and Goll fell out (went over each other). The law that Fionn made was, that they should drive bones through the wattled rods that were dividing the house, and the one with whom the bone should go, the marrow to be his."

This is the common partition in Highland cottages, rods woven into a kind of rude basket-work, and plastered with clay. Rob Roy's house at the head of Glenshira, near Inverary, is so divided.

They did that, and Goll dragged Coireall through the wattled rods with the bone.

After that they went to try each other to the strand (cladach), and Coireall won of Goll, and he left the woman's house."

> Cluiche ri cluiche nan soc,
> Cluiche nan corcan s nam bian ;
> A' chulaidh chomhraig a bh' aig an dis
> Cha 'n fhaca mi roimhe riamh.

Each game to the game of the ends,
The game of the whittles and skins,
The battle array that these two had,
I never before have seen.

This then paints the dwellings of the heroes as very rude, and gives the clue to another poem which I have : sixty lines of very good popular poetry, describing how Goll slew Coireall at a merrymaking, and how Fionn lamented over his son, and why he hated Goll thenceforth. I have not found this in any book as yet.

"It must be that the Feinn were strong ?"
"Hoo ! They were as strong as the horses. There

2 D

was one who was called Mileach Mor, and he sent word
for them once, and the chase fallen short. When they
arrived, they were put into a long house there, and
they were without anything. A big black girl came
in, and she asked a battle of warriors from them."

"Let me get to her," said Conan.

Conan went, and she seized him, and she floored
him, and she plucked three of her hairs, and she
bound his three smalls. Then she went out, and they
loosed Conan. She came in again, and she sought a
battle of warriors, "Let me get at her," said Conan.

"What canst thou do!" said they to him. They
let him go, and she floored him, and this time she did
something else to him, and then she went out.

They killed the Mileach Mor, and they had the
keep of a day and a year there.

This joins an Islay tradition to one published by Mr.
Simpson in 1857, as current in Mayo (see pages 220
and 227), and it also joins in with a great many other
stories which I have in manuscript, and with Magach
Colgar, No. xxxvi, and so to ancient MSS. now in
the Advocate's Library. And thus one old Highlander
with a failing memory, but who can still remember
some scraps of what he learned in his youth, and
could remember in his manhood, forms one mesh in a
net-work of tradition, and manuscript and print; history and mythology, prose and poetry, which joins the
whole Gaelic family together, extends over three centuries, and may be found to join them to the earliest
records of the Pagan world. This is no solitary case.
The man is a specimen of a class which survives in far-
away corners, but which must soon vanish before
modern ways, together with the Gaelic language.

No. LXXXVI.

NIGHEAN RIGH FO THUINN.

THE DAUGHTER OF KING UNDER-WAVES.

From Roderick MacLean (tailor) Ken Tangval, Barra, who heard it frequently recited by old men in South Uist, about fifteen years ago. One of them was Angus Macintyre, Bornish, who was about eighty years old at the time. Written by H. Mac-Lean, 1860. I have selected this, because it shews one of the Ossianic heroes in a very mythological character. I omit the Gaelic for want of room, and translate closely but more freely.

THE Fhinn were once together, on the side of Beinn Eudainn, on a wild night, and there was pouring rain and falling snow from the north. About midnight a creature of uncouth appearance struck at the door of Fionn. Her hair* was down to her heels, and she cried to him to let her in under the border of his covering. Fionn raised up a corner of the covering, and he gazed at her. "Thou strange looking ugly creature," said he "thy hair is down to thy heels, how shouldst thou ask *me* to let thee in ?"

She went away, and she gave a scream. She reached Oisean, and she asked him to let her in under the border of his covering. Oisean lifted a corner of his covering, and he saw her.

"Thou strange, hideous creature, how canst thou ask me to let thee in ?" said he.

"Thy hair is down to thy heels. Thou shalt not come in."

* A falt 's a fionna.

She went away, and she gave a shriek.

She reached Diarmaid, and she cried aloud to him to let her in under the border of his covering.

Diarmaid lifted a fold of his covering, and he saw her. "Thou art a strange, hideous creature. Thy hair is down to thy heels, but come in," said he. She came in under the border of his covering.

"Oh, Diarmaid," said she, "I have spent seven years travelling over ocean and sea, and of all that time I have not passed a night till this night, till thou hast let me in. Let me come in to the warmth of the fire."

"Come up," said Diarmaid.

When she came up, the people of the Finn began to flee, so hideous was she.*

"Go to the further side," said Diarmaid, "and let the creature come to the warmth of the fire."

They went to the one side, and they let her be at the fire, but she had not been long at the fire, when she sought to be under the warmth of the blanket together with himself.

"Thou art growing too bold," said Diarmaid. First thou did'st ask to come under the border of the covering, then thou did'st seek to come to the fire, and now thou seekest leave to come under the blanket with me ; but come."

She went under the blanket, and he turned a fold of it between them. She was not long thus, when he gave a start, and he gazed at her, and he saw the finest drop of blood that ever was, from the beginning of the universe till the end of the world at his side. He shouted out to the rest to come over where he was, and he said to them.

* This gives to Brat the meaning of the cover of a tent or booth, it generally means a flag, a rag, or a mantle.

"Is it not often that men are unkind! Is not this the most beauteous woman that man ever saw!"

"She is," said they, as they covered her up, "the most beautiful woman that man ever saw."*

Then she was asleep, and she did not know that they were looking at her. He let her sleep, and he did not awaken her, but a short time after that she awoke, and she said to him, " Art thou awake Diarmaid ?"

"I am awake," said Diarmaid.

"Where would'st thou rather that the very finest castle thou hast ever seen should be built ?"

"Up above Beinn Eudainn, if I had my choice," and Diarmaid slept, and she said no more to him.

There went one out early, before the day, riding, and he saw a castle built up upon a hill. He cleared his sight to see if it was surely there ; then he saw it, and he went home, and he did not say a word.

Another went out, and he saw it, and he did not say a word. Then the day was brightened, and two come in telling that the castle was most surely there.

Said she, as she rose up sitting, " Arise Diarmaid, go up to thy castle, and be not stretched there any longer."

"If there were a castle to which I might go," said he.

"Look out, and see if there be a castle there."

He looked out, and he saw a castle, and he came in. "I will go up to the castle, if thou wilt go there together with me."

* The very same idea exists in a Spanish legend of the Cid, who in like manner shewed kindness to, and shared his couch with a leper: in the night he changed into St. Lazarus, all bright and shining.

" I will do that, Diarmaid, but say not to me thrice how thou did'st find me," said she.

" I will not say* to thee for ever, how I found thee," said Diarmaid.

They went to the castle, the pair. That was the beautiful castle ! There was not a shadow of thing that was for the use of a castle that was not in it, even to a herd for the geese.

The meat was on the board, and there were maid servants, and men servants about it.†

They spent three days in the castle together, and at the end of three days she said to him, " Thou art turning sorrowful, because thou art not together with the rest."

" Think that I am not feeling sorrow surely that I am not together with the Fhinn," said he.

" Thou had'st best go with the Fhinn, and thy meat and thy drink will be no worse than they are," said she.

" Who will take care of the greyhound bitch,‡ and her three pups ?" said Diarmaid.

" Oh," said she, " what fear is there for the greyhound, and for the three pups ?"

* Na can. Cha chan. This verb is not common in some districts.

† This description of magnificence is very characteristic. The narrator, knowing nothing earthly about castles, describes nothing, but leaves everything to fancy, except the goose herd, and the food, and the waiters. An Arabian story-teller would have given a long detail of eastern magnificence, the Countess d'Aulnoy would have filled in the picture from her own knowledge of courts, and when all is done the incident is the same. It was the most magnificent castle that could be imagined, and there were lots to eat, and servants to work, and there is an end of it.

‡ Saighead mialchoin ; perhaps arrow, Greyhound.

He went away when he heard that. He left a blessing with her, and he reached the people of the Finne, and Fionn, the brother of his mother, and there was a chief's honour and welcome* before Diarmaid when he arrived, and they had ill will† to him, because the woman had come first to them, and that they had turned their backs to her, and that he had gone before her wishes, and the matter had turned out so well.

She was out after he had gone away, and what should she see but one coming in great haste. Then she thought of staying without till he should come, and who was there but Fionn. He hailed her, and caught her by the hand.

"Thou art angry with me, damsel,"‡ said he.

"Oh, I am not at all, Fhinn," said she. "Come in till thou take a draught from me."

"I will go if I get my request," said Fionn.

"What request might be here that thou should'st not get," said she.

"That is, one of the pups of the greyhound bitch."

"Oh, the request thou hast asked is not great," said she; "the one thou mayest choose take it with thee."

He got that, and he went away.§

At the opening of the night came Diarmaid. The greyhound met him without, and she gave a yell.

"It is true, my lass, one of thy pups is gone. But if thou had'st mind of how I found thee, how thy hair was down to thy heels, thou had'st not let the pup go."

"Thou Diarmaid, what saidest thou so?"

"Oh," said Diarmaid, "I am asking pardon."

* Flath a's failt.   † Miorun.   ‡ Righin.

§ This is characteristic of Fionn, as he always appears in these traditions; he represents wisdom, but crafty wisdom, and gains his ends by stratagem.

" Oh, thou shalt get that," said she, and he slept within that night, and his meat and drink were as usual.

On the morrow he went to where he was yesterday, and while he was gone she went out to take a stroll, and while she was strolling about, what should she see but a rider coming to where she was. She stayed without till he reached her.

Who reached her here but Oisean, son of Fionn.

They gave welcome and honour to each other. She told him to go in with her, and that he should take a draught from her, and he said that he would, if he might get his request.

" What request hast thou ?" said she.

" One of the pups of the greyhound bitch."

" Thou shalt get that," said she, " take thy choice of them."

He took it with him, and he went away.*

At the opening of the night came Diarmaid home, and the greyhound met him without, and she gave two yells.

" That is true, my lass," said Diarmaid, " another is taken from thee. But if she had mind of how I found her, she had not let one of thy pups go. When her hair was down to her heels."

" Diarmaid ! What said'st thou ?" said she.

" I am asking pardon," said Diarmaid.

" Thou shalt get that," said she, and they seized each other's hands, and they went home together, and there was meat and drink that night as there ever had been.

In the morning Diarmaid went away, and a while after he had gone she was without taking a stroll. She

---

* This is foreign to the character of Oisein in all other stories, but he was the son of Fionn, and he generally tells his own story.

saw another rider coming to-day, and he was in great
haste. She thought she would wait, and not go home
till he should come forward. What was this but
another of the Fhinn.

He went with civil words to the young damsel,
and they gave welcome and honour to each other.

She told him to go home with her, and that he
should take a draught from her. He said that he
would go if he should get his request.

She asked that time what request that might be,
" One of the pups of the greyhound bitch," said he.

" Though it is a hard matter for me," said she, " I
will give it to thee."

He went with her to the castle, he took a draught
from her, he got the pup, and he went away.

At the opening of the night came Diarmaid. The
greyhound met him, and she gave three yells, the most
hideous that man ever heard.

" Yes, that is true my lass, thou art without any
this day," said Diarmaid, " but if she had mind of how I
found her, she would not have let the pup go; when
her hair was down to her heels, she would not have
done that to me."

" Thou, Diarmaid, what said'st thou ?"

" Oh, I am asking pardon," said Diarmaid. He
went home, and he was without wife or bed beside
him, as he ever had been. It was in a moss-hole
he awoke on the morrow. There was no castle, nor a
stone left of it on another. He began to weep, and
he said to himself that he would not stay, head or foot,
till he should find her.

Away he went, and what should he do but take
his way across the glens. There was neither house nor
ember in his way. He gave a glance over his shoulder,
and what should he see but the greyhound just dead.

He seized her by the tail, and he put her on his shoulder, and he would not part with her for the love that he bore her. He was going on, and what should he see above him but a herd.

"Did'st thou see, this day or yesterday, a woman taking this way?" said Diarmaid to the herd.

"I saw a woman early in the morning yesterday, and she was walking hard," said the herd.

"What way did'st thou see her going?"

"She went down yonder point to the strand, and I saw her no more."

He took the very road that she took, till there was no going any further. He saw a ship. He put the slender end of his spear under his chest, and he sprang into her, and he went to the other side. He laid himself down, stretched out on the side of a hill, and he slept, and when he awoke there was no ship to be seen. "A man to be pitied am I," said he, "I shall never get away from here, but there is no help for it."

He sat on a knoll, and he had not sat there long when he saw a boat coming, and one man in her, and he was rowing her.

He went down where she was, he grasped the greyhound by the tail, and he put her in, and he went in after her.

Then the boat went out over the sea, and she went down under, and he had but just gone down, when he saw ground, and a plain on which he could walk.* He went on this land, and he went on.

---

* This notion of a land under the waves is very widely spread, and common to many nations. The Arabian Nights are full of stories about people who lived under the sea, but this was not taken from the Arabian Nights, for it is common to all the surviving branches of the Celtic family, and to other races.

In the story of "Rouge Gorge," Foyer Breton, 1858, a maiden

He was but a short time walking, when he fell in with a gulp of blood. He lifted the blood, and he

befriends a red-breast, and by his aid and advice gets magic sabots and a stick, walks over the sea to certain islands, where she knocks at a rock, and out comes Mor vyo'ch, the sea cow, which only varies from other cows in being better, and magical. In Gaelic it would be muir bho. By thrice repeating the name of Saint Ronan d Hybernie, and stroking the beast with a magic herb, the cow which had been sold, and had returned, was transformed to Marc'h mor, the sea-horse, which again is like other horses, only ten times better. The word Marc'h does not now survive in Gaelic, but riding is *Mar-cach*.

The horse is sold, and returns, and is transformed by the same means into Mor Vawd. Mer veau, muir bho, the sea-calf or cow, which is a sheep with fine red wool, which is sold also, but jumps into the sea, and escapes to the Seven Isles, and vanishes into a rock.

In the story of the Groach d l' ile de Lok (156), a man goes into a boat like a swan, and when he is on board the swan awakes, and dives down to the bottom of a pool in the middle of a Sea Island, and there he finds a magnificent dwelling, and a fairy, who treats him well for a time, but turns him into a frog at last.

In the Mabinogion it appears that Cardigan Bay was once dry land, and that the land sank, and the people survive, with their dwellings and possessions.

In a curious pamphlet which I picked up in Dublin—"The History of the Isle of Man," etc., " with a succinct detail of enchantments that have been exhibited there by sorcerers and other infernal beings," etc., 1780, I find the account of an English tourist, who, like Herodotus, wrote down all he heard, and seems to have believed a great deal of it. He mentions the "Mauthe doog," which a Gaelic scholar would spell Madadh dubh dog, black, who is a Celtic goblin still, and endless other stories and superstitions which are familiar to me; but amongst others, he tells a tale of Port Iron, where the people were quite familiar with mermen, and had caught a merwoman in a net one moonlight night on the shore. She would not speak till she was allowed to escape to her own people. She had a tail like a fish. So has put it into a napkin, and he put it into his pouch. "It was the greyhound which lost this," said he.

Abdallah of the sea in Lane's Arabian Nights.   But this is nothing. A company was formed for diving, "in glass machines cased with thick tough leather," and a man was let down near the Isle of Man to seek for treasure. The diver passed through the region of fishes, and got into a pure element, clear as the air. He saw the ground glittering with all manner of magnificence, streets and squares of mother of pearl. He hauled his diving bell into a house, and almost within reach of treasures, but there was no more line, and he was hauled back empty handed.

This is a "story" in every sense of the term, and it is so elaborate and ornamented that it must have been cooked for the stranger, or by him, but the main idea is that there is a world under the waves, and the Manks sailors then declared that they commonly heard at sea the bleating of sheep, the barking of dogs, the howling of wolves, and the distinct cries of every beast the land affords, and they now believe in the water horse, and the water bull, and the sea man.

Being lately in Ireland, I proceeded to pump a carman, who had the reputation of being full of stories, and after many vain attempts I got him started, as we drove home to Waterford in the dark. The first thing he told me was a story which was perfectly familiar, though told with an Irish brogue, and with Irish characteristics—a story of a man who grew rich by getting sea cows and sheep. His place of abode, and all particulars were given, but I knew that the same story was told in Orkney, Harris, and Barra ; here I had it at Waterford, and it was the same as the Breton story quoted above, for the end of it was that the cow and all her progeny ran off, and jumped into their native sea, because the man wanted to slaughter the cow.

The same idea is in Straparola's, Italian. A man is swallowed by a mermaid, and restored from the bottom of the Atlantic. It is in old Scotch ballads where men fall in love with mermaids. It is in German stories where men are carried off by Nixies. It is in Norse and Swedish, and it was in Greek and Latin, for there were sea gods of old, and from all this fiction I would gather one probable fact. The men whose minds first conceived

He was a while walking, and he fell in with the next gulp, and he lifted it, and put it into his pouch. He fell in with the next one, and he did the like with it. What should he see a short space from him, after that, but a woman, as though she were crazed, gathering rushes. He went towards her, and he asked her what news she had. "I cannot tell till I gather the rushes," said she.

"Be telling it whilst thou art gathering," said Diarmaid.

"I am in great haste," said she.

"What place is here?" said he.

"There is here," said she, "Rioghachd Fo Thuinn, Realm Underwaves."

"Realm Underwaves!"

"Yes," said she.

"What use hast thou for rushes, when thou art gathering them?" said Diarmaid.

"I will tell thee that. I perceive that thou art a stranger."

"Yes, a true stranger," said Diarmaid.

"The daughter of King Underwaves has come home, and she was seven years under spells, and she is ill, and the leeches of Christendom are gathered, and none are doing her good, and a bed of rushes is what she finds the wholesomest."

this idea were not bred near the sea, or used to it, they were not sailors. They surely came from some inland country to the sea, and peopled it with the creatures of the land. If they saw a seal they might fancy it a man. A walrus they might call a cow, and if the idea was so formed by those who first arrived at the sea, it has survived till now.

A mermaid was lately seen off Plymouth, according to a young sailor of my acquaintance, and Diarmaid went to the land under the waves to search for the daughter of the king.

"Well then, I would be far in thy debt if thou would'st see me where that woman is."

"Well then I will see that. I will put thee into the sheaf of rushes, and I will put the rushes under thee and over thee, and I will take thee with me on my back."

"That is a thing that thou can'st not do," said Diarmaid.

"Be that upon me," said she.

She put Diarmaid into the bundle, and she took him on her back.

(*Was not that my lass !*) When she reached the chamber she let down the bundle.

"Oh ! hasten that to me," said the daughter of King Underwaves.

He sprang out of the bundle, and he sprang to meet her, and they seized each other's hands, and there was joy then.

"Three parts of the ailment are gone, but I am not well, and I will not be. Every time I thought of thee when I was coming, I lost a gulp of the blood of my heart."

"Well then, I have got these three gulps of thy heart's blood, take thou them in a drink, and there will be nothing amiss."

"Well then, I will not take them," said she; "they will not do me a shade of good, since I cannot get one thing, and I shall never get that in the world."

"What thing is that ?" said he.

"There is no good in telling thee that ; thou wilt not get it, nor any man in the world ; it has discomfited them for long."

"If it be on the surface of the world I will get it, and do thou tell it," said Diarmaid.

"That is three draughts from the cup of Righ

Magh an Ioghnaidh, the King of Plain of Wonder, and no man ever got that, and I shall not get it."

" Oh !" said Diarmaid, " there are not on the surface of the world as many as will keep it from me. Tell me if that man be far from me."

" He is not ; he is within a bound near my father, but a rivulet is there, and in it there is the sailing of a ship with the wind behind her, for a day and a year, before thou reach it."

He went away, and he reached the rivulet, and he spent a good while walking at its side.

" I cannot cross over it ; that was true for her," said Diarmaid.

Before he had let the word out of his mouth, there stood a little russet man in the midst of the rivulet.*

" Diarmaid, son of Duibhne, thou art in straits," said he.

" I am in a strait just now," said Diarmaid.

" What wouldst thou give to a man who would bring thee out of these straits ? come hither and put thy foot on my palm."

" Oh ! my foot cannot go into thy palm," said Diarmaid.

" It can."

He went, and he put his foot on his palm. " Now, Diarmaid, it is to King Mag an Iunai that thou art going."

" It is, indeed," said Diarmaid.

" It is to seek his cup thou art going."

---

* This personage plays a part which is common enough, that of the ferrymen, of whom Charon was one. A little red-haired man rising in the middle of a river that was a year's sail wide, and taking a great hero over on the palm of his hand, is not to be reasonably accounted for, and he should be some marine divinity. He tells his own employment below.

" It is."

" I will go with thee myself."

" Thou shalt go," said Diarmaid.

Diarmaid reached the house of King Wonderplain. He shouted for the cup to be sent out, or battle, or combat ; and it was not the cup.

There were sent out four hundred Lugh ghaisgeach, and four hundred Lan ghaisgeach, and in two hours he left not a man of them alive.

He shouted again for battle, or else combat, or the cup to be sent out.

That was the thing he should get, battle or else combat, and it was not the cup.

There were sent out eight hundred loo gaishgeach, and eight hundred lan gaishgeach, and in three hours he left not a man of them alive.

He shouted again for battle, or else combat, or else the cup to be sent out to him.

There were sent out nine hundred strong heroes, and nine hundred full heroes, and in four hours he left no man of them alive.

"Whence," said the king, as he stood in his own great door, "came the man that has just brought my realm to ruin ? If it be the pleasure of the hero let him tell from whence he came."

" It is the pleasure of the hero ; a hero of the people of the Finn am I.   I am Diarmaid."

" Why didst thou not send in a message to say who it was, and I would not have spent my realm upon thee, for thou wouldst kill every man of them, for it was put down in the books seven years before thou wert born.   What dost thou require ?"

" That is the cup ; it comes from thine own hand for healing."*

* The resemblance which all this bears to mediæval romance,

" No man ever got my cup but thou, but it is easy for me to give thee a cup ; but for healing there is but the cup that I have myself about the board."

Diarmaid got the cup from King Wonderplain.

" I will now send a ship with thee Diarmaid," said the king.

" Great thanks (Taing mhor) to thee, oh king. I am much in thy debt; but I have a ferry of my own."*

Here the king and Diarmaid parted from each other. He remembered when he had parted from the king that he had never said a word at all, the day before about the little russet man, and that he had not taken him in. It was when he was coming near upon the rivulet that he thought of him ; and he did not know how he should get over the burn.

" There is no help for it," said he. " I shall not now get over the ferry, and shame will not let me return to the king."†

What should rise while the word was in his mouth but the little russet man out of the burn.

and to Welsh popular tales, is striking. The subject is referred to elsewhere. Fionn had a healing cup, which he refused to give Diarmaid after the fatal boar-hunt, and a great part of mediæval romance hinges on the search for a mystic healing cup. There is another story of which I have read in which Conan goes to Ifrionn ; the cold isle of the dead.

  * Some Saxon foe relates that a Mac—— had proved unwittingly that his family were older than the flood. The other objected that there were none of that name in the ark, to which the highlander replied—" The Mac——s had always a boat o' their ain."

  † The idea of the ferry is clearly that of one of the dangerous tidal fords which abound in the islands. One between North Uist and Benbecula is said to be six miles wide. It is crossed on foot, at low tide, and in a boat when the tide is high, and at night it is dangerous enough.

"Thou art in straits, Diarmaid."

"I am."

"It is this day that thou art in extremity."

"It is. I got the thing I desired, and I am not getting across."

"Though thou didst to me all that which thou hast done ; though thou didst not say a word of me yesterday ; put thy foot on my palm and I will take thee over the burn."

Diarmaid put his foot on his palm, and he took him over the burn.

"Thou wilt talk to me now Diarmaid," said he.

"I will do it," said Diarmaid.

"Thou art going to heal the daughter of King Underwaves ; she is the girl that thou likest best in the world."

"Oh ! it is she."

"Thou shalt go to such and such a well. Thou wilt find a bottle at the side of the well, and thou shalt take it with thee full of the water. When thou reachest the damsel, thou shalt put the water in the cup, and a gulp of blood in it, and she will drink it. Thou shalt fill it again, and she will drink. Thou shalt fill it the third time, and thou shalt put the third gulp of blood into it, and she will drink it, and there will not be a whit ailing her that time. When thou hast given her the last, and she is well, she is the one for whom thou carest least that ever thou hast seen before thee."

"Oh ! not she," said Diarmaid.

"She is ; the king will know that thou hast taken a dislike to her. She will say Diarmaid thou hast taken a dislike to me. Say thou that thou hast. Dost thou know what man is speaking to thee ?" said the little russet man.

"Not I," said Diarmaid.

" In me there is the messenger of the other world, who helped thee ; because thy heart is so warm to do good to another. King Underwaves will come, and he will offer thee much silver and gold for healing his daughter. Thou shalt not take a jot, but that the king should send a ship with thee to Eirinn to the place from whence thou camest."*

Diarmaid went ; he reached the well ; he got the bottle, and he filled it with water ; he took it with him, and he reached the castle of King Underwaves. When he came in he was honoured and saluted.

" No man ever got that cup before," said she.

" I would have got it from all that there are on the surface of the world ; there was no man to turn me back," said Diarmaid.

" I thought that thou wouldst not get it though thou shouldst go, but I see that thou hast it," said she.

He put a gulp of blood into the water in the cup, and she drank it. She drank the second one, and she drank the third one ; and when she had drunk the third one there was not a jot ailing her. She was whole and healthy. When she was thus well, he took a dislike for her ; scarcely could he bear to see her.

" Oh ! Diarmaid," said she, " thou art taking a dislike for me."

" Oh ! I am," said he.

Then the king sent word throughout the town that she was healed, and music was raised, and lament laid down. The king came where Diarmaid was, and he said to him,

" Now, thou shalt take so much by counting of

* This bit bears some resemblance to the German story of Godfather Death, in that the messenger of the other world instructs a man in the healing art, and he heals a king's daughter.

silver for healing her, and thou shalt get herself to marry."

"I will not take the damsel; and I will not take anything but a ship to be sent with me to Eirinn, where the Fhinn are gathered."

A ship went with him, and he reached the Fhinn and the brother of his mother; and there was joy before him there, and pleasure that he had returned.

MacLean quotes a Gaelic proverb—

"Cha d thug gaol luath nach d' thug fuath clis."
"None gave love quickly but gave sudden hate."

Which might be the pith of this curious story. Unless it is mythological it cannot be explained. At all events, here is one of the heroes of Ossian meeting with the messenger of the other world in the Realm under the Waves, and crossing a river like the pious Æneas, when he went below. The story is manifestly imperfect. Something should have been done with the greyhound, but I have no version which fills up the gap.

There is an Irish story which seems to bear upon the incident. Tuirreann, the sister of Fionn's mother, is married to Iollan Eachtach, and his fairy sweetheart transforms her into a hound, and takes her to Fergus. She there gives birth to a couple of puppies, " Bran" and "Sceoluing," Finn's favourite hounds, which were consequently his cousins. Diarmaid is one of the names mixed up with this strange Irish story, and this favourite hound might have been the transformed lady, and if so, Diarmaid's relative—his grand aunt. It is not easy, then, to accomplish the feat of making the

Fionn of the stories a real commander of mortal Irish militiamen.

The incident of the greyhound and her three pups, formed part of a story which was told to me at Polchar inn on the 3d of September 1860. The narrator was a slender middle-aged woman, with black hair and gray eyes, returning from durance at the jail at Loch Maddy; her offence had been the sale of unlawful whisky. I heard her crooning a very pretty old Gaelic love song to a baby, and went down into the kitchen. I found a whole tribe of black-haired girls, of all ages, barefooted, and barelegged, clustered about the peat fire with their bare arms all twined about each others' necks and waists, and their bright eyes and teeth glancing in the red light over each other's shoulders, as they peeped at the stranger. An old man was smoking on a bench, and the singer with black elf-locks was dancing the baby on her knee. We soon got friends, and the story was the result. It was a step-mother story, and the wicked muime gave away the pups to a captain of a ship, and accused the king's daughter of killing them, and broke candlesticks and laid the blame on the girl, till the king took her out to a lonely moor, and said—

"Whether wouldst thou rather that I slew thee outright, or that I should cut off one hand, and one breast, and one knee."

Here the old dame used action and great emphasis, and a shiver of horror ran through the junior part of the audience, who were listening intently.

The deed was done, and the girl crawled to a house where there lived three king's sons under spells, and she went in and found food. They came home and put off their cochal, that is their enchanted form; and one of them said, " Here is a drop of king's blood on the board ;" and he sought, and found her, and dressed her wounds, and washed her, and "dried her with a towel."

She married this one, had three sons, and by the help of a poor woman, and through the agency of a well, recovered her lost members.

She went home at last, and found her father with a wounded leg, which would never be well, till his daughter cured it with her two hands. She laid her recovered hands on the knee, the penitent father cut a caper quite well, and the muime was roasted.

This joins the traditions of the Feinne to Grimm's Handless Maiden.

The idea of a land under ground is also very common in Gaelic stories, and I had intended to give several illustrations of the belief. I had also selected a number of other specimens of traditions of the Feinne, popular history, and proverbs, stories of water horses, water bulls, and other such matters. The last number on my Gaelic list is 308, on my English list, 357, making about 665 stories, but the wish to give one long one as a specimen, and to preserve as much Gaelic as possible, has exhausted my allotted space.

In the oldest Gaelic manuscript in Edinburgh, an ancient scribe has written—"And I regret that there is not left of my ink enough to fill up this line ; I am Fithil, an attendant on the school." So I, like Fithil. must stop scribbling, though not for want of matter, and write

FINIS.

CPSIA information can be obtained
at www.ICGtesting.com
Printed in the USA
LVOW01*1702090217
523757LV00013B/203/P